THE

MERCERS' COMPANY

1579–1959

Decorated initial capital from the earliest surviving Company charter:
letters patent of Elizabeth I, 1560
Mercers' Company

THE MERCERS' COMPANY 1579–1959

By
IAN DOOLITTLE

With an Introduction by
PETER NAILOR

Edited by
ANN SAUNDERS

The Mercers' Company
1994

ISBN 0 9521515 1 0

PRINTED IN GREAT BRITAIN BY
W. S. MANEY & SON, HUDSON ROAD, LEEDS

CONTENTS

LIST OF PLATES

Unless otherwise stated, all photographs are from the Mercers' Company Archives.

LIST OF FIGURES

Unless otherwise stated, all illustrations are from the Mercers' Company Archives.

CHAPTER VII

CHAPTER VIII

CHAPTER IX

CHAPTER X

CHAPTER XI

CHAPTER XII

The Maiden, used as an end-of-Chapter ornament, is one of those depicted on a badge given by John Bancks and worn by the residents of Whittington College.

FOREWORD

In 1994, the Mercers' Company, first among the twelve great Livery Companies of the City of London, celebrates the sixth centenary of the granting of its first Charter by Richard II. This account of the Company's development from the late sixteenth century to the years immediately after the Second World War coincides happily with this celebration.

It traces the events, both internal and external, which transformed the Company over the centuries, from a working, self-regulating brotherhood of City merchants, trading in fine fabrics and luxury goods, to a group of individuals, still a brotherhood, involved in the administration of great charitable estates.

The Company of the present day is concerned with a wide variety of charitable activities: education, care of the elderly and needy, medical care and research, Church patronage, and support for arts and heritage projects. It also has a traditional association with the armed services.

During the twentieth century the Mercers' Company has published a number of diverse accounts of aspects of its history. Sir John Watney, Clerk from 1875 to 1906, compiled in 1914 *An Account of the Mistery of Mercers of the City of London otherwise the Mercers' Company*, relying for the early period on the researches of Dr R. R. Sharpe of the Guildhall Records Office. In 1936, the *Acts of Court of the Mercers' Company 1453–1527*, edited by Laetitia Lyell, was published under her name and that of the then Clerk, Sir Frank Watney. In 1968 *The Charity of Richard Whittington. A History of the Trust administered by the Mercers' Company 1424–1966* by Miss Jean Imray, Archivist of the Company from 1961 to 1981, was devoted to the Company's most important Trust. In 1991 she followed this with *The Mercers' Hall*, an exhaustive description of the development of the building and of the activities that went on in it.

This volume is a welcome addition to these histories, which together with a companion history of the earlier period (currently in preparation) will provide the most complete description available of the development of a City Livery Company.

The Company chose the historian Dr Ian Doolittle to write the history of its more recent past both for his knowledge of the civic institutions of the City of London, and his detachment as a professional historian. Our thanks go to him for his lively account of the Company, and to Dr Ann Saunders, also a historian, for her careful contribution as editor.

This history will surely be of great interest not only to members of the Livery, but also the wider public, for the light it throws on the unique role of Livery Companies in the history of the City of London.

Francis Baden Powell

Spring 1994

FRANCIS ROBERT BADEN-POWELL
Master of the Mercers' Company

AUTHOR'S ACKNOWLEDGEMENTS

A number of people have contributed, in their different ways, to the preparation of this book. Michael Wakeford, the Clerk, supported the project through its long gestation. Anne Sutton, the Archivist, and her successive Assistant Archivists, Ann Wingfield and Ursula Carlyle, responded efficiently and pleasantly to the demands on their time and patience. The work of the former Archivist, Jean Imray, proved invaluable in many respects. In addition to her various publications, Jean prepared many reviews, analyses and memoranda based on her intimate knowledge of the Company's records. The History Panel encouraged me to help the general reader with the historical background. Dr Roger Lane will recognise some passages in the introductions to certain Chapters. The help of two other Panel Members, Harry Hodson and Peter Nailor, is also acknowledged. Michael Berlin was employed by the Mercers' Company as my full-time research assistant throughout the project and without his hard work this book could not have been written. Dr Hana Sambrook has kindly compiled the Index. Ann Saunders has been a most efficient editor.

IAN DOOLITTLE

EDITOR'S ACKNOWLEDGEMENTS

The Editor wishes to thank Michael Wakeford, Clerk to the Mercers' Company, and the Editorial Committee for entrusting her with the task of seeing this book through the press; she is most grateful to the author, Ian Doolittle, for the confidence which he has shown in her. Professor Peter Nailor, Provost of Gresham College, has been an unfailing support throughout the undertaking.

She is grateful to Anne Sutton, Archivist to the Mercers' Company, for her help and advice, and to Ursula Carlyle, Assistant Archivist, for her cheerfulness throughout the selection of illustrations, and for her good ordering of them when found.

Many people have helped with these illustrations. At the Guildhall Library, Ralph Hyde, John Fisher and Jeremy Smith have given assistance beyond the call of duty, as has John Watts of Guardian Royal Exchange. Lord Gainsborough has responded enthusiastically in the search for a likeness of Sir Baptist Hicks, Viscount Campden. Livia Visser-Fuchs, David Jackson of the Department of Astronomy, Cambridge University, and A. V. B. Norman of the Wallace Collection have advised on interpretation of details.

The Company is most grateful to all those who have permitted reproduction of material, and especially to Her Majesty the Queen for gracious permission to reproduce the Hollar engraving of *Winter*.

The following institutions have been most helpful in making material available for illustrations; the individuals named have given willing co-operation: Abingdon School (M. St John Parker and Nigel Hunter); Dauntsey's School (Mrs Hilary Murray); Henry E. Huntington Library, San Marino, California, USA (Thomas Vlange); Imperial College Archives (Ann Barrett); Lambeth Palace Library (Dr Melanie Barber); Lamport Hall Trust (G. P. S. Drye); The Museum of London (Dr Mireille Galinou, Kay Staniland and Hazel Forsyth); National Portrait Gallery (Jayne Shrimpton and Ian Wallace); Royal Commission on Historic Monuments of England (Stephen Croad and Anne Woodward); The Royal Society (Sandra Cumming); The Society of Antiquaries (Bernard Nurse and Adrian James); St Paul's Girls' School (Mrs Jacquie Childs); The Warburg Institute (Paul Taylor). Additional photography was undertaken by P. J. Gates and Godfrey New.

Finally, the Editor wishes to thank Graham Maney and Linda Fish of Messrs Maney & Son, Leeds, who once again have seen a long and complicated book through the press with unfailing patience, cheerfulness and professional expertise.

ANN SAUNDERS

LIST OF ABBREVIATIONS

AC	Acts of Court
CEP	Colet Estate Papers
DEP	Dauntsey Estate Papers
GC	General Committee
GCM	General Court Minutes
GR	Gresham Repertories
K&H	D. Keene and V. Harding, *Historical Gazetteer of London before the Great Fire* (Chadwyck-Healey, Microfilm, 1987), I (Cheapside)
MSP	Mercers' School Papers
SPS	St Paul's School
SPS GM	St Paul's School Governors' Minutes
THG	Trinity Hospital Greenwich
VCM	Visitation Court Minutes
WPP	William Palmer's Papers

Note: Unless otherwise stated, all references to manuscripts are to the Mercers' Company archives at the Hall.

INTRODUCTION

BY PETER NAILOR

I

This account of the affairs of the Mercers' Company has been written to mark the sixth centenary of the granting of a charter to the Company. It begins at a time when the nature of the modern institution was beginning to take shape. In the 380 years or so which are described, we see the Company changing from a working guild, still concerned in part with the making and trading of fine fabrics, to a charitable organisation fulfilling the intentions of earlier benefactors in an altered society. The continuous theme that runs throughout the period is the Company's dedication to public service.

The book is not a complete history of the Mercers' Company from its first beginnings, nor does it attempt to be all-encompassing. The Company is fortunate enough to have a wide range of archive material which can be used to illustrate the ebb and flow of its fortunes during its long history, and it has recently sponsored a volume on Mercers' Hall by a former Archivist of the Company[A] and a study of the Company's plate by a former Master of the Company.[B] Additionally, an account of the early history of the Company is being prepared by Anne Sutton, the Archivist, and the Revd Gordon Huelin is writing an account of the Company's Church patronage.

This volume, then, is only one of a number of publications which it is hoped will be supplemented over the years and which, taken together, will give a fuller and more varied picture than one book alone could provide.

Nevertheless this volume, marking as it does a celebration of an important milestone in the Company's history, sets out the major themes and events which have shaped the Mercers' Company's fortunes in modern times.

II

The background against which changes in English society, and specifically life in London, developed in the sixteenth century encompasses the great events which affected the whole of Europe. The Age of Discoveries was no less significant in this respect than the Renaissance and the Reformation; gunpowder and printing were only two examples of what we would now call technological change which added to the excitement and ferment of the age. At one level, they produced intellectual and artistic achievements of great importance, and at another led to major political and religious shifts and to great wars. It was a century in which fundamental and often violent change occurred on a scale that altered the face of Europe and the fortunes of England.

One important marker about the way in which the Mercers' Company's interests would develop was put down early in the century. In April 1510 the Court of Assistants met with the Dean of St

[A] Jean Imray, *The Mercers' Hall*, London Topographical Society, No. 143 (London, 1991).

[B] Roger Lane, *The Mercers' Company Plate*, MC (London, 1985).

Fig. 1. John Colet, Dean of St Paul's Cathedral and founder of St Paul's School. By G. Arnold after a painting by William Segar, Somerset Herald (Pl. III).
Mercers' Company

Paul's, John Colet, to agree the arrangements whereby the Company would accept the charge of administering his new School.[C] Colet's purpose in proposing that the Company should be the trustee for his foundation is described graphically by his friend Erasmus, in words that have been often quoted but bear repetition here:

After he had finished all, he left the perpetual care and oversight of the estate and the government of it, not to the clergy, not to the bishop, nor to any great minister at court, but amongst married laymen, to the Company of Mercers, men of probity and reputation. And when he was asked the reason of so committing this trust, he answered to this effect: That there is no absolute certainty in human affairs; but for his part, he found less corruption in such a body of citizens than in any other order or degree of mankind.[D]

What is significant here is the emphasis that was given to the importance of education and to the desire to root it firmly in the fabric of secular

[C] 16 April 1510, f. clxxxiiij°, in L. Lyell and F. Watney, *Acts of the Court of the Mercers' Company 1453–1527* (1936), p. 382.

[D] T. Allen, *Erasmi Epistoli* (1922). IV, p. 518.

FIG. 2. Three examples of John Colet's handwriting from the Ordinances of St Paul's School, 28 June 1518.
Mercers' Company: photographs by courtesy of the Warburg Institute

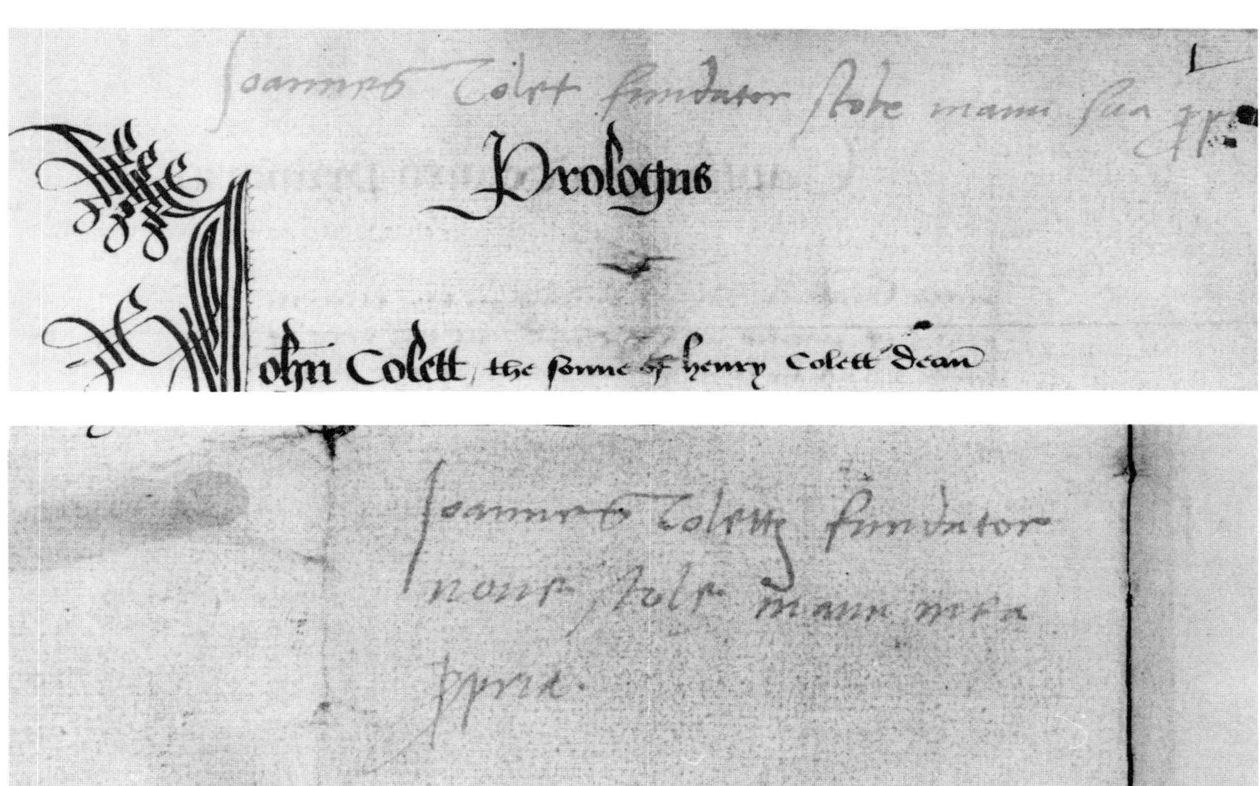

society. The Mercers' Company was being drawn to the ideals represented by the humanist movement which was one of the fundamental elements in the rebirth of arts and letters. The spirit of the Renaissance came later to England than to Italy, but by the end of the fifteenth century it had been absorbed by scholars, in London as well as at Oxford and Cambridge, who emphasised Platonism and the significance of the study of classical studies as a means towards a better understanding of literature and writing.[E]

[E] John Guy, *Tudor England* (1988), pp. 15–18.

John Colet himself was an influential figure in this movement, along with Thomas Linacre and Thomas More, and they played a major part in influencing Wolsey to support them in controversy, and to aid the movement by endowing schools. Wolsey, indeed, followed Bishop Wayneflete's example in suppressing religious houses to meet the cost of establishing new, or reorganised, schools. By the end of the fifteenth century there were already 114 endowed schools in England, of which 85 had been set up since 1450. In something of the same way, English humanism also encouraged the study of the law, with a similar result in promoting the development of the Inns of Court and, to a lesser extent, Inns of Chancery.

The advancement of education was also present later on, when the suppression of religious houses and institutions became so significant a feature of the Henrician Reformation and the later Protectorate. However, by this time education was only a part of the story, and in some ways an incidental factor by comparison with the challenges to traditional piety and theology. In 1538, the Hospital of St Thomas of Acon in Cheapside was closed, as part of the general dissolution of religious houses. The Mercers' Company had a long-standing connection with the Hospital, and used a part of the premises for its meetings. Almost immediately the Company began negotiations to purchase the site and buildings, and to continue the Hospital school. An agreement with the Crown was finally accomplished in 1542, and the School became the Mercers' School. The cloisters and chapter house were converted into a private dwelling, on the site now occupied by Frederick's Place. In 1547 the Company sold that property and some of the houses which lay between it and Old Jewry to meet the expenses arising from the dissolution of chantries, which was instituted by Protector Somerset. But by then, the Company's home was secure, and the School had been reconstituted in the ambulatory.[F]

In pre-Reformation times, 'living in charity' was a social and religious ideal that affected many aspects of daily life. But although levels of giving to the poor increased in the early part of the sixteenth century, the role of private benefactors began to change, and was accelerated by the effects of the Reformation. It moved from a personal desire to provide succour, often through legacies, to participation in the affairs of institutions which, much more often after the Reformation had taken hold, had an independent role.[G] The cure of souls was being overtaken by the care of minds. But Livery Companies provided support, in this connection, to preachers as well as to schools within their spheres of interest. In 1557 the Great Twelve Companies were approached by the Lord Mayor with a proposal that they should each support one scholar, to undertake regular preaching and to serve in parishes. Out of this, some notable developments arose but, as Ian Archer records, it was part of a general movement that had significant consequences:

> The changes in the religious culture of the [Haberdashers'] Company in the sixteenth and early seventeenth centuries had important implications for its future course of development. It was the godly who provided much of the impetus for the foundation of the charitable trusts which was to change the character of the Company from an organisation concerned with the regulation of a trade to one involved in the management of charities.[H]

This too was the experience of the Mercers' Company.

III

In the later part of the sixteenth century, London began a period of growth that proved to be faster than any comparable development in other European capitals, and was to be sustained for longer. A population of about 120,000 in 1550 grew to 200,000 by 1600, and to 375,000 by 1650. London had long outstripped other cities in England like Coventry and Norwich, and its dual role, as the national seat of government and a great seaport, accentuated the significance which it began to have in shaping the course of overseas trade, and in influencing agricultural and industrial change. It became the major centre of consumption for the

[F] Imray, *Mercers' Hall*, p. 16.

[G] See *London 1500–1700, the making of the metropolis*, edd. A. L. Beier and R. Finlay (1986), p. 19.

[H] I. W. Archer, *The History of the Haberdashers' Company* (1991), p. 45.

privileged classes clustering around the Court, the law and commerce, and developed a new importance as a centre for the nascent professions. Towards the end of the century, these influences brought about a great increase in building and land exchange which, after 1580, began to show up in the extent of the London townscape.[I]

The combination of political and mercantile roles which stimulated the growth of London was almost unique in Europe. No other capital shared them to the same extent, and there were links between the merchant communities and the gentry which drove the growth of the City and the development of economic centralisation.[J]

London began to dominate the cloth export trade early in the sixteenth century; in 1504 about 43% of the nation's cloth exports were invoiced and shipped through London, but by 1546 the proportion had risen to 86%. The direct impact of trade upon general prosperity was limited, since much of the business remained in the hands of small groups of Merchant Adventurers, but the spin-offs for London were considerable. It was a period when price inflation became marked; merchants sought to invest their money in new ways, though manufacturing continued to be one outlet, which generated a considerable expansion in industries, and the incorporation of a number of new craft guilds. It led too, to an increase in membership in others, and to a spread of production in the London suburbs. The profits of trade spread through to Whitehall, and generated conspicuous expenditure by the aristocracy, which was supported through loans and pawnbroking.[K]

Great merchants, like the Greshams, involved themselves in Government finance, but this was not a totally novel development; Richard Whittington, after all, had been a very early model for this sort of entrepreneurial activity. But after the 1540s, successive governments came to rely heavily upon London merchants for loans. This in return produced profitable consequences, in revenue-farming, grants of patents and the opportunity to bid for the operation of monopolies.[L]

But after the end of the 1560s, as the revolt of the Netherlands against Spain drifted into open war, the trade links between England and Antwerp rapidly declined and Antwerp lost its dominance. The growth in domestic trade continued, however, and London merchants sought new markets elsewhere in Europe, in the Mediterranean and further afield. This development was epitomised by the incorporation of new trading ventures which culminated in the organisation of the East India Company. The gains in all of these areas made up for the decline in the traditional cloth trade to northern Europe which, by 1614, had shrunk beyond reclaim. One significant result at home was a diversification in commerce and in the community of merchants, so that guild membership was much less important than it had been earlier as a prerequisite for success.[M]

I See E. J. Davis, 'The transformation of London' in *Tudor Studies*, ed. R. W. Seton-Watson (1924), and *London 1500–1700*, Introduction.

J See T. K. Rabb, *Enterprise and Empire: Merchant and Gentry Investment in the Expansion of England, 1575–1630* (1967).

K See *London 1500–1700*, and L. Stone's study of the career of *Sir Horatio Palavicino* (1956).

L See the magisterial study by R. H. Tawney, *Business and Politics under James I; Lionel Cranfield as Merchant and Minister* (1958).

M *London 1500–1700*, pp. 15–18.

CHAPTER I
THE ELIZABETHAN COMPANY

The reign of Elizabeth I (1558–1603) saw the Livery Companies of London at the height of their power and prestige. The capital's economy could still be harnessed (or strait-jacketed) by a guild system which obliged all those who traded in the Square Mile or its 'suburbs' to become free of a Company. Since London dominated the country by its size and prosperity, these controls placed the Livery Companies in an immensely favoured position. They were institutions of national significance.[1]

However, as the economy continued to expand, there were signs of strain. Guilds formed to regulate the activities of retailers and handicraftsmen found it difficult to assimilate wholesalers and merchants. This was especially true of the large Livery Companies which increasingly had to rely on wealth and civic standing rather than economic necessity to attract members. Most of the Great Twelve lost control over the trades whose names they bore.

The process by which the Mercers' Company lost its connections with the trade in luxury cloth known as 'mercery' is by no means straightforward,[A] but it remains the case that the late sixteenth century represents a turning-point for this Company as for so many of its fellows. 1579 has a domestic significance as the date of a bequest by Sir Thomas Gresham which had a deep (not to say deleterious) impact on the Company's development, but also has this wider significance. In both senses it marks the beginning of a new era in the Company's life.

THE MEMBERS

Who were Mercers in 1579? The question is easy to pose, but difficult to answer. There are lists, it is true, and by dint of a certain amount of effort it is possible to construct a roll-call of the Company for the beginning of the period. It is more difficult to put any flesh on the bones of these Elizabethans. Some prodigious fact-finding affords a little assistance,[B] but many of the names remain mere names. Accordingly, any conclusions drawn from the pen-pictures given below must be heavily qualified. The shafts of light really serve only to emphasise the darkness elsewhere. It is also important to realise that the sources, quite apart from being defective in coverage, are also selective. They reveal, generally speaking, the public and not the private side to an individual's achievements and activities.

At the head of the roll stood the great merchants, men who had few, if any, equals in the business world of their day. Pre-eminent was Sir Thomas Gresham, merchant and financier, who receives special treatment in the following Chapter. Then should be noticed Lionel Duckett, whose activities were scarcely less impressive. He was a member of the Merchant Adventurers' Company (which controlled the vital cloth trade with Europe), imported goods from the Mediterranean, lent money to the Crown, financed slave-trading between Africa and the Caribbean, was involved in copper-smelting in the north of England and supported attempts to find the North-West Passage.[2]

Sir Thomas Ryvett, like Duckett, was a friend of Sir Thomas Gresham. He too was a cloth trader and he too was accorded the dubious honour of being asked to lend money to the Crown. Sir William Allen was another who sent cloth to

[A] See below, pp. 18–20.

[B] A. N. Willson, the historian of Collyer's School, compiled valuable reference-cards for a large number of Elizabethan Mercers.

Europe (Antwerp, of course, but also Danzig and Emden), but he participated additionally in the Russia and Spanish Companies. In 1570 he was granted commercial privileges by the Shah of Persia. John Marsh was a prominent member of the Merchant Adventurers', Spanish and Muscovy Companies.

Beneath these major figures came a clutch of middle-ranking men. First, perhaps, was Edmund Hogan, Sir Thomas Gresham's factor, who rose to be not only a considerable merchant in his own right but also a diplomatic agent for the Queen. Matthew Field, a partner of Hogan's, was particularly involved in Frobisher's voyages (searching for a North-West Passage) and the production of copper (through the Mines Royal Company). Edward Castelin had multifarious interests: African ventures, shipowning, cloth exporting and mining. He was another of those merchants whose influence led to their nomination for the task of raising money for the Crown. Anthony Hickman worked with Castelin in the Canaries, shared Castelin's interests in the African slave trade, ship ownership and cloth exporting, and also imported sugar. William Byrde, apart from a controversial term as a Petty Customs official, was a subscriber to the Frobisher voyages, a member of the Mines Royal Company and a cloth trader. Robert Hilsdon, a founder member of the Eastland Company and an intermittent inhabitant of Danzig, imported rye, flax and pitch from there and exported cloth. Henry Isham was another founder member of the Eastland Company and he too, not surprisingly, exported cloth to Danzig. Thomas Cordell traded mainly in the Mediterranean, both in the conventional manner and as a privateer, though Elizabethans acknowledged no clear distinction between the two forms.

Finally, there was a third category comprising traders important enough to have left traces of their activities in the records, but clearly not on a par with those already described. In some instances these men were factors for their superiors in the Company. Thomas Nicholls the younger, for example, was factor for Hickman and

Fig. 3. Sir Lionel Duckett, Lord Mayor in 1572–3, aged 76. Oil painting on board by an unknown artist, executed 1586, the year before his death. During his year of office, he tried to restrain extravagant hospitality in the Companies and in the City generally. Sir Lionel was also Master of the Mercers' Company four times.
Mercers' Company

Hilsdon in the Canaries. Thomas Cranfield, father of the famous Lionel,[C] was the former Antwerp factor for Vincent Randall, Master of the Company in 1574. In other cases they were members of firms run by Mercers. John Barker and Edmund Burlase, for example, were members of the Isham firm (headed at this time by the brothers Henry and John, though the latter was now in semi-retirement in the country).[3]

Outside the conventional framework of the mercantile community are to be found a handful of men who also deserve to be mentioned. John

[C] For whom see below, pp. 43, 94.

Dee was a compound of astrologer, philosopher, chemist, mathematician and geographer.[4] Anthony Jenkinson, an 'honorary' freeman, was a 'traveller' who sailed to forbiddingly distant lands in what today is Russia, and tried to find a North-East Passage to China. He had the good fortune to be liked by Ivan the Terrible, and secured privileges for English merchants from other potentates in that part of the world.[5] Michael Lock was another 'traveller', though a less successful one, who found himself in and out of debtors' prison. Twenty-five years of journeying also gave him a taste for map-making, but again his labours were ill-rewarded; his cartography of the north Atlantic was highly inaccurate. George Nedham deserves, perhaps, to be included among the merchants proper, but he is now chiefly remembered for his persistent penmanship aimed at persuading English merchants to set up a new cloth mart at Emden in place of Antwerp.[6] Thomas Copley was a wealthy and well-born convert to Roman Catholicism who spent a large part of his adult life in rather pathetic exile on the Continent, devoting a little energy to ineffectual service for Spain in the Netherlands and a great deal more energy to correspondence in order to secure the release of his forfeited property in England and to make his peace with the Queen. His pen had as little effect as his sword.[D7] Finally, there may be mentioned William Oldborough, who came from a well-known seafaring family and was shipmaster for the Muscovy Company. He lived in a Company house in Stepney and became an honorary freeman in 1573.[8]

Of course, these men were not merely Mercers and merchants. They had other roles as well. A number were members of the City Corporation. Lionel Duckett, for example, was Alderman of Bassishaw Ward and William Allen Alderman of Bridge Ward. A substantial number were Common Councilmen, though only a dozen or so served for any length of time. Edmund Hogan, for instance, was a Councilman from 1565 to 1593, Robert Hilsdon from 1574 to 1583, and Henry Isham from 1576 to 1593. (The inter-connections, in fact, between the Mercers and the Corporation were not as numerous or as deep as might have been expected, and the reasons for this are discussed later in this Chapter.)

As far as 'public' offices are concerned, the instances are few and far between. There is certainly a smattering of customs posts (controllers, surveyors and so on), but otherwise the list is thin. There are also a number of MPs, but none of them evidently played a prominent part in Commons debates: they were MPs as merchants and not as public, still less political, figures. Two alone in this category attract more than passing mention in the records, and then for the wrong reasons. Sir William Damsell was the Crown agent at Antwerp until replaced by Sir Thomas Gresham in 1551 for alleged incompetence (though his attempt to combine the position with the governorship of the Merchant Adventurers was probably the real reason), while Thomas Egerton had been Under-Treasurer at the Mint until imprisoned in 1556 on a charge of misappropriating Crown money from captured treasure ships.

Such, then, were the men who joined the Mercers' Company in Elizabethan times. A typical Mercer did not exist, but if he did he would no doubt have been a cloth exporter who had served for a time as a factor in Antwerp, with interests also in the Muscovy Company and the Mines Royal. He had a healthy suspicion of public office, avoiding Parliament and the City Corporation alike. He lent money to the Crown when, but only when, he had to and otherwise he devoted himself to making sufficient money for a rural, if not necessarily landed, retirement. The typical Mercer, it seems, was a merchant *semple* and felt no need to be anything more. Hence the difficulty in tracing his activities.

THE STRUCTURE OF THE COMPANY

Not many years before this volume takes up the story, in 1562, a valuable list of Company

[D] In his Company, as well as his country, Copley was a misfit. If anything, the Mercers in the early part of Elizabeth's reign were of a Puritan persuasion. See P. Collinson, *Godly People* (1983), p. 46 n. 6 and p. 278.

members was compiled. As revised in 1581 it comprised 271 names in the following categories: 4 Wardens, 4 Aldermen, 20 Assistants, 45 Liverymen and 198 freemen 'out of Livery'.[9] What did each office involve, and how did a man pass from one rank to the next?

Unlike some of the smaller, craft-based Companies, the Mercers had no 'journeymen' class of tradesmen who, though not 'free' of the Company, were nevertheless obliged to submit to the Company's rules and regulations. All members of the Mercers' Company were 'free' of it, that is to say they had been formally and individually admitted. There were three ways of obtaining the freedom: by apprenticeship to a freeman; by patrimony or direct descent from a freeman; and by redemption or purchase. By a long way the most common method was apprenticeship. Between 1561 and 1600, of 798 freemen admitted, 578 were apprentices, 167 sons of freemen and 53 redemptioners.

It is difficult to penetrate beneath the formalities and establish precisely what an apprenticeship meant at this time, but there are many indications that it meant a good deal more than the empty charade it undoubtedly later became. Take, for instance, Sir Thomas Gresham's remarks on his apprenticeship to his uncle Sir John:

> I myself was bound apprentice eight years to come by the experience and knowledge that I have [of trade and commerce]. Nevertheless I need not to have been apprentice, for that I was free by my father's copy, albeit my father, Sir Richard Gresham, being a wise man knew [that] although I was free by his copy it was to no purpose except I were apprentice to the same whereby to come by the experience and knowledge of all kinds of merchandise.[10]

A scholarly study of the Isham firm suggests that other Mercer apprentices shared Gresham's experience of a real, practical and sometimes demeaning training.[11] Young men destined for the cloth trade evidently had to live abroad for a number of years, coping with the hurly-burly of the Antwerp market and perhaps eventually acting as factor for their masters.

The Company itself reflected the views and experience of its members. In 1576, for example, it opposed the City Corporation's attempt to obtain exemption from the apprenticeship controls of the Statute of Artificers (1563). The Mercers rehearsed the following points: there was a need for experienced merchants and craftsmen; each man should confine himself to the trade in which he served his apprenticeship; and the 'intermeddling' of unskilled men in other trades only led to higher prices and poor-quality goods. A statute of Edward III had also discountenanced 'intermeddling', and London, of all cities, should not press for exemption from Parliament's decrees. Not content with mere opposition, the Company also put forward a bill designed to reinforce the principle of 'one man, one trade'.[12] The City's bill, and the Company's, came to nothing; but the attitudes revealed are most interesting. It is also worthy of notice that one of the Company's favourite ploys to enforce discipline was the threat to prohibit defaulting members taking on new apprentices.[13]

The other methods of obtaining the freedom deserve less attention. Of patrimony there is only a little to be said. As already indicated, there were many members like Sir Richard Gresham who could have taken advantage of patrimony for their sons but decided not to do so. A few did, however, and prominent members such as John Marsh, Sir Richard Mallory and Sir Roger Martin are all found admitting their sons *en bloc* on payment of the 2*s*. patrimony fee.[14] Redemptioners were less numerous but more interesting. They were admitted by special Act of Court and in many cases the 3*s*. 4*d*. fee was waived. Entrants fell into various categories. First, there were the great officers of State or courtiers, as witness the Earl of Pembroke, the Earl of Bedford and Robert Dudley, the future Earl of Leicester, who were all admitted in 1562.[15] Their freedoms were granted quite simply *honoris causa*. Secondly, there were those who became free in connection with some particular event or problem. When an Exchequer dispute over concealed chantry lands was settled in 1573, the protagonist, Henry Knyett, a

FIG. 4. Impression of the common seal of the Mercers' Company, first made in 1425 and subsequently destroyed in the Great Fire, 1666. The origins of the Maid as the Company symbol are obscure. The second Royal Charter of 1424 granted the Company a common seal (as shown), although the symbol was in use even earlier. The arms were registered by the College of Heralds in 1568, but it was still possible for the Maid herself to vary as time passed; it is worth noting the changes over the years — see later illustrations.
Mercers' Company

Gentleman of the Privy Chamber, and the orchestrator of the settlement, Sir Walter Mildmay, a Privy Councillor, were both made honorary freemen.[16] Thirdly, there were experts (notably lawyers) who had given or were expected to give the Company assistance in dealing with pressing problems. Thomas Owyn, who was made free in 1571, went on to give the Company legal advice in relation to the concealed lands dispute and other matters.[17] Then there were men who had performed notable service to trade and whom the Mercers wished to reward. Anthony Jenkinson (1560) and William Oldborough (1573) are obvious cases. Next, and in a similar category, were those colleagues, relatives and servants of prominent Mercers who sponsored their applications. Sir Lionel Duckett was responsible for three such admissions: in 1573 (a silkseller), 1580 (a servant) and 1584 (another servant).[18] Finally may be noticed those appointees of the Company, from a St Paul's High Master (1578) to the Under-Clerk (1571), who qualified, if not automatically, then certainly ex officio.[19]

Once admitted, a freeman was known as a Young Man, a 'yeoman' or (the favoured term) a Bachelor. In some Companies Bachelors had their own separate organisation, but there is no sign of this in the Mercers'. The only real information about them as a group comes from the intermittent service of a few of them whenever a member of the Company became Lord Mayor. Sixteen 'chief' or Master Bachelors, selected by the Wardens, had to bedeck the Company barge and attend in appropriate gowns on the Lord Mayor during his procession to St Paul's. This, it may be imagined, was an expensive assignment and, though the Master Bachelors obviously tried to get contributions from their fellow Bachelors, they were personally responsible for meeting the cost. Predictably enough, there were squeals of anguish. In 1571 three Master Bachelors

> desired to be allowed of the Company something of their liberality towards their charges for so much as they have borne and laid out more this year than other Bachelors heretofore, by reason that all things are so chargeable and men's contributions of this Company not so liberal as heretofore and withal brought forth a bill of diverse Bachelors' names that have not yet borne any charges with them by reason of their absence out of the town.

The response was twofold: first, to pursue the defaulting Bachelors with threats of fines and, secondly, to increase the number of Master Bachelors to twenty in order to ease the burden.[20]

The Master Bachelors were rewarded for their trouble by elevation, in due course, to the Livery, and it may be assumed that the selection of

Master Bachelors was carefully monitored. From the experience of other Livery Companies, it is not hard to envisage some form of cleavage between Master Bachelors and potential Master Bachelors on the one hand, and the rest of the Bachelors on the other. Relations between the Assistants and the ordinary Bachelors never became as acrimonious as they did in other Companies, where there were often surges of populist pressure from below, but there is a little evidence that similar tensions were present in the Mercers' Company. The attempts to get Bachelors to pay for the Master Bachelors' expenses on Lord Mayor's Day represent one such hint. Another, possibly, is a memorandum in 1578 to the effect that six Bachelors should meet with the Wardens to establish the names of their fellows against the 1562 roll and to arrange for the calling of a meeting of the yeomanry 'that they may be the better known to the Company and to each other'.[21]

The Livery calls for little comment. It was no more and no less than the stepping-stone between the yeomanry and the Court of Assistants. Periodic 'calls' on to the Livery by the Court were made, usually in groups (as in the case of Master Bachelors), but sometimes singly. The only controversial point concerned precedence on the Livery roll, because it was by rote that Liverymen were nominated for service as Wardens and Master. The 'calling roll', as it was sometimes known, was also used for all ceremonial occasions.[22] Hence the displeasure of one Liveryman who thought that he had been misplaced in the roll by a mistake of the Clerk.[23] Usually men were brought on to the Livery in strict order of admission to the freedom, but occasionally a favoured individual was allowed to jump the queue.[24]

The Assistants formed the executive committee of the Company, meeting as regularly as it was necessary to do so in order to deal with major business. It was the Assistants who granted leases, disciplined members and made representations to the Crown or Parliament. The General Court of the Company, including the Livery and Bachelors, met only quarterly and merely ratified *some* of the decisions already made by the Assistants. The Assistants were a powerful Cabinet, the General Court a toothless Commons.

In 1562 there were twenty-four Assistants. Four were Aldermen of the City and were Assistants ex officio; twenty were Assistants because they had served the three executive offices which made up the Company's 'cursus honorum' or rather 'laborum', namely (in ascending order) the Renter Warden, House Warden and Upper Warden. The Renter (or Fourth) Warden looked after the Company's estates; the House (or Second) Warden dealt with domestic finances; and the Upper (or Third) Warden, recently elevated in status, supervised the important St Paul's School trust.[25]

Each year the six most senior Liverymen would be nominated for Renter and House Warden and two of them (not necessarily the most senior)[26] would be chosen by the Assistants. The Upper Warden was chosen from those who had already served as Renter and House Warden. The Master (i.e. Master Warden) was chosen by the previous year's Master, and he had not only to have served all three junior Wardenships but also to have been or be a City Alderman or Sheriff (or at least to have fined-off or been formally excused such offices).

It may be imagined that members qualified to be Masters were not always easy to find and this explains why Gresham, Duckett, Ryvett and others all served multiple Masterships. Service as Master or Warden evidently placed heavy demands on an individual's time and resources. No specific information is available, but the prospect of the Upper Wardenship so daunted one member in 1561 that he made a spirited attempt to avoid election and was only coerced by threats of severe retribution.[27] However, most members destined for high office were ready to make the necessary sacrifices. The prestige outweighed the inconvenience.

The picture of an oligarchical hierarchy, with power vested in the Wardens and the Assistants at the expense of the Livery and Bachelors, is reinforced if the question of attendance is considered.

Attendance at meetings was a constant problem and at first sight it appears to have afflicted the whole Company. Indeed, in March 1565 an order concerning 'late appearance and slack coming to the Court and Quarter Days' complained that 'every man from the highest to the lowest kept not order in coming as in old time the ancient fathers did ...'.[28] However, as the order went on to indicate, there were special circumstances which were at least partly to blame. The plague had prompted men to flee the capital, particularly in the summer months; and in July of the previous year there were no Wardens, old or new, to be found at all at election-time. They were all lying low at their country houses.[29] The order was evidently a belated attempt to avoid a recurrence of the embarrassment. It certainly does not appear to reflect a general waywardness on the part of the Wardens: the instance stands alone. The same may be said of the Assistants. The only occasion when the quorum of twelve was not achieved came in 1573 when there was a clash with a meeting of the Merchant Adventurers.[E] [30]

Attitudes seem to have been very different among the lower ranks. One of the rare attendance lists at a General Court, in July 1573, reveals the following: Sir Lionel Duckett (Lord Mayor), Sir Thomas Gresham (Master), three old Wardens, two new Wardens, thirteen Assistants and only two Liverymen, John Barefoot and Henry Isham.[31] The latter are, in fact, exceptions which reinforce the rule. Barefoot was a former Master Bachelor, whom only death prevented reaching higher offices, while Isham was a future Warden and Master.[32] It may reasonably be supposed that the fines periodically laid down for non-appearance, though avowedly applicable to all ranks,[33] were really aimed at the Livery and Bachelors, and also that, when in 1571 John Isham suggested recruiting 'certain persons of the Livery' as Assistants to bolster the 'small appearance' at 'those courts', he was referring, not to the Courts of Assistants, but to the General Courts.[34] Liverymen, and still more so Bachelors, had no reason to attend Court meetings when their voice meant so little. 'Ratification' and 'confirmation' had become empty words.

A concluding word is required on the officers. By far the most important was the Clerk, but little information about his day-to-day work emerges. The Acts of Court concentrate on the unusual rather than the commonplace and, although there is information on the misappropriation of money which landed Clerk Foster in prison in the 1560s,[35] there is next to nothing about legal or routine endeavours. The Clerk acquired during these years, and for the first time, a deputy or Under-Clerk who was to be the registrar of the Company's writings and to stand in for the Clerk when the need arose, with a view eventually to replacing him.[36] The first two Under-Clerks, Richard Stockbridge and Thomas Dalby senior, did indeed become full Clerks. The only other important official was the Under-Officer or Beadle who, on the initiative of John Ramidge, became rent-gatherer as well.[37] Apart from his obvious responsibilities, the Under-Officer had to supervise the conduct of the Bachelors.[38] Below this triumvirate came the customary assortment of domestic servants, including a butler, cook and storekeeper. Appointments were usually by personal application and there was rarely much excitement. However, in 1587 the Queen herself intervened in the election of the Under-Officer, and the Company was obliged to persuade the successful candidate, Southern, to resign and appoint the royal favourite, Norton, instead. Unfortunately Norton soon displayed a taste for 'drunkenness, brabbling[F] and evil company' which eventually took him to prison, and he was replaced by Southern in 1593.[39]

FINANCE

An introductory survey of this kind should ideally include a balance-sheet of the Company's finances. This, unfortunately, is out of the question.

[E] This provides interesting evidence of the continuing connections between the two Companies (or at least their members). See below, p. 18.

[F] Brabbling = quarrelling.

The records are neither full enough nor clear enough to permit such calculations. Only one set of accounts (the Renter Warden's) survive for this period, and in the absence of the others, and without a clear distinction made between corporate and charitable funds, reliable figures cannot be produced. It is necessary to make do with references in the Acts of Court. Even these are intermittent and sometimes infuriatingly laconic. In 1576, for instance, there is recorded the return made to the subsidy or tax assessors. The clear yearly revenue of Company land, after the deduction of repairs, quit-rents,annuities and pensions, was declared to be £44 15*s.* 11*d.* As for 'money' (i.e. capital) the Company said it had none at all 'for that little we have is bestowed on [a store of] armour and gunpowder' ready for the defence of the realm.[40] This is effectively the only summary of the Company's financial position for the period,[G] but it leaves many questions unanswered. Tax returns, unfortunately, are not noted for their candour.

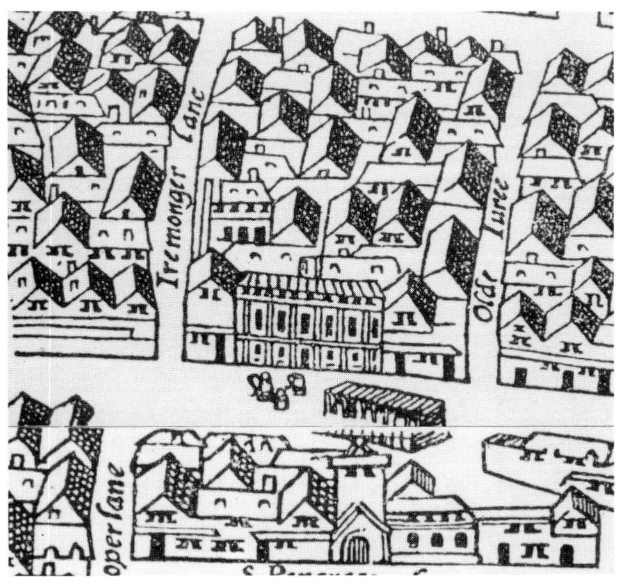

FIG. 5. Detail from the woodcut map of London, drawn during the 1560s and commonly, though erroneously, ascribed to Ralph Agas. The façade of Mercers' Hall can be seen clearly, facing on to Cheapside; in the middle of the road is the Great Conduit, market stalls packed closely around it, with tall wooden water cans, wrapped with osier, nearby. Professional water carriers used these to take fresh water from house to house.
By courtesy of Guildhall Library, Corporation of London

There is, however, enough other evidence to indicate that the Company was worried that its estates were producing insufficient rental income. In 1581 there was ratified an Act of Court for 'improvements of rents, setting of fines and granting leases etc.' The preamble spoke of 'the great decay and afterdeal'[H] of the Company and ascribed the situation to three factors: the tenants-at-will not repairing their properties, uneconomic rents and heavy legal charges. A committee had made a 'taxation and improvement' of all the Company's property not under lease, and had made a register of their suggestions. The Act prohibited leases of property for more than twenty-one years (save in cases of rebuilding) or for less than the rents and fines set out in the register. The same rules were to be applied, *mutatis mutandis*, to all property which subsequently fell vacant.[41]

Likewise there are signs that the Company was indeed short of ready cash. A brief reference in 1575 to there being 'no money presently in the House' is supplemented by a sequence of entries in 1578.[42] In April of that year a committee was appointed 'to survey the state of the House and [discover] how the afterdeal thereof hath grown and by what means the same may be conveniently restored again . . .'. It can scarcely be coincidental that at the same court an exhibition (i.e university grant) was stopped and eight men taken on to the Livery.[43] The committee's recommendations are not recorded, but its influence may easily be traced at the next Court meeting in June. First, steps were taken to secure repayment of, or better security for, loans made to young freemen starting up in business. Secondly, money was taken from

[G] A 1563 subsidy return gave £69 11*s.* 6*d.* 'in lands' and £55 6*s.* 8*d.* 'in money'. Whether the former figure amounted to clear revenue, thus making the return directly comparable with the 1576 figures, is not apparent. AC, 1560–95, ff. 45v–6.

[H] Afterdeal = disadvantage, especially financial (*OED*).

the St Paul's School account to make up a deficiency in the House account. Thirdly, it was decided to grant a lease of certain Company properties (both vacant and reversionary) to a group of Company members in order to raise money for the repayment of debts totalling £600 or more. Finally, and perhaps most eloquently, the customary dinner at the Wardens' election was cancelled in favour of wine and spice cakes only, and at the confirmation of the election on the following day the Wardens were to bear the entire costs of dinner themselves 'because the House is at such an afterdeal'.[44]

The conclusion, therefore, appears to be that the gloomy complaint to the subsidy-men in 1576 was not without some basis in fact. The Company was finding it difficult to balance the books. Whether this was due to unbridled expenditure or inadequate revenue is impossible to say.

ESTATES

The Company's estates in 1579 are most conveniently set out in a survey compiled in the previous year by John Cheke, the Second Warden.[45] The Renter Warden's 'charge' lists the Company's lands (excluding St Paul's School) under the following heads:

		Rent		
		£	*s.*	*d.*
1.	Property in the City of London attached to the dissolved Hospital or College of St Thomas of Acon	83	2	8
2.	The Whittington estate in the City	168	4	3
3.	Property in the City given by Lady Isabella Gresham	14	6	4
4.	The same, Richard Lakin	8	0	0
5.	The same, William Dauntsey	34	6	0
6.	The same, Thomas Windout	6	0	0
7.	The same, William Estfield	20	14	4
8.	The same, Nicholas Widdowson	5	0	6
9.	The same, William Browne	10	6	8
10.	The same, Richard Collyer	22	0	0
11.	The same, Sir James Yarford	30	10	0
12.	The same, Robert Chertsey	13	0	0
13.	Property in Long Acre [now Covent Garden] given by Lady Joan Bradbury	3	6	8
14.	Quit-rents	7	4	6
	TOTAL	£426	1*s.*	11*d.*

For the 'discharge' it is necessary to turn to the Renter Warden's accounts.[1] [46] In 1578–9 against an income of £477 12*s.* 6*d.* there is recorded expenditure of £273 15*s.* 2*d.*, leaving a healthy surplus of £203 17*s.* 4*d.* How typical was this? The figures suggest that for much of the Elizabethan period £200 was indeed not uncommon. Rents produced a reliable gross income which rose from some £400 in the 1560s to £700 in the 1590s. Expenditure was a good deal less regular: repair bills were quite unpredictable. Nevertheless, even in the worst years, the 'discharge' rarely rose above £400 at the beginning of the period and £500 at the end.

Only on three occasions, the early 1560s, the early 1580s and 1589–90, was this pattern upset. In 1560–1, 1561–2 and 1562–4 there were actually deficits of between £20 and £30; in 1582–3 the surplus fell to £30 or so from consistently much higher figures; while in 1589–90 a deficit of £70 was recorded. The last occasion was an aberration attributable to the cost of both repairs to the Hall and Chapel and also the rebuilding of properties in Mitre Alley; but the other two periods were more serious and it will be seen below that the Company recognised the danger signals and reacted accordingly.

The St Paul's School estate was the responsibility of the Third Warden. The 'charge' com-

[1] A word of warning is needed. The personal responsibility which the Renter Warden bore for his accounts means that the figures include money he *should* have received and not merely what he *did* receive. However, on the apparently reasonable assumption that rent arrears did not vary a great deal from year to year, the figures quoted may be regarded as at least an approximate guide to the true state of the finances. It should be noted that the fines or premiums paid for the grant or renewal of leases, as opposed to the annual rents, were rather anomalously allocated to the Second Warden's account.

prised lands in the City, Whitechapel, Stepney, Buckinghamshire, Hertfordshire, Cambridgeshire and Essex, and in 1579 it amounted to £166 19*s*. 2*d*. The 'discharge' covered the payments to the High Master and Under-Master and other expenses, and totalled £86 9*s*. 4*d*. This left some £70 for repairs and other 'extraordinary' items. Unfortunately, no account books for the Third Warden have survived and it is not possible to repeat for St Paul's the year-by-year analysis given for the rest of the Company's property.

Turning now to the administration of the estates, indications have already been given as to the main theme which emerges from the evidence. It was the pressure of financial difficulty which lay behind the main developments. Consider first the early 1560s. In March 1561 the General Court heard of various 'scandals' involving Company members, including a lessee who persuaded the Company to waive his entry fine, two lessees who sublet to a 'stranger' or non-Mercer, and a reversioner who assigned his future interest. The Company, it is reported,

> marvelled not a little to see how and in what manner those that had their minds accomplished to their desires pondered and weighed not no more the good minds of this fellowship, seeing so freely beneficially they consented and granted at their suits and desires to their requests and this so slenderly regarded and weighed by them

and it was determined to take remedial steps in order to ensure that in future such cases were 'better forseen and circumspectly looked into'. In the first place, it was agreed to incorporate in any future lease a provision against subletting or assignment to anyone not free of the Company by apprenticeship or patrimony. Secondly, no grants or promises of reversionary or future leases were to be made, whether to Mercers or non-Mercers.[47] At the same Court proposals were made for the sale of some dilapidated cottages which were 'more painful and chargeable than profitable'. After inspections had been made and tenants asked to contribute to the cost of repairs, some at least of the cottages appear to have been sold.[48] It is hard not to link these sales and the clamp-down on subletting and so forth with the deficits recorded in the Renter Warden's accounts at this time.

The same is surely also true of the early 1580s. The Act for 'improvement of rents, setting of fines and granting leases etc.' has already been noticed. This was plainly designed to increase rental income on the basis of a thorough review of all the Company's properties. There were, in fact, two other Acts passed in 1581 which pointed in the same direction. An 'Act for Balloting' was designed to avoid the recriminations and embarrassment caused by open voting. The Act covered every kind of decision, but it must have been leases in particular which the Company was trying to protect.[49] Favours to the great men at Court or to fellow members of the Company were a constant problem and, as the decision of 1561 made plain, rental income suffered in consequence. The ballot box protected revenue as well as freedom. Another Act made a similar point: no suitor was allowed to remain in Court while his case was discussed.[50]

The new rents naturally met with a good deal of resistance, and the Company was obliged to make concessions for some of its poorest tenants and to reduce registered rents for country properties which were deemed too high.[51] Most tenants, however, appear to have complied, and though the results were not spectacular rental income did rise steadily. Save for the unusual case of 1589–90, the excess of revenue over expenditure was never seriously threatened again.

CHARITIES

The Company's most notable charity in 1579 was Dean Colet's magnificent benefaction, St Paul's School, situated next to the old Cathedral. The other schools in the Company's custody were Richard Collyer's School at Horsham in Sussex (jointly administered with the local vicar, churchwardens and parishioners), Alderman William Dauntsey's School at West Lavington in Wiltshire, and the Mercers' own Chapel School in Cheapside. In addition, there were university exhibitions created by the gift of Lady Margaret North.

The Whittington almshouses near the City church of St Michael Paternoster Royal for thirteen needy men or women should also be noticed. Finally, there were a large number of lump-sum legacies from which either yearly payments were to be made to worthy objects, including the poor, hospitals, prisons and parish churches, or loans made to young men starting up in business with an obligation merely to make 'interest' payments in the form of cash or coal to the poor.

FIG. 6. The Leigh Cup. This magnificent covered cup, made in 1513, was presented to the Company in 1571 by Sir Thomas Leigh, expressly to be used at the election of the Master of the Company. The hallmark of this cup was previously believed to be 1499, until it was reinterpreted by the Antique Plate Committee of the Goldsmith's Company in 1983. The words inscribed around the cup are:
To elect the Master of the Mercerie, hither I am sent, and by Sir Thomas Leigh for the same entent.
Mercers' Company

The Company became increasingly popular with legators throughout the Elizabethan period. The most celebrated was Sir Thomas Gresham whose bequest is discussed in the next Chapter, but there were many other benefactors. Sir Thomas Ryvett (1582), Robert Hilsdon (1582), Sir William Damsell (1582), Alderman John Haydon (1583) and Sir Lionel Duckett (1585), all gave £200 or more. In fact, the Company showed signs of disquiet at this flood of munificence and examined proposals carefully before accepting. On at least four occasions potential trusts were actually deferred or turned away. In 1560 John Roysse's proposals for what became Abingdon School were regarded as likely to give rise rather to 'travail, labour and pain' than benefit for the parties involved;[52] in 1568 the Company was reluctant to accept an encumbered gift of property from Lady North because the houses concerned were in a 'ruinous' state;[53] in 1577 Sir Thomas Gresham's suggestion of a Gresham and Mercers' College at Oxford or Cambridge met with no encouragement; and in 1583 the chance of establishing scholarships at Robert Taylor's Emmanuel College in Cambridge were passed by as 'smally profitable nor commodious'.[54]

The Mercers, then, were popular and indeed rather fastidious trustees. Did they deserve this reputation? Some decades earlier Colet had reportedly declared, when asked why he had entrusted his benefaction to the Company, that 'while there was nothing certain in human affairs he yet found the least corruption' in such a body of citizens 'of approved reputation'.[55] Was this still true?

The answer may well be that it was. Only one instance of the misapplication of trust funds has been discovered, and the bequest concerned, Sir Rauf Warren's, was at least partly to be spent on Company dinners.[56] However, young men's loans were also involved and the criticism, which came from Sir Rauf's son, evidently pricked the corporate conscience, for in 1581 there was ratified (as one of the five Acts mentioned elsewhere in this

Chapter) an Act for the use of benefactors' money. In the first place it made the general statement that monies were only to be spent in accordance with the wills and testaments of the benefactors. Secondly, it established the qualifications for a loan: recipients had to be freemen (not Liverymen) retailing or trading in merchandise and residing in the City of London, and loans to those who did not so qualify had to be repaid.[57] As far as personal peccadilloes were concerned, again the record is almost unblemished. The instance of a Renter Warden accepting £4 in bribes for admitting men to a Whittington almshouse stands alone.[58]

Nevertheless it is important not to assume that, because it was not corrupt, the Company was therefore even-handed. This would be to fall victim to twentieth-century preconceptions. When the Company could exercise discretion in its charitable works, it did not hesitate to give a preference to its own members. In 1564, for example, the Company agreed to establish two University exhibitions but hoped to be able to appoint scholars from St Paul's School 'and specially Mercers' children'.[59] The list of the recurrent 'doles' to the needy tells the same story. For every Italian preacher or military veteran who received Company money,[60] there was a score of 'in-house' beneficiaries. Whether it happened to be an ex-Clerk's widow, the former servant of a prominent Mercer and benefactor, an erstwhile Second Warden fallen on hard times, or a freeman trying to get out of prison, the Court was ready to help.[61] Outsiders had to take second place. When application in 1567 was made on behalf of the bankrupted ex-Lord Mayor and Grocer, Sir Thomas Lodge, the Company replied that 'great impoverishment had lately happened [also] to diverse brethren of their own fellowship that had like need of supportation and help of the Company which the Company are to relieve'.[62]

There was one ironic consequence of this domestic largesse. The ordinances for Whittington's almshouses provided for a preference to be given to Mercers in the admission of the thirteen poor men or women. Yet when the figures are examined no undue proportion of Mercers is found. The explanation is not that the Company was unprepared to give first consideration to its own members. In 1568 the Court decided to defer the selection of two new almsmen until it could be seen 'whether any brother of this fellowship will sue for the same' and if none did so then the Wardens could 'place such other honest poor men there as they shall think most meet for that room and place'.[63] The answer is almost certainly that any Mercers who might have been able to make use of the almshouses were adequately provided for out of the Company's own resources.[64]

It is worth re-emphasising that this favouritism was neither illegal nor dishonourable. The Company was entitled to distribute its unencumbered resources in whatever way it saw fit, and former members who had given land and money would have found it strange, not to say disloyal, had current members not benefited when need arose. Indeed, when benefactors did attach charitable obligations to their bequests they frequently stipulated that Mercers should have preference. The point is simply that 'charity' then was not the same as now. The concepts are quite different.

Any verdict on the Mercers' Elizabethan charities turns on the quality of the Schools, particularly St Paul's. Unfortunately, though the records are quite full (at least for St Paul's and Collyer's), they tend to reveal the abnormal rather than the normal, conflict rather than harmony. Nevertheless, even when the bias is discounted, a rather unhappy picture remains.

The longest-serving High Master of St Paul's during this period was John Harrison (1581–96) and his was a turbulent turn in office. Numbers and standards both fell until eventually Harrison was removed. The boys seem to have been used as pawns in Harrison's power-struggle with the Company, literally mouthing his arguments in the masque or 'dialogue' at the yearly visitation.[65] The difficulties at Collyer's were almost as acute, and again revolved around a controversial Head Master, James Alleyn (1571–1617). Alleyn's misdemeanours ranged from assuming too many outside duties to charging fees for the 'free' School;

and numbers declined as a result. Local parish pressure elicited a full review by the Company in 1596–7 and the situation seems to have improved.[66]

There are, of course, two possible conclusions: that the Company deserves blame for the faults or praise for the remedies. On balance, praise is more appropriate. There was really little that could be done if the all-powerful Head or High Master chose to abuse his position. Only heavy-handed sanctions such as removal (St Paul's) or re-drawn ordinances (Collyer's) could be employed by the Company, and by then the damage had been done. The reputation of a School could not be reclaimed by executive action; it had to recover by natural processes. Accordingly, the problems of its Schools should not too readily be used to indict the Company's performance as trustees. As far as it is possible to establish, the Mercers' charities were in the custody of vigilant and honest men.

TRADE

It was in Elizabeth I's reign that the Company fought its last and unavailing battle to retain control over its eponymous trade. 'Mercery' was the name given to the more specialised end of the cloth trade, and encompassed linens, velvets and (most notably) silks. Until the beginning of the sixteenth century, Mercers had dominated the import trade in such luxury cloths and they had been the acknowledged élite of England's most important trade.

The Company had also been closely connected with the Merchant Adventurers' Company which governed the activities of English cloth merchants trading in the crucial market of Antwerp.[67] However, by the beginning of this period the situation had changed dramatically. Although City regulations required that men became freemen before trading in the Square Mile, the so-called 'custom of London' meant that there was nothing to prevent new men carrying on trades which had no connection with the Company of which they were free.

It may easily be imagined that those who became free by patrimony or redemption could well pursue 'foreign' trades, and as generation succeeded generation the tidy divisions between City Companies became hopelessly blurred. The Mercers thus lost their monopoly on merceries. They also lost touch, at least on an institutional level, with the Merchant Adventurers. From 1527 the latter no longer met at Mercers' Hall and their minutes were no longer recorded in the same book as the Mercers' (though they continued to have an office and storage-space at the Hall); and from 1555, in what was almost a ritualistic step, the bond between apprenticeship in the two Companies was severed.[68] Of course, the personal interconnections were many and deep, as witness the biographical sketches given earlier; but as a Company the Mercers were undeniably losing economic influence and the gradual divorce from the Merchant Adventurers was both symptom and cause of the process.

At the beginning of Elizabeth's reign, therefore, the Company was in a sensitive, defensive mood. In 1561 the Master and Wardens were summoned before the Privy Council to explain why the price of silk was so high. Ten years earlier the response to the same question had been that high costs had obliged them to pass on high prices to customers. Now, however, the answer was quite different.[69] The Master and Warden simply disclaimed responsibility on the grounds that the Company's members were 'the least and smallest number that do retail and sell silks in all the whole City of London'. Upon further questioning the officers explained that 'all those that do sell silks upon London Bridge be not Mercers nor free thereof nor also a great number of persons that do sell silks in Cheapside, Milk Street End and Wood Street be not Mercers neither, but some be Grocers, some Merchant Taylors, some Haberdashers, some be Clothworkers and some of other Companies and no Mercers at all . . .'. In the face of all this the Privy Council was obliged to adopt a less aggressive attitude and merely asked the Company to provide a list of all the silk traders among its members and to enjoin such traders to charge less. The Company, of course, complied; but it also decided to try to seize the opportunity to regain lost ground. A committee was set up to devise the best means of applying to the Queen and Privy Council

for the reducing and bringing again into this fellowship the whole order, traffic and trade of the retail of silks and mercery wares as it was and hath been in times past, and no long time since it was wholly in this fellowship and none others . . .[70]

Nothing is heard of the committee's deliberations, but the scheme was not jettisoned entirely. In May 1571, the Court was treated to a draft bill drawn up by the Upper Warden, Thomas Colshill, which was also designed to bring all silk retailers into the Company. The Wardens were asked to have the draft improved by the lawyers and then (with Sir Thomas Gresham's help) to place it before Cecil and Leicester with a view to submitting it to the Queen. The 'improved' draft attributed the 'decay' of the Company as well as the high price and poor quality of silk and other mercery wares to the Company's inability to control trade. Men could join the Merchant Adventurers' Company or other Livery Companies and yet still practise trades which were formerly, and properly, the preserve of the Mercers. The draft provided that all importers and retailers of silk or other merceries, present and future, would have to become free of the Mercers' Company if they were to continue their trade. In return, all Mercers who were retailers in the trade of other Companies were to leave that trade or join the appropriate Company. Every Company, in other words, was to have its 'own' trade and thus be able to control and discipline its member-traders.[71] Again it is unclear what happened to this proposal. Evidently it received no warm response at Court, though it appears to have made some headway in the City Corporation.

A year later, in 1572, Lionel Duckett was given £100 not merely to offset his expenses during his mayoralty but also 'to the end that he might be the better willing to do the Company's pleasure in reducing of all retailers of silk to be of this fellowship, wherein he had already well begun for the setting forward thereof . . .'.[72] In fact, the City Corporation was being asked at this time to take general measures to 'reduce' all traders into their appropriate Companies, and though it may be imagined that the Mercers actively supported the campaign, there is no positive evidence of this.[73] Next came a simple *cri de cœur*. In 1573, when asked to contribute loan-money towards the City's corn supply, the Company asked for a reduction in its usual assessment on the grounds that it was 'in much worse estate now, both in substance by decay of occupying and also in number, than heretofore they have been . . .'.[74] The reasons were twofold:

In primis, the Mercers in times past had the only trade of linen cloth and the chief trade of uttering silks by grate [i.e. wholesale] and by retail, and now the trade of linen cloth is wholly in other Companies' hands and of silks the Mercers have the least trade for the retail thereof. Also, they were the cheapest and in manner the only Merchant Adventurers and shippers of cloth, and now by the great number of redemptioners that have been made free there are more cloths in greater quantities shipped by other Companies than by our Company.

The last in this series of episodes occurred in 1576. It began with a resolution to follow the example of the Vintners, who had recently won the support of the Privy Council in their application for exclusive control over the wine trade, by drafting a Parliamentary bill to deal with silk.[75] Three weeks later, however, this plan was lost in the concern aroused by the City Corporation's attempts to amend the Statute of Artificers (1563) in such a manner as to permit City freemen to carry on any trade they pleased. This was certainly no radical proposal: it merely ensured that the 'custom of London' was not overridden by statute. However, the Mercers naturally saw the move as 'hurtful to the Company's suit for the bringing the retail of silks into this Company' and, as seen above, not only opposed it but also, in a bill presented to the House of Lords, advanced some counter-proposals. These latter deserve some attention. The 1563 Act was to remain in force, but it was to be applied to cities and boroughs in the following manner: existing freemen were to continue in the same trade for the rest of their lives (but with no obligation to join the appropriate Company); present or future apprentices were to practise only the trade they were apprenticed in *and* to join the appropriate Company; while those entitled to the freedom by patrimony were to confine themselves to the trade of which their fathers were free.[76]

In one sense the Company was successful in its tactics: the City's bill was lost in the House of Lords and the Statute of Artificers remained intact.[J] In other respects, however, it was a defeat. The Company's attempt to reassert trade controls was lost without trace and the City was left at liberty to apply its own interpretation to the 1563 Act. The status quo, in other words, favoured the City Corporation and the erosion of the distinctions between Companies continued apace.

The effort of 1576 appears to have been the Company's last attempt to stem the tide. Certainly the next reference to the problem comes some twelve years later and takes the form of an impotent complaint. When the Queen asked for a loan in 1588, the Wardens spoke of the 'great decay of the Company, as well in the trade of retail, whereof there was not above six in the Company of any ability, as also that the trade by wholesale was now in a manner nothing because of this troublesome time and that the number of the Company was small and poor . . .'.[77] No doubt 1588 was an unusually bad time for trade and no doubt the Wardens were likely to have exaggerated the Company's difficulties, but it will be clear that real problems did exist. The interesting thing is that the Company no longer seems to have thought it worth while fighting to resolve those problems.

The truth was that the Mercers simply could not force Elizabethan trade into a medieval straitjacket. Indeed, because so many of their potential members worked in overseas trade, the Mercers' Company was especially vulnerable, either to the rival claims of the Merchant Adventurers or to the other members of the Great Twelve. The kind of sophisticated and multi-faceted commerce undertaken by the great Elizabethan merchants could not be assimilated at all comfortably within the London guild system.

It will be noted that the Company effectively confined its demands to a monopoly over the *retail* silk trade, and yet even in this respect its efforts were unsuccessful. In fact, at the very time it was calling for a reinforcement of trade controls at Guildhall and in Parliament, the Company was quietly abandoning its own domestic controls. In 1571, it is true, a member was fined for trading with a retailer who was not free of the Company, contrary to the Company's ordinances (though the fine was commuted to three fat cygnets for the Election Dinner!) and in the following year another member was warned for the same offence.[78] However, in 1573 the Wardens were ordered to refrain from imposing further such penalties for members 'occupying' with men free of other Companies until further notice.[79] There the matter rested. The Company accepted the inevitable and resigned itself to a slow but steady metamorphosis from a trading guild into a charitable society.

RELATIONS WITH THE CITY CORPORATION

Relations between the Company and Guildhall existed on two levels, the institutional and the personal. Into the first category fell the series of fiscal demands which occur so frequently in the Acts of Court in these years. By far the most important were the loans for corn in fulfilment of the City's obligation to maintain an adequate supply of food in order to mitigate the impact of those periodic dearths which regularly swept the country. The Mercers and their fellow Livery Companies were required by the City to contribute at first money and later grain itself to central stores. This gave rise to long and complicated disputes. In 1560, for instance, members protested about the repayment of part only of the

[J] Dr Ian Archer of Keble College, Oxford, kindly supplied information on the bill's progress through Parliament.

An.reg.1. Sir Thomas Lee *Mercer.* 1558

THis ſir Thomas Lee (or Leigh) gouerned this worthy Citty of London, in the yeare 1558. He was not long in this authoritye, but God ſent vs our gracious and Noble queene Elizabeth to raigne and gouerne ouer this happy land. At the ſolemnization of her Maieſties Coronation, it pleaſed hir highneſſe to make this lord Mayor Butler for that high feaſt, & gaue vnto him a cup of golde for his dilligent paines and diſcharge of his high office. Alſo in this yeare the cittizens of London had a muſter before the queene at Greenewich of 1400. men, all furniſhed and ſet forth by the ſeuerall companies of the citty of London. Sir Thomas Lee lies buried in the Mercers chappell.

Sheriffes. John Hlaſe. Richard Champion.

An.reg.7. Sir Richard Mallary *Mercer.* 1564

SIr Richard Mallary was according to auncient cuſtome by the common conſent of this citty elected and choſen Lord Mayor for this yeare, in whoſe time I finde little recorded. In this yeare was the great Froſt, being very ſharpe & extreame, and continued many daies, inſomuch as the Thames was ſo frozen vp, that from London bridge to Weſtminſter, diuers courtyers ſhot at prickes vppon the yce. It continued till the third of January, and then came ſo ſwift a thaw, that within two daies the yce was ſo cleane conſumed, as if no ſuch froſt had hapned, but in the farewel thereof it bare downe Owſe bridge, and did much hurt. The Watch was this yeare continued on ſaint Peters euen, Nothing can I ſay further of this knight as yet, He lies buryed in the Mercers chappell.

Sheriffes. Edward Jackman, Lyonell Ducket.

An.reg.10. Sir Roger Martin *Mercer.* 1567

SIr Roger Martin was now Lord Mayor of this citty, who diſcharged the ſame very grauely and as the place required, His bringing vp was not very great, but by his diſcreet carriage and good dealing, became in time a great merchant in this citty and of great wealth, He was very courteous, and of a very pleaſant and ieaſting ſpirit, He was ſo well taken amongſt men, that hee was choſen an Alderman firſt, after called to be ſheriffe of London, and in his due place mayor, this knight married a Grecian dame, and lyeth buried in the pariſh church of ſaint Antolines, vnder a very faire monument erected, This yeare there happened ſuch ſcarſitie of fodder and hay, that in diuers places the ſame was ſold by waight for fiue pence the ſtone. No further can as yet be ſet downe of this knight.

Sheriffes. Thomas Ramſey. William Bond.

An.reg.14. Sir Wilam Allin *Mercer.* 1571

THis yeare ſir William Allin was called to this high place, by the whole conſent and cuſtome of this citty, He was a man of no greater birth then a Citizen of this cytty, and borne without Byſhopſgate, He had ſo tender a feeling of the many neceſsities of the poore, that he would buy wood from the carte and diſtribute it with his owne hands, Beſides he would walke often through the ſaid pariſh, and ſuch poore as ſtood in need he gaue reliefe vnto, and at his death gaue a weekly porcion of bread to the poore of the ſame pariſh vpon euery ſabbaoth day for euer, and was buried in the pariſh church wherein hee was chriſtened. This yeare the citizens trained three times a weeke, the number of 3000. and on May day muſtred before the Queenes Maieſty at Greenwich.

Sheriffes. Henry Mylles. John Branch.

An.reg.15 Sir Lyonell Dvcket *Mercer.* 1572

IN this yeare of our Lord abouesaid, the choiſe of the lorde mayor of this cittye, was appointed to the gouernment and charge of ſir Lyonell Ducket, who ſo behaued himſelfe in this high place, that hee gained vnto himſelfe great credite all the reſt of his daies, It ſhould alſo appeare by circumſtance, that he had a deſire to raiſe the needy poore, by leauing a taſt of his bounty behind him, beſtowing largely vpon the poore of the pariſh of Buckland in Barkſhire, in which place he reſted him, and gaue a farewell to London, and in that towne and pariſh ended his daies, and there lies buried. Many bi-matters happned in his yeare, but nothing concerning himſelfe or this citty, can I finde as yet of certainty, but if any true notes come to hand, they ſhall be ioyned hereunto.

Sheriffes. Rychard Pype. Nicholas Wodroffe.

FIG. 7. In 1601, William Jaggard published a small book entitled *A View of all the right Honourable the Lord Mayors of this honorable Citty of London*; a single copy survives and is now in America. The five Mercers who had of recent years risen to the City's highest office are shown here: Sir Thomas Leigh, 1558; Sir Richard Mallory, 1564; Sir Roger Martin, 1567; Sir William Allen, 1571; Sir Lionel Duckett, 1572. As the reader will note, Jaggard often reuses his woodcuts, changing only the text below.

By courtesy of the Huntington Library, San Marino, California

loan; in 1567 they resented the repayment being made in kind, not cash; in 1573, as already noticed, the Company requested a reduction in its quota; and in 1576 it resisted a request to make good a loss incurred on poor foreign corn and urged that the deficit be supplied from sales of existing corn and, if necessary, a general tax.[80] Behind these public statements lay a private struggle to get Company members to pay their due share of the levies. Assessments were made on the usual rank-by-rank basis, but equity did not ensure compliance. Warnings of double-payment penalties had to be issued on at least two occasions, and at the time of the 1573 protest there was compiled a book of defaulters who had to pay their dues before they could benefit in any further way from the Company.[81]

Other demands from the City were less onerous. Sometimes the requests were civic in nature (clearing the town ditch or building a pest house),[82] sometimes national (repairing Yarmouth Harbour).[83] The sums involved were not large, but the Company did not acquiesce meekly. On one occasion it thought it had been assessed unfairly, and on another it simply refused on the grounds that the money should be raised as a tax and not a Company levy.[84]

The personal relations with the City have already been touched upon. Fewer Mercers were submitting themselves to the expensive rigours of municipal office. The most notable example is afforded by Sir Thomas Gresham who, with the backing of the Queen, managed to secure exemption from civic duties as Sheriff and Alderman in 1563.[85] Gresham, of course, was unusual — his work as royal agent kept him abroad for long periods — but others followed his lead. Indeed, the Company commented on the phenomenon in 1571 in the preamble to one of the draft bills for bringing all retailers of silk into the Company. The contrast was drawn between the 'six or eight' Aldermen who were members of the Company in Henry VIII's time and the two Aldermen then.[86]

The figures may be in dispute (nine Henrician Aldermen are listed in the margin of the manuscript and there were at least three, possibly four, Aldermen at the time of the draft bill),[87] but the trend is not. There certainly *were* only two Aldermen in 1579 and, to take another significant sample year, two only again in 1603.[88] Later pages will introduce two prominent Mercers of the early seventeenth century whose abstinence from civic office was as notorious as Gresham's.[K] In other words, there can be detected in Elizabeth's reign the beginnings of a disengagement of Mercers from the City Corporation. The trend was to continue for many generations and it had a deep significance.

It is clear, therefore, that relations between Company and City were not what they had been. On an institutional level there were regular bickerings over imposts and on a personal level there was a loosening of ties. In the face of common threats in the following century the two bodies were to join forces again, but the seeds of a longer-term separation, however gentle and polite, were sown.

RELATIONS WITH THE CROWN

The Company's contacts with the Crown chiefly arose from its role as a potential source of wartime aid. Whether it was money, soldiers, armour or gunpowder, or whether the enemy was in Ireland, France or in the Channel, the Mercers were asked to assist. Every two or three years, on average, the request would come. On occasion the Company would try to resist, as witness the protest registered in 1588; but invariably it had to bow to royal pressure, and the problem became a familiar one of prising the money out of members. In 1578 an ordinance was passed providing for fines to be levied on those who refused to contribute towards assessments, particularly for musters;[89] while in 1580 a 'Black Book' was instituted for much the same purpose. The preamble to the Black Book Act, one of the celebrated five Acts, declared that 'in times past this Company has been very sore charged and greatly burdened by the sending out of soldiers into the wars for the service of the Prince in the defence of the realm and also with

[K] See below, pp. 94–5.

diverse other charges and prests from time to time'. Accordingly a register of debts was to be maintained, on the basis of which a Company member might be refused certain privileges and benefits.[90] The signs are that the Black Book was not well used (at least not for its original purpose, since it contains a good deal of other miscellaneous information), but its mere institution is evidence of the regularity with which the Company was subjected to royal exactions.[91]

The Crown's other dealings with the Company took the form of patronage — less burdensome and less frequent than taxation, perhaps, but sometimes just as difficult for the Company to satisfy. In 1574 came the first direct request for such favours from the Queen. One Scudamore wanted leases of two houses in Cheapside, and the Queen, together with Leicester and Burghley, wrote on his behalf. This threw the Company into deep perplexity, but to its credit it did not capitulate. One house was already committed, while the other was intended for use by the Company itself and in any event could not, by Company ordinances, be granted in reversion until the expiration or surrender of the existing lease. A further letter on the Queen's behalf from Leicester brought forth a suggestion for compromise, but no retreat. In the end Scudamore was bought off (albeit with the substantial sum of £125) and in due course the second property was indeed used to provide supplementary premises for the Hall.[92] The second such intervention by the Queen occurred in 1578, and again the Company stood its ground quite well. To begin with, it thought it would be unable to comply with Elizabeth's request that a lease be granted to the brother of one of her Privy Councillors because of a previous commitment, and it was only when the grantee surrendered his interest (after a negotiation superintended by Sir Walter Mildmay) that the Company did as it had been bidden to do.[93] Next came an application by the Queen in 1582 on behalf of a would-be tenant of a St Paul's School farm. On this occasion the combined blandishments of Elizabeth, Walsingham and Hatton succeeded in persuading the Company to break its recently restated prohibition on long leases of country property.[94]

FIG. 8. The handsome Wagon and Tun, made in 1554 by Jeronimus Orth, was presented to the Company in 1573 by William Byrde. The wagon can travel along a surface by a clockwork mechanism which is in good working order.
Mercers' Company

Finally, there is the reaction to the Queen's support for Edward Norton as Under-Officer in 1587. At first the election for Southern was defended as free and fair, but after an expression of royal displeasure Southern resigned and Norton was selected in his place, with the unfortunate consequences already described.[95] Patronage, of course, was a feature of the age and it should cause no surprise, nor undue censure, if the Company succumbed to its pressures. In many ways the measure of independence it maintained deserves greater attention than the occasional capitulation.

The general impression is that relations with the Crown were as harmonious as they could have been, given the Queen's determination to sustain her hard-pressed exchequer with Company money and satisfy her courtiers with Company leases. The importunity, though considerable, was kept within tolerable bounds. The Queen's personality and her policies (or lack of them) earned her the respect or at least the tolerance of her City 'victims'. Attitudes changed, however, at the end of her reign when the style of government altered, and there was positive antagonism under the early Stuarts. It was not that the Mercers had been immune from royal demands in the past: these pages should show the fallacy of that assumption. It was rather that the demands became more intense, more arbitrary and, most importantly of all, less obviously justifiable. It was one thing to give money, albeit under protest, to defeat the Armada in the Channel; it was another to do the same for dubious and humiliatingly unsuccessful adventures abroad.

THE HALL: FEASTS AND CEREMONIES

The Company's Cheapside home, acquired from the Hospital of St Thomas of Acre in the first half of the century, has been the subject of meticulous research,[96] but it is still difficult to envisage. A mid-century representation does survive (Fig. 5), though it is impressionistic in the extreme. John Stow spoke of the 'fair and beautiful chapel, arched over with stone, and thereupon Mercers' hall, a most curious piece of work'; but this description omitted the Hospital church, which became the Company's chapel in 1542 (leaving the old chapel, controversially, to be used as shops). There were a large number of minor improvements and alterations during these years, but the only major development involved the acquisition of additional accommodation in 1580.

The grandest occasion of the Company calendar was the Election Dinner, held at first in July and then from 1590 onwards in September. During the 1580s, it is true, the Company's financial difficulties dictated restraint and only drinks appear to have been served;[97] and in another year the plague had the same effect. Generally, however, the 'superfluity' (as it was once disarmingly described)[98] went unchecked.[99]

The main fare (subject to the occasional Mayoral precept)[100] was usually venison donated by the Wardens' friends, and this gave rise to a certain amount of 'one-upmanship', as witness the following illustration of John Isham's 'liberality' as recalled by his son:[101]

> In those days they that were chosen Wardens of the Company of the Mercers did [yearly] against their feast, which was at St. James's tide [25 July], procure of their friends as much venison as they could to make their brethren good cheer. Now this man, having had great goodwill and liking of gentlemen, did against the time of the feast gather together 33 fat and large bucks, which he showed to divers of his Company, lying altogether in a gallery where he dwelt. Which seemed unto them most strange, as by their speeches I might perceive, being then a youth and standing by as others did. Yea it was thought that not one before his time nor since, until the writing hereof, had the like by a great many.

All members of the Company, except those 'out of the Livery', would be invited, together with a number of distinguished guests from the City and Westminster. In 1564, for instance, the Lord Mayor, the two Sheriffs, several Aldermen, the French Ambassador (in recognition of a recent Peace), a number of peers and a few other public notables all attended.[102] In 1560 there was even the prospect of the Queen appearing , a possibility which prompted a flurry of anxious activity and a determination to make Sir Thomas Gresham, 'the beginner and doer of all this', meet the extra expense.[103]

The wives of guests and members were not excluded, though they were seated in a separate room. There was indeed a good deal of stratification by 'estates', from the High Table in the Hall down to the 'gentlewomen waiters'' own table in an ante-room.[104] The chief waiters, in fact, were a selected group of Bachelors fulfilling another of their pre-Livery duties and liable to fines for non-appearance.[105]

Towards the end of the meal there took place the celebrated 'garland ceremony', during which the new Master and Wardens were adorned with diadems of thirty gilly flowers and toasted by their predecessors from standing cups of hippocras or spiced wine.[106] Such rituals were not uncommon among the Livery Companies, and when the change of date from July to September made flowers difficult to obtain the Mercers modelled their velvet substitutes on those used by the Grocers and Drapers.[107]

Other dinners were less splendid and less regular. In December there was held a Surveyors and Audit Dinner for St Paul's School, to which from 1567 (when the date was changed to February) the academic examiners were also invited.[108] There was also meant to be an annual dinner paid for out of Sir Rauf Warren's bequest, but this was sometimes merged with other events — for example, a Mercers' School 'apposition' in 1581, and the election of Sheriffs from 1592 onwards — and occasionally, or so it would seem, not held at all.[109] A special dinner was held in 1576[L] but there were no others.[110] Doubtless the Election Dinner was thought to be the appropriate occasion to entertain the great and the good, particularly at a time when the Company was short of money. As for innovations, Quarter-day Dinners for all save those 'out of the Livery' were instituted briefly in the late 1560s, but suspended for reasons of cost in 1570 and then evidently dropped;[111] while a proposal in 1577 for a Young Men's Dinner came to nothing.[112] Enduring novelties had to await Sir Thomas Gresham's Quarterly Dinners for the whole Company which began in 1597.[113]

In addition to such 'domestic' affairs there were, of course, also times when the Company played an important part in civic or City events. On the five occasions during Elizabeth's reign when a member of the Company became Lord Mayor and, somewhat less significantly, on the six occasions when a member became Sheriff, the Company played a prominent role in the celebrations which surrounded the commencement of the new incumbent's term of office.[114] Members of the Company, from Assistants to Bachelors, were pressed into service, whether as supervisors at the Lord Mayor's feast, bargemen for the Lord Mayor's Show, bearers of the Company's emblematic Maiden or Virgin,[M] [115] or simple footmen processing to and from Guildhall. The rituals were the subject of detailed precedents and careful planning. The colour of the Master Bachelors' hoods and gowns, the duties of the waiters and the plate to be provided, all were laid down in the records.[116] The Company also participated in the Midsummer Watch procession around the City in 1568, but this was no more than a brief resuscitation of a dying tradition and the Mercers' contribution (in the form of lights and bearers) probably owed more to a desire to support their Lord Mayor, Roger Martin, than genuine enthusiasm.[117] The real hub of the City's ceremonial year was now the Lord Mayor's Show, and to it the Company contributed manfully.

CONCLUSION

The most difficult question has been left to last. How did the Company regard itself? Was it conscious of its history and its future, or did it live only for the present, treating traditions as routines and turning a blind eye to posterity?

At an 'official' level at least there were indications of a consciousness of the Company's obligations to past and future generations of members. In 1566, for example, it was resolved to erect monuments to Whittington, Colet and other notable benefactors in order 'to keep in memory their worthy facts and to encourage others to follow them in the like'.[118] When in 1573 further such 'personages' were placed in the Hall, the reason was again stated to be the need to ensure that the benefactors' good deeds were kept in 'continual memory'.[119]

[L] Possibly in acknowledgement of the defeat of the City's apprenticeship bill.

[M] The identification of the Maiden who appears in the Company's arms as the Virgin Mary was doubted by Sir John Watney in his *History* (pp. 27–9), but J. Bromley presents a strong counter-case in *The Armorial Bearings of the Guilds of London* (1960), pp. 168–72. It was certainly assumed by subsequent generations of members that the Maiden was the Virgin Mary: see, for example, AC, 8 October 1701.

Whether such stratagems had the desired effect is another matter. Benefactions did certainly continue to be directed towards the Company. Indeed, as seen earlier, the Company even turned some away. It will, however, have been noticed that the benefactors were invariably former Masters or Wardens, or their widows. It seems very doubtful that outside the Court of Assistants, and still more so outside the Livery, members were nearly so conscious of the Company's role. In view of the oligarchical tendencies identified above, dividing Wardens and potential Wardens from the long-serving Bachelors and confining Company festivities very largely to the Livery, to the exclusion of the Young Men, it would seem that Company loyalty went so far and no further.

This should not be a matter of great surprise. At a time when the Livery Companies still retained, even among the Great Twelve, a certain residue of their economic *raison d'être*, some of the lowlier members at least were bound by necessity, not affection, to their Companies. Only when the City's trading regulations were further relaxed would the Mercers' Company find itself composed entirely of those who had *chosen* to join its ranks. Only then would all members be committed to the Company's charitable ideals. One of the compensations for the loss of the Mercers' guild past would be a heightened consciousness of their charitable future.

CHAPTER II
THE GRESHAM LEGACY

SIR THOMAS GRESHAM

Sir Thomas Gresham (1517–79) was one of the great merchants and public servants of Tudor times. The success of his endeavours, on behalf of both his country and himself, was prodigious. For nearly two decades, through the reigns of Edward VI and Mary as well as the early years of Elizabeth I, he was the Crown's most important financial agent abroad, coaxing and indeed manipulating the foreign exchanges to protect the Crown from the effects of fluctuating trade and currency rates, and trying to secure credit and loans on the best possible terms. He was effectively an ambassador without portfolio and, like his royal employer, had sometimes to use style to hide the lack of substance in his negotiations. The shortage of ready cash was a constant and worrying limitation for the Tudors. Historians may now question whether Gresham's achievements were really as remarkable as was once believed; there are indications that legerdemain and bullying played as much part as shrewd negotiation; but, whatever the methods, the results were undoubtedly impressive.

Contemporaries were plainly aware that Gresham was a figure of the highest significance. With prestige came wealth. Gresham, like other public servants, was not paid directly by the Crown, but he exploited his advantageous position to the full. He amassed a large fortune and died reputedly the wealthiest commoner in England.

The first considered appreciation of Gresham's life came in the nineteenth century with the publication of Burgon's *Life and Times* (1839).[1] Not unnaturally, Burgon saw Gresham as a model for his own age, a prototype of the enlightened entrepreneur. Here was a man, it was claimed, who without the benefit of noble birth earned great wealth by virtue of skill and application, and then at his death distributed that wealth for the benefit of his fellow citizens. This view survived until quite recently, but now a more sceptical attitude prevails.[2] Gresham is now seen as a hard-headed and occasionally dishonest financier, unencumbered with moral sensitivity; not a little of his spectacular rise to fame, it is said, was the result of a readiness to thwart rivals and deceive the Crown. This historical reappraisal is important in the context of this story because there has been a good deal of debate about the motives for, and also the generosity of, the legacy which forms the subject-matter of this Chapter. The details will be given in their proper place below, but it may be stated here that in his capacity as benefactor of the Mercers' Company, Gresham conforms more to the picture painted by recent historians rather than to the didactic model of the Victorians.

A few words are needed on Gresham's links with the City and the Mercers. It is one thing to explain how he accumulated the money for his benefaction, but another to show why he placed it in the joint custody of the Corporation and the Company. Gresham was the son of Sir Richard Gresham, who became both Lord Mayor and Master of the Mercers' Company; and he was apprenticed to his uncle, Sir John Gresham, another Lord Mayor and Master. Thomas himself, though he never served in the City Corporation, was a fully fledged Mercer: he was made a freeman in 1543, was admitted to the Livery in the following year and served as Master in 1569–70, 1573–4 and 1579. Even his wife's first husband was a Mercer.

As far as benefactions were concerned, his uncle John founded the well-known Grammar School at

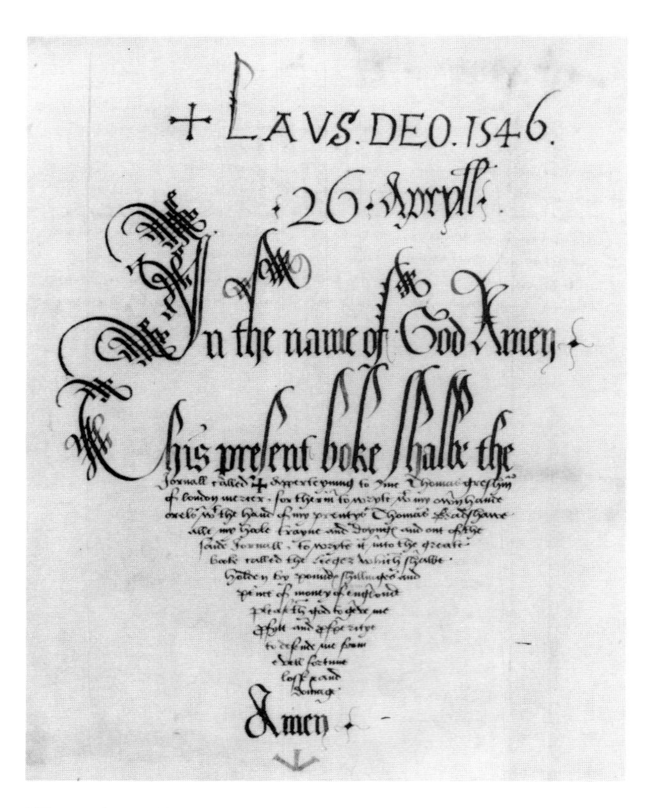
+ LAVS. DEO. 1546.

26 Aprill.

In the name of God Amen

This present boke shalbe the

Amen

FIG. 9. The first page of Sir Thomas Gresham's Day Book. Gresham kept his accounts from 1546 to 1552 in this large volume, measuring 18 × 12 in. Though, unfortunately, it pre-dates the building of the Royal Exchange, the entries make clear what a systematic businessman Gresham was, even at the start of his career.
Mercers' Company

Holt in Norfolk (administered by the Fishmongers' Company), while his stepmother Isabella gave a substantial legacy to the Mercers themselves.

THE ROYAL EXCHANGE[A]

The origins of Thomas Gresham's legacy may be traced to his father's time when it became a matter of general concern that the City of London could not boast a proper bourse (i.e. a money or trading market) in the continental style. Merchants met publicly in Lombard *Street*, and that meant quite literally in the open air, with no protection for their persons or indeed their dignity. The lack of a bourse was regarded as both a symptom and a cause of London's failure to dominate European trade in the way that first Antwerp and later Amsterdam did. Various plans were put forward, notably in the late 1530s, during and after Sir Richard Gresham's mayoralty. These foundered partly because of difficulties in acquiring the necessary land and partly because of differences over the best position for the site. Demands for action continued, however, despite the set-backs. In 1561, for example, Sir Thomas was treated to the following remarks in a letter from his agent in Antwerp:[3]

> ... indeed it is [a] marvel that we have so good orders as we have, considering what rulers we have in the City of London; such a company that do study for nothing else but for their own profit. As for example, considering what a city London is and that in so many years they have not found the means to make a bourse! But [we] must walk in the rain when it raineth, more like pedlars than merchants; and in this country, and all others, there is no kind of people that have occasion to meet but they have a place meet for that purpose. Indeed, and if your business were done and that I might have the leisure to go about it and that you will be a means to Mr Secretary [Cecil] to have his favour therein, I will not doubt but to make so fair a bourse in London as the great bourse is in Antwerp without molesting of any man more than he should be well disposed to give.

[A] This section in particular owes much to the unpublished researches of Miss Jean Imray, the Company's former Archivist. See in particular Misc. MS 2. 12.

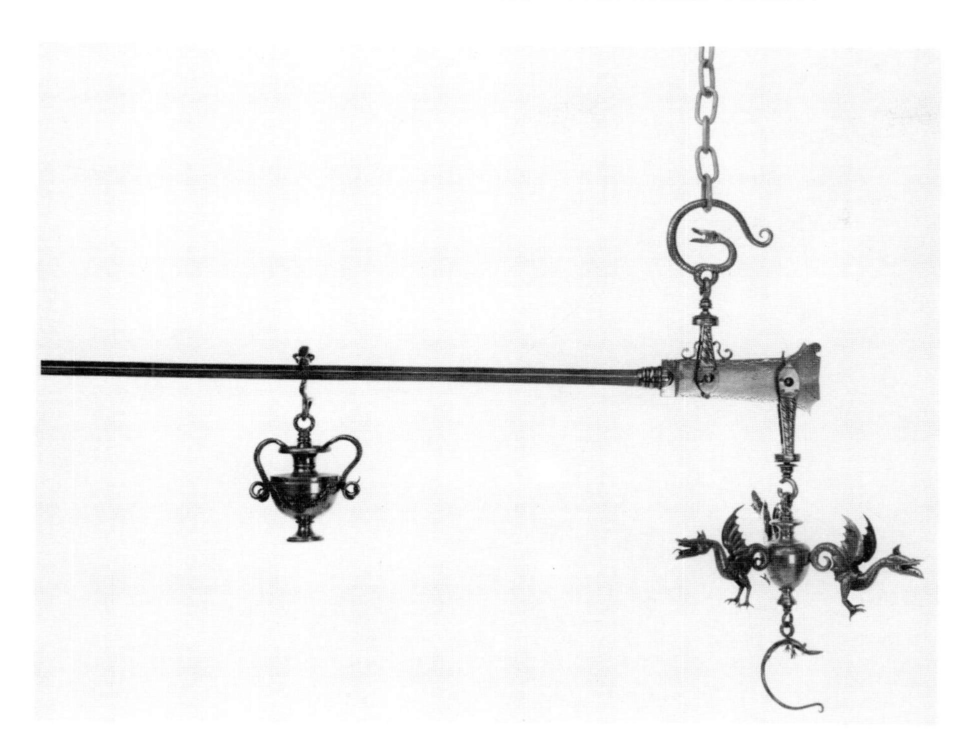

FIG. 10. Gresham's Steelyard. This handsome weighing instrument bears Gresham's own arms; he may have given it to the Royal Exchange.
By courtesy of the Museum of London

Gresham did not evidently release his man from his duties nor did he immediately take up the challenge himself, but the idea did not disappear from sight. In January 1565, under what impetus it is impossible to say, Gresham is found offering to pay the costs, and organise the construction, of a bourse (or Exchange, as the English term had it), provided that the City Corporation gave the site. The City at once responded to the suggestion and, after one attempt had been defeated by reason of the Merchant Taylors' dogged refusal to sell (notwithstanding a good deal of rather unseemly pressure), a suitable and available site was found in Cornhill. Then there was the question of paying for it. Something over £3,000 had to be found, and as usual in such circumstances individuals were asked to contribute. The Mercers submitted a list of 128 possible donors, of whom 83 did eventually give some money (in total £296).[4] These 'voluntary' sums, however, were not sufficient and, among other devices to make up the shortfall, the Corporation imposed a forced loan on the Companies themselves, and in April 1566 the Mercers duly paid £70.[5]

At the same time as these efforts were being made to fulfil the City's side of the bargain, other, but unfortunately less successful, attempts were made to ensure that Gresham kept his part of the deal. In February 1566 Gresham attended a meeting with the City's representatives and it was reported that[6]

> [he] did most frankly and lovingly grant and promise that within one month after the building and fully finishing of the bourse and bourse pawns [i.e. shops] and other buildings intended he would assure to the City for the City's use the moiety of all the said bourse, pawns and other buildings, as well of those buildings planted within the circuit of the bourse as without; the profits thereof to come to the said City, to the use of the Mayor and Commonalty of the said City, after the decease of the said Sir Thomas Gresham and of his wife, so that it happen that the said Sir Thomas do die without issue of his body lawfully begotten. And the other moiety he hath like promised to leave to the Mercery with like estate and like condition as aforesaid; and for the sure performance of the premises the said Sir Thomas ... did give his hand to [Alderman] Sir William Garrard and drank a carouse to Thomas Rowe [a kinsman who had been involved in the acquisition of the site] ...

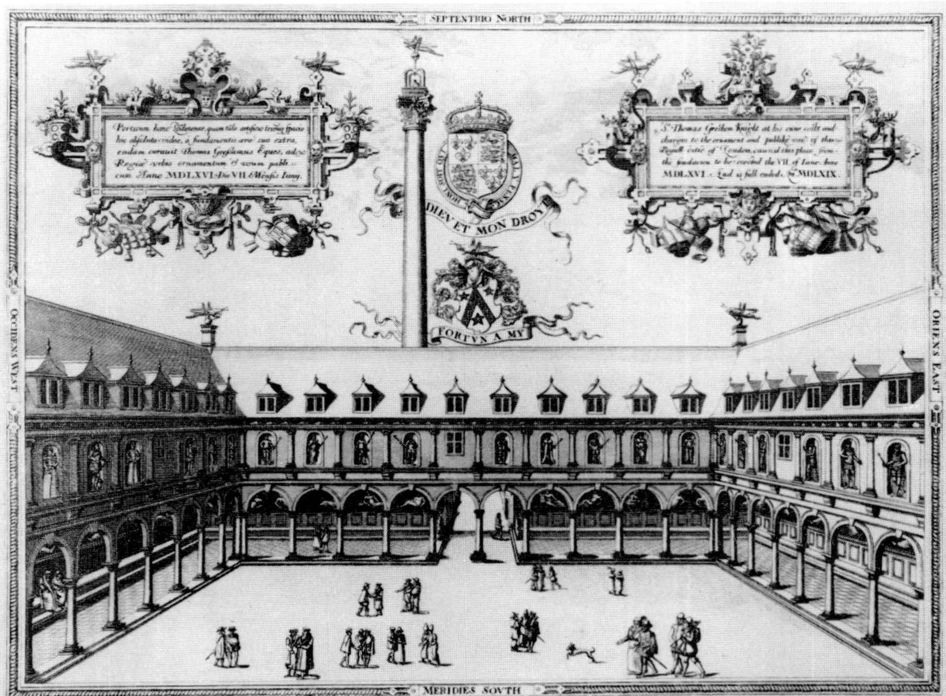

FIG. 11. The exterior and interior of the Royal Exchange, *c.* 1569, by Frans Hogenberg, re-issued by Robert Wilkinson, 1810. Note the Gresham grasshoppers which adorn every possible vantage point.
By courtesy of Guardian Royal Exchange Collection

In the following May the City tried to consummate this arrangement in legal form, but though it sealed its own part of the agreement (with provision for a £5,000 performance bond from Gresham), the counterpart was evidently never executed. The significance of this was only to become apparent a number of years later when Gresham grafted his celebrated College on to the Exchange benefaction. If matters had remained as the City had intended they should in 1566, then separate provision for the funding of the College would have been necessary and the proceeds from the Exchange would have been the City's (and the Company's) to do with as they pleased. The failure to conclude the agreement with Gresham was a serious one; the City and the Mercers should have known better than to rely on a mere understanding with such a tough negotiator.

For a few years all was well. The building work got under way in June 1566 and three years later it was completed. The Exchange was an imposing structure, built, significantly enough, in the Flemish mode and with Flemish labour (much to the disgust of the English workmen). An arcaded courtyard was surrounded on its outside and on the second storey by 120 'pawns' or shops from which first the Greshams, and later the City and Company, would draw their income. Gresham's emblematic grasshoppers stood on the four corners of the steeply pitched roof and also on top of the high tower, the bell of which summoned merchants to the concourse. Despite the grandeur, lettings were sluggish at first, but then in 1571 Gresham arranged what can only be described as a publicity stunt. The Queen's visit gave the Exchange (or, as it was thereafter called, the *Royal* Exchange) the prestige it had hitherto lacked.[7] The remaining leases were quickly disposed of and rents rose commensurately. The Royal Exchange did not fulfil the wishes of its backers in emulating its models on the Continent, but at least it was solvent and did not look likely to become a burden to its future custodians.

FIG. 12. Queen Elizabeth I opening the Royal Exchange, 23 January 1571. Tapestry designed by Richard Beavis, 1887, for the Mansion House.
By courtesy of Guildhall Library, Corporation of London

The City and the Mercers were shaken out of this complacency by the news in 1575 that Gresham was planning not only to establish an educational College, but also to require the City and Company to pay for the proposed foundation out of the Royal Exchange rents. This must have come as a bolt from the blue. As far as can be established, the first indication the trustees had of any such intention came in a letter from the Vice-Chancellor of Cambridge University in March 1575 hoping to divert the rumoured benefaction in his University's direction. In the same month and again in April, there were meetings between the City and Gresham which, though stated to have been concerned merely with 'the assurance of the Royal Exchange', almost certainly dealt with the newly planned College. Three months later all doubts were dispelled with the making of Gresham's will. Its provisions confirmed the City's, and the Mercers', worst fears.[8]

THE WILL

In the first place, the Royal Exchange was granted (subject to Lady Gresham's life interest) to the City and Company for a period of fifty years. If during that time a licence in mortmain was obtained (and Gresham urged this upon his legatees), then the City and the Mercers were to have the Royal Exchange in perpetuity. Thus far Gresham fulfilled his promise. However, he went on to make the income arising from the Royal Exchange subject to various charges. Out of its half of the proceeds, the City was to provide £50 per annum for each of four lecturers in Divinity, Astronomy, Music and Geometry in what was to become Gresham College, as well as £53 6*s*. 8*d*. per annum to eight almspeople and £50 per annum to five prisons. The Mercers' half was committed in similar ways: £50 per annum for each of three lecturers in Law, Physic and Rhetoric; £50 per annum to hospitals and a prison; and rather more attractively £100 per annum for quarterly Company Dinners. Finally there was the devise of Gresham's Bishopsgate house, in which the College was to be established, to the City and

FIG. 13. Sir Thomas Gresham's tomb, St Helen's Bishopgate. A grasshopper surmounts the helm.
By courtesy of English Heritage

Company jointly for fifty years, again with provision for a licence in mortmain. The result was that a legacy, which the City and the Mercers had expected to be encumbered only by Lady Gresham's life interest, was subjected further to payments totalling £603 6*s*. 8*d*. per annum. The disappointment must have been heightened by the fact that more than half of the outgoings were to be devoted, not to the traditional objects of charity, but to salaries for lecturers at the Bishopsgate College.

Gresham's reasons for founding his College were once thought to have been farsighted and his motives idealistic. However, as the verdict on his character has altered, so has the assessment of his educational aims. 'Farsighted' the benefaction certainly was not. There were a number of enterprises offering practical non-academic education and catering especially for the daily needs of London's merchants and tradesmen. Most were on a small scale but there were some schemes and suggestions of a like kind which might have matched Gresham's own plan had they come to fruition. No direct link between these abortive ideas and Gresham College can be traced, though there are some suggestive personal and Company connections. John Dee, for example, in an introduction to a translation of Euclid in 1570, spoke of the practical value of mathematics, particularly for those who shunned more rarefied studies at Oxford or Cambridge, and also emphasised the need to have works on the subject available in the vernacular. It has always to be remembered that Gresham's own formal stipulations for his College were extremely vague and that the assertion that the College was 'a characteristic product of the Elizabethan Age' must be interpreted in the light of the trustees' subsequent amplification and implementation of the bequest.[B] None the less even the rudimentary framework gives some idea of Gresham's intentions and these were plainly *not* original. The College was noteworthy only because, unlike so many such plans, it actually came into being. Nor is it reasonable to describe the founder's motives as 'idealistic'. The foundation of Gresham College is now seen in prosaic terms, namely, in part as merely the intellectual complement of the Exchange (itself a practical attempt to foster economic nationalism) and in part also as the manifestation of a London merchant's desire to leave a permanent mark in the City.[9]

Sir Thomas Gresham, therefore, died not the magnanimous benefactor of vision but rather, as he had lived, a calculating and opportunistic businessman. The publication of the will must have made the City and the Company ponder the wisdom of becoming entangled with the great man's financial affairs. The bargain of 1566 had every prospect of becoming one-sided indeed.[C]

LADY GRESHAM'S TENURE (1579–96)

In the meantime, before the legacy came into the City's and the Company's joint control, there was the question of Lady Gresham's life interest. The apparently innocuous provision in Gresham's will turned out to be a source of major difficulties and, for the seventeen years which elapsed between the death of Sir Thomas in 1579 and the death of his widow in 1596, the Company, and the City, were driven close to distraction by the behaviour of this extremely formidable lady.

The first contretemps arose in 1580 when the City and the Company approached Lady Gresham with a view to obtaining from her an 'assurance' of their joint future interest in the Royal Exchange. Lady Gresham declared herself 'very ready and forward' to acquiesce in the request, but made her consent conditional upon the grant of a lease to her late husband's associate (and Mercer) Edmund Hogan.[10] Without any testamentary evidence to support her case, Lady Gresham claimed that her husband had intended that the City and Company should not have the Exchange unless provision were made for Hogan.

[B] See below, p. 37.

[C] Little wonder that, when in 1577 Gresham suggested the additional foundation of a 'Sir Thomas Gresham and Mercers' College' in Oxford or Cambridge, the Company declined the honour. SPS AC, 1513–1622, f. 180v.

Doubtless for the sake of the larger end in view and not, it is to be hoped, because Hogan was a Mercer,[D] the condition was accepted and the lease granted. The quid pro quo came in an Act of Parliament passed in March 1581.[11] The main purpose of the Act was twofold: to settle differences which had arisen between Lady Gresham and another branch of the family and to provide for the discharge of Sir Thomas's debts. The City and the Company were able to secure the inclusion of a proviso which excepted the Royal Exchange from the settlement in the rest of the Act and confirmed the arrangements contained in the will, save that now the legacy was assured to the City and Company for ever. The licence in mortmain had been obtained, at least as far as the Royal Exchange was concerned.[12] (It was to be thirty-six years before the Bishopsgate house was similarly secured.[13])

The next round of negotiations with Lady Gresham came later in 1581 when there was concern about the Exchange's poor state of repair. The City at least asked her to fulfil her (alleged) obligations and invoked Privy Council assistance in an attempt to prick her conscience. Whether anything resulted is unclear. Probably not, because more than a year later the City, presumably with Company support, instigated an inquiry into the question of responsibility for repairs to a further decaying fabric and to see whether Lady Gresham could be 'charged and compelled' to act. This time there was evidently some success, but her workman was so inept or worse that only three years later matters were as bad as before. In 1586 the Privy Council had again to be asked to intervene, which it did by warning Lady Gresham that 'the Queen will take great offence if so beautiful a monument is suffered to decay'. Less satisfactorily from the Company's point of view, the Privy Council ordered that the cost of repairs be divided into three equal shares, though in the event Lady Gresham appears to have paid for all the work herself.[14]

Further recalcitrance was evident in 1590 when Lady Gresham refused to contribute to the costs involved in the Chancery suit brought by one Jacques who laid claim to some of the land on which the Exchange had been built.[15] She argued that, since the site had been purchased by the City and not by her husband, it was not her concern. This was literally true, of course, but it hardly became her to take such logic-chopping points when she had done so little to maintain the fabric of the Exchange, an obligation which was, at least on the basis of her reasoning, undoubtedly hers alone to discharge. Her niggardliness, in fact, appears almost breathtaking when considered in the light of her conduct over the next few years.

Lady Gresham had a son, William Reade, born to her during her previous marriage. As the end of her life drew near, she became anxious to make the best possible provision for him and her other dependants. One ruse was to extract as much money as she could from the Exchange before it fell into the hands of the City and the Mercers. Early in 1593 Lady Gresham petitioned the Privy Council proposing an Act of Parliament, the chief effect of which would have been to enable her and her heirs to grant leases for twenty-one years or three lives, taking the fines for themselves and reserving merely the then current rents to enable the City and Company to carry out their obligations under the will. To add insult to injury, the bill stipulated further that if the City or the Mercers failed to fulfil those obligations then the bequest would pass to another trust corporation. The Company's reaction to all this can only be surmised, but the City's response does survive and, as a reflection of the mounting indignation and concern about the entire legacy, it deserves lengthy quotation. Even the formal language fails to mask the message:[16]

> ... her demand is utterly against both the last will and testament of Sir Thomas Gresham, her late husband, as also expressly against an Act of Parliament made in the twenty-third year of her Majesty's reign [1581]. Unto which Act the said Lady Gresham was privy, and

[D] The Acts are equivocal. Hogan is described as 'a good brother of the Company and furtherer of the gift of the Exchange'. AC, 1560–95, ff. 347v–8.

her counsel was heard, what they could say, before the said Act passed. And they say also, the same request of the said Lady Gresham is against all reason and equity: for that the citizens of the City of London purchased in fee simple, in the name of divers feoffees, the soil whereupon the Royal Exchange is builded, and paid for the same above four thousand pounds; and in the eighth year of her Majesty's reign [1566] conveyed the same to Sir Thomas Gresham, upon condition to have reassurance made according to certain covenants, which was not done. And albeit the citizens might lawfully have entered for breach of the said condition, and presently taken the rents and profits of the whole, yet they have contented themselves to accept of the same according to the last will and Act of Parliament and have suffered the said Lady Gresham to take the whole profits. And yet they have been at great charges in defending of title made to some part of the same, and in paying of quit rents, tithes and widows' dowers, which they still continue to this day.

Touching the employment of the profits of the Exchange, according to the purport of the testament of Sir Thomas Gresham, it is thereunto answered that it is meant, and so it shall be performed, that the same, after the death of the Lady Gresham, shall be employed justly and truly according to the trust and confidence in them reposed. Which if they should break, there are Courts of Equity that can take order for the remedy thereof. But for as much as the said Lady Gresham is to have the same during her life and the employments are not to be made until after her death, therefore this complaint is now made before any injury be offered.

These cogent arguments seem to have scotched Lady Gresham's attempt to be given the right to grant leases, but the idea of a 'default' provision in case the City and the Mercers should fail to fulfil their trust obligations took root and the Privy Council pressed for a further reply on this point. Either because of brave obstinacy or because of a touch of indifference towards a troublesome bequest, the Company at first stood its ground and refused to accede to any condition not already imposed by the will or the 1581 Act of Parliament.[17] However, when the Company joined in the formal answer to the Privy Council, it adopted a subtler position. Without any recognition of the merits of the argument, it agreed to offer some form of bond for the due performance of its obligations in return for a further assurance of the Exchange by Lady Gresham and royal backing for the College to prevent any conflict with Oxford and Cambridge Universities.[18] There the matter appears to have ended. With her main aim lost Lady Gresham evidently backed away from the commitment required and the Privy Council presumably had no desire to have the Crown involved in the imbroglio.

Lady Gresham, however, had one last card to play. It so happened that just as she was coming to the end of her life many of the twenty-one-year leases granted by her husband when he first set up the Exchange fell due for renewal. Lady Gresham inevitably saw this as a golden opportunity to collect large fines before her death. The corollary, of course, was that the City and Mercers, when they came into possession, would be confronted with a set of tenants most unwilling to endure further fines or increases in rent. It was said that Lady Gresham collected a total of £4,000 in her timely 'raid'.[19] Unfortunately there was little the City or the Company could do. Lady Gresham was simply entitled to the proceeds of the Exchange until her death. In one case, it is true, the Mercers came to an arrangement with two canny and persuasive tenants who came to them for protection against the predatory widow,[20] but for the most part they, and the City, had simply to wait for Lady Gresham to die.

LADY GRESHAM'S 'LEGACY'

Lady Gresham's death in November 1596 must have been greeted with great relief by her late husband's legatees. However, relief turned to exasperation during the two years of legal wrangling which followed. There were two main problems, both the direct cause of Lady Gresham's systematic exploitation of Sir Thomas's Royal Exchange property.

In March 1597 Lady Gresham's son, William Reade, made a predictable bid for part of the estate. He petitioned for the benefit of all the leases granted by his mother, amounting to £504 per annum in rental income. The Company's reply was equally predictable.[21] It first rehearsed not merely the ordinary expenses to which the

Company and City were committed (i.e. £603 6*s*. 8*d*.) but also the extraordinary expenses — tithes, wages, fees, repairs and so forth — for which the two corporations additionally found themselves liable (calculated at £238 13*s*. 4*d*.). If Reade were to draw off the income he proposed, then on the basis that other leases produced £120 per annum there would be a shortfall, according to the Company's figures, of £118 per annum. The Company further pointed out that a large sum had been spent in acquiring the site for the Royal Exchange, and the Greshams had enjoyed the benefit of that investment for many years. Additional heavy expenditure on repairs to the Exchange and Gresham's house was anticipated in the near future. The reply concluded: 'sure we are that neither the City nor Company of Mercers shall be any gainers by Sir Thomas Gresham's will, but [rather] take upon them a charge without profit'. On this trenchant and indeed prophetic note the matter appears to have rested. Reade admitted defeat.

The second problem was much more difficult to resolve. It first materialised in a formal fashion in the spring of 1598 when a number of tenants petitioned the Lord Keeper, Sir Thomas Egerton, with an angry tale. They had been obliged to renew their leases with Lady Gresham shortly before she died, and had paid her hefty entry fines for doing so. On Lady Gresham's death they were promised by 'certain Aldermen' favourable treatment if they did not go to law to assert any rights they might have. Instead they now found themselves faced with substantially increased rents, terms limited to ten years and other onerous provisions. At their expense, the tenants claimed, the City and the Company were making £500 'profit' each year.

The reply to all this, via the Lord Keeper, was as vigorous as the reply to Reade had been.[22] The promise of favourable treatment was flatly denied and the £500 surplus was dismissed as an exaggeration which took no account of various extraordinary payments. The real surplus was £121. The rent increases were therefore necessary to maintain the trust, and in any event were modest by comparison with the profits made by the tenants through subletting. The complainants were derided, inevitably perhaps, as a minority of 'busy and factious persons' caring only for themselves. Most of the tenants were allegedly content to pay their fines and rents.

The tenants were more formidable adversaries than Reade and refused to accept this initial rebuff. They followed up their petition to the Lord Keeper with a similar one to the Privy Council itself.[23] Again a reply had to be formulated. The main points were much as before, though there were two new ones which deserve notice.[24] In the first place, the Privy Council was told that tenants had been warned that any leases made with Lady Gresham would not stand after her death. Those who had gone ahead none the less had done so at their own risk, 'knowing that if [she] should fortune to live but three years they should have good recompense in the easiness of their rents for the fines required'. The second point was less grandiloquent, though more practical, being an offer to grant tenancies-at-will to poor young tenants of single shops at low rents and without fines.

The Privy Council mediators must have appreciated that further exchanges of this kind were pointless and decided to introduce some specific proposals into the dispute.[25] The 'articles' were simplicity itself: all rents were to be set at £7 or between £6 and £8; all tenants with leases from Sir Thomas or Lady Gresham were to have the benefit of them until expiration; and there was to be no subletting without permission. Needless to say, it was the second article which made the City and Company blench and the impasse remained. It was, however, clear that some form of settlement would have to be reached. The City and Company could perhaps have stood firm in the face of the hectoring demands of the tenants and defended its position in the Courts (to which at least one tenant took his case),[26] but the pressure exerted by the Privy Council was irresistible. There was nothing to be done, save to fight for as satisfactory an outcome as possible. Hence the petitions despatched in the summer of 1598 to a clutch of notables which put the trustee-landlords' case in forceful terms and suggested a legal resolution of the quarrel.[27]

In fact, the matter never came to trial because Privy Councillors Knollys and Fortescue managed to effect a settlement, though it took a good deal of further 'negotiation' before success was achieved. Faced with the rejection of the 'articles' by the City and the Company,[28] the Privy Council tried to persuade the tenants to surrender, but the new tenants proved unwilling to co-operate.[29] In late September 1598 the trustees made another attempt at their own solution by trying to establish what fines tenants would pay for leases of eighteen years with a right to alienate.[30] However, the interesting proviso was added that if no conclusion could be reached Fortescue was to be approached with a view to 'ending the matter'. Sure enough the trustees' initiative came to nothing and in no time an 'official' agreement was reached.[31] It looks very much as if the City and the Company had found the Privy Council pressure too much, for the terms were not very favourable to them and differed little from articles already rejected. Rents were to be set at a basic £7 per annum, though evidently with some flexibility; the Gresham leases were to continue or be redrawn in similar terms; future leases were not to be alienated without landlord's consent, though the Gresham leases could be assigned in accordance with their terms, provided the assignee was 'a citizen of good behaviour'; and during the term of the Gresham leases, the shops could be 'enjoyed' as before. The third provision was of some benefit to the City and the Company, but the first, second and last were most disappointing. The articles may have been less than precise and indeed somewhat repetious, but their effect was plain enough. Lady Gresham, as her husband had done, had had the last word.

The Company did at least have the consolation of knowing that its immediate difficulties with the Exchange leases were over. Apart from two further petitions to the Privy Council in 1600 from aggrieved tenants (successfully parried, it would seem),[32] the Company was henceforth able to enjoy its estate free from legal challenge.

GRESHAM COLLEGE

At the same time as the Mercers were struggling with the revenues of the trust, they were also attempting to deal with its object, Gresham College itself. Sir Thomas's will was unhelpfully vague on the question. It merely stated that the Company and the City were to

> permit and suffer seven persons by them from time to time to be elected and appointed ... meet and sufficiently learned to read ... seven lectures, to have the occupation of my ... mansion house [in Bishopsgate], gardens and all other appurtenances for them ... there, to inhabit, study and daily to read the said general lectures ....

Apart from also requiring that the lecturers be and remain unmarried, that was all Sir Thomas said about his proposed College. The rest was for his trustees to determine.

The first task was to draw up some ordinances. There are some difficulties in establishing precisely what happened, but after some debate and revisions the trustees seem to have settled on rules which broadly provided as follows.[33] Lectures were to be public and to be given in English as well as Latin to assist the ordinary City dweller. The practical as well as the theoretical aspects of each subject were to be tackled, again to help citizens in their daily avocations. The divinity lectures were to uphold the tenets of the Church of England and to refute the doctrines of Roman Catholicism on the one hand and sectarianism on the other, while the other lectures were also to follow certain syllabuses and schools of thoughts (rehearsed in some detail). Finally, there were a number of quite precise regulations concerning the day-to-day discipline of the College, including residence, meals and entertainment.

Unfortunately, the ordinances did not meet with the approval of the Gresham professors and the dispute which ensued brought the College to a halt before it had even begun to function. The initial set of lectures were due to be given in 1597, first in June and then in October.[34] They clearly did not take place, doubtless because of the plague then raging in London. Then the bitter wrangle with the Royal Exchange tenants occurred and this could possibly be the reason why the start of lectures was postponed during 1598.[35] By 1599, however, only the ordinances, it was clear, were delaying matters. In February of that year, when the lecturers were asked to subscribe to the ordinances, they requested time for consideration.[36] Three months later four of them made the same request, notwithstanding the fact that their stipends were now being withheld for so long as they held out.[37] By June the number of rebels had increased to five, and a full-scale quarrel surfaced. Some detailed objections were laid before the committee. The main grievance appeared to be that the trustees were attempting to interfere with the internal affairs of the College. To take one example, the lecturers took exception to the planned twice-yearly visitations. The committee responded by threatening the recalcitrants with dismissal.[38]

The next stage, as so often was the case in such instances, involved the intervention of the great officers of State. First, the Archbishop of Canterbury and the Lord Keeper, and then the Privy Council itself, all weighed in and, probably swayed by the fact that one of the rebels, Music Professor John Bull, was a royal favourite, they exerted strong pressure on the committee to back down.[39] The result, inevitably, was a victory for the professors. In November 1599 the committee was obliged to pay the salary arrears.[40] Then in April 1600, when another attempt was made to secure agreement on the ordinances, there was a further letter from on high calling the dispute into Star Chamber.[41] Quite what happened there, or at a (presumably) less formal hearing at Francis Bacon's Chambers, is unclear;[42] but the result is evident enough. No ordinances were ever signed by the professors, and the college was left without detailed rules and regulations. The professors had 'won', but the price was a heavy one, namely a rudderless College and a disillusioned committee. From this point onwards the City and the Company can be seen losing interest in the burdensome College and its troublesome members.

FINANCES

No account of the early years of the Gresham foundation can fail to grapple with the question of its financial viability. It has been seen how nervous the trustees were that the rents from the Exchange would be insufficient for the charitable burden placed upon them. Was the benefaction indeed a 'charge without profit', as the Company claimed in 1597?[E] Or was this special pleading and were the tenants more accurate when they spoke of hefty surpluses?

The answer, needless to say, is that both were right, in their different ways. It all depends on the perspective. To begin with the Company was certainly out of pocket. Deficits amounted to £67 in 1597 and £146 in 1598, while in the following three years the accounts merely balanced.[43] The shenanigans of Lady Gresham at the end of her life and the disputes with the tenants in 1596–8 obviously took their toll on rental income. Thereafter, however, the situation improved considerably and, apart from two 'break-even' years in 1606–7, increasingly substantial surpluses were recorded. In the 1620s income was invariably exceeding expenditure by £500 and in the late 1630s by £1,000. There were oscillations and lurches, of course, characteristic of any leasehold estate, but the general pattern is clear. The explanation is that after the initial difficulties rental income leapt ahead. £600 to £800 became over £1,000 in the 1620s and over £2,000 in the 1630s. By contrast, and despite the Company's earlier fears, expenses remained, if not static, then at least under control. It is true that there were occasionally large repair bills (for example in 1636–7), but the general maintenance charge increased only slowly. Hence the 'profit'.

How, then, was the money used? A good deal was evidently kept back for contingencies. The spectre of repairing costs quite properly haunted the committee. Some, however, was considered available for use, and the way it was spent throws light on the Company's attitude towards the

[E] See above, p. 36.

benefaction. In the first place, there was little compunction in devoting money to purposes quite unconnected with the College. The following gifts or loans may be noted: in 1612–13 £310 for the Irish plantation;[44] in 1620 £100 for the Palatinate;[45] in 1627–8 a total of £400 for Crown lands;[46] and in 1640 £500 for a loan to Charles I.[F] [47] Secondly, and in marked contrast, there was a deep reluctance to spend any more money on the College than the will expressly obliged the Company to spend. In 1606, for example, the committee gave a cool reception to a request for a contribution towards a divinity lecture in St Helen's Bishopsgate Church. 'It is not thought fit', ran the minutes, 'for precedent's sake to bring a new burden in [*sic*] this kind'.[48] The committee had the excuse, perhaps, of speaking in a year when the accounts merely balanced but, after four years of surplus with every prospect of surpluses to come, the comment is more than faintly disingenuous. In 1627, it is true that the professors were given an additional 20 marks (later £20 per annum) as a contribution towards their 'common charges',[49] but this was the only material increase in the trustees' regular disbursements. Certainly the treatment of the College was very different from the treatment of the Company. It will be recalled that Gresham also left £100 a year for quarterly Company Dinners. On at least two occasions that sum was exceeded, first by £28 and then by £72.[50] No concern about precedents here!

All this is not to say that the Company's suspicions of the benefaction were unfounded. There was a sting in the tail, as later pages will show. For the present the benefaction was showing a healthy surplus, and certainly the Company could have been more generous towards its College had it so chosen. However, what if a sudden calamity were to strike and the Exchange were to need, not merely repairs, but reconstruction? Would not the Company's fears be amply justified then? The melancholy answer was to be given in 1666 and then again in 1838.[G]

THE EARLY LIFE OF GRESHAM COLLEGE

After all the vicissitudes, what kind of College was it that finally emerged? Did Gresham College reflect the bitter wrangling behind the scenes and founder even before it had begun? The signs were certainly not propitious. Buffeted by the legal and financial problems which beset the benefaction, the Gresham Committee showed a distinct lack of interest in the educational side of the College's endeavours. The minutes are lifted out of their general torpor only by estate management matters. On the functioning of the College itself they are almost silent. There is, in fact, an exception which graphically proves this rule. In 1616 the professors petitioned the committee with four requests; to be made a body corporate in order that they might receive benefactions for a College library or other purposes; to be allowed to institute a collegiate 'commons' or victualling system; to be given an allowance to pay for such 'commons' since £50 per annum had been eroded in value by inflation; and that the pulpit in Gresham House be repaired and a bell rung to announce lectures.[51] Two months later, after taking legal advice, the committee solemnly declined all these requests, save one — the bell in the Royal Exchange would be rung at lecture times![52] When, four years afterwards, mention is made of a readiness to pay for the construction and stocking of a library in the College, it is plain that this was a purely private initiative. The committee merely gave permission for it and then considered which room or rooms would be best.[53] It did nothing more. The only material response to the professors' requests came in 1627 with the grant towards 'common charges'. Otherwise the College was obliged to fend for itself, not so much independent as neglected.

[F] For these payments generally see below, pp. 60–4.

[G] See below, pp. 78–82 and 133–40.

The College's other main handicap was one every Tudor and Stuart institution had to endure, namely the corrosive effects of patronage. It has already been seen how often the Company and the City had to deal with interference from Privy Councillors. If tenants were able to enlist well-placed support for their rent squabbles, so were academics striving to become Gresham professors; and elections were regularly the occasion for a positive bombardment of orders masquerading as 'recommendations'. The committee invariably had to succumb, whether or not better candidates were available. In 1607, for example, the Company found itself faced with four candidates for its Physic chair, two of whom were backed by James I, the third by the King's chief minister, the Earl of Salisbury, and the fourth by the Lord Chamberlain.[54] The first vote, by a show of hands, produced a shrewd equal split between one of the royal choices and Salisbury's. A subsequent ballot led, just as prudently, to the selection of the King's man, Dr Mounsell. Such pressure became less insistent in the second half of James's reign (a fact not unconnected, presumably, with Salisbury's death in 1612); and Charles I appears to have championed only one candidate, and for one of the City's chairs at that. However, the damage was done. Some of the professors at least were men who lent the College no lustre whatever and whose elections gave the impression that the College could be hijacked by political or religious opportunists. For an embryonic institution on the eve of the Civil War this was indeed an unfortunate reputation to have acquired. What was worse, where the Crown and its servants led, the committee, at least occasionally, followed. This was notoriously true of the Company's chair of Rhetoric.[55] The second, third and fourth incumbents were all related: Charles Croke was followed by his cousin Henry Croke, who in turn was succeeded by his brother-in-law Edward Wilkinson; and Charles was himself closely connected with such influential members of the Mercers' committee as Sir Thomas Bennett and Baptist Hicks. The fifth Rhetoric professor was, at least, not a Croke kinsman, but he was not much better qualified for all that. John Goodridge was elected in 1639 at the very senior age of fifty-eight, and he appears to have commended himself rather on the grounds of faithful service to the Company as Warden of Trinity Hospital Greenwich than his expertise in the subject on which he was supposed to lecture.

However, despite all these difficulties the College did not, in fact, sink without trace or even without dignity during these pre-Civil War years. The College it is true, never became a College in the proper sense: its performance as an educational establishment turned solely on the quality of the lecturers and the lectures. It is also true that some of the lecturers were nonentities or worse. Some, however, were leading authorities in their fields and they lent distinction to the College which employed them. At least three of the City's professors, Henry Briggs (Geometry, 1597–1620), Edmund Gunter (Astronomy, 1620–7) and Henry Gellibrand (Astronomy, 1627–37), and at least one of the Company's professors, Thomas Winston (Physic, 1615–43, 1652–5), all did quite as much as Gresham and his trustees could have desired.[56] They made contributions to learning, but did not lose sight of the practical applications of their discoveries.[57]

The professors thus participated in the development of scientific and intellectual curiosity that was beginning to grow and become fashionable by the time the Restoration took place. The period up to and including the Civil War was not an easy time for the scholarly community any more than for men of affairs, but Gresham College provided a useful forum for the personal contributions of its professors and the growth of the Royal Society owes something to it as a model.

That, however, lay somewhat in the future. The fact remains that the Civil War forced a hiatus in the development of Gresham College, and it never fully recovered.

PLATE I

Sir Thomas Gresham, 1544. This magnificent full-length portrait, which hangs on the landing of the present Hall, was probably painted in Flanders: current research suggests that it may have been the work of William Scrots. It was executed at the time of Gresham's marriage to Anne Ferneley, when he was 26 years of age. His clothes are rich, though unostentatious; the skull at his feet shows the young man's consciousness of mortality.
Mercers' Company

PLATE II

Sir Thomas Gresham and his wife, Anne Ferneley, widow of Sir William Reade, Mercer. The portraits were probably painted during the 1550s and are ascribed to Antonio Mor. The expression on her face hints at her forceful personality.
By courtesy of the Rijksmuseum, Amsterdam

PLATE III

John Colet, 1467(?)–1519, Dean of St Paul's Cathedral and founder of St Paul's School, which opened in 1509. The Ordinances of 1518 (see also Fig. 2) were rebound in 1585, when this miniature portrait of Colet was added to the cover by William Segar, artist and Somerset Herald.

Mercers' Company

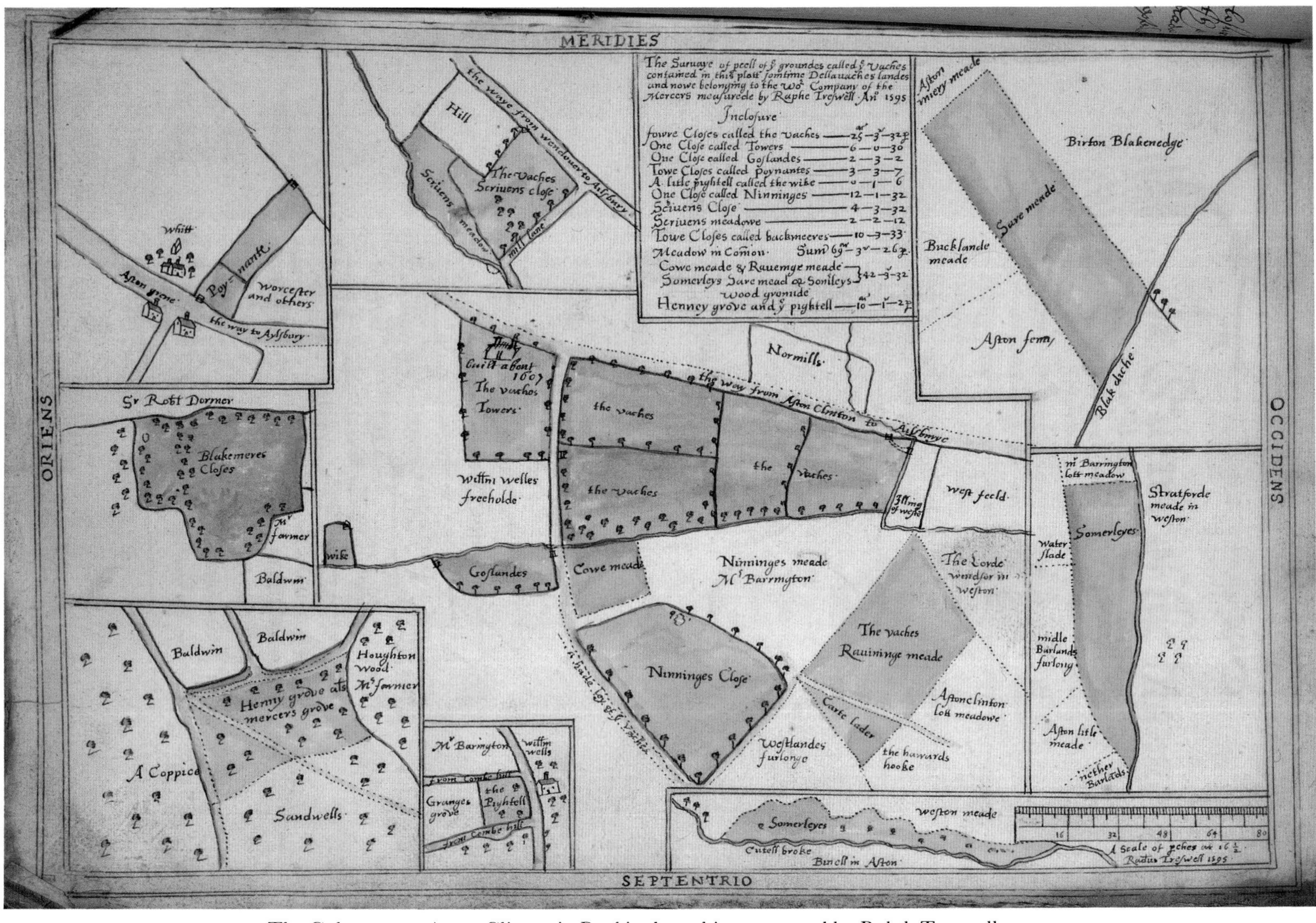

The Colet estate: Aston Clinton in Buckinghamshire, surveyed by Ralph Treswell, 1595.
Treswell was among the first of the modern land-surveyors, pioneering techniques in a science which expanded rapidly in the sixteenth century. The Company no longer owns the property.
Mercers' Company

CHAPTER III
TWO BENEFACTIONS

The dissolution of the monasteries and other Catholic objects of charitable endowment might have been expected to cause a post-Reformation decline in philanthropy. In fact, charitable activity continued on a formidable scale, particularly in London.[1] If confirmation were needed, the details set out in Chapter I, in relation to the generosity of Tudor Mercers and the popularity of the Company as a trustee, serve to provide it. Nevertheless, although the Reformation did not stifle generous impulses, it certainly channelled them in different directions. The process was plainly not a rapid one and is not easy to describe, but benefactors began to turn from the institutional to the personal, from the commemorative to the practical. To some extent this merely reflected the demise of the monasteries, but in large measure also it was based on a sense of impatience with the moral condition of society.

It so happened that in the early seventeenth century the Company was entrusted with two substantial benefactions, both with charitable objectives but with very different emphases. The first, from a Roman Catholic non-Mercer, looked back to a monastic past; the second, from a Protestant Mercer, looked forward to a Puritan future. Both benefactions have an intrinsic importance for the Company's development, but they also illustrate the more general themes outlined above.

PART I. TRINITY HOSPITAL, GREENWICH

THE BENEFACTOR

Henry Howard (1541–1614) was a member of that ill-fated Catholic family whose confrontations with Henry VIII and Elizabeth I led to imprisonments and deaths. Henry's grandfather, the 3rd Duke of Norfolk, escaped execution in 1547 only by reason of the King's death a matter of hours before the appointed time; his father, the Earl of Surrey, was not so lucky and had died on the block earlier in the same year; his brother, the 4th Duke, was executed in 1572; and his nephew, the Earl of Arundel, died in prison in 1597. Henry himself led a hazardous existence under Elizabeth, always proscribed and occasionally imprisoned; but, by a mixture of caution and good fortune, he survived. When the accession of James VI of Scotland loomed large, Howard made his bid for power and, after steering a devious course through the Essex-Cecil feud, he found himself among the favoured few in 1603. James made Howard Earl of Northampton and a Privy Councillor, and from then until his death in 1614 Northampton was one of the most powerful men in the country.

Northampton was not an attractive man. 'Proud, pedantic and cynical' is the verdict of his most authoritative, and not unsympathetic, biographer.[2] Scholar, sycophant, homosexual, Northampton conforms to the stereotype Jacobean courtier. Of course, this is not the whole story: he was also an administrator of energy and ability; but after living for sixty-three years in constant expectation of imprisonment or death Northampton was not going to let his chance of power, and wealth, slip from his grasp. The 'cautious pilot' who had 'brought his bark safe out of the broken seas' would not allow anything, scruples included, to stand between him and the

FIG. 14. Henry Howard, Earl of Northampton (1540–1614), aged 54. Portrait on board; the identity of the artist is uncertain. The Earl was an important benefactor of the Company, though he was not a Mercer himself. He was a friend of Lionel Cranfield (see Fig. 23). He holds an armillary sphere or mobile representation of the solar system. Around the base of the sphere are the words 'Knowledge Follows' in Latin. *Mercers' Company*

promised land.[3] He certainly had no qualms about changing religion. A Catholic throughout Elizabeth's reign (though emphatically of the Anglo-Catholic, not the Jesuitical kind), Northampton became a Protestant under James. That his 'conversion' was purely a matter of expediency became apparent when he reaffirmed his Catholicism shortly before he died.

Such was Northampton's acquisitiveness during his decade in power that he was worth some £80,000 when he died. For a penurious, proscribed Roman Catholic this was a remarkable achievement. Much of the wealth was vested in worldly trappings, in particular the grand Northampton House in the Strand; but some was devoted to charitable works.[4] In 1607 Northampton founded a hospital at Clun in Shropshire, and in the following year he endowed an almshouse at Castle Rising in Norfolk. His most generous benefaction, however, was Trinity Hospital, Greenwich.

THE BENEFACTION

Northampton had spent much of his youth and some of his adult life in Greenwich and so when, as an old and wealthy man under James I, he looked for a country retreat it was natural that he should build one there. It was equally natural, having established benefactions at Howard bases in Shropshire and Norfolk, that Greenwich was chosen for Northampton's most ambitious foundation. The first steps were taken in 1610 and 1611 by the purchase of property for the site of the hospital from his nephew, the Earl of Suffolk, and Lady Lumley respectively. The next significant transaction came in 1613 with the acquisition of the following as endowments: land at Lee, Lewisham, Bankers and Swaffield in Kent, subject to a tenancy for life of Sir Nicholas Stoddard; property in St Martin-in-the-Fields in London leased back to its former owners; additional property in the same parish; and, after the death of Lady Kildare, Beckloe and Lowells farm in Kent, with an annuity payable out of Sir John Daccombe's lands in Dorset making up the shortfall in the meantime.[5]

In February 1614 Northampton laid the foundation stone of Trinity Hospital, but he did not live to see it built. In June of that year he died. His will provided not only for the endowment of the Hospital with the property listed above but also for the administration of the Hospital: 'and I will ... the Company of Mercers in London [shall have the nomination, placing and displacing] of the poor of the Hospital at Greenwich yet so as they choose twelve out of Greenwich and the other eight out of Shotesham in Norfolk, where I was born'.

Why did Northampton choose the Mercers? He was not, after all, a member, and appears to have had no direct contact with the Company. The answer is almost certainly to be found in Northampton's association with one of the most important Mercers, Lionel Cranfield (see Fig. 23).[6] Cranfield, an extraordinarily successful merchant, had first come to Northampton's attention when presenting the Company's case against its assessment for the plantation of Ireland to the Privy Council.[A] [7] Thereafter Northampton gave support and patronage to Cranfield, who rapidly became the Crown's expert on trade and finance. What is even more significant, in his capacity as a Receiver of Crown Revenues, Cranfield was able to assist Northampton in his land acquisitions in Greenwich.[8] By 1612 Northampton was describing Cranfield as 'a special friend', and it would not be at all surprising if the friendship had extended to entrusting Trinity Hospital to Cranfield's Company.[9]

The initial formalities involved in instituting the Hospital were quickly completed. In May 1615 the Company was read Northampton's will and duly accepted the trust,[10] while in the following month John Griffith, Northampton's former secretary and executor, obtained Letters Patent confirming the foundation and making the Hospital a body corporate.[11] It took much longer to set up the Hospital on a formal basis. Even after the first almsmen were admitted in February 1617, it was still another four years before the Hospital acquired the ordinances by which it was to be governed and on which the Mercers' authority was to rest. Accordingly, apart from a ceremonial appearance at its opening, the Company had little to do with the Hospital until 1621. Interim control was in the hands of Griffith the executor and Robert Swale the Warden.[12]

THE ORDINANCES

After much labour the hard-pressed Griffith presented his draft ordinances to the Company in January 1621. The Mercers persuaded Griffith not only to alter 'many things' but also to pay for a legal opinion on the best way to ensure that the Company was 'kept free and without danger and damage in this business'. 'Some doubt' had arisen that

> the Company by accepting the government of the Hospital may make themselves liable to make good the miscarriage of the Wardens and poor men of the hospital, especially considering the Company is by the statutes directed to take sufficient surety to be bound with the Warden for his just accounting and payment of his rests [i.e. balances].[13]

Evidently the point was settled to the Company's satisfaction (though in what manner is not clear), because in March the ordinances or statutes were agreed upon and in May Griffith presented the Company with its sealed copy.[14]

The ordinances laid down, in close detail, a regime for the life of the Hospital.[15] Quasi-monastic in its character, the crowded daily timetable kept the almsmen to a strict routine of humble devotions and wholesome chores. Of more immediate importance here is the role allotted to the Mercers. There were three main tasks. The first was to select twenty almsmen. The parish authorities of Greenwich and Shotesham were to nominate two men for each vacancy, certifying their suitability as to age, residence, poverty and character. The Mercers then selected one of the two names put forward, not on quite the same basis as the parishes, but in accordance with the following rather coy injunction in the ordinances:

> in which election to be made by as grave a Company trusted by the Founder, we cannot suspect either affection, partiality or corruption and trust that it will be done and performed with all sincerity according to the trusts reposed in them.

The second task was to elect the twelve Visitors who were to make the annual visitation to the Hospital. Two had to be Wardens of the Company and six Assistants. The Visitors were to call the Hospital Warden, almsmen and servants before them, punish offences, examine the accounts, check the inventories and examine the state of the property. Thirdly, the Company was to manage the Hospital estates, though this power

[A] See below, p. 57.

FIG. 15. The Earl of Northampton's tomb, as originally erected at Dover Castle. It was the work of the celebrated sculptor, Nicholas Stone, and cost £500. This drawing by Sir Edward Dering was made in the second quarter of the seventeenth century, when the monument was still whole and complete. Damaged by time, such portions of it as are still intact are cherished in the Chapel at Trinity Hospital, Greenwich; the figures of the Cardinal Virtues, Temperance, Fortitude, Prudence and Justice, now stand at the doorway under the portico.
By courtesy of the Society of Antiquaries (MS 497A, f. 53r)

(or task) was limited to the extent that it was the Hospital Warden who collected the rents and the Hospital seal could not be affixed to deeds without the consent of ten of the almsmen.

How did the Company discharge each of these tasks? The selection of almsmen at first imposed no burden whatever because empty places were simply not filled in order to save money during a financial crisis which is discussed later. Then in 1628 there were seven Greenwich and six Shotesham vacancies to be supplied. The Greenwich selection caused no problems, perhaps for the simple reason that the Company knew the parish officers and something about the candidates. The Shotesham choice was more difficult, for two reasons. Back in 1623, when the Company had contemplated filling a vacancy (but had not eventually done so), Shotesham had seen fit to present only one name, and the Company had deemed that nomination forfeit and had selected a substitute from Castle Rising.[16] Accordingly in 1628 the Company felt obliged to honour that commitment and gave one of the six places to a Castle Rising man. The other difficulty was that, notwithstanding the certification procedure, the Company did not feel content merely to rely upon the Shotesham nominations and select five of the ten names 'blind'. The Earl of Arundel, Northampton's great-nephew and heir, was therefore asked to assess the candidates for the Company.[17]

On other occasions Arundel's intervention in the choice of almsmen was less welcome. During the interim regime of Griffith (1617–21), Arundel had tried his best to exercise his influence, but eventually went too far and affronted Griffith with the unsuitability of a particular nominee.

We cannot expect due performance of the trust committed unto [the Mercers], if his Lordship, that is patron and protector of the poor Hospital, and we, in execution of the will, should make such a breach, and in this time when I labour so much to settle it according to my Master's will and directions and to put the government into the hands of the Company.[18]

Arundel evidently had a thick skin because he made life as difficult for the Company as he had done for Griffith. In 1628 Arundel recommended one of Northampton's old servants, William Hest (or Hast), for the Castle Rising place, but Hest admitted that he had never lived there and he was passed over.[19] None the less a visitorial deputation had to be dispatched to appease the angry Earl, taking with them the ordinances and a letter from Shotesham in support.[20] A few years later two supernumerary almsmen were installed in the Hospital at the Earl's insistence, though admittedly also at his expense.[21] Finally, in 1635, 'out of the Visitors' great desire to gratify his Lordship', an unqualified Greenwich man was selected, at least temporarily.[22] Patronage was a fact of life in the early seventeenth century and patronage exerted by a man in Arundel's special position was particularly hard to resist. That must be the Company's excuse for allowing such interference.

The Visitors' disciplinary duties were made the more difficult by reason of the overly strict regime which the ordinances sought to impose. More than one almsman made it clear that he could not cope with such irksome restrictions. One Cordell Brewster declared that 'he would not be kept in like a boy or a slave, and that he and the rest of the almsmen were more restrained than all other almsmen of other places and, being told the Founder's Statutes required so much, he replied [that] the Founder's Statutes were not agreeable to God's Laws or man's laws'.[23] Brewster was expelled for this outburst and other evidence indicates that he was an obstreperous man.[24] It is significant therefore that his statement receives some corroboration elsewhere. One Martin, when told that he could not leave the Hospital for fear of the plague, declared that 'they should not make water without leave'.[25] Little point would be served by rehearsing all the cases of admonishment, punishment and expulsion in the visitation records. Fascinating though such glimpses of the lifestyle and attitudes of ordinary people are, they do not really help in assessing the effectiveness of the Company's disciplinary role, nor how the Company perceived that role. The Visitors were, in any event, dependent for their information on the Warden, and their annual chastisements were no more than a supplement to the Warden's weekly 'corrections'. The most that can be said is that between them, the Visitors and the Hospital Wardens adhered sufficiently to the intricate ordinances to provoke at least some of the almsmen into vociferous protest.

The Company's third task, the management of the Hospital's estates, should have been a simple matter of negotiating leases and collecting rents. However, as already indicated, the endowment properties were, in two cases at least, conditional or contingent upon other interests or events, and predictable problems arose. The first and less serious difficulties concerned the Stoddard tenancy. Unfortunately, Stoddard's own lands adjoined those held on lease from the Hospital and the boundaries became a matter of contention. The Hospital claimed that[26]

of purpose to confound the said [Hospital] lands ..., that the same might not be distinguished from his own proper lands of inheritance, [Stoddard] did to that end take and pull down all the mounds, hedges and fences wherewith the said several parcels of land ... were enclosed ... and did for the space of divers years afterwards hold and enjoy the same intermingled with his own.

The Stoddards denied the charge and the dispute lasted for some twenty years after the death of Sir Nicholas Stoddard in 1618 until it was settled by independent assessors.[27] There was, however, no discernible impact on the finances of the Hospital and there is no need to follow the quarrel any further.

Much more significant was the contemporaneous struggle to secure payment of the annuity of £150 per annum due from Sir John Daccombe during the life of Lady Kildare. When Daccombe died in 1625, he left a debt to the Crown and the surety for that debt put a stop on the Trinity Hospital annuity to secure his own reimbursement. It took some while before a solution was found. This involved the Earl of Arundel taking a lease of Daccombe property and repaying the Crown and the Hospital out of the proceeds.[28] Further financial problems arose in 1629 when the farm fell into the Hospital's possession on the death of Lady Kildare. It was not so much the fact that, once again, there was a challenge to the Hospital's title (for that was successfully rebuffed),[29] nor that the Daccombe annuity ceased (for the farm eventually matched the £150 per annum in rent exactly),[30] but rather that extensive and expensive repairs were necessary and a new lease could not be granted until 1631.[31]

The Daccombe troubles placed a great strain on the foundation. It has already been noticed that no new almsmen were admitted until 1628, seven years after the Company took control of the Hospital. Thames flooding added to the financial difficulties and as late as 1632, when there were still ten vacancies, 'it was thought meet' to fill only six of them 'in regard the house is behind hand by reason of the many assessments that have been and are to be levied upon the same by reason of the repair of the banks of the river running by the marsh lands [forming] part of the [Hospital's] possessions . . .'.[32] In the following year, when more vacancies had occurred, the Visitors were still only prepared to admit replacements in view of the cost. The Hospital thus remained four short of its intended twenty almsmen.[33] Such a device

FIG. 16. The Trinity Hospital cup. Given to the Hospital at Greenwich, on 24 February 1617, the day the Hospital was consecrated, by Thomas, Earl of Arundel and Surrey, great-nephew and heir of Henry Howard, Earl of Northampton and founder of the Hospital.
Mercers' Company

FIG. 17. The Trinity Hospital seal matrix of 1616, with its casket.
Mercers' Company

was merely the most conspicuous of a number of cost-cutting measures. Under-paying the almsmen,[34] suspending the Warden's salary,[35] abandoning the common kitchen (until tavern-eating obliged a resumption),[36] even doing without dinner on visitation,[B] [37] all these devices were employed in the cause of economy. The Hospital may not have been quite 'dissolved', as the Warden and poor men claimed in a submission during the Daccombe case,[38] but it was certainly given a severe jolt. The endowment, in truth, was a little too conditional and contingent for comfort. Only after 1629, or rather 1631, when Beckloe and Lowells farm was repaired and leased out profitably, could the Hospital look to the future with confidence.

The Company's role in the early years of Trinity Hospital is quite an impressive one. It may have allowed the Earl of Arundel more influence than his strict entitlement, but Arundel was both powerful and intimately concerned with the benefaction. In other respects the Mercer Visitors acted vigorously and scrupulously. Discipline was maintained in the way Northampton would obviously have wished. Moreover, the funds of the Hospital were husbanded with care. It is possible, perhaps, that the Visitors succumbed over-readily to the Warden's calls for economy, but when surpluses did build up they were used with a keen regard for the benefactor's wishes. 'Dead' cash was made to earn interest[39] and loans for extraneous purposes were secured and repaid.[40] By 1642, at the outbreak of the Civil War, Trinity Hospital was securely established in good hands.

PART II. THE FISHBORNE LEGACY

Richard Fishborne was a native of Huntingdon, a well-born and well-educated 'gentleman', who first found employment in a noble household.[41] However, he did not enjoy 'the candied happiness of the Court' and after a short while turned to trade,[C] serving his apprenticeship with the celebrated Mercer Sir Baptist Hicks and becoming free of the Mercers' Company in 1596. Of his subsequent career as a merchant only a little is known, namely that he had an extremely successful trading partnership with the Merchant Taylor John Browne. His public offices are inevitably better documented: apart from a string of directorships in the main trading Companies, he was a Common Councilman, a prominent parishioner of St Bartholomew Exchange (where he lived in some style),[42] and Warden of the Mercers' Company in 1615 and 1624.

Fishborne was a committed Christian, 'a true-woven Protestant and a natural son of the Church of England', who was deeply conscious of the need to take the Gospel in an active, proselytising way to those 'dark corners of the land' where ignorance or, worse, Catholicism still prevailed.[43] He was also conscious of material as well as spiritual needs, and during his lifetime assisted the poor and the sick. Accordingly, when Fishborne died in April 1625 a single man, there was every reason to expect that he would leave considerable sums to charity and, given his connections with the Company, that he would ask the Mercers to administer at least some of the bequests. The extent of his munificence, however, must have come as a great surprise.

Towards the end of his life Fishborne gave a box to the Company's Wardens and it was only a matter of hours before he died that Fishborne told

[B] Cf. a later order which simply prohibited second courses — save when Arundel was present! AC, 1631–7 (rough), f. 167.

[C] Theodore Rabb (in *Enterprise and Empire*, p. 291), identifies Fishborne as the Captain Fishborne who was a Spanish privateer in the 1580s (and whose activities are mentioned in the works of K. R. Andrews and J. S. Corbett). The absence of any allusion, however delicate, to these activities in the biographical eulogy of Nathaniel Shute, *Corona Charitatis* (1626), is certainly not conclusive, but there must remain some doubt as to the accuracy of the identification.

FIG. 18. The tomb of Richard Fishborne, Mercer and benefactor to the Company. The effigy now rests in the Ambulatory of the Hall just outside the Chapel door; it has survived both the Great Fire of 1666 and the destruction of the Hall in 1941.
Mercers' Company

Warden Banks that the box contained his will.[44] When the will was duly revealed in the presence of the Assistants it was found to contain a series of remarkable bequests.[45] The legacies totalled well over £12,000 in cash, quite apart from considerable quantities of silver. Some were purely personal in character, but a large proportion were charitable. Christ's Hospital, St Bartholomew Exchange and other London parishes, certain prisons and a large number of ministers and lecturers all benefited; but the largest bequests were made in trust to the Mercers. There were nine in all:

1. £500 to purchase property worth £25 per annum for sermons in Mercers' chapel.

2. £2,800 to buy livings for worthy preachers in northern counties. The terms of this provision were the subject of such debate later that Fishborne's actual words deserve quotation.

Item, I give and bequeath to the said Wardens and Commonalty of the Mystery of Mercers in the City of London the sum of two thousand eight hundred pounds therewith to buy and purchase two or more parsonages, rectories or church livings anciently appropriated to some abbey, monastery or religious house or houses and now commonly called impropriations, the same to be in Lincolnshire, Yorkshire or some other northern county or counties of this land where the said Company of Mercers shall best fit themselves with such a purchase, and find most want of the preaching of the Word of God to be, and the same church livings or impropriations as purchased and as my will is shall be from time to time successively for ever by the said Wardens and Commonalty of the Mystery of the Mercers of London after their wonted custom of elections by most votes at their General Courts conferred, bestowed and conveyed upon two or more ministers respectively for and during such term and terms and in such manner and form and with such cantle[D] and provision that if they or any of them prove not-resident or have any other benefit or church living with cure of souls beside them the said Wardens and Commonalty and their successors from time to time for ever shall and may remove, displace, dismiss, deprive and eject them or any of them out of the said impropriation or any of them and elect and place another or others in this or their rooms according to their good discretion and I heartily entreat the said Wardens and Commonalty for God's sake that they be very careful from time to time to make choice of such as be well known to be honest, discreet and learned, fearing God and painful in their ministry that by their life and doctrine they may win many souls to Christ Jesus. And although I hope the sum of two thousand and eight

[D] Cantle = slice, portion (*OED*), but obviously here meaning stipulation.

hundred pounds thus by me bequeathed will purchase such church livings or impropriations by the value of two hundred [pounds] by the year or thereabout, yet because my confidence is that the Company of Mercers will husband it to the best for the performance of my good intent and purpose herein, my meaning is not to enjoin them to a precise yearly value nor that they shall bestow the said whole sum but that they fit the purchase to the money by me thus bequeathed as well as they conveniently then may, reserving and retaining in their hands sufficient to bear and defray the charge of travail, counsel and conveyances incident about such purchases.

3. £1,000 to provide five loans of £200 each to Young Men of the Company for a period of five years free of charge. Preference was to be given in the first instance to shopkeepers in the mercery trade, secondly to silkmen and finally to merchants and other traders. If the Young Men were called on the Livery during the five-year period then they were to repay the loan within three months.

4. £1,000 to purchase property worth £50 per annum. £25 was to be used to maintain a lecture or sermon at St Bartholomew Exchange. The Company did not have to select the minister, and if the opposition of a slighted incumbent meant that the lecture could not take place the Company was to distribute the £25 among the poor, whether its own members or not, taking care to select those who were 'aged, orderly and religious'. £20 was to be distributed among the poor of St Bartholomew, though the Wardens were to ensure that this did not merely lead to a drop in the parish poor rates. The remaining £5 went to the Second Warden and Clerk for their trouble.

5. £420 to purchase property worth £21 per annum. £20 was to be spent on a Livery dinner and £1 on a sermon beforehand.

6. £300 to defray legal costs incurred by the Company. Fishborne added a proviso at this point to the effect that the Company would no longer be obliged to fulfil his trusts if any property producing income for those trusts were seized or forfeited.

7. 100 oz. of gilt silver plate or the same value in white silver plate, at the Company's choice.

8. £1,000 to purchase property worth £50 per annum to be spent on clothes and shoes for 30 'poor brethren' of the Company or their widows.

9. £2,000 to buy property worth £100 per annum to be spent on worthy causes in

FIG. 19. Badges presented to another Mercers' almshouse, Whittington College, in 1626 by John Bancks; his motto runs beneath the Mercers' Maiden. The badges were worn by the residents. *Mercers' Company*

Huntingdon. Again, the subsequent controversies surrounding this provision call for a quotation:

> Item, whereas I am desirous to do good unto the town of Huntingdon where I was born and yet am not acquainted or informed of the state or wants of the same town I do give and bequeath to the Wardens and Commonalty of the Mystery of the Mercers of the City of London aforesaid the sum of two thousand pounds upon this trust and confidence that they the said Wardens and Commonalty shall and will therewith buy and purchase lands and hereditaments to the clear yearly value of one hundred pounds and bestow and distribute the same to some good and charitable uses in the said town as in the maintenance of a lecture out of a grammar school [or] in erecting and endowing of an almshouse. In any or all of these or such other good and pious uses to have [in] perpetuity and yearly forever in such manner, form and proportion as the said Wardens and Commonalty together with the advice of my executors hereafter named [John Browne, Fishborne's partner, was in fact the *sole* executor] shall upon the information of the state and wants of the town devise and ordain.

When the Assistants heard the will for the first time on 8 April 1625 three points will have made an immediate impact. First, Fishborne's bequests to the Mercers, totalling £9,020, were on a grand scale, worthy of comparison with the charities of those far more celebrated figures, Sir Thomas Gresham and the Earl of Northampton. Secondly, Fishborne had given his bequests a very personal and deeply religious stamp. 'Puritan' is a word that historians use cautiously now, but Fishborne's legacy was certainly a Puritan one in the sense that he wanted to supplement the Church's ministry and to give a body of laymen the right to choose and remove his preachers. Thirdly, and on a more domestic note, it was plain that Fishborne had utter confidence in the integrity and capability of the Company. The legacy of £2,800 was not tied to a yearly income figure, but rather the Mercers were given discretion to make the purchases they saw fit with express permission to cover their expenses; £300 was given to the Company to meet legal charges (in addition, be it noted, to the right to deduct expenses from the £2,800); and an almost gratuitous 'indemnity' was given in case the encumbered lands were taken away from the Company. The will in fact concluded with a provision that if a licence in mortmain could not be obtained and the money placed in some form of stock, then the Company was to suffer no liability if the stock were to be lost by reason of bad debts or other reasons:

> for as my trust and confidence in the Company is that they will be very careful and circumspect for the preserving of the said stock and sums of money for the maintenance of the said good uses so my desire is that they be no losers by that which may casually happen beyond the foresight and care of provident men . . .

This may seem only reasonable, but it was most unusual for trustees to be given comfort in such express terms. Fishborne was quite obviously bound closely to the Company by affection and respect. The way in which the will was deposited is evidence enough. It is equally obvious that the Company responded in like fashion. The story of the Fishborne charity is significantly different from that of its two main predecessors. The Company did not treat it with the sense of injustice felt towards Gresham College nor even the concern for potential liability with which the Trinity Hospital ordinances were greeted. Instead the Company, having been given a virtual indemnity for the consequences of its actions and an almost unfettered discretion, accepted the Fishborne trust with manifest enthusiasm.

IMPLEMENTING THE BENEFACTION

It took the Company no less than five years to complete the purchases set out in Fishborne's will. A great deal of time and trouble was spent investigating the value and security of possible lands, livings and tithes. Potential vendors bombarded the Company with proposals and offers, and reports, 'views' and legal investigations followed in equal volume.[46] Then there were problems of interpretation: how could the Company best retain the power to remove unsatisfactory preachers, and how was it to select the Young Men entitled to loans?[47] Finally, the Company had to assess the claims of potential beneficiaries. One moment it would be the worthy burgesses of

Huntingdon suggesting ways of spending the £100 per annum, next inhabitants of the north-east asking for a preacher or lecturer.

Eventually the benefaction was disposed of in the following way. The £2,800 for livings (bequest number 2 above) was spent on:

(i)	the tithes of Swinborne, Repwick, Errington, Bingfield and Colwell (Northumberland) from Sir John Fenwick and used to endow a lectureship at Hexham (1628)	£880
(ii)	the rectory of Canwick (Lincolnshire) and its tithes from Richard Bures (1628)	£550
(iii)	the rectory of Repham (Lincolnshire) and its tithes from Lady Frances Wray (1631)	£1,000
(iv)	the tithes of Chollerton and Beresford (Northumberland) from Sir John Fenwick and used to endow a lectureship at Berwick-on-Tweed (1631)	£550
	TOTAL (omitting legal expenses)	£2,980

The £500 for sermons (bequest number 1), £1,000 for the poor of St Bartholomew Exchange (4), £420 for a dinner and sermon (5), £1,000 for Mercers' clothing (8) and £2,000 for Huntingdon (9), totalling £4,920 in all, were devoted to the part-purchase of an estate at Chalgrave in Bedfordshire comprising the manor, a farm and other property. The purposes for which the income produced by the estate was earmarked were described satisfactorily enough in the will, save in the case of Huntingdon. The 'good and charitable uses' were the subject of much debate until the Company agreed to the town corporation's suggestion of £60 per annum for the poor and £40 per annum for a lecturer.[48] As far as the remaining bequests were concerned, the first loans to Young Men (bequest number 3) were made in 1627,[49] a silver 'voider' bearing Fishborne's arms (7) was bought in 1628,[50] while the £300 for legal costs (6) disappeared with predictable speed, Chalgrave alone accounting for £135.[51]

A fitting conclusion to this first stage in Fishborne's benefaction came in 1633 when a monument to him was erected in one of the niches in the Hall and he was entombed, together with his partner John Browne, in the Chapel.[52]

TROUBLES

No benefaction as valuable as Fishborne's was likely to be immune from legal difficulties, and it can have come as no surprise when the Company's title to one of its newly-acquired livings, Canwick, was challenged by someone claiming the right to an annuity. The Company

FIG. 20. One of three beakers adorned with the Mercers' Maiden, presented to the Company in 1604 and 1605 by John Bancks. He had been apprentice to Sir Baptist Hicks (see Fig. 26).
Mercers' Company

FIG. 21. Embellishments, possibly unauthorised, to the Renter Warden's Accounts of 1605/6 (vol. 1603–24, f. 40). One figure is clearly shooting at a bird, the musket propped on its stand, an arrow appears to fly backwards from a bow, while another figure scrambles up the letter, a horn lantern swinging from his girdle.
Mercers' Company

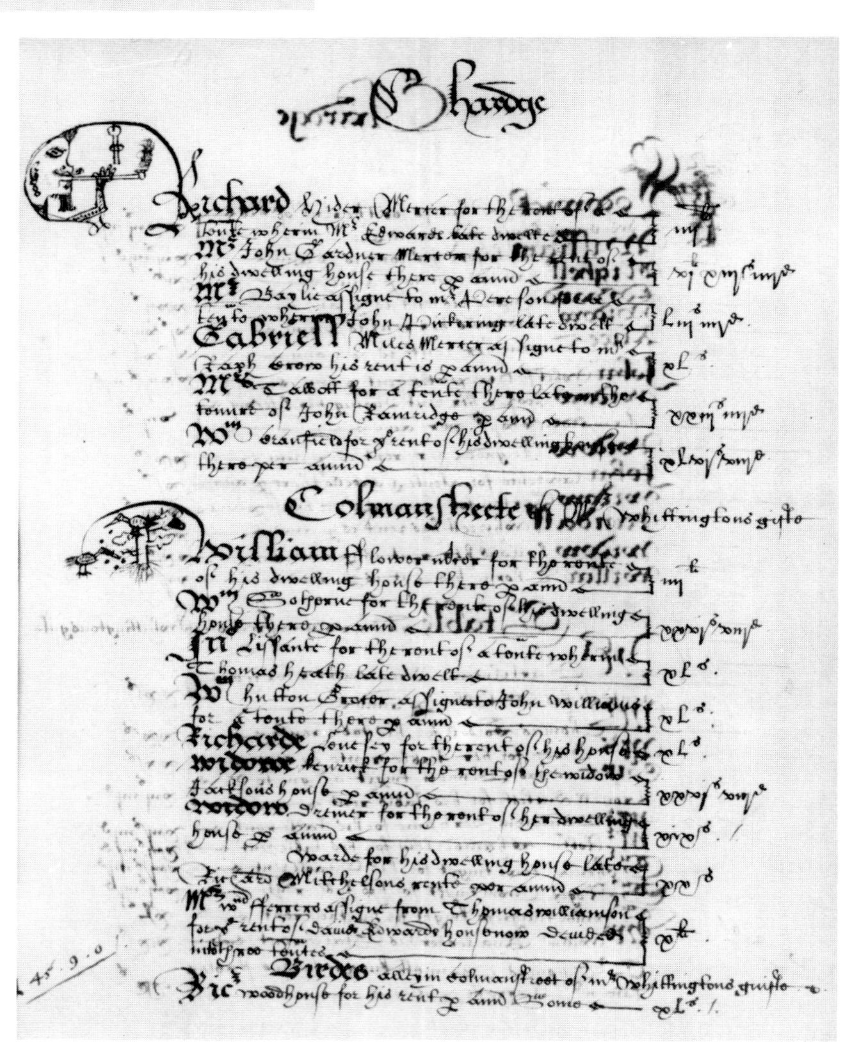

FIG. 22. More marginal drawings from the Renter Warden's Accounts, 1605/6 (vol. 1603–24, f. 41). The punkish figure at the top appears to be smoking a pipe, while below a bird sits on its nest.
Mercers' Company

was obliged to push its vendor into Chancery to resolve the question and later to sue him for compensation.[53] Less predictable, and more interesting, were the religious and political problems arising from the Huntingdon and Berwick lectureships.

The Huntingdon difficulties began with the very first appointment. The town's corporation urged the Company to give the lectureship to Dr Thomas Beard, the celebrated Puritan who already held a living there and had indeed taught the young Oliver Cromwell at the Grammar School.[54] This support was powerfully reinforced by a letter from Charles I — a rather surprising intervention which is difficult to explain.[55] Nevertheless, despite this pressure, the Company stood firmly by Fishborne's intention. The lecturer had to be a *new* preacher, an addition to the existing ministry. Beard was acknowledged to be a worthy man, but he did not meet Fishborne's requirements.[56] Accordingly the Company chose one Robert Proctor.[57] However, it was still necessary to obtain the Bishop of Lincoln's permission for Proctor to preach, and the bishop declared there to be no need for a lecturer, and if one were to be appointed then he would only give the necessary licence to Beard.[58] Again the Company resisted and wrote to the bishop explaining its position. When the bishop reiterated his views, so did the Company. In 1631 the Company got its way, though only at a price. A gratuity of £40 was given to Beard by way of compensation, and Proctor was allowed to preach.[59]

The Company's next dispute with the bishop was much less successful, mainly because on this occasion Archbishop Laud himself intervened. Laud was on principle opposed to lay interference in Church affairs and the Mercers' right to remove its preachers (which he assumed included the Huntingdon lecturers) angered him deeply. This is how he reported to the King in 1633:[60]

My Lord Bishop of Lincoln signifies that the Company of Mercers of London, trusted with the gift of one Mr Fishborne, set up a lecturer at Huntingdon, with the allowance of forty pounds per annum to preach every Saturday morning (being market day) and Sunday in the afternoon; with a proviso in his grant from them that upon any dislike they may have of him, he shall, at a month or at a fortnight's warning, give over the place, without any relation to Bishop or Archbishop.

My most humble suit to your Majesty is that no layman whatsoever, and least of all companies and corporations, have power to put in or put out any lecturer or other minister.

When Charles had responded, Laud wrote in the following terms to the Bishop of Lincoln:[61]

My Lord, I take this occasion also to signify to you that I represented to his Majesty the care that your Lordship took in your diocese according to your certificate which you sent to me, and particularly that which concerns the Company of Mercers in London, who by the gift of Mr Fishborne, a brother of theirs, and by a proviso in his gift, take upon them to place and displace a lecturer at Huntingdon, upon any dislike, at a month or a fortnight's warning, without any relation to Bishop or Archbishop. This, his Majesty says, your Lordship did justly dislike, and gave his answer to that passage in writing in his own hand and in these words: 'That he could not hold fit that any lay person or corporation whatsoever should have power these men would like to themselves, for he would have no priest have any necessity of dependence upon their people and commanded me to signify to your Lordship that he would have this remedied.' I pray to your Lordship therefore, in his Majesty's name, to take present order that the Mercers either relinquish the grant and submit to the orders of the Church or else that you admit no lecturer there, unless your Lordship can think of any better way to remedy this new lay encroachment upon your Church.

The bishop, of course, responded quickly to this royal command and the lecturer, John Squire (who had succeeded Proctor), was duly prohibited from preaching. This time the bishop was not prepared to compromise. Encouraged by the local inhabitants, the Company tried hard to get first Squire and then his successor, John Pointer, reinstated, but with no success. Even the alternative strategy of purchasing a local living for the lecturer met with episcopal obstruction. The dispute dragged on for the rest of the 1630s, notwithstanding petitions to the Archbishop and the Lord Keeper, as well as the Bishop's commissary, Sir John Lambe.[62] Only the outbreak of Civil War resolved the problem. The Puritans in the Long

Parliament, needless to say, supported the Company in its stand: in 1640 the House of Commons even sent Huntingdon's own Oliver Cromwell and the Mercer William Spurstow to the Hall to make its views known; and eventually, in 1644, Pointer was given formal sanction to continue as lecturer.[63] By then no less than ten years had elapsed since his election.

The Berwick story is not dissimilar from the Huntingdon one, though Berwick's location on the Scottish border at a time when Charles was fighting the Bishops' Wars made this lectureship an even more sensitive subject. In 1637 a potential problem was converted into an actual one by the election of John Jemmat. Jemmat had previously been presented by the Company to St Michael Paternoster Royal, but had been refused admittance by Laud.[64] He owed his nomination to Berwick, at least according to a hostile witness, to the pressure of a local Puritan faction led by Robert Fenwick.[65] When Jemmat set off northwards he went (or so he later claimed) with a warning from Laud 'that he would have an eye upon him whithersoever he went' and to have 'no hand in disturbing the King's preceedings in the north' (which Jemmat later understood to mean the King's Scottish affairs). Laud evidently also wrote ahead to the Bishop of Durham 'to signify what a one was arriving in his diocese'.[66]

Two and a half years later this formidable disapproval had its effect. The King wrote to the Company that Jemmat had 'not behaved himself so orderly and peaceable [*sic*] . . . as he ought and as these times in that place do more especially require'. Jemmat was to be prevented from preaching and should receive no further salary. In his place the King recommended George Sydeserffe, 'an orderly clergyman and one very well affected both to our service and the discipline of the Church of England and who has suffered for us in the troubles in Scotland . . .'.[67] The Company duly complied with this request and Sydeserffe was elected *vice* Jemmat in February 1640.[68] Unfortunately, Sydeserffe did not meet with the approval of his flock. They, or perhaps the Puritans among them, deemed that Sydeserffe could neither be understood nor indeed heard in church. In February 1641 they urged the Company to find 'a painful and profitable lecturer' to replace him.[69] A few weeks later, in April 1641, the Company responded to the complaints and removed Sydeserffe.[70] The contrast with the meek acceptance of the royal nominee little more than a year earlier is instructive. Was it because the Company had become less prepared to accept royal or episcopal authority, or was it merely that the Company had been emboldened by Parliament's own stand against the Crown? The following Chapter will afford some clues.

At this point it suffices to make two brief points. First, the Company's trusteeship of the Fishborne legacy had brought it face to face with the authoritarianism of Charles and Laud, with obvious consequences for both corporate and individual political attitudes. Secondly, during that confrontation the Company revealed itself warmly committed to the ideals embodied in Fishborne's will and prepared to resist even the Crown itself to see those ideals implemented.[71]

CHAPTER IV

THE CROWN, PARLIAMENT, AND THE CIVIL WAR

A change of monarch, even a change in the form of government, does not necessarily mean a change to the daily lives or prospects of ordinary citizens. None the less the accession of James I in 1603 meant more than a change of personality, skills and style. It is true that before the old Queen died, the mechanisms of the Tudor system, and the compromises of the Tudor political framework, had begun to crumble, and the new government inherited a difficult position. It still remains the case that James and his son made matters not only worse, but intolerable, by their own fatal combination of arrogance and incompetence. The Personal Rule of 1629–40 may have been a brave and not necessarily doomed attempt to do without a fractious Parliament, but it was also an admission of defeat. In one generation, the Stuarts had moved from at least a form of representative government to an attempt at absolutism.

The citizens of London in the early years of the seventeenth century were only too aware that they were living in times of unusual uncertainty and difficulty. This was especially true of the Livery Companies whose privileges and assets were always vulnerable to royal caprice or impecuniosity.[1] Political turbulence was bound to increase that vulnerability, and whatever the long-term significance of the changes at Westminster might turn out to be, the short-term effects in the City were undeniably serious. The legal subversion of the Company's chartered rights could be rectified by Act of Parliament or another royal decree, but it was more difficult to provide for the reparation of financial depredations. Long after the turmoil of the Interregnum of 1649–60 had subsided, the Mercers found themselves 'paying' for the financial exactions of these years.

PART I. IRELAND

MONEY

Throughout the period from the accession of James I to the outbreak of the Civil War, the Livery Companies were inundated with demands for money from the Crown. The first two Stuart Kings, labouring under the twin handicaps of unrealistic pretensions and an unsympathetic Parliament, regularly turned to the City for 'loans' to relieve their financial embarrassment.[2] Most of these exactions can be adequately described *en masse* below in Part II of this Chapter, but the money raised for Ireland deserves separate treatment, partly because of the scale of the demands and partly because the estates which resulted played an important part in the life of the Company for 300 years.

In 1608, following an unsuccessful rebellion of the native Earls, the Crown seized control of six Ulster counties and put in hand a scheme of 'colonisation'.[3] The aim was chiefly defensive, to prevent future insurrections and deny England's enemies a potential base for invasion; but there were also more positive objectives: namely to reform the ignorant Catholic peasantry, relieve over-population in England, and reward soldiers who had helped quell the recent rebellion. The original aim was for individual 'undertakers' to acquire land on a piecemeal basis, but in the

FIG. 23. Lionel Cranfield (1575–1645), created Earl of Middlesex in 1622, Master of the Mercers' Company in 1615–16 and 1622–3. This print was drawn by W. Haines and engraved by E. Scriven, from an original portrait by Daniel Myttens.
Mercers' Company

Sir Thomas Gresham's gift of the Royal Exchange to the City of London and the Mercers' Company. An imaginative reconstruction, painted in 1851 by the German artist, Edward Henry Wehnert, of the occasion when Gresham gave his hand to the Lord Mayor, Sir William Garrard, in token of his intention regarding the Royal Exchange. Among the company is Sir Lionel Duckett, whose portrait appears in Figure 8.

By courtesy of Guardian Royal Exchange Collection

John Isham, Mercer, 1525–96. This painting on wood by an unknown artist hangs at Lamport Hall, Northamptonshire. The clock was presumably included as one of his most valuable possessions; it is unusual in that the highest point of the chapter ring lies between XII and I, instead of XII being vertical. Isham rose to be Upper Warden in 1576; he and several of his brothers were involved in the cloth trade with Antwerp.

PLATE VII

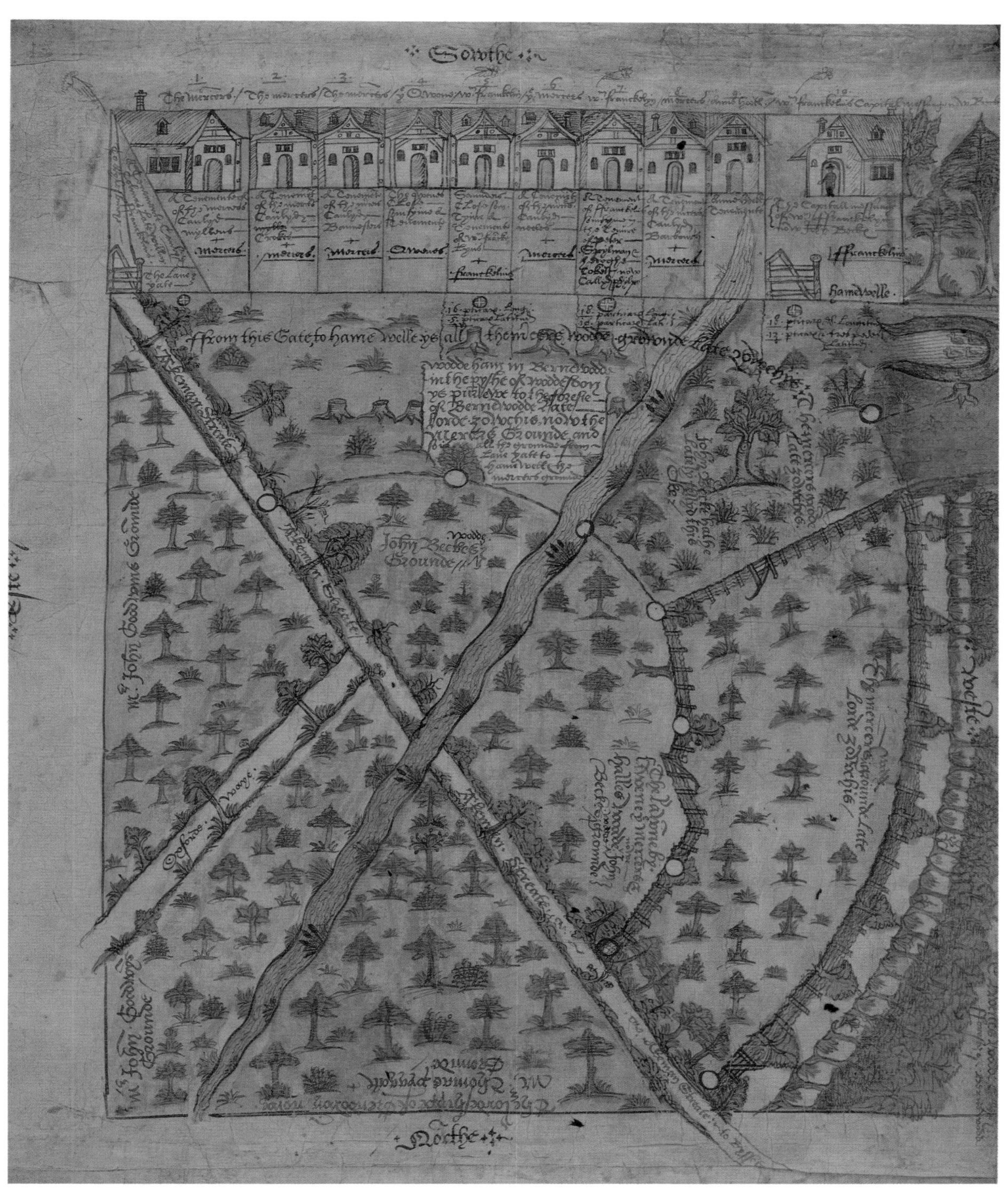

The Colet estate: Woodham, Buckinghamshire, an early seventeenth-century pictorial map on parchment by an unknown hand. The north is at the bottom of the survey and it lacks a scale. Notice the houses drawn out along the top, the detail of the hedgerows and of the rushes by the stream, the ducks swimming on the pond. Beside a large tree is a rueful reminder: 'John Becke hath lately fellyd this Oke'. Akeman Street follows its inexorable Roman line; the road to Oxford turns off it. The Company no longer owns the property.
Mercers' Company

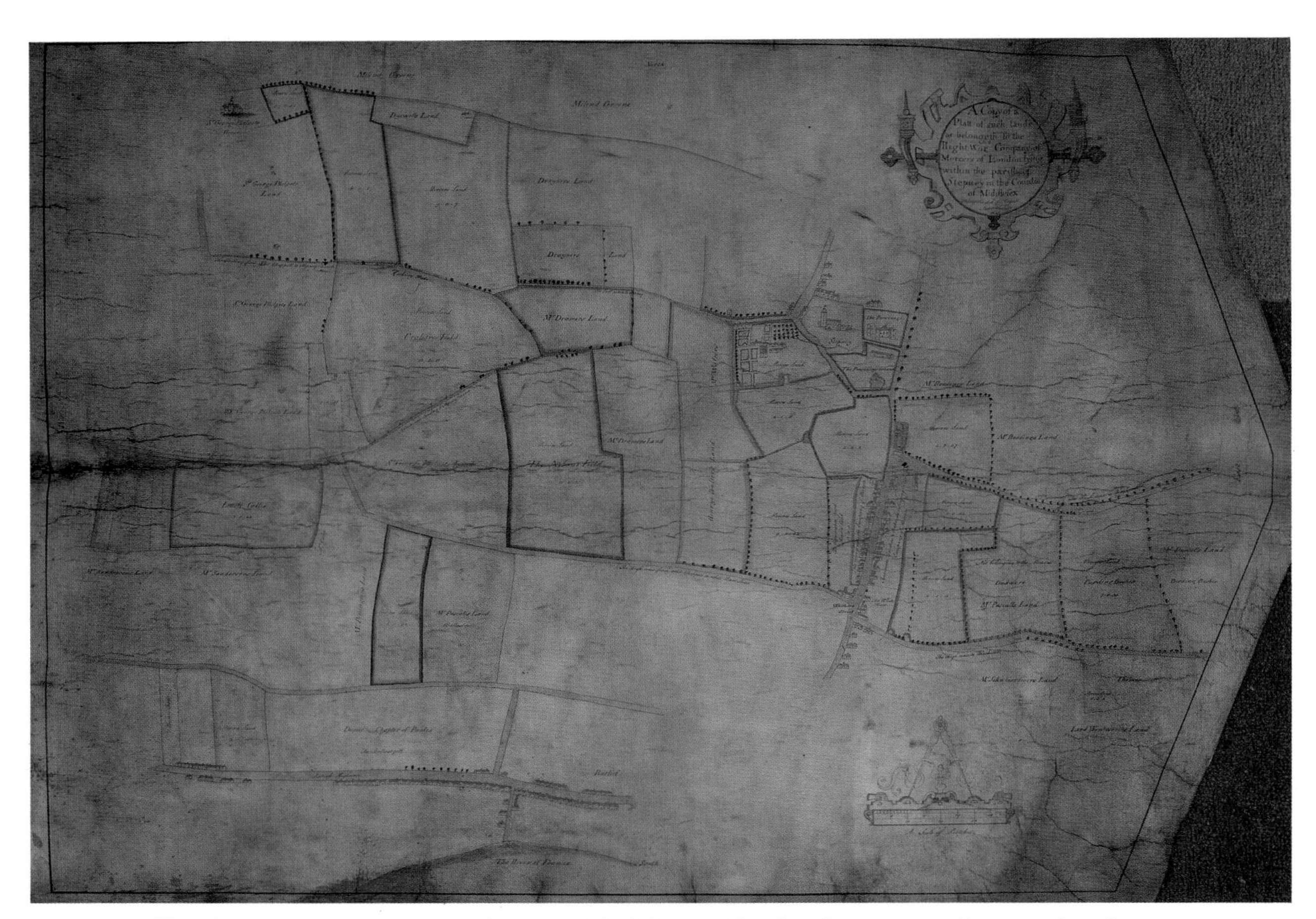

The Colet estate: plan on parchment of the Mercers' land at Stepney, 20 August 1615, by an unknown surveyor. The Colet family had a long association with Stepney; John's father, Sir Henry, still lies in his canopied tomb in St Dunstan's Church which can be clearly seen towards the centre of the map. The Company no longer owns the estate.

Mercers' Company

spring of 1609, when the plantation appeared to be in danger of failing for lack of support, the King approached the City of London to persuade it to take up a large tract of the escheated land, namely the county of Coleraine and neighbouring areas. In due course the request, in the form of a mayoral precept, was passed on to the Companies for their consideration. The Mercers replied:[4]

> That in all humility they return thanks to His Majesty in the gracious remembrance of them in the offer of the same precept, but forasmuch as they are for the most part men that live by merchandize and therefore are inexperienced in managing a business of that nature and withal want means and ability for the accomplishment thereof this Company are not willing to have a hand or intermeddle in the same.

Such an outright refusal was unusual, though there was a good deal of scepticism and reluctance among the other Companies. None the less, when a second precept was issued asking for names of contributors, sufficient support was forthcoming to encourage the City Corporation to agree terms with the Crown at the turn of the year. The unwilling Mercers would have to accept the majority verdict.

In January 1610 came the first request for money. £20,000 was to be raised from the Companies on the basis of the corn quota, and the Mercers' share was £1,640, of which one-quarter (£410) was required immediately.[5] The Company were 'very much aggrieved at the inequality of the taxation in regard of their small number of householders and the great cost rated upon them, being a full 12th part of the £20,000 levied upon the whole City'; and they decided to ask the Lord Mayor for relief.[6] This plainly had no effect, for little over a week later it was resolved to petition the Privy Council on the matter.[7] Their Lordships were told that the 'great decay in number and estate' of the Mercers and the 'great increase of some other Companies of late years' made the corn rate quite out of date and utterly at variance with such other assessments as the subsidy.[A] The petition concluded with the following 'causes manifesting the great decay of the Company of Mercers':

> 1. In times past their Company were the sole shippers of cloth and Merchant Venturers. Now the most part of the Merchant Venturers are not of the Mercers' Company.
> 2. The whole trade of retailing linen cloth was in the Mercers. Now not above eight linen drapers [are] free of the Mercers and very many of other Companies.
> 3. The whole trade of retailing silks was in the Mercers. Now not above ten retailing Mercers [are] free of the Mercers' Company. The residue being very many are free of other Companies.

Later pages will suggest that these protestations have to be treated with at least some scepticism, and it was perhaps fortunate for the Company that the Privy Council declined to meddle in what it regarded as the internal affairs of the City and said that the Company should make payment as requested.[8] None the less, it urged the City to consider adopting a more equitable system of taxation.

This was not, however, the end of the affair. Attempts by the Company to have a Common Council summoned to consider their grievance failed, and a second quarter assessment at the old rate duly arrived.[9] This sent the Mercers back to the Privy Council 'for ease', but again their Lordships were unwilling, or unable, to help.[10] This was followed, remarkably enough, by the imprisonment of Wardens Barnes and Thwaites on the order of the Court of Aldermen. The Wardens' ordeal lasted only a few days because, on the understanding that the Mercers' future assessments would be reduced, the Company agreed to the second sum of £410 as originally demanded.[11] The assessments were indeed revised and the Mercers paid £310 as their last two contributions towards the £20,000 and on the same lower basis thereafter.[12]

The first assessment had been passed on to individual members, but the three further demands, and the prospect of others in the future, prompted discussion in this as in other Companies whether it was better to continue with individual

[A] The grievance went back many years, of course. See above, p. 19.

assessments or transfer the obligation to 'domus', i.e. corporate funds. In August 1610 the Mercers resolved on the latter course. Members decided to relinquish claims arising from their contributions to the first quarter payment of £410 and accordingly resolved that 'the House should undergo the whole burden and that the profit that should hereafter arise should rebound unto the body of the same'.[13] This decision acquired significance a few months later, in January 1611, when the City asked the Companies whether they would adopt a proportionate share of the land in Ulster in lieu of the money they had contributed, and would in future contribute, and discharge the cost of the plantation themselves, or whether they would prefer to leave the disposal of the land to the City's own standing committee, the Irish Society.[14] It was made plain that declining the offer would not exempt Companies from further contributions; and it is a measure of their suspicion of the scheme that the Mercers' first reaction was indeed to refuse,[15] though ten days later they changed their minds and accepted their share.[16]

Before the Company was allotted its land, it was confronted with a precept requesting contributions towards a second sum of £20,000.[17] The Mercers, in common with the majority of their fellow Companies, were not ready to accept forfeiture of their existing rights as the price for not advancing more money, and duly paid a total of £1,240 (i.e. at the new rate) between July 1611 and May 1613.[18] It was in December 1613 that the allotment of lands took place, with the plantation being divided among twelve groups of Companies (each headed by one of the Great Twelve) constituted in such a way as to make the collective contribution of each group one-twelfth of the £40,000.[19] The Mercers, associated with the Innholders, Cooks, Embroiderers and Masons, drew Lot number 8. This was some 21,000 acres to the west of the River Bann to the south-west of Kilrea. The allotment, however, did not mark the end of the Companies' financial contributions. At the same meeting of Common Council the first instalment of a third payment of £20,000 was requested[20] and during the following three years the Mercers paid a further £1,240. This brought the Company's share of the total payment of £60,000 to £3,920.[21] Such was the 'burden'. What now of 'the profit that should hereafter arise'?

THE MANOR OF MERCERS

The formalities of vesting the various 'proportions' took some time. First, it was necessary for a licence in mortmain to be obtained, and then the Irish Society created twelve manors, replete with the usual legal powers and tenurial categories. It was not until October 1618 that 'the Manor of Mercers' was conveyed to the Company. In the meantime, however, work on the plantation began. A standing committee was set up as early as February 1614 for that purpose.[22]

Information on these early years of the Irish estate is scanty. This is especially unfortunate because the Mercers adopted what proved to be a unique approach. Instead of farming out their land to a single undertaker they kept it under direct control. Quite why they did not follow the example of their fellow Companies is not clear. It was not a matter of fundamental principle, because in 1621 they seriously considered accepting an offer for a lease of the whole estate, and did not do so merely because the terms were not attractive enough.[23] (Indeed, they even encouraged one aspirant 'farmer' to see whether he could obtain a grant in fee simple and allow the Company to drop out of the arrangement altogether.)[24] Even when they reassured tenants in 1631 that the latter 'need not doubt or fear the Company's letting their whole proportion to any one man', they did not rule out the possibility entirely. The idea was simply 'altogether contrary to their present disposition and resolutions which if they change hereafter they will give notice to their agent beforehand and take his information of the inconveniences there against'.[25] The decision was doubtless a pragmatic one, based on the Company's satisfaction with 'their agent'. In 1631 the incumbent was Thomas Church, with ten years' evidently commendable service behind him. In 1621, by contrast, the Company was in the midst of the turmoil created by the 'negligence and ill-husbandry' of Richard Vernon, Church's predecessor.[26] Little wonder that they nearly seized the opportunity of a carefree, assured down-payment and rental, and little wonder also that the mood changed as Church eased the burden in the following years.

If the methods were different on the Mercers' estate, the results were very similar. No more than on any other manor did the Mercers make the kind of progress with the plantation that the Crown had desired. The 'Conditions to be observed by the British Undertakers of the escheated lands in Ulster' involved the building of sturdy and fortifiable homes, the settlement of resident English and Scottish tenants, and the exclusion of the native Irish from the new landholdings. On none of these points did the Mercers achieve any great success. The inhospitality of the land and a corresponding lack of enthusiasm combined to make progress very slow indeed. A few houses, and a castle, were built, and three- or four-score immigrants were settled; but it was so much easier to allow the local people, under cover of a few head leases, to remain on the land. The Irish were hungry for land and paid well; the British were indifferent and paid badly. Market forces, suitably camouflaged, triumphed.[27]

The net result of this modest opportunism was a rental income of between £140 and £200 per annum.[28] A mediocre return, it might be thought, on a capital outlay of £4,000 and regular supervision. Worse was to come, however. The failure of the Companies to adhere strictly to the 'Conditions' imposed upon them was regarded by the Crown as sufficient grounds for a comprehensive legal attack.

STAR CHAMBER (1635)

The instigator and orchestrator of the Crown's assault was Sir Thomas Phillips, an Irish 'adventurer' who had been thwarted in his (not unreasonable) hopes of advancement and profit by the City in its management of the Londonderry plantation, and thereafter waged a lifelong battle to discredit the planters. Two brief sequestrations of rent, in 1625–7 and 1628, were the direct result of Phillips's endeavours, but his crowning achievement was the Star Chamber lawsuit of 1631–5. The City, or more accurately the Irish Society, was charged with obtaining the grant of exorbitant rights and privileges under false pretences, violating its contract with the Crown and otherwise betraying the King's trust. The Companies were not themselves joined in the proceedings, but they were well aware that they stood or fell with the City, and requests for money to meet the Irish Society's expenses met with a ready response from each of the Twelve.[29] Attempts to find a compromise took up two years or more but came to nothing, and in January 1635 the trial began. It mattered not that the City was able effectively to exonerate itself on all material charges save that of failing to install sufficient British settlers. The Crown was determined to obtain the 'right' verdict, and Charles I's judges did not lightly ignore such 'guidance'. With a rather disturbing degree of unanimity, the twenty-two judges pronounced the case proven and ordered that the City surrender its patent and pay a fine of £70,000.

It was quite clear that the King's chief motive in responding to Phillips's representations was financial. Not content with coercing the landowners into paying for the dubious privilege of administering a dangerous part of its kingdom, the Crown now resolved to make them pay yet more for not adhering strictly to its rather fanciful conditions of settlement. Charles was certainly not concerned with any point of principle.[B] In fact, the Star Chamber decree signified no more than the Crown's opening gambit in a lengthy haggle over terms. The negotiations embraced some other points of dispute between the Crown and the City, but the upshot, as far as the Irish

[B] In July 1636 the King even recommended a would-be tenant of the Company's proportion! AC, 1631–7 (rough), f. 215.

lands were concerned, was that, though the surrender remained as the Court had pronounced, the fine was reduced to £12,000. The Companies, including the Mercers, strove hard to avoid, or at least to mitigate, the consequences of the settlement, but to no avail.[30] In February 1638, when the City's Londonderry charter was formally revoked, the Companies lost their title too.

It remained only for the Mercers to find its £520 share of the £8,000 levied by the City on the Companies to pay for the £12,000 fine.[31] It is a measure of the Mercers' indignation that they subsequently steeled themselves to disobey both the Attorney-General and the Lord Mayor, and refused to deliver up their original Irish deeds.[32]

Two years later there was a glimmer of hope. The summoning of the Long Parliament in 1640 provided the Mercers and their fellow victims with an opportunity for drawing attention to their maltreatment.[33] Their story was readily taken up by reformist Members as further evidence of Stuart oppression, and in August 1641 the Commons formally vindicated the City and Companies and called for the restoration of the status quo ante. An increasingly vulnerable King was inclined to agree, or at least professed to be so inclined, when he was attempting to win much-needed support from the citizens of London in November 1641. 'One thing [he declared] I have thought of as a particular affection to you, which is to give back unto you freely that part of Londonderry which heretofore was evicted from you'.[34]

However, as so often, Charles gave too little, too late. In the month before he spoke the Irish Rebellion had broken out, engulfing the country in such sectarian savagery that no further colonisation could be contemplated until Cromwell had exacted his bloody vengeance almost a decade later. In the intervening years the Mercers could do no more than contribute money and arms to the beleaguered Irish Protestants.[35] Even when order was imposed, it took many years before Cromwell's Parliament could be persuaded to follow the Long Parliament's lead and restore the Irish estates. The necessary Letters Patent and deeds of conveyance did not transpire until 1657–8.

This first chapter in the story of the Irish estate closes with the disposition of the restored Lot 8. This time the Company succumbed to the temptation of letting the entire property to a 'farmer' in line with their fellow Companies. One Gervase Rose was granted a forty-one-year lease at £300 per annum subject only to a lease of part of the estate to the former agent, Thomas Church.[36] Lessees were to retain control of the Irish estate until 1831, and the 'Manor of Mercers' thus passes out of the mainstream of the Company's history, save only for those occasions when the grant of a fresh lease assumed financial importance.[C]

PART II. FINANCE

TAXES, LOANS AND GIFTS

The Company was plagued with repeated demands for money during this period, the Irish affair being only the most brazen of a score of such exactions. The others are best presented in tabular form which gives a clearer impression of the incidence as well as the size of the levies. How did the Mercers react to these repeated demands? It would be easy to assume from a glance at the anxious discussions and prevarication recorded in the Acts of Court that there was mounting anger, and then to connect that apparent anger with the outbreak of Civil War. Closer inspection, however, reveals a more complicated picture, and emphasises that *post hoc* is not always *propter hoc*.

The first sign of resistance came in 1604, but all the Company did was to appoint two members to discuss with representatives from other Companies the fairness of the assessment of the corn rate and other matters. There was no complaint against the Crown loan itself.[37] In 1611 the Company did actually refuse to make a contribution to

[C] For the most striking instance, see below, pp. 106–8.

Whereas the wardens and comynaltie of the Mistery of the Mercers of the Cittie of London have paid in ready money to Sr Thomas Smyth knight Treasurer for Virginia the some of [illegible] poundes for their adventure towardes the said voyadge It is agreed that for the same they the said wardens and comynaltie and their successors shall have ratablie according to their adventure their full parte of all such landes tenements and hereditaments as shall from tyme to tyme be there recovered planted and inhabited And of all such Mynes and Mynerall of gold silver and other mettalls or treasure Pearles precious stones or any kinde of wares or Marchandizes commodities or proffitts whatsoever which shalbe obteyned or gotten in the said voyadge according to the porcon of money by them imployed to that use in as ample manner as any other adventurer therin shall receave for the like some
Written this 22th of Aprill Ao: 1609

Richard Atkinson

FIG. 24. Virginia Company bond, 1609.
Mercers' Company

the Virginia Company, but the Lord Mayor's request was an informal one and the reasons for declining (namely, that the Company, and its members, had already ventured substantial sums) were evidently accepted without demur.[38] The 'benevolence' for James I's son-in-law, the Elector Palatine, came at a time when the Company at least professed to be £3,000 in debt by reason of its Irish expenditure. None the less it was prepared to give £200 (partly from the Gresham account but partly also from the sale of plate), and further pressure to match the sum in 1614 elicited a further £110 (largely from the St Paul's School account), though it was accompanied by a protest to discourage further demands.[39]

The most determined resistance arose in 1627–8 in relation to the Royal Contract loan. The first Mayoral precept, in December 1627, was for £3,720 and gave rise to intense debate at no less than three General Courts before it was accepted. However, the Company does not seem to have opposed the loan on point of principle. Rather, it was concerned about the authority of Common Council to impose such a levy on the one hand and the security for repayment on the other. Thus at the first General Court, on 24 December,

> after long and serious consideration and debate about power of the Court of Common Council to impose such a matter of this nature upon the Company and about security for the repayment of the money it [was] at last by erection of hands declared that this Court does not conceive this Company to be liable to furnish the same sum by virtue of the said precept or upon command thereof grounded upon the Act of Common Council. Nevertheless the inclination of this Court is of its own accord for the furtherance of his Majesty's service to furnish the said sum by way of a treaty and not of compulsion.

At the third General Court, on 8 January, the Liverymen were satisfied by a speech from the Recorder that Common Council did indeed have the necessary authority. They then proceeded to a vote, and though the motion to comply with the precept was lost by 38 votes to 32

> afterwards the Court joined together [i.e. considered] a means of accommodation and a good issue of this difficult business. At last the general inclination of the Court being to furnish the money and all the difference remaining being about security . . . it was moved and voted that the money [be] given and security obtained at the next meeting of Common Council.[40]

Much the same can be said of the reaction to the second precept, in July 1628, for £1,240. Again three General Courts were necessary before payment was authorised, but again fundamentals were not involved. There was doubt once more as to the authority of Common Council, and also the form of the Lord Mayor's precept. Members were worried that a dangerous precedent might be established.[41] Another concern was whether payment would prejudice rights 'so lately allowed and

TABLE 1
COMPANY LOANS AND GIFTS, 1596–1643

	DATE	DESCRIPTION OF PAYMENT	METHOD OF PAYMENT
(1)	1596	£492 loan to the City for ships	Domus (i.e. corporate funds)
(2)	1598	£1,600, part of £20,000 loan to the Crown for Irish war	Freemen
(3)	1603	£54 'loan' to the City to purchase patent from Crown	Domus
(4)	1603	£250 gift to the City for the Coronation	?Domus
(5)	1603	£68 for same	?Domus
(6)	1604	£1,200, part of £15,000 loan by the City to the Crown	£1,200 loan from Sir William Craven, repaid by interest-bearing assessments on freemen
(7)	1609	£200 for the Virginia plantation	Domus. (Any shortfall was to be drawn, if necessary, from the Gresham or St Paul's School accounts, but the former were certainly not drawn on and there are no contemporary accounts for the latter.)
(8)	1612	£50 for the same	?Domus
(9)	1614	£50 for the same	?Domus
(10)	1614	£310 for the Palatinate	Domus, out of cash or from loans (no indication as to which method was used).
(11)	1620	£310 for the Palatinate	In roughly equal one-third shares from the Gresham account, the St Paul's School account and the sale of plate 'not given by notable benefactors'
(12)	1627–8	£4,960, part of £120,000 loan to the Crown via the City (the so-called 'Royal Contract' loan)	The Lord Mayor's precept asked first for £3,720 and then for £1,240. Towards the first sum Sir Baptist Hicks contributed a year's loan of £2,700, the balance being taken and the repayment of the loan being made from various sources, including a repaid East India Company debt and loans from the Gresham, Fishborne and St Paul's School accounts. The second sum was to have been raised entirely from an assessment on members but at least some of it was evidently borrowed on the Company's seal
(13)	1629–30	£266, part of £4,300 gift for the Royal Pageant	Domus
(14)	1632	£62, part of £1,000 fine on the City for not arresting the murderers of the Duke of Buckingham's creature, Dr Lambe	Nearly £31 from members and the remainder from domus
(15)	1635	£55 for Ship Money	?Domus
(16)	1639	£100 for the same	?Domus
(17)	1640	£3,250, part of £50,000 loan for the Crown	The accounts show the following borrowings: £1,050 from the St Paul's School account; £500 from each of three members (Spurstow, Gardiner and Flyer); £200 from the Trinity Hospital Greenwich account; and £500 from the Gresham account

TABLE 1 (*cont.*)
COMPANY LOANS AND GIFTS, 1596–1643

	DATE	DESCRIPTION OF PAYMENT	METHOD OF PAYMENT
(18)	1642	£6,500, part of £100,000 loan for the relief of Ireland	£5,810 from loans by members; the balance evidently from domus
(19)	1643	£3,250, part of £50,000 loan for the 'safety and defence' of the City against the King	Loans from individuals (chiefly members or widows)

(1) AC, 1595–1629, ff. 4v–5v.
(2) Ibid., ff. 21, 27v.
(3) Ibid., f. 29v. The sum was to be described in the Second Warden's accounts as a *loan* in case the City were subsequently to exploit the patent.
(4) Ibid., f. 46v.
(5) Ibid., f. 51.
(6) Ibid., f. 56v. See also R. Ashton, *The Crown and the Money Market 1603–40* (1960), pp. 116 and 117n.
(7) AC, 1595–1629, f. 96.
(8) Ibid., f. 124.
(9) Ibid., f. 133.
(10) Ibid., f. 133v.
(11) Ibid., ff. 213–14; Second Wardens' accounts, 1617–29, ff. 87v, 101v; St Paul's School Surveyor's accounts, 1620–38 (1620/1); Renter Wardens' Gresham accounts, 1619–36, f. 419.
(12) AC, ff. 322–3v, 324, 337–v, 344; Second Wardens' accounts, 1617–29, ff. 304v, 320, 322, 329, 331v, 344, 363–v, 371; Renter Wardens' Gresham accounts, 1625–54, pp. 57–8; St Paul's School Surveyor's accounts, 1620–38 (1627–8 and 1628–9). See also Ashton, *Crown and the Money Market*, pp. 135–41.
(13) AC, 1595–1629, f. 358v; 1625–31 (rough), ff. 232v, 259v–60: Second Wardens' accounts, 1629–38, f. 34.
(14) AC, 1631–7 (rough), ff. 64v–6, 69–v; Second Wardens' accounts, 1629–38 (1632/3). The episode is studied in L. M. Goldstein, 'The Life and Death of John Lambe', *Guildhall Studies in London History*, IV (1979), pp. 19–32.
(15) AC, 1631–7, f. 51; Second Wardens' accounts, 1629–38 for 1635/6 and 1636–7.
(16) AC, 1637–41, ff. 91, 93, 94v.
(17) Ibid., ff. 178v, 179v, 180v–5; Renter Wardens' accounts, 1638–48, f. 92v; Second Wardens' accounts, 1638–48, ff. 112v–13, 114v–15, 119; SPS accounts, 1634–54 for 1640; Trinity Hospital Greenwich accounts for 1641/2; Renter Wardens' Gresham accounts, 1636–58, pp. 348–9, 371.
(18) Second Wardens' accounts, 1638–48, ff. 155v–7v, 168; Cash Book, 1642–58.
(19) AC, 1641–5 (rough), ff. 84v–7; Second Wardens' accounts, 1638–48, ff. 211, 242–3, 254; Cash Book, 1642–58. There is evidence at this date that the Company owed £1,090 to the Gresham account: AC, 1641–5 (rough), f. 73. Whether this means that part of the £3,250 was in fact borrowed from this source is unclear.

declared' in the Petition of Right and the declaration of the House of Commons in the case of a recalcitrant Vintner, Nicholas Clegate.[42] There was no suggestion that the loan itself was unacceptable, and in any event ten days after uttering its brave words the General Court voted to make payment in full.[43]

Similar tactics were employed in 1629–30 when the Company was ordered to contribute towards the costs of a pageant for Charles I. The Act of Common Council authorising the levy was said to be conditional upon a review of the City's own finances, and such a review had not taken place before the precept was issued. The Company therefore refused to pay until a further Act had been passed.[44] Once again the City had the last word: the Chamberlain adopted the simple tactic of deducting the £266 from the £3,720 outstanding debt in his books. The Mercers squealed but gave way:[45]

> And albeit they found that the £3,720 was gotten from them at first by undue means and also that the defalcation of the said charge towards the payments is conditioned against equity and fair dealing, yet forasmuch as they see that unless they will yield to this unreasonable condition they shall not get the rest of their money, they condescended as in a necessity and for avoiding of a great inconvenience to receive their money according to the terms propounded as aforesaid; but wish that this dealing may be ever hereafter remembered by this Company whensoever they shall be demanded to disburse any sums by certificate of Act of Common Council for any loan whatsoever.

There is no denying the anger here, but it would be wrong to interpret it in political terms. The legalistic challenge to the City's legislative powers smacks rather of the exploitation of 'rights' by a sorely-tried creditor than the assertion of rights against the Crown by an aggressive parliamentarian.

Even Ship Money, that most controversial of Charles's demands, did not rouse any obvious partisan anger. In 1637, it is true, an objection was made, but only on the grounds of double-assessment,[46] and as late as 1639, when at least some truculence might have been expected, the concerns were mild and pragmatic, namely the fact that the Company was still owed more than £1,000 for similar loans and the absence of any security.[47] Only in July 1640 did the Company finally refuse to pay Ship Money.[48] By this stage, however, the entire City was turning a deaf ear to the King's entreaties for more money. In a sense the refusal, coming as it did so close to the final slide into Civil War, is the exception which proves the general rule of compliance. The Company shared the general reluctance to deny money to the Crown. It showed a robust determination to avoid whatever exactions it could, and certainly cannot be regarded as royalist in persuasion. Yet neither was it parliamentarian: it seems to have been incapable of *political* opposition. In fact, as later pages will indicate, the Company was content to wait upon events. The real consequences of the taxes, loans and gifts listed above were not political but financial.

DEBT

For the state of the Company's finances between 1603 and 1660 it is necessary to study both the Renter Wardens' and Second (or House) Wardens' accounts.[49] The two sets of figures have to be viewed together because the distinction between 'property' and 'other' matters was an arbitrary one and never really worked in practice. Fortunately the joint pattern is quite clear. After many years of largely uninterrupted surpluses, the late 1630s and early 1640s (in the case of the Renter Wardens' accounts) and the 1640s and 1650s (in the case of the Second Wardens') saw recurring deficits. This is the background against which the Company's efforts to mitigate the problem have to be seen.

The struggle began in 1643 with the drastic decision to sell almost £700 worth of Company plate.[50] This constituted (in weight, at least) approximately three-fifths of the Company's entire collection.[51] In the following year the first steps were taken to recover the public 'loans', namely resolutions to ask the Mayor and Aldermen for the repayment of the 'City' monies and to enquire of the other Companies to see whether a petition should be presented to Parliament in relation to 'State' monies.[52] These latter initiatives deserve credit for a little success: between 1644 and 1646, £650 and £1,083 of the loans of 1640 and 1643 respectively were repaid.[53] That was all, however, until 1651 when there is mention of efforts (*inter alia*) 'to procure in the monies the Company heretofore lent to the State . . .'.[54] Again some results were achieved: nearly £300 of the 1640 loan trickled in between July 1651 and December 1653; but there remained more than £11,000 in unpaid principal alone from the three great loans of 1640–3.[D] [55]

Little wonder, therefore, that for much of the 1650s the Company concentrated on self-help measures. In May 1651 consideration was given to the best course 'to bring the Company out of debt . . .'.[56] The result was a committee which was first deputed to 'treat with the Company's tenants and to let leases of property' and then, in view of 'the great debt the Company oweth', to examine the financial problem generally.[57] Regular meetings were held and detailed property reviews compiled,[58] with a marked impact on rents (as an

[D] Nearly £2,000 of this debt derived from the Gresham fund, as witness an eloquent resolution in 1645: 'whereas £1,949.6.10½ has been heretofore borrowed out of [the] Gresham account lent to the use of the State of the Kingdom in a greater sum it was now thought fit that mention of that debt be left out of the Gresham account with a note that the sum was paid into the Company's stock for the aforesaid purposes'. AC, 1645–51, f. 10.

A. Trinity Hospital, Greenwich, founded by the Earl of Northampton, 1616. Early nineteenth-century watercolour by an unknown artist. The buildings remain substantially unaltered.
Mercers' Company

B. Lady Mico's almshouses, at their first location opposite St Dunstan's Church, Stepney. The almshouses were founded by Lady Mico, widow of Sir Samuel Mico, Alderman and Mercer, by her will of 1670, and were built in 1690. They were rebuilt in 1857, and again in 1976, but still remain in Stepney. We do not know the name of the artist who produced this watercolour in the nineteenth century; he may also have been responsible for the painting of Trinity Hospital, Shotesham (Pl. XIXA).
Mercers' Company

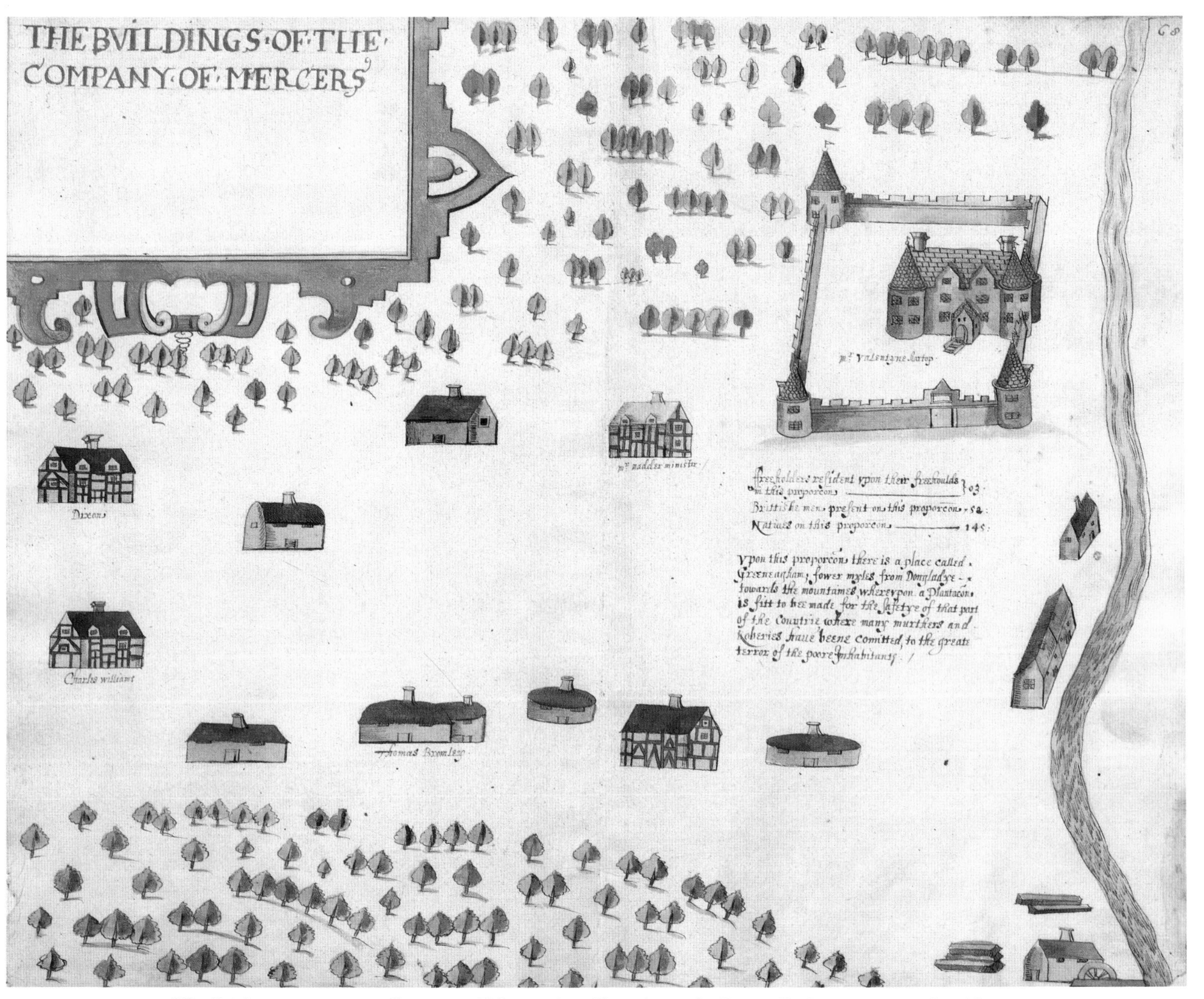

The Irish estate: survey of houses at Kilrea, 1622. Note the encircling wall, there as protection (Carew MS 634, ff. 64v–65).

By courtesy of Lambeth Palace Library

FIG. 25. The Dethick Salt, 1638. John Dethick was admitted a Mercer in 1630 on payment of a fine of £30. £20 was returned to him and the remaining £10 was spent on the purchase of the Salt.
Mercers' Company

FIG. 26. Tomb of Sir Baptist Hicks (1551–1629) and his wife, created Viscount and Viscountess Campden in 1628, at Chipping Campden. He was Master of the Mercers' Company in 1603, 1610 and 1621. He and his wife left money in trust to the Company to provide exhibitions to Oxford and Cambridge for boys from St Paul's School. He purchased the Manor of Campden in Gloucestershire, and at Chipping Campden built a mansion at a cost of £29,000, which was destroyed in the Civil War. Sir Baptist also built twelve almshouses for the little town, which still flourish. Having no son, his title was allowed to pass through his daughter, Julian, to his son-in-law, Edward Noel.
By courtesy of Oxfordshire County Council Leisure and Arts

increase in the Renter Warden's revenues signifies).[59] Such increases were welcome, but unfortunately insufficient. The Renter Warden may have been recording surpluses, but the Second Warden was not.[60] In December 1657 another committee was chosen, this time with a brief to 'purge the books of hopeless debts and to settle a way to lessen the common charge'.[61] The bad debts were duly expunged and transferred to the Black Book,[62] but the other task, of course, proved more difficult. Two provisions were made, but neither was likely to prove any kind of panacea. One was to restrict the expenditure on dinners to certain levels and to require the appropriate Warden to bear any excess. The other was to abolish the gratuity customarily given to members who had been elected Sheriff or Lord Mayor for the decoration of their houses.[63] Such assistance, said the committee,

> was judged a work very necessary during such times as the Company were in a condition able to perform the same without prejudicing their other more necessary affairs. But now, finding the common stock of the Company to be very low, and much in debt, and therefore unable (if any such occasion should again happen) to allow any such gratification, unless by taking up money at interest (which may tend to the ruin of the Corporation). Wherefore the Committee, holding it very necessary, have ordered that for the future all such gratifications to any such person or persons that shall or may be hereafter chosen either Lord Mayor or Sheriffs of this City shall cease until it shall please God to raise the estate of this Corporation into a more flourishing condition.

Divine intervention took some while to transpire. Indeed, as the next Chapter will show, the Great Fire of London, which some contemporaries at least interpreted as God's vengeance for a sinful capital and which itself represented a financial calamity even more disastrous than the Stuart 'loans', came upon a Company still labouring under a burden of debt. James I, Charles I and Parliament combined to leave the Mercers extremely vulnerable to the kind of misfortune which occurred in 1666.

PART III. THE CIVIL WAR

London's part in the outbreak (and the outcome) of the Civil War has been the subject of much scholarly debate. A pioneering account published in 1960 argued that, notwithstanding the conduct of Charles I, particularly during the Personal Rule, the City remained fundamentally committed to the Crown, and it required an election 'coup' by radicals in December 1641 to capture the City for Parliament.[64] Since then, scholars have examined the picture in other parts of the country and a synthesis has emerged which suggests that in 1640 Parliament could call on widespread support for its stand against Charles I and his chief ministers, Laud and Strafford. This support, however, was emphatically not ideological in nature, but rather born of a conservative resistance to Charles's new centralised style of government in both Church and State. Such support was unlikely to survive any subsequent lurch into constitutional novelties and, if war were ever to present the traditional governors of the country with a choice between King and Parliament, the former would not have to do much to regain their allegiance.

In 1979 the evidence for London was re-examined and found to bear the same interpretation as the rest of the country.[65] Londoners were as troubled as those elsewhere by Charles I's conduct, and it was only the radicalism of 1640–2 (of which the 'coup' of December 1641 formed part) which pushed them away from Parliament and back to the Crown.

The evidence for the attitude of the Mercers, both as individuals and corporately, is not extensive and is often difficult to interpret.

The preceding Part of this Chapter reveals a Company which fought hard to resist the repeated demands of both the Crown and the City, but did so on grounds which were strictly apolitical. Whether this betokens a Company sorely tried

FIG. 27. *Winter*, one of a set of engravings of the Four Seasons by Wenceslas Hollar, 1643–4. The masked fur-clad lady stands with her back to Cornhill, the tower of the Royal Exchange, and the Tun, as the prison for night vagrants was called, visible to the right; she faces towards Cheapside, in the direction of Mercers' Hall.
The Royal Collection, copyright 1993: Her Majesty the Queen

but still committed to the Crown or a Company alienated (albeit on a non-ideological basis) from it, is really impossible to say. The absence of any personal records, taking the historian beneath the formal Court minutes, precludes a firm answer to the question.

It remains here to consider how the Mercers reacted to the political and religious events of the Civil War period. The following pages reinforce the impression created by the financial story in Part II, namely a Company and its members reacting to, rather than guiding, events and more concerned to survive the turmoil than profit by it.

INDIVIDUALS

A consideration of the Mercers' allegiances during the turbulent years 1640 to 1660 begins with the distinction between the individual and the corporation. A number of members are known to have made quite definite choices between King and Parliament. For instance, Sir John Cordell, who was Master of the Company in 1631–2, 1642–3 and 1648–9, and City Alderman from 1635 to 1647, was a Royalist who suffered imprisonment certainly once, and possibly twice, for refusing to accede to Parliament's financial demands.[66] Robert Gardiner, Master in 1641–2, was another supporter of the King. He was voted off Common Council in the December 1641 elections which swept the Parliamentarians into power in the City and two months later he was sent to the Tower for promoting a petition attacking the radicals on the City's influential Militia Committee.[67] Sir William Russell, a wealthy merchant who acquired the lucrative Treasurership of the Navy and lent money to Charles I, is also known to have been a Royalist.[68]

On the other side there was Thomas Atkins, who became a City Alderman (1638–61) and Master of the Company (1637–8, 1644–5), after some years as a prominent merchant and civic leader in Norwich. Atkins was certainly a pragmatic man not above making a healthy profit out of the war, but nevertheless was undeniably a Parliamentarian, with a spell in prison to prove it for having refused to supply names for a forced loan to the Crown.[69]

William Spurstow was also a Puritan, in both the religious sense (he was a vestryman of St Stephen's, Coleman Street, which was well known for its radicalism) and the political sense (as MP for Shrewsbury in the Long Parliament).[70] Samuel Moyer was a younger man than Atkins and Spurstow, and his parliamentarianism, which in his case was really republicanism, did not manifest itself until the 1650s (he was MP for London, for example, in the notorious Barebones Parliament of 1653).[71]

It is possible that this roll-call could be extended, though probably not by much. The inability to identify more than a handful of Mercer partisans in the 1640s and 1650s could, of course, be attributable simply to failures of evidence. However, it appears to reflect also a reluctance by most Mercers to commit themselves. It is additionally noteworthy that those few who did so seem to have been divided, with rough equality, between the two sides. On the basis of individual allegiance, at least, the Mercers cannot be said to have been either Royalist or Parliamentarian.

THE COMPANY

What now of corporate allegiance? There is certainly evidence of Puritanism in *religious* terms. The difficulties at Huntingdon rehearsed in Chapter III may perhaps be attributed merely to the Company's determination to observe Fishborne's wishes (though the strength of that determination, as evidenced by the long battle to secure its nominees' reinstatement, may betoken something more). There can be no denying, however, the significance of the Company's actions at Berwick. The appointment of Jemmat to the lectureship, after Laud's refusal to admit him to St Michael Paternoster Royal, was almost brazenly defiant, and if the Company later agreed to remove Jemmat on Laud's insistence, the replacement Sydeserffe did not long survive the Archbishop's eclipse before the Company bowed to local pressure and ejected him.[E] Indeed, the very enthusiasm with which the Company approached the inception and administration of Fishborne's Puritan bequest appears to afford a guide to the Company's religious attitude.[72]

Whether this Puritanism spread into the political arena as well is rather doubtful. A study of the Haberdashers' Company's 'active Puritanism' in these years remarks that 'the Assistants were not pleased when the constitutional religious Puritanism of the pre-1640 period developed into the revolutionary political puritanism of the 1640 decade' and adds that 'there is every indication that the Liverymen's interest in promoting Puritan preaching did not carry over to voluntary support of a rebellious Parliament'.[73] Such a clear-cut pattern is not discernible for the Mercers' Company, but the distinction between religious and political Puritanism is clear enough.

It is significant that the Company's political allegiances are much more difficult to categorise

[E] See above, p. 54.

than its religious attitudes. Such evidence as there is points in no particular direction. In 1628 Alexander Gill junior was dismissed as Under-Usher at St Paul's School for slandering the late Duke of Buckingham, Charles I's assassinated favourite, and also the King himself. Gill was pardoned in 1630 and even taken back as High Master (in succession to his father) in 1635, but was then dismissed in 1640 for the brutal treatment of two boys and general insubordination, despite interventions by the King and Laud.[F] [74] In 1629–31 the Collyer's School Headmastership was the subject of a King-and-Parliament quarrel, but the Company does not appear to have taken sides.[75] In 1640 the Company elected as Gill's successor at St Paul's School a Puritan, John Langley, whom Laud characterised as 'sectiously set against the government of the Church of England'; but the motivation may well have been not political but domestic: one of Langley's sponsors was the aged Lord Cranfield.[76] Two years later the former High Master Gill was summoned by the Company to explain his part in the publication of a pamphlet attacking one of the City's Aldermen,[77] but whether the displeasure was primarily caused by the pamphlet's political message or by the fact that the Alderman in question was a Mercer is not clear. In 1643 the Company favoured the nominee of its influential member Thomas Chamberlain for the Gresham Chair of Physic rather than the candidate recommended by the leader of the City radicals, Sir Isaac Pennington.[78] In the next year the Mercers agreed to remove the Royalist Headmaster of Collyer's School, though this did not prevent them subsequently from paying him for some part-time teaching in 1647.[79] In 1650 the Presbyterian Joshua Cross was ejected from his Gresham Professorship of Civil Law (on a casting vote) for absenteeism and a general failure to perform his duties, but he was replaced by a man, John Bond, not noticeably different in his political views.[80] Two years later Thomas Winston, who had left the country in 1642, ostensibly for health reasons but probably in reality for political ones (he certainly had a thriving practice among Royalist exiles on the Continent), was reinstated in the Gresham chair of Physic in 1652, but his patron, confusingly enough, was Speaker Lenthall.[81]

This catalogue should be sufficient to indicate the eclecticism of the Company's politics in these years. No pattern is discernible. Patronage was bestowed in much the same way as it had always been: due deference was paid to the claims of the country's rulers (whether King or Parliament), but the candidates' personal merits and the wishes of the benefactor were always considered as well. The irresistible impression is that the Company was bewildered by the political turmoil rather than attempting to turn it to its own purpose. In 1643 the Acts of Court referred to the Civil War as 'the distraction of the times'.[82] It was an eloquent phrase which accurately reflected, in suitably neutral terms, the Company's attitude.[G]

[F] Laud's support for Gill was evidently based less on personal attachment than on his distaste for the Mercers' exclusive control of the School. In a campaign which is strikingly similar to (and was conceivably inspired by) his assault on the Company's right to remove Fishborne's appointees, Laud in both 1637 and 1639 encouraged the Dean and Chapter of St Paul's to investigate the Company's powers, and the Company was sufficiently perturbed to consider in 1640 whether to 'prefer a bill in Parliament for the establishing of the sole government of St Paul's School upon them . . .'. As an example of his alleged predilection for canon law, Laud's role in the Gill affair was made one of the charges against him at his trial and his defence throws some incidental light on the episode. AC, 1637–41, ff. 136–v, 189. See also M. F. J. McDonell, *The History of St Paul's School* (1909), pp. 187–8, 190–3, and *The Annals of St Paul's School* (1959).

THE RESTORATION

The Restoration was not inevitable. It was a haphazard affair, very much in the hands of George Monck as the commander of the only disciplined army in the country. The Mercers' records certainly endorse this view. In March 1660 the Company held a lavish 'entertainment'

[G] For similar evidence, in relation to the Drapers' and Salters' Companies, see A. H. Johnson, *The History of the Worshipful Company of Drapers of London* (1914–22), III, pp. 118–19, and J. S. Watson, *A History of the Salters' Company* (1963), pp. 78–9.

FIG. 28. Interior of the Royal Exchange by Wenceslas Hollar, 1644. To the left of the foreground, we can see a Dutch merchant with fur hat and padded breeches, and a woman selling news-sheets or ballads nearby, while two Turks can just be distinguished in the centre of the front rank of the throng. To the right, on the façade of the upper storey, we can see two statues, the nearer one intended for Charles I; when the plate was re-issued in 1668 another figure was added for Charles II, and the Latin dedication to the Lord Mayor, John Wollaston, was replaced by the Royal Arms.
By courtesy of Guardian Royal Exchange Collection

for Monck and his officers in celebration of the restoration of the City's Common Council (which had been dissolved by order of the Rump Parliament). £397 was devoted to an enormous feast, with the only concession to the Company's 'straightness of ... room' (as its financial deficits were termed) being a request that Monck's life-guards satisfy themselves with £5 for drink.[83] Little more than two months later the Company was faced with a precept from the Lord Mayor for £780 for Charles II, to which it responded 'readily and cheerfully' as its 'free-will offering'.[84] On 29 May the Mercers contributed men and decorations for the King's entry into London.[85] In the following month the Company lent £195 to meet the cost of the City's own feast for the King on 5 July.[86] Again, the Company was asked to play its part on the day with attendants, escorts, Liverymen lining the King's route to Guildhall and so forth. For the King's Coronation in April

1661 the pattern was repeated a third time: contributions in money (£390 paid to the City) and in kind (a facelift for the Hall and the Royal Exchange).[87] For a Company labouring under serious financial difficulties these were heavy demands and, though the sums were said to have been offered 'readily and cheerfully', there must also have been at least a little anxiety. The burden of debt left by the Interregnum was given additional weight by the Restoration.

There is a cameo which highlights the transition from Republicanism to Monarchy. During the Interregnum the *Royal* Exchange was called the *Great* Exchange, and in 1650 there was daubed on it the slogan: 'Exit Tyrannus Regum Ultimus'. In March 1660, when the Long Parliament was dissolved and the return of the dead King's son imminent, the message was obliterated and plans set in hand to replace the nearby statue of Charles I which had been destroyed by order of the Council of State.[88] *Multum in parvo.*

CHAPTER V

THE GREAT FIRE AND ITS AFTERMATH

In the short space of four days at the beginning of September 1666, much of the City of London was destroyed by the Great Fire. Contemporaries observed the spectacular devastation with a mixture of fear and wonderment, and succeeding generations have been scarcely less impressed. Pepys' own chronicle of the progress and effects of that 'most horrid, malicious, bloody flame' has inspired and indeed formed the basis of a small library of historical reconstructions, ranging from the superficial to the painstaking. There are, of course, numerous aspects of the Great Fire worthy of investigation, but perhaps the most important of all has been largely neglected. With the notable exception of T. F. Reddaway, who gave a magisterial account of the rebuilding of the City,[1] historians have tended to overlook, or perhaps more accurately shy away from, the long-term impact of the wholesale destruction. Even after Reddaway's work, there are still many questions concerning the property market after 1666 which remain unanswered. The pace of the rebuilding after the Fire may have been remarkable, but what about the price which had to be paid for encouraging such enterprise? At a time when fire insurance was virtually unknown, landlords could only rebuild their property either by finding the money themselves or, more usually, by inducing tenants to do so with the grant of long leases at low rents and often without fines. Either method necessarily placed heavy and continuing burdens on a landlord's resources. The effects were felt, not merely during the term of the initial post-Fire leases, but in many cases for a long while thereafter, for the simple reason that the concurrent expiration of so many 60- to 90-year building leases in the early and mid-eighteenth century (when there was also a good deal of competition from the burgeoning estate developments in the West End) led to a severe depression in property values. It was probably not until the early nineteenth century that the City property market finally threw off the malaise which the Great Fire created.[A] [2]

Such is the backcloth to the Livery Companies' experience. As important City property-owners they were bound to be badly affected; indeed, they were likely to be in an even worse position than most. Already reeling from the royal exactions before 1640 and the political turbulence thereafter, they found the impact of the Great Fire particularly hard to absorb. 1666 set in train a long period of financial difficulty for almost all of them. Their determined struggle to fight free of the shackles thus imposed were later dubbed 'the Second Foundation', and a general study of this process, exploiting the enormous amount of evidence which lies largely unstudied in the Halls and at Guildhall, is badly needed.[3] The findings would constitute an important element in that general account of the London property market which is still awaited. The Mercers offer a good example of the response of one large Company with substantial City property-holdings, which even before the Great Fire was finding it difficult to balance the books. It was unusual only in the sense that in its attempt to escape from its post-1666 predicament it made a gross error of judgement which nearly had disastrous consequences.

[A] Outside the City, of course, there were profits to be made, and in 1670 the Earl of Castlemaine claimed that the Mercers were trying unfairly to exploit the situation by imposing exorbitant terms for the renewal of his Charing Cross lease. By influence and eloquence he beat the Company down to a £1,200, not £1,800 fine: AC, 1669–75, f. 15v and T. F. Reddaway, *The Rebuilding of London after the Great Fire* (1951 edn, p. 30, n. 2). Such opportunities, however, were few and far between.

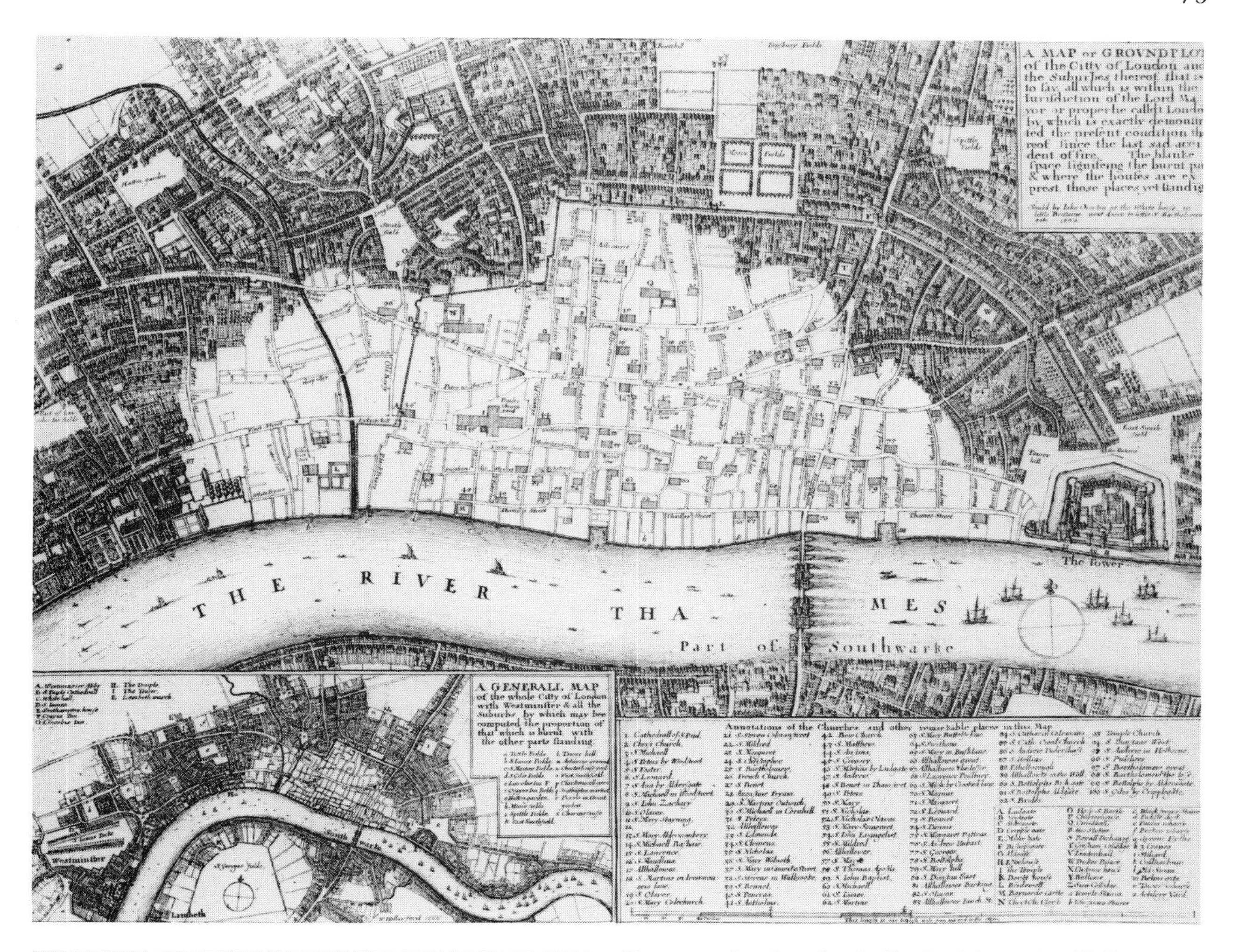

FIG. 29. *London after the Fire* by Wenceslas Hollar, 1666. The burnt area is shown white; the sites of St Paul's, the churches and other important destroyed buildings are indicated.
By courtesy of Guildhall Library, Corporation of London

FIG. 30. The seal matrix of the Company, made by Matthew Johnson in 1666–7, to replace the medieval matrix destroyed in the Great Fire (see Fig. 4). This seal is still in use.
Mercers' Company

There is indeed a direct link between the Great Fire and the bankruptcy which overwhelmed the Company in 1745. However, for a detailed assessment of the impact of the events of September 1666 it is necessary to consider the Mercers' various properties under separate heads.

THE HALL SITE[4]

The Company's own buildings were totally destroyed, though the stone of the Hall and Chapel did actually halt the progress of the Fire for a time.[B] By Wednesday 5 September, there was nothing left but ruins, and Pepys, stepping warily through the embers, found the coloured glass from the Chapel window lying about in heaps 'so melted and wrinkled by the heat that it looked like parchment' and took a piece home as a souvenir.[C] [5] The Company, therefore, was faced with *tabula rasa* and, after the initial shock at 'the late, lamentable fire' had subsided,[6] it commissioned Edward Jerman to

> survey the ground where the Hall and Chapel stood, with the Company's contiguous ground which fronts Cheapside, Old Jewry and Ironmonger Lane and to plot out such of the same as may serve to build a Hall, Chapel and Schoolhouse with the appurtenances for the Company's own use and what is fit to be let out to building.[7]

By July 1667 the 'draft or scheme' was ready and approved as a 'model' for the development of the site.[8] So much was easily accomplished. More difficult were the tasks of persuading tenants to rebuild in the approved manner on acceptable terms, winning the acquiescence of neighbouring landowners (particularly the powerful and difficult Sir John Frederick) and, above all, finding the necessary money.

It was obviously essential to begin with the shop tenancies, because the site had to be made to produce some income again as soon as possible. Negotiations were started in March 1667 and continued for the following three years.[9] In return for covenants to rebuild their properties not only substantially but also in accordance with Jerman's plan, existing tenants were granted longer leases (often up to 61 years) at the former rent until the expiration of the old lease, and at a higher rent thereafter. New tenants were to be granted long leases with the higher rent payable from the outset. In neither case was an entry or renewal fine paid.

The result was that, although the rent from the Hall site properties actually increased from £87 per annum before the Fire to £200 shortly afterwards (with a further £50 on its way when old leases expired and the higher rents came into force), no further additions in rent and, still more disturbingly, no capital sums could be expected until well into the eighteenth century.[10] The income from fines had always fluctuated wildly, but the receipt of £7,501 in the years 1657–8 (admittedly for all the City property, including the Whittington estate) gives an idea of the extent of the Company's sacrifice.[11] It was not that the Mercers had been unduly generous. Their leases were much the same as those granted by other corporations in the Square Mile as well as those embodied in the decrees of the Fire Court which adjudicated rebuilding disputes.[12] It was simply that the price to pay for rebuilding leasehold property quickly was a heavy one.

As far as the Company's own buildings were concerned, the progress of rebuilding was much slower, as witness the following chronology:

Clerk's house	1668–9
Cheapside archway	1669–71
Kitchen	1670
Schoolhouse	1671
Chapel	1672–4, 1679–82
Hall	1674–6

[B] It proved possible to rescue the Company's records and plate, but not the seal, which had to be replaced: AC, 1663–9, f. 76v.

[C] Compare a member's uncannily similar experience almost 300 years later when the post-Fire Hall was destroyed: 'It was just getting light. There was glass everywhere. Burnt paper fell like black snow on to my [motorcycle] goggles. As I bumped over the coils of firemen's hoses, I could see that an enormous amount of damage had been done. Mercers' Hall, or rather its site, for very little seemed to be standing, was still smouldering when I got there'. Imray, *Mercers' Hall*, p. 405.

A comparison of Figure 5 with Figure 35 gives an impression of the post-Fire changes. There was now a uniform frontage of shops along Cheapside, broken only by an elaborate porchway leading into an ambulatory, surmounted on the west and east sides by the Hall and Parlours. The Chapel and School now occupied the north-east corner of the site. The Hospital Church of St Thomas, the Mitre Tavern and St Mary Colechurch all disappeared.

The cost was £13,716[13] and the lapse of eight years between the construction of the Clerk's house and the completion of the Hall indicates how difficult it was to raise the money. The Company had recognised the problem as early as October 1666 when it resolved to sell all but a few favoured pieces of plate to reduce its borrowings;[14] and, when the expense of rebuilding the Hall site became fully apparent, the Company knew it could not cope out of its own resources and turned to its members for help. The results were not, however, all that might have been desired. Despite repeated and at times rather desperate pressure upon members,[D] a protracted subscription raised only £1,900; gifts of other kinds totalled somewhat more than £1,100; and calls on the Livery around £500.[15] This still left almost £10,000 to be found and there was no alternative but to borrow. It is clear that a large number of short-term loans at 5% to 6% were secured by bonds under the Company's seal in 1667–8 and 1668–9, and it may safely be assumed that this pattern was repeated in the following years.[16] The Company was obviously saddling itself with onerous commitments for the future, without the prospect of increased revenue to throw off that burden. In 1675 the Mercers spoke of themselves being 'involved in much debt since the great loss sustained by the late general Fire' and also of 'the vast charge which they have been at in their several buildings'.[17] They spoke no more than the truth.

[D] In 1675 the Master and Wardens were asked to 'employ further pains to stir up' those who were 'backward in contributions', while three years later it was resolved to make a public list of those who had contributed *and* those who had not. AC, 1669–75, f. 159; 1675–81, f. 61v.

THE WHITTINGTON ESTATE[18]

The entire Whittington estate was situated in the City and most of it, including the almshouse itself, was destroyed in the Fire. Some indication of the extent of the damage is afforded by the fact that rents in 1666–7 were only one-sixth of the pre-Fire yield of about £400.

The process of rebuilding was much the same as at the Hall site, though on a smaller scale. The first task was to restore rental income, and rebuilding on new or extended leases was soon under way. A little later, in 1670, the almshouse itself was rebuilt, at a cost of £600. The sum was not daunting and the estate was well able to sustain the expense, at least by borrowing, out of a rental income which by 1676 had been restored to its pre-Fire level.

There was, of course, a price to be paid. In the absence of fines and any material increase in rents for 60 years or so (rents of £461 in 1682–3 were only £6 higher in 1713–14), the estate did not yield the surpluses (whether for the benefit of the almshouse or the Company) which it would have been expected to provide in the normal course. However, this was not a heavy price and the charity emerged virtually unscathed from the drama of 1666. The real impact of the Fire came later, in an indirect fashion, when the Company's disastrous attempt to escape from its post-Fire difficulties threatened to engulf the Whittington estate as well. That, however, is a story which will be told in Chapter VII.

ST PAUL'S SCHOOL

The flames which consumed old St Paul's Cathedral also devoured Colet's adjacent School. In October 1666 the Company was obliged to make the following order:[19]

that for this juncture of time (wherein the School and schoolmasters' houses are down and the children for the most part dispersed) the said School shall cease, and the Masters shall have the liberty of betaking

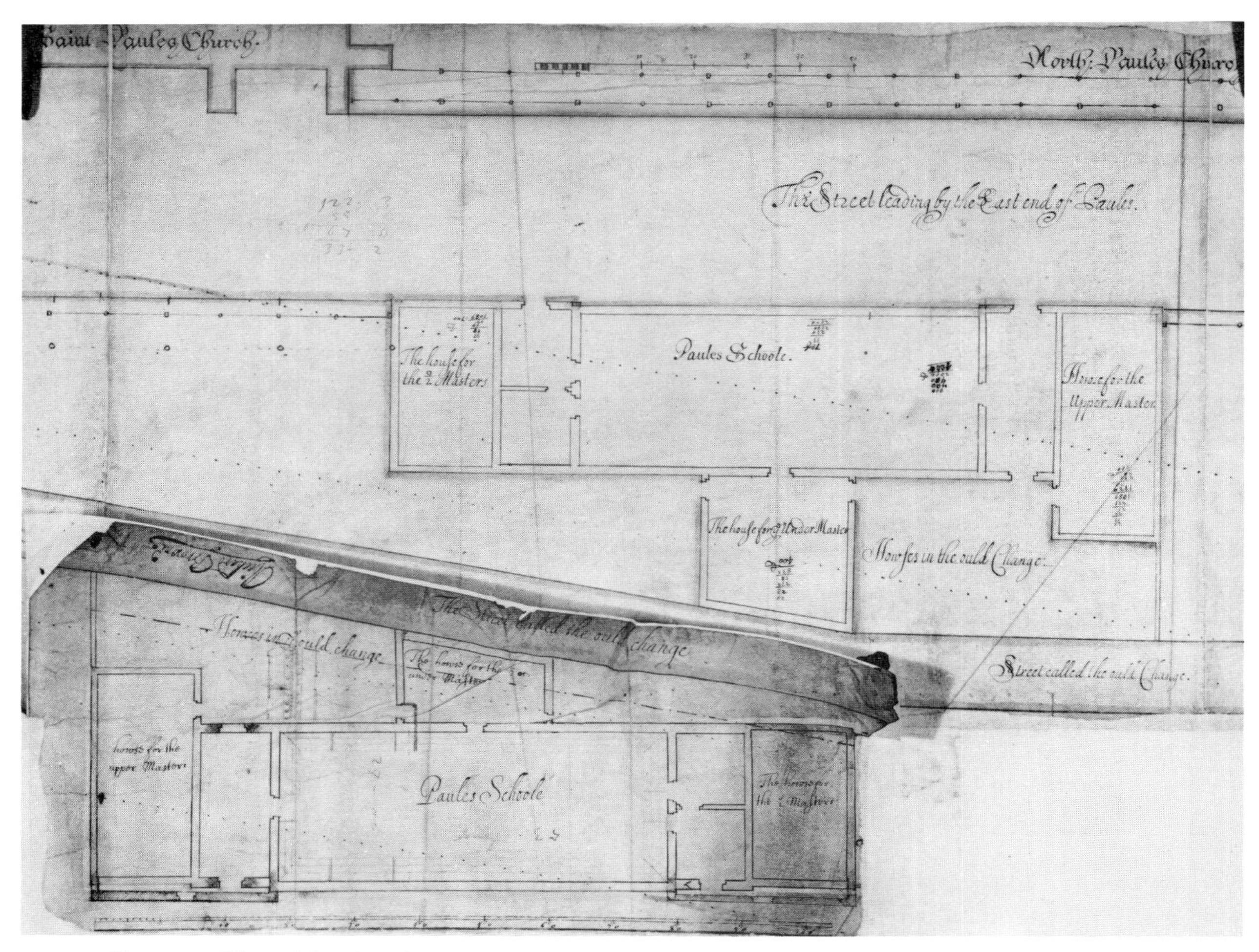

FIG. 31. Plan of the site of the second St Paul's School, as it was laid out after the Great Fire of 1666. It shows the site in relation to the east end of the pre-Fire St Paul's Cathedral. The four round dots to the left of the site mark the stakes erected by the City authorities in an unsuccessful attempt to widen the road.
Mercers' Company: photograph by courtesy of the Warburg Institute

themselves to what they shall judge most fit for their own advantage. And upon condition they promise to return to the service of the School when the Company shall call them thereunto it was further ordered that during the time of the School's cessation they shall quarterly receive the salary appointed them by the Founder together with their licences.

The 'cessation' lasted four-and-a-half years, and although this was not inordinately slow progress it was certainly a much longer interruption than the Company envisaged. Surprisingly enough, the explanation for the delay is not connected with money. A substantial part of the St Paul's School estate was situated outside London, and even some of its City property escaped the Fire. The Surveyor's 'charge' gives no indication of a slump in rents in 1666.[20] Even the expenditure of £6,190[21] on rebuilding the School does not seem to have caused major difficulties. There are references, it is true, in the Acts to the 'sale' of surplus rental income to assist in the rebuilding and to the School estate being 'much in debt to the

FIG. 32. St Paul's School as rebuilt after the Great Fire, engraved by Wenceslas Hollar, 1670.
By courtesy of Guildhall Library, Corporation of London

Company',[22] and there are certainly deficits in the Surveyor's accounts for 1669/70 to 1673/4 which are no doubt attributable to the same cause. However, after that date, with income rising and expenditure virtually static, surpluses recurred and soon reached unheard-of levels.[23]

The real explanation lies with the difficulty which attended the establishment of the site of the new School. On the one hand, there were plans to widen the street between the Cathedral and the School, entailing the loss of almost half the latter's ground, and on the other, there was the Company's own desire to take the opportunity afforded by the Fire to enlarge the School.[24] At one stage it looked as if the street-widening would prevail and there was talk of moving the School. In May 1667 Pepys had a conversation with Sir Richard Ford (a Mercer) and Sir John Frederick:[25]

> [they] did talk of Paul's School which they tell me must be taken away; and then I fear it will be long before another place, as they say is promised, is found; but they do say the honour of their Company is concerned in the doing of it and that it is a thing they are obliged to do.

This proved unnecessary for, after much agitation (including applications to Surveyor-General Denham and the Privy Council itself), the official scheme was dropped and the Company's own plan (devised by Jerman) adopted instead. The building itself was very similar to its predecessor ('built up again much after the same manner and proportion as it was before' is the verdict of the old Pauline and famous antiquary, John Strype),[26] but the site was larger. The School was ready for use again in March 1671, and High Master Cromleholme returned from his spell of private enterprise at Wandsworth (where doubtless he had been joined by at least some of his displaced staff and pupils) for the formal re-opening after Easter. Cromleholme did not, however, enjoy his new surroundings for long, for he died in July 1672 — a death attributed by some to the destruction of his precious library in the Fire.

THE ROYAL EXCHANGE[27]

The destruction of Gresham's Exchange was vividly described by an anonymous observer:[28]

> When the fire was entered, how quickly did it run round the galleries, filling them with flames, then descending the stairs, compasseth the walls, giving forth flaming volleys and filling the Court with sheets of fire! By and by, the Kings [in the niches overlooking the quadrangle] all fell down upon their faces, and the greater part of the stone building after them (the Founder's statue alone remaining) with such a noise as was dreadful and astonishing.

Fortunately, the Fire did not also consume Gresham's former house in Bishopsgate, and it was decided to give the shopkeepers and traders at the Exchange temporary accommodation there, the professors being informed that[29]

> since the Exchange was down the City and the Company had no other means of raising money to support the Founder's uses than by letting of this house [i.e. the College] (which the present extreme necessities of the City doth also require from them).

The Company and its joint trustee were both acutely conscious of the need to rebuild the Exchange as quickly as possible. In January 1667, for example, the Gresham Committee acknowledged 'how necessary it is, as well for the general encouragement of all citizens, as also for the profit it will bring to the City and Company, and their tenants, to hasten with all speed the rebuilding of the Royal Exchange'.[30] Yet it was September 1669 before the merchants were able to return to the floor of the Exchange and March 1671 before the shopkeepers followed suit. Why the slow progress?

There were various reasons. Some were technical and to a large extent unavoidable. It proved difficult to secure the services of the Surveyor Jerman, who then died before the work was completed;[31] a few problems were encountered in obtaining and transporting the necessary stone;[32] and there were lengthy, often exasperating, negotiations with the owners and tenants of land required for the enlargement of the Exchange. However, the main reason, as the 'chief workmen' pointed out when asked in November 1668 'why they have of late proceeded so slowly in the work of the Royal Exchange', was quite simply 'the uncertainty what should be done'.[33]

The Exchange was no ordinary building and the Gresham Committee could not easily decide how it was to be rebuilt. Was it to be a grander building than its predecessor and, if so, would it be financially viable? They were not able to resolve such questions on their own because the King himself took an interest in the project. Charles was firmly of the opinion that the Exchange should be 'set free' from the surrounding buildings 'in regard it is of so public and eminent a concern for the honour of the City'.[34] Such a 'suggestion', of course, carried enormous weight, but could the committee justify the expense? It would cost thousands of pounds to buy out the persons affected.[E] The King was also known to favour an elaborate design involving porticoes on all sides of the Exchange.[35] Again this would mean considerable expenditure. Would the money be recouped? The only revenue, of course, was the rents from the Exchange shops, and it was extremely difficult to calculate what a new and enlarged building would be able to charge its tenants. The existing tenants, needless to say, claimed that additional shops would be ruinous, not merely for themselves but also for the Exchange.[36] The committee, however, took the optimistic view: trade would expand with the additional facilities and everyone would benefit.

None the less, when they decided to proceed with the whole scheme, it was clear that royal pleasure as well as economic logic was an important consideration. In September 1668 'the Committee seemed to incline to the building of a double pawn of shops [outside as well as inside the building] because it will be more magnificent and pleasing to his Majesty, and because it will better answer the charge of building';[37] and in October,

[E] The King, with an evenhandedness which may have caused Committee members at least some exasperation, had also expressed his desire that 'no private person may be wronged in his inheritance without having just satisfaction given him for the same'. GR, 1626–9, p. 303.

when ratifying the recommendation, the General Court spoke of the committee being 'induced thereunto as well by his Majesty's declared will and pleasure as well as it [i.e. the plan] bears the most apparent show of profit to the City and Company'.[38] The future was to reveal how heavy a price the Company had to pay not only for its financial miscalculation but also for its deference to royal wishes.

Once the 'uncertainty what should be done' had been removed, the work proceeded apace, though there was still time for another assessment of the cost-effectiveness of the 'outward' shops and for the omission of the porticoes on the east and west sides (with the King's permission, of course, duly obtained through the good offices of Surveyor-General Wren).[39] In September 1669 the Lord Mayor performed a modest ceremony and the Exchange began its business again.[40] The shops were not so easily re-opened, and there were more complaints from the old tenants and some haggling with the new before that part of the exercise was completed at the end of March 1671.

The finished building (Fig. 34) was indeed impressive. The sub-committee's assertion that the Exchange had been restored 'plusquam antiquum splendorem' was something of an understatement.[41] Gresham's monument had been completely revamped: a free-standing, double-sided structure in the classical style replaced its unpretentious Dutch-inspired predecessor.

The total cost was the enormous sum of some £66,000. £7,000 was spent on acquiring the additional land and the remainder on the building itself.[42] This was a far cry from the £4,000–£5,000 estimated in November 1666 as the likely cost of rebuilding the Exchange in its former style (no matter how unrealistic that early figure may have been) and it indicates the cost of making the building 'more magnificent'.[43] It was also very considerably more than the £47,600 contemplated in 1669 for the fully porticoed design.[44] The committee's complaint in February 1669 concerning 'the greatness of the charge given in by the workmen since Mr Jerman's death, far exceeding the estimate made by him' was obviously fully

Fig. 33. Sir Christopher Wren, by Johann Baptist Closterman. Wren served as Professor of Astronomy at Gresham College from 1657 to 1660. After the Fire, he was one of the Commissioners for Rebuilding the City of London, with particular responsibility for St Paul's Cathedral and the City churches.
By courtesy of the Royal Society

FIG. 34. The Royal Exchange, drawn by J. Donowell and engraved by A. Walker, *c.* 1680. The floor plan indicates the particular position of each nationality or trading group.
Mercers' Company

justified.[45] The costs quite clearly got out of control. Hence the Mercers' bill for a formidable £29,000. Hence also some pardonable exaggeration by City representatives and Mercers alike.[F]

In the first instance the Company raised the money ('the only engine that can give vigorous motion to that great and needful work', as the sub-committee pompously described it)[46] by borrowing on the Company seal. Most of the loans were made at 6%, and accordingly the Company needed something over £1,700 for the interest charges.[47] Unfortunately earlier estimates that shop rents would produce £5,200 per annum (and hence £2,600 to the Company)[48] proved far too optimistic and £3,000 was the more usual figure.[49] This was insufficient even to service the loans, let alone discharge them (save by fresh ones). Nor was there any prospect of improvement. Indeed, all the signs were that the Exchange shops would

[F] London's eighteenth-century historian declared of the Royal Exchange that 'this most magnificent of structures cost the City and the Company of Mercers between them £80,000, as I have been told by a judicious citizen who knew, and a Mercer': J. Stow, *A Survey of the Cities of London and Westminster and the Borough of Southwark*, ed. J. Strype, (1754), I, p. 462.

A. The Maiden's head. The Company's arms adorn the title-page of the Book of Wardens' Arms which the Company ordered to be made in 1634.
Mercers' Company

B. The Book of Wardens' Arms, folio 11, showing the arms of Ralfe Stinte, Thomas Sarocolle, Francis Flyer and Robart Gardener, Wardens for the year 1635.
Mercers' Company

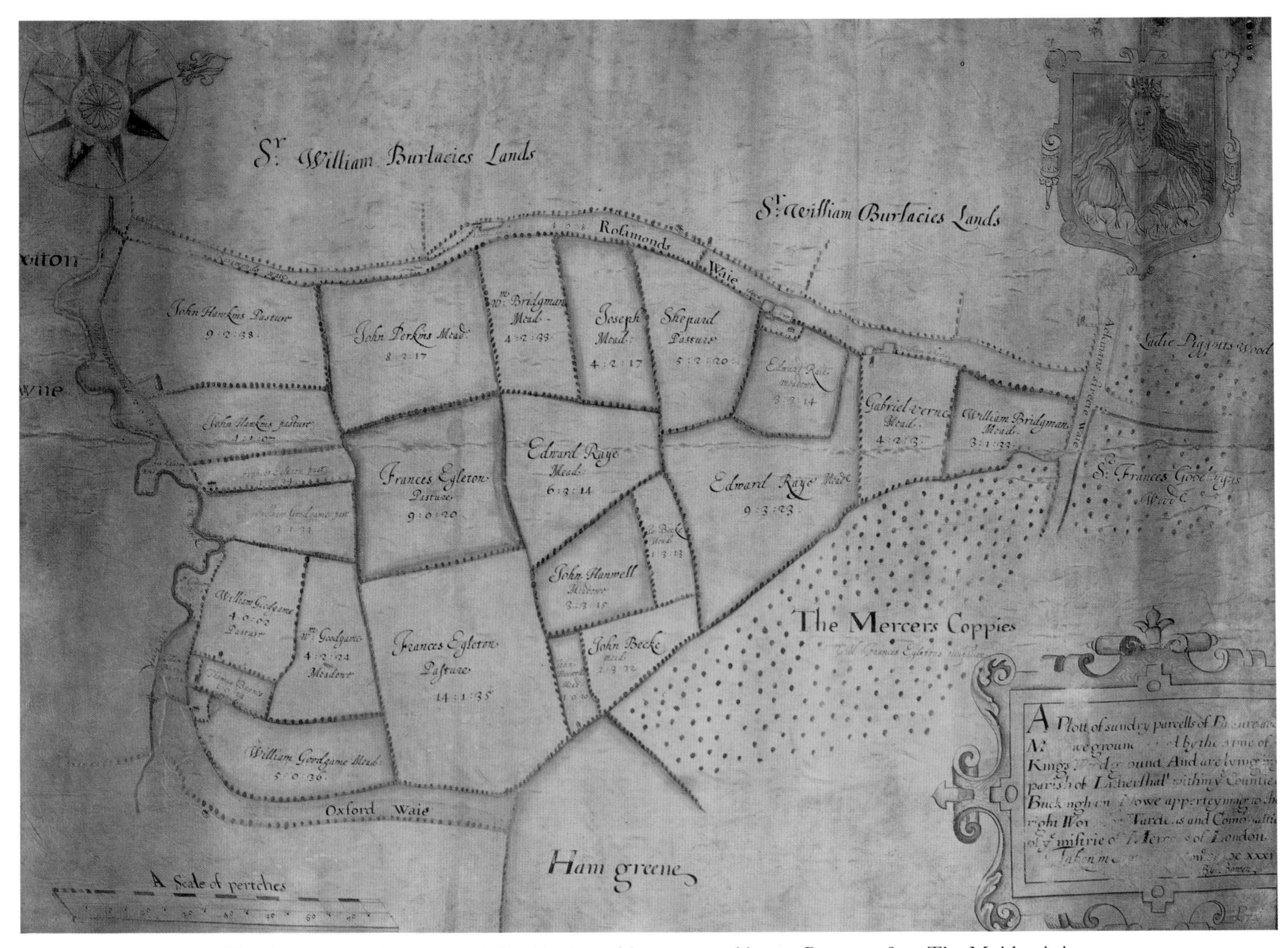

The Colet estate: Ludgershall, Buckinghamshire, surveyed by —. Bowen, 1631. The Maiden is in fashionable seventeenth-century dress — note her slashed sleeves and compare her crown of roses with the powdered wig of the eighteenth-century Maiden in Plate XIVA. The Company no longer owns this property.

Mercers' Company

FIG. 35. The Cheapside frontage of the post-Fire Hall. Engraved by Emery Walker from *A Prospect of London and Westminster* by Robert Morden and Philip Lea, 1677.
Mercers' Company

never be profitable enough to sustain the cost of their lavish construction. The whole of the western 'outward' pawn remained unlet and, despite strenuous efforts to find an appropriate use for it, it was closed off in 1684.[50] There were also problems with some of the other 'outward' shops.[51] It really did appear that the former tenants had been right: there were too many shops. The sub-committee acknowledged that 'it is a known maxim that plenty of any commodity makes it cheap and contemptible'.[52]

By 1681 the Company was anxious enough to look to Parliament for assistance. The celebrated Rebuilding Acts had enabled the City Corporation to apply some of the revenue from additional duties on coal entering the Port of London towards the cost of constructing the Royal Exchange. There seemed no reason why the Mercers, who had borne half the cost, should not enjoy a like benefit in any future such Act renewing the grant, particularly since 'the Company have been great losers by that building'.[53] As a precedent for future applications this was a portentous move,[G] but it had no immediate result. The Company was left to face its problems unaided.

The figures in the Gresham account indicate the extent of the difficulties. There may have been

[G] See below, pp. 99, 103–6.

a surplus from 1669/70 to 1682/3, but this was simply because no attempt was made to reduce the loans incurred in the rebuilding. Indeed the principal debt had increased from the original total of £29,000 to £45,800 by 1682.[54] The deficits which occurred after 1682/3 arose precisely because efforts were made to discharge some of the debt.[55] The account proved unequal to the task and by 1690/1 the borrowings were rising again, notwithstanding continued deficits. Disaster loomed, not merely for the trust, but also (because it had affixed its seal to the bonds guaranteeing repayment of the loans) the Company itself.

CONCLUSION

How could the Company shake off this heavy burden? Reducing expenditure to essentials was one answer, and certainly supplicants for the Mercers' charitable assistance had little success. For a time no petitions at all could be put before the Court, and later only after endorsement by the officers.[56] When they did obtain a hearing there was often no more than sympathy available. The rebuilding of a parsonage, buying corn and coal for the poor, church repairs[57] — all met with a response of the following kind:

> this Company is in no condition at present to bring a further charge upon themselves, because their loss by the late dreadful fire and their charge since upon several public buildings in this City hath not only exhausted their stock but set them much in debt and thereby rendered them incapable not only of remoter acts of charity but of relieving even their own distressed members.[58]

Even existing charitable commitments suffered: many payments were suspended for at least a few years, while others were simply reduced.[59]

However, retrenchment was never likely to be enough. Despite the Court's efforts, the combined Second Wardens' and Renter Wardens' accounts were in deficit for all but one of the ten years from 1675/6 to 1685/6.[60] An investigating committee may well have been right in believing that 'the Company's estate may be sufficient to pay the debts and other incident charges provided they do not run into any extraordinary expenses' (and certainly the accounts returned to surplus in 1686/7),[61] but merely balancing these books was not sufficient. The bond debt had still to be dealt with, and no amount of good husbandry would make much impact on that large, and growing, problem. Radical measures were needed.

It took an inordinately long time for the Company to grasp this truth. In June 1668[62]

> Deputy [Thomas] Dawney [appointed the Surveyor's assistant in the previous year] now declared that the Company's manifold occasions for money to carry on their building of the moiety of the Exchange, the Hall and Chapel, St. Paul's School and the Schoolmasters' houses, and Whittington's almshouses, would call for greater supplies of money than can well be raised either out of their revenue or upon the credit of their seal, and then moving that a committee might be appointed to consider of such ways and means as may probably give assistance whereby the Company may be preserved from running too far into debt. It was resolved that all the Assistants or any seven be authorized as a committee to enquire into and make a calculation of the charges of the building and then to propound and consider of all lawful ways for raising money for the same.

However, it was one thing to 'resolve' and another to act. The committee does not appear to have met. It certainly has left no trace of its proceedings. Six years later another committee was appointed 'to look into the estate of the Company and to consider such expedients as may conduce to their welfare'.[63] Again there is no reference to any subsequent proceedings. Only when the bond-holders began to demand repayment of the loans or receive extra interest did the Company really confront the difficulty. In April 1684 a committee was asked to consider how the Company's creditors could be assured of repayment and, unlike their predecessors, they reported back with specific proposals.[64] The scheme was nothing less than a kind of corporate mortgage, involving the vesting of the Company's estate in a set of trustees charged with the task of repaying the creditors. The lawyers blessed the arrangements and drafted the necessary documents; the committee elegantly certified the scheme as 'the best way to secure the creditors and the honour of the Company'; and all that was required was the approval of the General Court.[65] There the scheme foundered. Various objections were raised, including the reliance which would have to be placed on the integrity of the trustees, particularly in view of the sixty-year term envisaged ('too long a time', it was thought, 'for their estate to lie at hazard subject to the practices of ill men which may arise') and also the difficulty of accommodating new creditors. After 'a mature debate', piecemeal arrangements to satisfy individual creditors gained favour as 'much safer' than the proposed trust. Even then members hesitated and the Master suggested a 'still more safe [*sic*] expedient', namely a members' loan (towards which he immediately offered £1,000). Still the Court dithered and, as the Acts put it, 'on the whole (without resolving anything) the matter was referred for further consideration ...'.[66] There was to be no mortgage (wholesale or otherwise), nor even a members' loan.

The rejection of the trust device was doubtless no disaster. It was a drastic remedy indeed. However, *something* had to be done: the problem would not simply disappear. Creditors continued to press for satisfaction and the standard reply, that 'they could not pay [the principal] at present but they doubted not but that the Company would take care for the paying of it in some short time', became less and less convincing.[67] For the foreseeable future the Company's revenue would not be able to sustain, let alone discharge, the bond debt. The corporate estate was chiefly in the City and was subject to rebuilding leases which would not expire until around 1730.

The only important exception, Elmfield (or Long Acre) in Covent Garden (which the Company quite rightly regarded as 'the best jewel in their estate'), was similarly tied up, though for different reasons: Lords Cranfield and Clarendon had been granted leases which together would last until 1760.[68] It therefore remained essential for the Company to find some method of escaping from its debt. Unfortunately, as Chapter VII will show, when the Company did decide upon a course of action, the cure proved to be worse than the disease.

CHAPTER VI

THE COMPANY ON THE EVE OF THE GLORIOUS REVOLUTION

PART I: QUO WARRANTO

The Company's vulnerability in the late seventeenth century is hard to over-estimate. The previous Chapter showed the Company's dependence on Parliament for the authority to set up financial arrangements to secure its future; and, almost at the same time as the drastic mortgage scheme of 1684 was being considered, the Crown itself threatened to challenge the Company's very existence.

The opposition which King Charles faced in his later Parliaments had focused on the Catholicism of his brother and heir. Charles's policies had been framed to ensure his brother's succession, and in the years after the Oxford Parliament of 1681, and the Rye House Plot to assassinate the King (which enabled Charles to implicate some of the Whig grandees), he was able to mount a counter-offensive against his political and religious opponents. One of the centres of opposition was the municipal corporations. When the Earl of Shaftesbury was acquitted of a charge of treason by a Grand Jury in London in November 1681, the King determined to bring the unruly towns to heel, and at the same time to gain influence over their choice of MPs. Crown lawyers turned their ingenuity to discovering lapses or errors that might render the municipal charters forfeit, in order that more strictly drawn charters could be substituted and Crown nominees installed.

In January 1682, the City Corporation was served with a writ of Quo Warranto, asking by what warrant it held its chartered rights.[1] At first, Charles tried to orchestrate a voluntary surrender of the Charter, but though the Shrieval election in the summer eventually, after a furious and unsavoury struggle, went the Crown's way, the Common Council elections in December did not, and in February 1683 the Quo Warranto case was begun. The Stuart judiciary was not unduly fastidious in cases of this kind (as the Company had discovered to its cost in the Irish case of 1635) and found for the Crown in June. After the City had voted to surrender its Charter, judgment was 'entered' in October 1683 and Charles was free to do as he pleased not merely with the foremost Corporation in the land, but also, because once London had capitulated resistance elsewhere was useless, with every other corporation as well — the Livery Companies included.

The Mercers' attitude towards these disturbing events is hard to determine. Individual members, of course, took sides and are identifiable as Tories or Whigs. Some, indeed, played leading roles in the Guildhall dramas. Dudley North, newly returned from successful trading in Constantinople, was one of the two Court candidates in the Shrieval election battle of 1682 and he was opposed by another Mercer, Thomas Papillon, whose Whiggery eventually obliged him to retire to Holland to evade legal retribution. Michael Godfrey, a fellow exile, who had served with his friend Papillon on the Grand Jury which had 'acquitted' Shaftesbury in 1681, was also a member of the Company.[2] However, in a corporate sense it is hard to discern where the Mercers stood. A contemporary asserted that the Company resolved to forbid its members to accompany North rather than Papillon to Guildhall after the

FIG. 36. Charles II's triumphal entry into the City at his Restoration, 1660.
By courtesy of Guildhall Library, Corporation of London

controversial Shrieval election,[3] but there is no evidence of this in the Acts. North was in fact later given the customary one hundred marks towards 'beautifying' his house during his year in office.[4] It is most likely that the Company simply waited on events, neither wishing nor daring to play any positive part in the dangerous political game which threatened to destroy its corporate integrity.

The Mercers' Quo Warranto writ was served on the Master towards the end of March 1684, and the Assistants naturally called a General Court to consider the matter.[5] It is tempting to

FIG. 37. Thomas Papillon (1623–1702), by Sir Godfrey Kneller.
By courtesy of the National Portrait Gallery, London

ascribe a vote in favour of considering the debt problem first to independence of spirit, but the terms of the response to the writ suggest that the importunity of the creditors was the real reason. The 'humble' petition of Charles's 'humble subjects, the Company of Mercers of London' was embarrassingly obsequious:[6]

whereas your Majesty hath been pleased now of late in your princely wisdom to issue out your writ of Quo Warranto against your petitioners (who are fearful they have given your Majesty some cause of displeasure) and being sensible how great an unhappiness it is to your petitioners to lie under your Majesty's disfavour, in tender sense therefore of the duty they owe to your most sacred Majesty, your petitioners in most humble manner pray that your Majesty would be graciously pleased to signify your royal pleasure to your petitioners and they shall as in duty bound entirely submit themselves to your royal will and pleasure.

FIG. 38. Initial detail from Charles II's Charter of Confirmation to the Company, 1670, restoring its rights and privileges.
Mercers' Company

A few days later Charles told the Company what he told all the other Companies, that he required them to surrender to him their 'governing part' so as to give him power to appoint and remove the Master, Wardens, Assistants, Liverymen and Clerk — all with a view, of course, to controlling votes at City elections (and particularly the parliamentary elections as part of his stratagem to ensure James's unopposed accession to the Crown). By sixty-eight votes to fifty-one it was decided to comply, and the Master, Aldermen and Wardens were asked to settle the legal formalities with the Attorney-General.[7]

It was not in fact till October 1684 that the instrument of surrender came before the Court for approval (when again a vote was needed) and December before the new Charter was sealed.[8] The contents of the latter were interesting not so much for the legal provisions (for these faithfully reflected Charles's stated intention only to control removals and appointments) as for the names of the Masters, Wardens and Assistants. There had been a purge of the Company's Whigs, including Papillon and Godfrey.[9] The approved members' first decisions were to authorise the payment of £192 to discharge the cost of the new Charter and (on the 'humble' motion of the Tory Alderman Sir John Chapman) to arrange with Lord Chief Justice Jeffreys how best to thank the King for his kind offices.[10]

The new Charters were first used in May 1685 to weed out Exclusionists from the Liverymen voting in the elections for James II's first Parliament. The Tory Mercers drew up their Livery list and then submitted it for approval by the Lord Mayor and Aldermen.[11] The political complexion of those Liverymen included and those excluded can be imagined.[12] The first *direct* experience of royal interference arose in March 1686 when James intervened in the choice of a new Clerk.[A] [13]

[A] The royal nominee, Francis Guy, did not in fact serve. The Company objected to the royal stipulation that Guy be required merely to make oath for the due execution of his office. This, the Company argued, afforded inadequate security against default. There is nothing, however, to suggest opposition in principle to the King's intervention and Guy's replacement, Joseph Sainsbury, was presented for, and received, royal approval. AC, 1681–7, ff. 124v–5v, 126v–7.

Then in November four out of sixty-six new Liverymen selected by the Assistants were found to be unacceptable to the Lord Mayor and Aldermen.[14] However, wholesale changes did not occur until October 1687 when James decided on a dramatic 'volte-face', involving a switch from Anglicans to Dissenters, in his attempt to secure Parliament's approval for the repeal of the penal laws against Catholics. Tory Assistants and Liverymen were removed *en bloc*, and many of the Whigs left out when the old Charter was surrendered (including Papillon and Godfrey) were restored.[15] The new complexion of the Company was such that a petition was presented to the King thanking him for his Declaration of Indulgence earlier that year which had suspended the penal laws against non-conformists of all kinds, Dissenters as well as Roman Catholics.[16]

The new stratagem, of course, was no more effective than its predecessor, and James's brief reign lurched towards its denouement. There was still time, however, for some further removals and restorations in February 1688[17] and an ingratiating invitation to Lord Chancellor Jeffreys's brother to preach a Company sermon,[18] before James's panic-stricken restoration of the status quo ante of early 1684 in October 1688.[19] By then, however, it was too late for James to recover his position. William of Orange landed at Torbay on 5 November 1688 and James's 'abdication' became only a matter of time.

After William and Mary's accession in January 1689, there came the inevitable settling of accounts. Sir Dudley North narrowly escaped prosecution for allegedly 'packing' juries during his Shrievalty, while Thomas Papillon returned from Holland to office and profit. More significantly, an Act for 'restoring and confirming of corporations' was passed by Parliament in January 1690 to put into legislative form James's last-minute reversal of his Quo Warranto interventions. This alone would have given the Mercers comfort that they would be spared a repetition of the nightmare of 1684–8; but the Act was no more than an outward sign of an inner resolution on the part of the governing class never to tamper with chartered privileges. It became almost an article of constitutional faith that charters, like property, should be immune from political attack; and not until the constitution itself came under critical scrutiny in the early nineteenth century did corporations like the Mercers find anyone questioning their right to an unfettered existence. The Company thus entered a period of constitutional calm which lasted 150 years. After the storms created by James I, Charles I, the Civil War, the Interregnum, Charles II and James II, this was a relief indeed. Had it not been for the financial crisis, these would have been happy times.

PART II. INTERNAL DEVELOPMENTS, 1595–1688

Before reverting to those financial troubles, the conclusion of at least one phase in the Company's life makes this an appropriate point at which to review the more important internal developments which took place after 1595 and which have not been described in the preceding four Chapters.

TRADE

In 1641 the Mercers were required to make a return of all their members for the purpose of levying a poll tax. The size of the Company revealed by the return was startling:[20]

at least	9	past and present Masters (including those who had fined off)[21]
	10	past and present Wardens likewise[22]
at least	24	senior Liverymen who had not yet served as Wardens[23]
	64	evidently junior Liverymen[24]
perhaps as many as	573	freemen[25]
	680	

Even allowing for the inclusion of two dozen or so 'pensioners', 'prisoners' and so forth among the freemen, these are unexpectedly high figures which are impossible properly to explain. Of course, it may be that the roll-call of 271 in 1562 is defective; but it has to be remembered that a careful revision of that list was made in 1581 and, since the purpose was to make sure that all members met their financial obligations to the Company, it is hard to imagine that serious undercounting would have occurred.[26] Again, the 1641 total may be too large, and certainly the Company would have been tempted to scour its books for any possible tax-payer for fear of official reprisals; but, although the list derives from a year-by-year summary of the admissions register and some of the early names are open to question, it has obviously been scrutinised to some extent.[B] [27] It is, of course, possible that the disparity is attributable to a genuine expansion in numbers. However, it will be recalled that during these same years the Mercers were at least claiming to be in decline. Indeed, in 1610 they declared that there were no more than '80 persons of any ability' in the Company.[28] It is possible that the 'decline' was in personal wealth rather than overall numbers and it is true also that such lamentations were convenient ways of minimising contributions to the Irish plantation and similar imposts; but however much the pleas and complaints are discounted they seem to rule out the possibility of significant expansion (and there is certainly no sign of any marked increase in those admitted to the freedom).[29] In the absence of further information, the exact pattern of the Company's membership between 1562 and 1641 remains something of a mystery.

Nevertheless the 1641 figures do at least provide evidence that the Company, if not expanding, was certainly replenishing its numbers without difficulty. If it really was true in 1610 that the Company was suffering 'great decay', it was true no longer. Indeed, the Company was actually restricting entry into its ranks by insisting that only merchants and retailers bind apprentices, and refusing to enrol apprentices in the manual or handicraft trades.[30] It was quite prepared, in 1636–7, to brave a full-scale public quarrel in defence of its position.[31] Even if the trade was acceptable, there was a stern prohibition against 'colourable' (i.e. sham) or otherwise irregular apprenticeships.[32]

Such exclusivity strongly suggests a backdrop of prosperity, or at least corporate well-being; and certainly the evidence makes the gloomy assertions of the 1610 petition hard to believe. It was, of course, true that the old cloth trade with the Continent had fallen away, but (as already observed) other trades, particularly with the Levant and India, had taken their place and offered great rewards to the enterprising, particularly as the century wore on. William Spurstow, Sir John Cordell, Sir Richard Ford, Sir Thomas Chamberlain, Thomas Papillon, Sir Samuel Mico and Sir Dudley North (in roughly chronological order) were all successful members of the East India Company or the Levant Company, or both.[C] Spurstow, in fact, who started his career in the Welsh wool trade, and graduated to exporting from London the light 'New Draperies' introduced by the Huguenots and other fine fabrics, personifies the transition.[33] The Company was also well represented in the Russia Company.[34]

As to the complaint that the retail of silk and linen cloth was slipping out of the Company's control, that too rings false. Even as the petition was written, two of the Company's members, Sir Baptist Hicks and William Ferrers, were effectively silkman and linen-draper respectively to the King. Hicks indeed was probably the most famous retailer of his time, disdaining to close his

[B] It is also possible that some of the poorest members would have been excluded from the list. The historian of the Drapers' Company for this reason considers that the returns omit a large number of that Company's freemen: Johnson, *Drapers*, III, p. 194.

[C] In a Company context, Chamberlain is perhaps the most interesting of these men. The references to him in the Papillon records suggest that he was a most important figure. Some determined research into his trading activities is undoubtedly merited.

shop in Cheapside merely because of his social success, and content to make a fortune from selling ribbons and silks (as well as supplying loans) to the Court and courtiers.[35]

It is impossible directly to challenge the figures given in 1610, but when two fairly full lists of trades do first appear, in the 1680s, the picture is rather different. The first list is dated November 1686 and, of the fifty-three Liverymen whose trades are given, fifteen were silkmen, eight linen-drapers and two 'mercers' simpliciter. A further list of thirty-six Rich Bachelors, also compiled during the Quo Warranto period (but with a few names which appear in the Livery list), includes ten silkmen, six linen-drapers and six mercers.[36] The specialised textile trade, especially the silk trade, is known to have expanded rapidly in the late seventeenth century to meet the needs of increasingly sophisticated London consumers,[37] but it is tempting also to think that the 1610 figures were too low. Certainly the impression they created of a permanent decline in the Company's retailing connections was quite incorrect. By 1688 the Mercers' link with the trade of mercery was still strong.[D]

COMPANY SERVICE

The basic structure of the Company remained as it had been in Elizabethan times. Members were still confronted by hierarchical ranks and offices to be served strictly by rote and according to 'seniority'. Newly-made Rich Bachelors or Liverymen were placed in order, usually (though not invariably)[38] by reference to their 'antiquity' (i.e. the date they were bound as apprentices, or seven or eight years prior to the date of their freedom in the case of those admitted by patrimony or redemption);[39] and mistakes or injustices were as keenly felt as they had ever been. In 1625 the Company was faced with a bitter quarrel between two 'misplaced' Liverymen who were ready, for a time at any rate, to forfeit their positions on the roll altogether rather than give way.[E] [40] The importance of seniority, of course, was that it determined a Liveryman's service as a Warden and Assistant. In 1634 a Deputy Governor of the Merchant Adventurers who had been serving abroad for many years discovered that he had been overlooked as Warden, and was in fact a good deal senior to the current Renter Warden. He was allowed to fine off from all the Wardenships in order, evidently, to correct the irregularity.[41] Assistants were usually chosen from those Liverymen who had already served as at least a junior Warden, but occasionally more were needed and again it was the seniority of those Liverymen who had not served as Wardens which determined the issue.[42]

Where the seventeenth century differed from the sixteenth was in the extent of 'fining off' from office. Rich Bachelors, of course, had always been reluctant to serve,[F] [43] but now Liverymen, even Wardens, regularly tried to be excused office.[44] Even Masters had occasionally to be persuaded.[45] The Company had to accept this state of affairs and, at a time when it was hard-pressed to balance the books, try to turn it to its own advantage.[G] Members were allowed to pay a fine for their discharge, and though a pretence was made that only those with worthwhile excuses would get permission, some fairly flimsy applications were accepted[46] and genuine hardship became instead a pretext for a reduction or waiver of the fine.[47] Payment of a fine was not merely sufficient to relieve a member of his obligations, it also entitled him to receive the privileges accorded to the seniority thereby gained.[48] In other words, a fine was as good as service. In a way which is hard to particularise, a further step in the transformation from guild to clubbish society had been taken.

[D] For a rare glimpse into the life of an 'ordinary' trading mercer at this time, see the unpublished study of Daniel Thomas by C. G. Lewin (1979).

[E] The Quo Warranto tergiversations, it may be imagined, gave rise to peculiar difficulties, see AC, 1681–7, ff. 99, 115.

[F] See above, pp. 10–11.

[G] Wardenship fines were vigorously pursued, particularly in the aftermath of the Fire. A search of the records for defaulters in 1675 led to claims against three deceased members' executors: AC, 1669–75, ff. 150v, 169.

39

40

FIG. 39. A Beadle's stave, one of two purchased by the Company, 1669–70; the other is now in the Museum of London.
Mercers' Company

FIG. 40. One of two Beadle's staves, purchased in 1679–80. These are carried by the Beadle and Under-Beadle on ceremonial occasions.
Mercers' Company

A similar tendency is discernible in the further signs of oligarchy evident in the seventeenth century. On the one hand, few of the 'generality' troubled to attend General Court meetings (only ten did so in 1613, and City dwellers at least were threatened with fines for non-appearance),[49] while, on the other, when an unusual number of Liverymen did appear at a Court in 1621, trouble arose and it was ordered that only six Liverymen who had not been Wardens could attend in future.[50] The effects may easily be imagined: Court meetings became the preserve of the few (not long after the report of the poor General Court attendance in 1615, there appears an order that Courts be held in the Hall and 'not at any private houses or any other place'[51]) and senior members lost touch with the junior (in 1660 the Assistants told the poll tax commissioners that they did not know where most of the freemen lived).[52] It may not seem significant that in 1645 and 1658 the Company was obliged to take steps to prevent members coming only to dinners and not to the preceding Court meetings;[53] but, in the light of the other evidence set out above, the members' behaviour may well reflect something rather more than natural human weakness. The Company was increasingly seen by its more junior, somewhat reluctant, members as attractive only as a source of occasional conviviality. Court business could happily be left to others and there were few Liverymen who bridled at their seniors' oligarchical rule.[H]

CHARITIES

The verdict on the Company as trustee is much the same as for the earlier period.[I] There are certainly no signs of corruption: the splenetic charges of two former High Masters of St Paul's, John Harrison and Alexander Gill junior, are

[H] At the time of the Star Chamber case in 1635 some Liverymen asked why the Company's Irish affairs were in the hands of the Assistants and not the generality. This could be regarded as an exception which proves the rule. AC, 1631–7 (rough), f. 160.

[I] See above, pp. 15–18.

difficult to take seriously.[54] All that can be uncovered is a failure to maintain a strict distinction between charitable and corporate funds. The way in which the Company drew upon the former to meet the demands of James I and Charles I has already been noted, the repayment of Hicks's £2,700 from sources which included the St Paul's School, Gresham College and Fishborne accounts being the most striking example.[J] The Company certainly attempted to repay these sums, with interest, to the charities concerned, but it is impossible to say whether the debts were all properly discharged. In similar fashion, there is at least one instance of a failure to account from one trust to another: Lady Mico's almshouses (discussed below) were built on land at Stepney belonging to St Paul's School without any attempt at compensation being made.[55] Finally there were some occasions on which disbursements from charities were suspended, although there was invariably good reason for such action. In 1644, for example, the Fishborne payments (except for the Huntingdon lecturer's salary) were withheld for a time because tenants' arrears made revenue insufficient.[56] Nevertheless the moratorium did not last long, in spite of the fact that the Company was continuing to lose what by 1660 had become 'a great sum of money'.[57] Another, even more striking, example is afforded by the Bennett charity. When a kinsman complained in 1667 about a suspension of payment to the poor of Wallingford, the Company disengaged itself from its own onerous post-Fire deliberations and dealt with the matter in the following manner:[58]

> The Court being very sensible of any thing that may touch their reputation as to the faithful dispensing of the charity committed to their charge, commanded their Clerk forthwith to wait upon Sir John Bennett and to acquaint him that the said Sir Thomas Bennett about fifty years ago did entrust the Company with the rectory of Kirton in Lincolnshire which he had let at the utmost value without any fine for £150 a year and placed uses upon it amounting to £149 12*s* per annum whereof the £20 to the said town was part. All which uses they have paid and maintained till Lady Day which was in the year 1664 and particularly that to Wallingford, notwithstanding the considerable losses the Company have sustained by the tenants, the payment of all taxes and charges for light horses and foot arms since the beginning of the late troubles, and repairs of the parsonage house and barns thrown down by the great wind in February 1661 and notwithstanding the premises will not now yield the old rent. But this Court then finding themselves run far out and that account (which is kept apart) considerably indebted to them and having no other way of reimbursing themselves but by suspending the payment of all the uses, excepting his Majesty's fee farm rent of £29 2*s*. per annum. Since which time of Lady Day 1664 their tenant hath scarce paid any rent, complaining that he can make no money of almost three years profits of the rectory which lie by him. Nevertheless the Company have put his bond in suit and do proceed against him. And the Clerk was further ordered to assure Bennett that when they shall have any money in their hands they do then forthwith resolve to make a just and equal dividend, the donor requiring no more from them.

Of course, the Company was scarcely the disinterested custodian present-day readers might have in mind. No more than in Elizabethan times was it above looking after its own members first, and outsiders afterwards.[K] Provision was made in the Mercers' School regulations of 1607 (evidently a revision of a set made in 1592) for a preference to be given to Mercers' children, especially the poor.[59] Likewise, in 1673 and 1685 certain exhibitions in the gift of the Company were earmarked specifically for St Paul's School and Mercers' School.[60]

As far as the progress of existing charities was concerned, no general picture emerges. On the one hand, there is Gresham College which slid from bad to worse in the latter part of the century.[61] Most of the professors neither lived in the College nor indeed lectured there; and their apathy was more than matched by the public's: audiences for those lectures that *were* given were pitifully small. What little prestige the College had came from its association with the Royal Society which was housed in the Royal Exchange until 1711.[62] In 1680 and again in 1686 the Company suspended the professors' salaries, and even

[J] See above, p. 62.

[K] See above, p. 17.

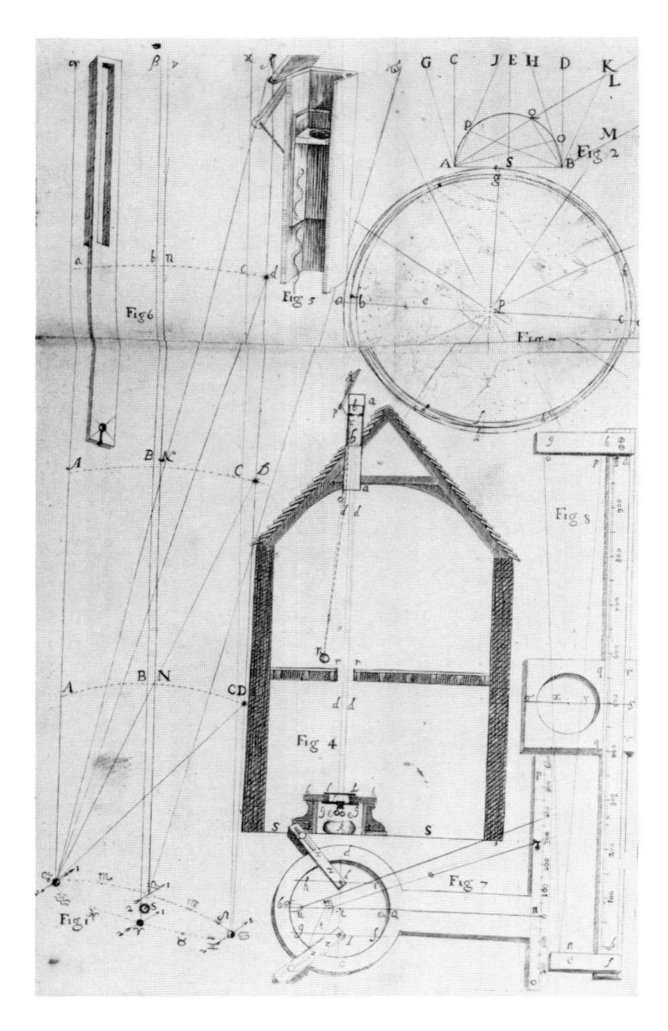

FIG. 41. Robert Hooke's zenith telescope, built into his rooms at Gresham College, from his *Attempt to Prove the Motion of the Earth*, 1674. Hooke was Professor of Geometry at Gresham College, 1665 to 1704.
By courtesy of the Royal Society

tried an advertising campaign to revive interest in the College; but neither the stick nor the carrot seemed to have much effect, and at a time when the expensively rebuilt Royal Exchange was proving a financial disaster, both in terms of long-term debt and current rental income, the Company began to look critically at the College's function. On the other side of the picture, St Paul's School enjoyed a period of considerable success. After the turbulence associated with Gill senior and junior, three successive High Masters, John Langley (1640–57), Samuel Cromleholme (1657–72) and Thomas Gale (1672–97), steered the School through the Civil War, Interregnum and the rebuilding after the Fire with great skill.[63]

New charities continued to arrive at the Company's door. Sir Thomas Bennett's gift of Kirton rectory charged with various small charitable commitments (as well as a payment to the Crown) has already been noticed. In addition (to note only the more important): Lady Campden (Hicks's widow) left £3,100 to be used to establish lectureships at Grantham and Wakefield and £1,000 for Young Men's loans;[L] Sir Samuel Mico

[L] The Company, in fact, did little to implement the trust: tithes were thought too risky an investment during the Interregnum and payments were suspended after 1666. Despite a Chancery decree in 1684, the charity was not fully implemented until the nineteenth century (see below, pp. 128, 148–9).

FIG. 42. Design for a fan-leaf depicting the Maid's Chariot of the Mercers' Company in the Lord Mayor's procession of Sir John Peake, Mercer, 1686.
By courtesy of the Museum of London

gave £500 for Young Men's loans; Jane Savage £2,000 for the relief of debtors in prison; and Lady Margaret Hungerford £1,000 for young apprentices. Some would-be donors were disappointed, for the Company remained nervous about assuming ill-funded or otherwise risky commitments.[M] Judge John Fuller was unable (posthumously) to persuade the Company to take on the administration of his almshouses in Stepney and Shoreditch;[64] while Alderman Perry's marginal note in his will was insufficient to persuade the Mercers to adopt a Young Men's loan scheme originally entrusted to the City of Gloucester Corporation.[65] Even caution, however, was no guarantee against error, as the example of Lady Mico's charity makes plain.

In 1670 Lady Mico, Sir Samuel Mico's widow, left £1,500 for the foundation of almshouses for needy women.[N] The money was regarded as insufficient for the purposes intended, and by agreement (and with the sanction of the Court of Chancery) the money was lodged with the Company with interest accruing for the benefit of the trust.[66] In 1690–1 some £700 was spent on the construction of the almshouses on land in Stepney, owned (as noted earlier) by St Paul's School, and the remainder invested.[67] Unfortunately the interest yield on the remainder of the bequest was barely enough to cover the almswomen's yearly pensions, and the prospect of serious financial losses, as and when the almshouses should require

[M] For a proposed condition to be attached to the Bennett bequest, dealing precisely with the difficulty highlighted in 1667 (see above, p. 91), see AC, 1595–1629, f. 161v; and for reservations about the Hungerford bequest, see AC, 1669–75, f. 124v.

[N] The Company nearly accepted another bequest, namely £1,000 to redeem slaves: AC, 1687–93, ff. 32v, 47v, 55–v.

repair or rebuilding, immediately presented itself. The Company had miscalculated and later had cause to rue its mistake. That, however, lay in the future. For the present, there remained the question of securing the yearly payments. The Court of Chancery had required that the surplus money be invested in land, but the Company, disenchanted for the present with property returns, tried to persuade Lady Mico's sole surviving executor to release it from that obligation with a promise that the pension money would be secured on the Covent Garden estate when the long leases there finally expired in 1760:[68]

> by which proposition [the Company] apprehend they offer a better and more certain maintenance for the said poor than any purchase of land which that money can assure them of. And they desire you to believe also that they should not offer the best jewel in their estate [Covent Garden by this time being fully developed] unless they had an end of their own in the case, viz. that in regard so great an estate is in one lease they resolve to charge it that so they may prevent [*it being a morsel fitted for the mouth of some powerful and greedy courtier and*[O]] other inconveniences that they forsee may happen in future by what hath happened formerly in their memory.

This, of course, provides a fascinating insight into the way in which the Company, or at least its indiscreet Clerk, viewed the long leasehold interests of the Cecils, Cranfield and Clarendon;[69] but it also gives yet another example of the way in which the trust and corporate estates were used to support one another. Sometimes the trust estates suffered from the association, but at others they benefited. The Mercers may not have been scrupulous trustees in the legalistic sense; but they certainly were in the ethical sense.[P] Little wonder that benefactors continued to seek their services so regularly.

GUILDHALL

The disinclination of members to assume the burdens of civic life, described in Chapter I, may not have actually increased in the course of the seventeenth cenury, but it was certainly no less marked than in Gresham's day. The total roll-call of Aldermen between 1595 and 1688 was twenty (not including those who fined-off and/or served for a very short time) and at any one time there were rarely more than three Aldermen in the Company and often fewer, as witness the following sample years:[70]

1620	Sir Thomas Bennett, Thomas Bennett and William Halliday
1640	Rowland Backhouse, Sir John Cordell and Sir Thomas Atkins
1670	Sir Richard Ford
1700	Sir William Gore and Sir William Hedges

Gresham's own example of reluctance to serve as Alderman and Sheriff was followed by three almost equally eminent businessmen in this period. Lionel Cranfield (later the Earl of Middlesex), in the words of his most authoritative biographer, was 'always ready to be a rogue elephant in the City and was never content to be a member of the City establishment . . .'.[71] Sir Baptist Hicks

[O] The words in italics are struck through. Similar feelings emerged a few years later when the annuity scheme (see Chapter VII) was under consideration. Offering the Company's unencumbered estate (including Covent Garden) as security for payment was thought to 'tend much to the benefit and advantage of the Company by fixed [*sic*] and settling their lands to be made the best improvement of [and] not so liable to have the advantage made by private persons' (AC, 1693–1700, f. 146). Of course, there was a degree of special pleading here. The Company was not quite the helpless victim of opportunistic ministers. There was at least acquiescence on the Company's side, and sometimes more. The renewal of Burghley's lease in 1597, for example, appears to have resulted from Baptist Hicks' encouragement: see his undated letter to his brother Michael (Burghley's Secretary) Lansdowne MS 107, no. 106 (in the British Library).

[P] The reluctance of the Company to commit trust monies to the purchase of property not only in the case of Mico but also in the case of Campden, and the coincidence of this reluctance with the Company's financial difficulties, does raise the possibility that the Company wanted to be able to call on such funds if need arose. This cannot be formally refuted. On balance it seems that the Company's own explanations should be accepted. It had, after all, suffered badly from the under-funded Gresham bequest (indeed it was a root cause of its financial impasse) and in the aftermath of the Fire it was difficult to pretend that property was a sound investment.

(later Lord Campden) emulated Gresham to the extent of invoking royal assistance in order to evade City offices. He made it quite plain that he valued his shop more highly than an Alderman's regalia.[72] Thomas Papillon had similar views: Judge Jeffreys conceded that 'I know Mr. Papillon's humour so well that I am confident he would much rather have been contented to sit in his counting house than in Guildhall in a scarlet gown'.[73] Having fined-off as Sheriff in 1673, Papillon was only pressed into service as the Whig nominee for that office in 1682 because he was persuaded that it was essential to make a stand against the King's attack on chartered rights; and when he returned from exile in 1689 he refused all entreaties to become an Alderman, though admittedly his reasons were many and varied.[74] Of the twenty Mercers who did serve as Aldermen, seven became Lord Mayor:

Sir Thomas Bennett (1603–4)
Sir Henry Rowe (1607–8)
Sir Thomas Atkins (1644–5)
Sir John Dethick (1655–6)
Sir Richard Ford (1670–1)
Sir John Peake (1686–7)
Sir John Chapman (1688–9)

This, of course, meant seven occasions on which the Company could have enjoyed the prestige, and suffered the expense, of arranging the Lord Mayor's Show. However, no show was held in 1603 by reason of the plague, Rowe's was evidently a modest affair, the Civil War put paid to Atkins', while Ford's and Chapman's both suffered from a combination of the Company's lack of money and the inappropriateness of celebrations at times of crisis. 1670 was held to be 'no fitting season for a pompous show, neither as it relates to the disunion of the times [presumably the aftermath of the Fire rather than affairs of state] or the condition of the Company . . .';[75] while in 1688 the Company referred to 'the present condition of the nation, now lying under the apprehension of a sudden and powerful invasion' and 'the present state of the Company's affairs, who [*sic*] are labouring under the weight of a great debt contracted by the rebuilding of the Exchange'.[76] However, in 1655 (despite the 'disunion' of *those* times) and again in 1686 (despite the Company's debt, which was obviously deemed by the Company's approved Tory membership less important than the need to 'show our respect to the Government'[77]) elaborate spectacles were organised, involving in particular the Maiden or Virgin on a triumphal chariot.[78] Accounts survive of both[79] and even (in the case of the latter) a pictorial representation (Fig. 42).[80] Individual Mercers may have decided to distance themselves as much as possible from Guildhall, but the Company itself still clearly felt that it had an important role to play in civic life.

CHAPTER VII

THE ANNUITY SCHEME

Once the political storms created by Quo Warranto and the Glorious Revolution had subsided, the Company was again obliged to grapple with its financial crisis. Frequent shuffling of the bond debts by repayment and creation, repayment and creation, kept the Company afloat, but only just;[1] and a long-term solution seemed as remote as ever. Then in 1698 there appeared a possible saviour, not, strange to say, a Papillon, Godfrey or other City magnate, but a clergyman from Beckenham in Kent.

DR ASSHETON

Dr William Assheton was possessed of a fluent pen and fertile imagination, and as part of his campaign to improve the lot of his fellow clergy he had devised a scheme by which clergymen (and others, too, if they wished) could ensure that, when they died, their widows were properly provided for.[2] After failing to convince the Corporation of the Sons of the Clergy and the Bank of England of its merits,[3] Assheton took his idea to the Mercers.[4]

It is easy to see why the Company did not follow suit. The mere fact that Assheton had been rebuffed elsewhere was not particularly significant. There were financial schemes aplenty in the 1690s, and there was little experience by which to distinguish the good from the bad. Assheton's scheme was certainly beguiling. The prospect of raising at once a large a sum of money by subscription against future smaller payments had obvious attractions for a corporate body so heavily in debt. Indeed, some of the money would be entirely unencumbered, since clergymen whose wives predeceased them would forfeit subscriptions. None the less, the commitment to pay a yearly sum equal to 30% of the sum subscribed was extremely onerous;[A] indeed, if Assheton's actuarial calculations were wrong (even supposing they existed[B]), it could prove disastrous. It is therefore little short of astonishing that the committee to which the General Court referred the proposals did not rigorously examine this crucial percentage.[5] Actuarial science may have been in its infancy, but such mercantile experts as Papillon and Sir William Hedges could have been expected to detect the flaws in the figures. Their only substantive changes or propositions concerned the minimum size of the total subscription (£100,000 not £50,000), the maximum (£300) and minimum (£50) sums which individuals could subscribe for a single annuitant, and the age (not above 60) and health of the subscribers.[6] Otherwise the committee's deliberations dealt simply with the need to give security for the payment of the annuities, and as soon as a schedule of much of the Company's corporate and trust property (with St Paul's School and Trinity Hospital Greenwich as the only notable exceptions) producing a rental income of £2,888 (with a potential income of £13,500) had been drawn up, Assheton professed himself satisfied.[7] When the committee reported back to the General Court with these revised proposals, it blessed them with the fateful

[A] The assumption that this crucial provision was included in Assheton's original proposal is based on the absence of any reference or challenge to it in the entries in the Acts of Court which deal with revisions and amendments to other aspects of the scheme; but it has to be acknowledged that it was not until the proposal was submitted to the General Court that the percentage was mentioned.

[B] There is nothing to suggest that Assheton had any mathematical ability. His previous publications had been on exclusively religious matters.

words that 'if the £100,000 mentioned be subscribed it would be to the interest, credit and reputation of the Company to accept thereof'.[8]

The General Court, to *its* credit, did not endorse the scheme straight away. After 'several debates' it resolved to call another Court and warn all members of the business to be debated.[9] It was that second General Court, held in January 1699, which appointed a committee to draw up a formal set of proposals for adoption.[10] Three weeks then elapsed, during which time the committee obtained counsel's comfort on the use of trust property in the proposed deed of settlement (subject, of course, to the due payment of the charitable commitments) and drafted proposals in a form suitable for publication.[11]

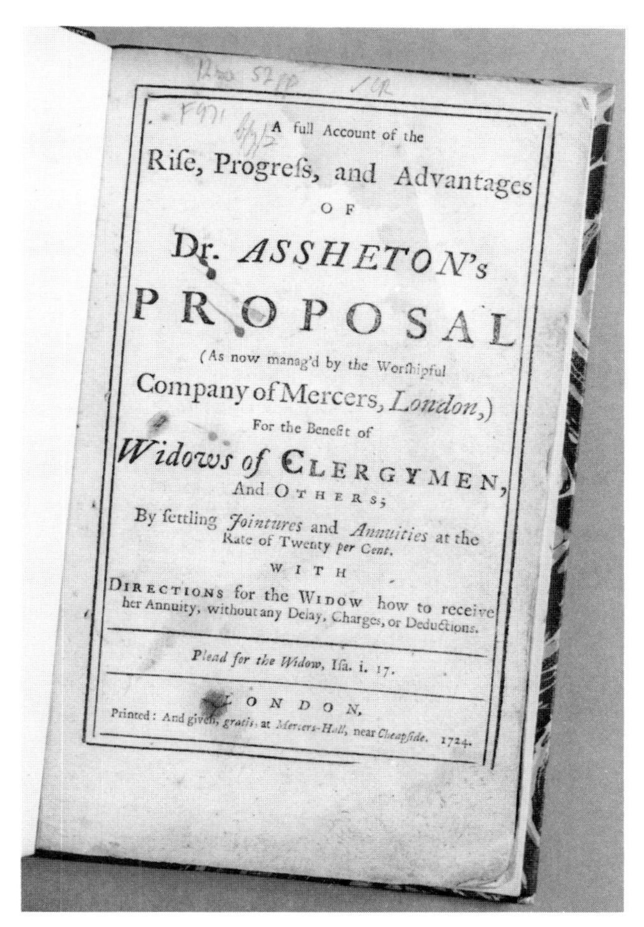
A full Account of the
Riſe, Progreſs, and Advantages
OF
Dr. *ASSHETON's*
PROPOSAL
(As now manag'd by the Worſhipful
Company of Mercers, *London*,)
For the Benefit of
Widows of CLERGYMEN,
And OTHERS;
By ſettling *Jointures* and *Annuities* at the Rate of Twenty *per Cent.*
WITH
DIRECTIONS for the WIDOW how to receive her Annuity, without any Delay, Charges, or Deductions.
Plead for the Widow, Iſa. i. 17.
LONDON,
Printed: And given, *gratis*, at *Mercers-Hall*, near *Cheapſide*. 1724.

FIG. 43. The title-page to the 1724 edition of Dr Assheton's unfortunate *Proposal* for an annuity scheme. The little prospectus was published by the bookshop in the Mercers' Chapel porch.
Mercers' Company

'The General Proposal for Widows' was accepted by the General Court without demur[12] and was printed for distribution as *An Account of Dr. Assheton's Proposal, as improved* [sic] *and managed by the Company of Mercers, for the Benefit of Widows of Clergymen and Others* ....[13] The preamble is interesting only for its disingenuousness: 'Dr. Assheton, considering where the ... subscription money might be lodged safely and reasonable security given for the due payment of the widows, did think it could not be better secured than in the hands of the Worshipful Company of Mercers of London ...';[14] while the actual terms contain nothing of significance which has not already been noted, though they certainly omitted a number of matters which should have been included (most notably conditions relating to the age of subscribers' *wives*).[C]

By June 1699 it had become clear that the scheme had not been a great success. Subscriptions had fallen well short of the £100,000 target.[15] The Company assumed the cause to be 'the uncertainty of things taking effect in the manner proposed' and resolved to put the deed of settlement in hand immediately and call for subscribers' monies as soon as the deed was engrossed.[16] At the same time various amendments were made to the scheme to make it more attractive: younger men could subscribe larger sums (£1,000 in the case of those aged 30 or under, £500 if 40 or under); subscriptions could be declared to be for the benefit of persons other than wives (though only for the lifetime of such wives);[D] the subscribers' bond for due

[C] The Company was not unaware of the significance of any marked disparity in age between subscribers and their wives, and a 59½-year-old Worcestershire clergyman with a 40-year-old wife was turned away in 1701 partly for this reason (AC, 1700–7, f. 34v); but the absence of any formal restrictions is most striking.

[D] In January 1700 Assheton evidently tried to persuade the Company to allow subscriptions for the benefit of third parties on an unrestricted basis, but this was considered a 'direct deviation' from the settlement and thus rejected: AC, 1693–1700, f. 184v.

compliance was halved; and the widows' first annuity instalments were to be paid somewhat earlier.[17] The consequence was that, when the scheme became effective after the finalisation of the deed of settlement in October 1699,[18] it did so on terms even less satisfactory than those resulting from the insufficiently severe examination a few months earlier. The relaxation of the terms may not have been particularly culpable (though the invitation of larger subscriptions from younger men opened up disturbing possibilities), but the discarding of the £100,000 minimum is hard to excuse. The merit of the scheme from the Company's point of view was that it offered a large capital sum to discharge the Royal Exchange debt and leave a sufficient surplus to generate income which, when taken together with increased rents from the Company's own property, would be adequate for future annuity payments. Such a prospect was now jeopardised. What was worse, by waiving the £100,000 precondition, the Mercers were now committed to proceeding with the scheme. As events were to transpire, they could only hope that no further subscriptions were made, because the scheme was doomed and any additional monies would only make the eventual crash worse.[E]

THE EARLY YEARS (1699–1725)

For a while the Company was able to enjoy the pleasure of receipts without the pain of repayments. Initial subscriptions, disappointing though they were, did at least provide the means to discharge a good number of bond debts, and the Gresham account now found itself paying 5% interest, not to a collection of individual Mercers and financiers, but to the annuity account.[19] At a stroke the Company postponed the day of reckoning on the Royal Exchange debt. Not until the annuities fell due for payment in large numbers would there be any serious financial pressure. However, by using the subscriptions in this way the Company was taking an enormous risk. If the anticipated increase in corporate revenue did not materialise, or did not materialise in time, there would be no money available to pay the annuities; and, of course, with the Company's estates pledged to meet such commitments, any failure would have catastrophic results.

The first signs of anxiety appeared in January 1710 when, belatedly, limitations were placed on the age of subscribers' *wives*: a subscriber over forty-five years of age could not have a wife more than fifteen years younger.[20] Four years later the Master and Wardens were ordered to be wary of accepting anyone aged over fifty, particularly when large sums of money were involved.[21] Even more significant was the adoption, in 1716, of a new accounting method designed to afford the officers the means of establishing quickly the state of the balance sheet. Receipts and payments for the House, Gresham, St Paul's School and annuity accounts were to be recorded in one cash book before being transferred into separate ledgers.[22] The prior system, involving each Warden giving and receiving his personal 'charge' and 'discharge', was evidently regarded as too cumbersome for the perilous times with which the Company was now confronted. When these arrangements were formally accepted the Court also asked the Clerk to improve the Company's cash position by buying Government stock 'with as much good husbandry as he can'.[23]

A few months later 'good husbandry' dictated a rather more dramatic move. Early in 1717 the Company obtained counsel's opinion on a reduction in the interest rate for future subscriptions from 30% to 25%.[24] The justification was the proportionate fall in national interest rates since 1699, but this has to be seen as an excuse not a reason. The Company was quite simply becoming uncertain of its ability to repay. As if to confirm the point, the restriction on elderly subscribers

[E] Assheton might have saddled the Company with still more treacherous commitments. In 1702 he contemplated a scheme for the widows of those clergymen who could not afford to subscribe themselves. Contributions from better-paid clergymen would be collected by the bishops and then paid to the Mercers in £50 portions for the benefit of nominated wives. Fortunately the scheme was not taken up by the Church, still less presented to the Company. See N. Cox, *Bridging the Gap* (1978), pp. 67–8.

FIG. 44. Cups presented by the Bank of England in 1694, as a token of gratitude for the use of Mercers' Hall during the first months of the Bank's existence. *Mercers' Company*

now hardened into a prohibition on any over fifty years of age.[25]

It is instructive to set these modifications to the annuity scheme alongside a debate on Gresham College which occurred little more than two months later. It will be seen below that at the turn of the century there were plans to rebuild the College on a smaller scale and let out the surplus land for building. This seemed a promising way of recouping at least some of the Royal Exchange losses. However, it proved impossible to obtain the necessary Act of Parliament and the idea was abandoned for a time. When it was revived in 1717 the General Court decided that the plan was too expensive. Instead it recommended the Gresham Committee[26]

> to consider some other method, and whether it might be proper for the City or the Company, either out of coal duties or otherwise, to endeavour to obtain some relief towards reimbursing the great expense and loss they have sustained in building the Royal Exchange, which was done to encourage the trade of England, and a duty on coals was appropriated by Act of Parliament after the Fire for widening the streets and other public uses in the City of London, and therein for the building of the Royal Exchange, but fell so far short that it did not answer the other uses and nothing was received towards the great expense of the Exchange.

Members were clearly beginning to feel the grip of financial difficulty tightening, and it is interesting to see them turning, as others had done in 1681 and were again to do later, to Parliament and the coal dues for salvation.

Concern about the health of both the annuity scheme in particular and the Company's finances in general recurred briefly in 1720–1[27] and then more seriously in 1723.[F] For a time in 1723 it

[F] Thomas Guy chose this inappropriate time to offer the Company £20,000, subject to an obligation to pay 4% per annum to St Thomas's Hospital. The Company was only prepared to accept on the basis of 3%, and Guy withdrew his offer. AC, 1721–8, f. 48–v.

looked as if the Company would decide to accept no further subscriptions, but finally it resolved simply to reduce the percentage once more, this time to 21%.[28] Again a fall in interest rates was advanced in justification and again the real reason clearly lies in the need to mitigate the adverse effects of the scheme. Another deed of settlement was engrossed and the scheme staggered on, still attractive (or rather, too attractive) to the investing public but causing palpitations to the Company.

CRISIS

The potential crisis became an actual one on 5 March 1725 when it was announced that the Company had insufficient money for the annuity payments due later that month. The Wardens were authorised to borrow £2,000 for the Company's needs and a committee was appointed to 'inspect the Company's books and accounts and consider of the general state of the Company's affairs'.[29] No sooner had the Committee begun its work than it recommended that a *standing* committee be established 'with a general power to inspect the Company's books and affairs as often as they think fit'.[30] Thus was formed the Committee of Accounts which was to guide the Company through the daunting times which lay ahead.

For many years the Committee's task was relatively easy, thanks to the generosity of the Company's members. Whenever there loomed a shortfall in the six-monthly payments to the widows, the Committee would arrange loans on bond either from its own ranks or the membership at large. In February 1726, for example, the Master (James Colebrooke) and the Second Warden (Wight Woolley) each promised £1,000 towards the £2,500 needed, with the remaining £500 to be taken up 'of such members of the Company as [the Wardens] thought meet'.[31] A year later Warden Joliffe offered £1,000 of the £3,000 deficit, 'the rest to be taken up of such members of the Company as will advance the same'.[32] And so the pattern was repeated, each spring and autumn, with only slight variations. It is quite clear that the Mercers were trying to keep their troubles to themselves, buying time in the hope that an increased rental income would give them release from the annuity burden. There is certainly nothing to indicate that the bond-holders were attempting to exploit their Company's predicament. The 4½% interest was not excessive (bearing in mind the increasingly doubtful security afforded by the Company's seal) and in any event it was reduced to 4% in 1736.[33] The Company had every reason to be grateful to those members, particularly Sir William Joliffe, Richard Chauncy and James Colebrooke, who advanced very considerable sums in these years.

Apart from such temporary measures, and a little revenue raising in the form of calls on the Livery[34] and Government stock investment,[35] the Committee could do nothing save hope that the books would begin to balance. They did not. Indeed, they became even more lopsided. In October 1739 the Committee referred to 'the Company's affairs and the great charge they are at by the annuities to widows';[36] and in the following year the Company decided to reduce the percentage payable on new subscriptions from 20% to 15%.[G] At the same time still more adjustments to the qualification rules were introduced, involving both restrictions and relaxations: on the one hand, subscribers aged fifty or under could proffer any sum between £50 and £500 provided their wives were no more than ten years younger; while, on the other, those between fifty and sixty could subscribe the same amounts provided their wives were no more than five years younger.[37]

This admission that the annuity scheme was again proving a grave disappointment seems to have swept away the Company's resolve to keep its problems to itself. Or perhaps members began to jib at placing their money at risk. Whatever the reason, there now appeared an unashamed readiness to take up money on bond wherever it could

[G] This followed a recommendation of a 'committee appointed to treat with tenants' (AC, 1735–42, f. 196v). Generally speaking, however, the Accounts Committee appears to have remained in control of the annuity problem.

be found.[38] Provided lenders would accept 4% interest and the security of the Company's seal, their loans were welcome.[H] Those members who did continue to make advances usually did so only in peculiar circumstances. On 5 April 1742 the Select Committee was told of an immediate need for £3,000 to cover the payments due on 25 March last, and Colebrooke (£2,000), Nathaniel Newnham senior (£500) and Nathaniel Garland (£500) responded to the call but, though they were ready to take out six-month bonds, they were to be repaid out of the first receipts which came to hand after the payments had been made.[39] Colebrooke was certainly ready to place his banking services at the disposal of the Company,[40] but he had clearly decided that with £5,000 already at risk any further personal money was best placed away from Mercers' Hall. How right he was! Despite an increase in the percentage payable from 15% to 20%[41] and a tougher attitude to subscribers' appeals for indulgence,[42] the scheme remained hopelessly under-financed. The legerdemain of six-monthly bond borrowings could not last for ever.

BANKRUPTCY

On 1 November 1745 the Accounts Committee made a series of bleak resolutions: that a breakdown of the Company's finances, present and future, be prepared and laid before members; that the Clerk be ordered to suspend payments of interest on the bond debts and to pay the annuitants only when rents came in; and that no more subscriptions for widows be accepted and no more money be taken up on bond.[43] These were fateful decisions. Whether they are regarded as the Company finally crying halt to the spiralling increase of debt or the reluctant acknowledgement that its credit was exhausted, they brought the financial crisis dramatically to a head. Some kind of arrangement with creditors would have to be devised if the Company was not to be confronted with the unthinkable, namely the enforcement of the security afforded by the estates contained in the deed of settlement (in the case of annuitants) and represented by the Company's seal (in the case of the bond-holders).

The Accounts Committee's views were endorsed by the Court of Assistants, and a General Court was summoned for 8 November.[44] The membership were given the current year's figures, which amounted to the following:

Expenditure	£	*s.*	*d.*
'Ordinary' charges and expenses	3,285	7	0
Annuity payments	8,107	15	0
Bond interest (4% on £85,500)	3,420	0	0
	14,813	2	0
Income			
Rents	7,327	15	0
Deficit	7,485	7	0

The General Court's decisions were wholly predictable: no further subscriptions or borrowings; further consideration of the Company's 'present situation' by the Assistants; notification to the bond creditors in the hope that 'an amicable accommodation may be effected'; and a full financial account to be prepared.[45] The last task was given to a committee which came to be known as the General Committee and which now took over from the Accounts Committee the regular supervision of the debt problem.[46]

With the aid of general legal advice from the Company's Solicitor, Nathaniel Cole,[47] and written opinions from eminent barristers,[48] the General Committee was able to give its considered views to the General Court in mid-January 1746. A long report (with even longer statistical appendices) on the annuity scheme confirmed the bleak summary given two months

[H] Details of undischarged bond debts were set out in the schedule to the 1763 Act of Parliament (for which see below, p. 109. Insofar as the identities of the creditors can be established, it is clear that members lent less and outsiders more as time passed. (The fact that these are only the undischarged debts seems unimportant: the likelihood is that members would have been repaid first.)

earlier.[49] The Company's total debt was estimated at £111,017. Lands in the deed of settlement were producing £4,814, of which £666 was committed to charities and other outgoings. Increases could be expected in due course from Ireland and particularly Long Acre, where £30 per annum could become £6,000 when the lease expired fifteen years hence. Lands not in the deed of settlement were less promising: express obligations accounted for £1,043 out of £1,959 per annum, and the committee thought that some of the property, notably the St Paul's School estate, could not be used for any general corporate purpose.

There was plainly little hope of any early or easy solution to the Company's difficulties. All the committee could do was recommend a judicious defensive tactic. It suggested that the *whole* of the Company's estates be placed in trust, not only for the repayment of the bond creditors but also for the payment of the certain charges on the Company's income, including money legacies, the Gresham and St Paul's School trusts, House expenses and bond interest arrears. This would not jeopardise the annuitants' position, and if not done the Company could find itself subject to legal claims from the bond-holders for priority repayment, which would, of course, absorb all the Company's available income and effectively destroy its corporate independence. The General Court heeded this call for pre-emptive self-preservation and ordered the necessary conveyance to be drawn up forthwith, requiring only to see the draft before it was executed.[50]

By this stage, however, the Company could not proceed without trying to accommodate the wishes of creditors. On the one hand, the annuitants had to be reassured that the proposed deed would not affect their position, while at the same time being told effectively that it was a matter between the Company and the bond-holders. On the other hand, the bond creditors were not content merely to have their principal debts secured in this way; they wanted the interest included as well.[51] This the committee accepted, though they were careful to provide also for the interest due on the Company's other debts.[52]

This triangular tussling became more serious in May 1746 when the annuitants began to hint at legal redress if they did not get satisfaction.[53] The General Court immediately urged formal discussions between the three committees to 'consider of a method to give [the creditors] satisfaction and if possible to prevent any suits between the Company and the bond creditors or annuitants'.[54] When the meeting took place Nathaniel Cole tabled a plan which involved a kind of tripartite receivership of the settled estates,[1] with a combined annuitants, bond creditors and Mercers' committee collecting rents and (effectively) granting leases, under powers conferred by deed and sanctioned by Parliament. Once the annuitants had been paid off, the estates would be pledged to discharge the bond debts under arrangements to be agreed at that stage between the Company and the bond creditors. Cole commended the scheme to the annuitants and bond-holders with a warning that only an 'amicable' [i.e. voluntary] solution would work: 'any legal [i.e. imposed] one will exhaust the whole or the greatest part of the [settled] fund, will be attended with infinite delay and most probably will not within [the] compass of any of the lives now in being answer the purpose which is desired by all the parties'.[55]

At the same time as it was fending off the demands of its creditors the Company was struggling to improve its financial position. The proposed sale of the barge and leasing of the bargehouse,[56] economising on staff[57] and suchlike were unlikely to make much impact; but the renting of the Hall to the Excise Commissioners for 21 years at £500 per annum certainly

[1] The assumption that Cole confined his proposals to the *settled* estate and not the whole estate is based on (a) a reference to the 'annuitants' estates' (in the context of the payment of outgoings) in the scheme itself (GC, 1745–7, p. 274), (b) the Company's subsequent reluctance to deal with the settled estate until it had a response to the scheme from the annuitants (ibid., pp. 303, 310–11) and (c) the use of a warning that the Company was under pressure to use the equity of redemption (or unencumbered element) in the settled estate as security for repayment of the bond creditors as encouragement to obtain the annuitants' assent to the scheme (ibid., p. 317).

would have done.[58] However, after serious negotiations the proposed rent evidently frightened the Commissioners away.[J] This rebuff, of course, made it still more imperative that some form of agreement be reached with the annuitants on the management of the settled estate. Leases were coming up for renewal, but the Company did not feel empowered to grant new ones without its creditors' authority.[59] It took the annuitants fully six months to decide that the scheme advanced in May was unacceptable;[60] and all the Company could proffer in response was a warning that the bond-holders were pressing for the conveyance of the equity of redemption in the settled estates (as well as the Company's other property) to secure their debts.[K 61] In December the annuitants finally put forward a proposal of their own: a Chancery decree by consent giving the Court wide powers of supervision over the management of the trust estate and of arbitration in case of disputes.[62] The Company, needless to say, blenched at such a prospect. The need for a Court application at all was doubted, but if made the annuitants' scheme would have to be amended. The annuitants were to be given powers of audit only and recourse to the Court would arise only in the event of disagreement.[63]

PARLIAMENT

The stalemate was still unresolved when some of the bond creditors took their case to Parliament. Dr Peter Shaw had been badly caught by the 'crash' in 1745[64] and he was determined to obtain recompense. He gathered as much information as he could[65] and then summoned a creditors' meeting at which he called for an application to Parliament.[66] The result was a petition presented to the House of Commons on 26 January 1747 by Shaw and other creditors of the Company 'on behalf of themselves and the rest of the creditors, subscribers for annuities and annuitants ...'.[67] The petition spoke of the annuity scheme being 'fraudulently' established and used to pay off the Company's debts rather than being preserved as a fund for future payments, and of the Accounts Committee 'fraudulently' sustaining the Company's credit after 1725 and 'unwarrantably' taking up not only further subscriptions but also large loans on bonds. The petition was referred, in the customary manner, to a committee, and the process of further petitioning and examination began. The Governors of the Charity for the Relief of Poor Widows and Children of Clergymen wished to support the annuitants' case for obvious altruistic reasons but were doubtless also anxious to prevent a rush of claimants from a failed Mercers' scheme; James Colebrooke wanted the chance to defend himself against the allegations in Shaw's petition; Huntingdon Corporation asked that no settlement be allowed to affect their entitlement to Fishborne money, payment of which had been suspended in 1745; laity and clergy in Wakefield sought renewed support for the Lady Campden lectureship, likewise cut off in 1745; and finally, early in March, the Company itself advanced its case:

> That the petitioners, the Wardens and Commonalty of the Mystery of Mercers of the City of London, under their present unhappy circumstances, are desirous to give their respective creditors all the aid, and do them all the justice, in their power; and in order thereto are advised it is proper for them to lay before the said Committee the following particulars: that the petitioners lent to his Majesty King Charles the First, and to the Parliament and City of London in the troublesome times of that reign, several sums amounting to £10,000 and upwards; that by the great expense of rebuilding the Royal Exchange after the same was destroyed by the Fire of London, Sir Thomas Gresham's charities and endowments are become indebted to the petitioners, the Wardens and Commonality of the Mystery of Mercers of the City of London, in the sum of £100,000 and upwards; which several facts the said petitioners conceived incumbent upon them to prove, and that they are able to do the same in a few hours from their books now before the

[J] The Excise Office stayed on in its adjacent premises in Frederick Mansion for a further 21-year term and then in 1768 acquired Gresham College (see below, p. 113).

[K] The bond creditors, in fact, were pressing for the implementation of the Company's own general settlement as suggested by the General Committee in January, though of course for different reasons.

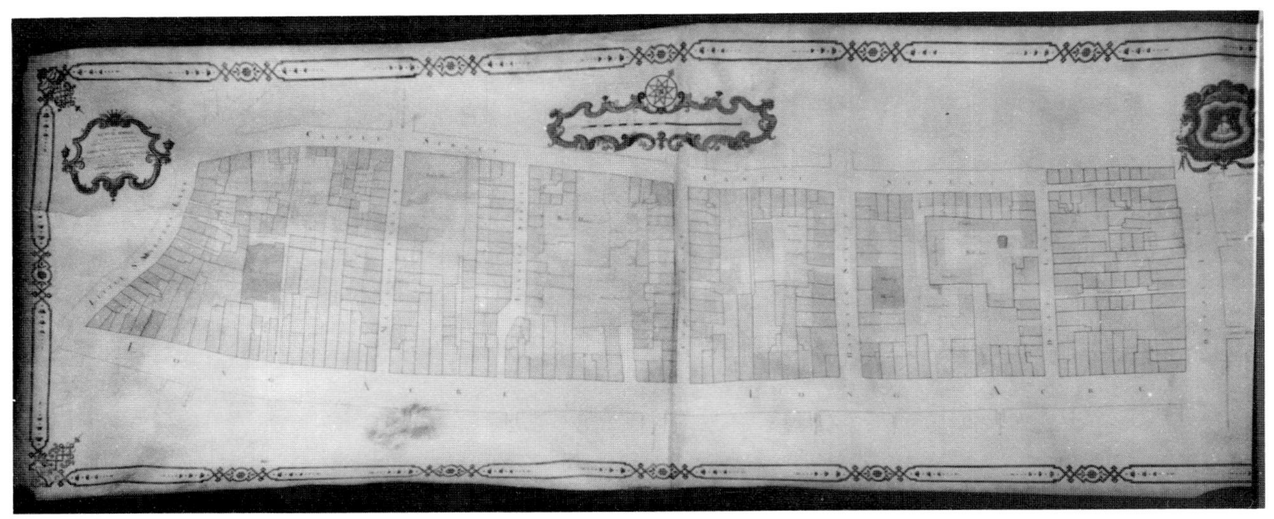

FIG. 45. Lady Bradbury's estate. Pen and wash survey on parchment of Long Acre in Covent Garden by Thomas Lediard, 1742. (For the Maiden from this plan, see Pl. XIV.)
Mercers' Company

Committee: and therefore praying that they may be heard before the said Committee touching the matters aforesaid, and that they may have such relief in the premises as to the House shall seem meet.[68]

The thoroughness of the ensuing examination may be gauged from the fact that the Clerk (or so he later claimed) took no fewer than 600 documents from the Hall to the House of Commons.[69] Details of the discussions do not survive, but it is clear that, despite some energetic lobbying by the creditors,[70] the Company got the better of the argument. The conclusion to the committee's report ran thus:[71]

Upon the whole it doth not appear to your Committee that there is any embezzlement of any of the Company's effects by any person whatsoever but all the money has been duly brought to account and it plainly appears that the causes of the Company's deficiencies are the great debt owing by the Company at the time of agreeing to Dr. Assheton's proposal, occasioned by the lending of large sums to King Charles I a little time before the Grand Rebellion, the losses the Company sustained by the Fire of London, the rebuilding of the Royal Exchange, the great deficiencies in Sir Thomas Gresham's estate to pay the annual salaries to lecturers and other charities, the fall of the rent of houses in which much the greatest part of the Mercers' estate consists, and above all by the disadvantageous bargain made with Dr. Assheton by granting of annuities in reversion at £30 per cent without proper limitation of age and allowing the parties to subscribe by proxy.[L]

The grammar was odd, but the verdict was clear enough. Whether by reason of the intrinsic strength of its case or because a number of friends sat on the committee,[72] the Company had been vindicated and Shaw vanquished.

It was, however, a hollow victory. In the first place, the report was never formally adopted by the full House: consideration was postponed beyond the date of what was first prorogation and later dissolution.[73] Secondly, a moral victory, however comforting, did nothing to help tackle the real problems which remained. The Mercers may have been encouraged by the appearance of 'so just' a report and the associated reflection that 'the Company's misfortunes arise from circumstances of a public nature' to hope that a joint application to Parliament for relief might meet with success, but in the meantime there remained the pressing need to manage the settled estate and thus find some money to meet the demands of not

[L] This last point was presumably a reference to the right to nominate third party beneficiaries (see above, p. 97).

only the annuitants and bond creditors but also the unpaid officers and lawyers.[74]

Nevertheless, it is possible to detect extra confidence in the way in which the Company tackled these tasks in the second half of 1747. The consent of the annuitant and bond creditors was finally obtained to enable the General Committee to grant new leases and accept surrenders 'in the manner usually practised by the Company' and also to permit the deduction of some money for expenses.[75] In October twenty vacant properties (including the bargehouse) were advertised,[76] while at the same time the Irish estate was reviewed and, on receipt of proposals for a new lease from the present tenant, a survey and account ordered.[77]

The same positive spirit was evident in the pressure for a petition to Parliament. Early in November 1747 the General Committee asked representatives of the annuitants and bond creditors, as well as the Company's Solicitor and Parliamentary agent, to 'meet and consider whether any and what application should be made to Parliament for the relief of the Company and their annuitants and bond creditors and they are also to consider a proper bill to be offered in Parliament for vesting the Company's estates in such manner as may be most beneficial for the Company's annuitants and bond creditors . . .'.[78] There are no details of the discussions but the Company was certainly given encouragement to proceed, and by the end of the year a petition to Parliament had been approved.[79] To a large extent it repeated the tale of woe set out in its predecessor of March. However, on this occasion the Company emphasised the sorry state of its rental income: 'the whole income of the petitioners' estate do [*sic*] at present amount only to £4,100 a year or thereabouts and consisting chiefly in houses in and about London and are liable to great repairs and are daily falling in their rents . . .'.[80] This was no less than the truth: the London property market was quite severely depressed at this time and landlords were genuinely concerned that tenants would not be encouraged to repair and rebuild;[81] but one cannot help noticing the absence of any reference to the additional income expected shortly from the Long Acre and Irish estates. The petition also contained a reference to the benefits its Royal Exchange partner had received from the coal dues, and Parliament was plainly invited to do something similar for the Mercers:[82]

> the City of London having, in 1693 [*recte* 1694], been reduced to great distresses, principally by money lent to the King and Parliament in troublesome times, the Fire of London, and the rebuilding the Exchange, obtained from Parliament a duty of six pence per chaldron upon coals for a term of years, which is at present near expiring . . . [and] your petitioners in a great measure owing their present unhappy situation to the same causes . . .

The City, in fact, was hoping to persuade Parliament to extend its coal dues for a further term and was ready to co-operate with the Mercers.[83] Parliament could easily resolve both problems at the same time.

Early in 1748 the usual Parliamentary procedure got under way: a delegation to the Speaker and the chief (i.e. Prime) Minister, Henry Pelham; the circulation of a Case to MPs; presentation of the petition to the House of Commons; and referral to a committee.[84] The examination of the Company's allegations involved not merely the checking of accounts but also the questioning of officials: the Clerk, for example, was forced to acknowledge that when the Long Acre lease expired in 1760 'some considerable improvement is expected therefrom, but how much he cannot ascertain'.[85] The verdict was sufficiently favourable for the Committee's report to be considered together with the City's petition for an extension of the coal dues,[86] and on 15 March the Commons ordered a bill to be drawn up which added 35 years to the coal dues term beyond the expiry date 1750 and appropriated from those dues

> the yearly sum of £3,000 [to] be applied . . . towards paying the annuities now payable, or which hereafter shall be payable, by the Company of Mercers of London, to several widows and others during their respective lives, in pursuance of contracts heretofore entered into by the said Company, and to such other creditors of the said Company as shall be deemed proper objects of relief. . .[87]

Three weeks later the Mercers' own relief bill was presented to the House. Various amendments were made during its passage through the Commons, but unfortunately details are hard to establish. There is, however, nothing to suggest the bill aroused much controversy. Dr Shaw, it is true, presented his own petition asking for special treatment as reward for his efforts in bringing the matter to its evidently successful outcome,[88] while a requisition for the production of deeds and books relating to the Colet charity briefly aroused fears of interference with property outside the settled estate, and prompted not only the speedy investment of some surplus cash expressly on trust for St Paul's School but also consideration as to how the Colet accounts should be kept in future.[89] Eventually, on 6 May 1748, the bill was passed by the Commons, and after a rapid, trouble-free journey through the Lords, received the Royal Assent a week later.[90]

'An Act for the Relief of the Annuitants of the Wardens and Commonality of the Mystery of Mercers of the City of London'[91] was primarily concerned with the manner in which the £3,000 per annum from the City's coal dues was to be used to meet the Company's obligations to its annuitants. In the first place, any shortfalls in current annuity payments arising from the inadequacy of the settled estate revenue were to be made good; secondly, interest at the rate of 3% was to be paid on annuity arrears as at 29 September 1750 (when the coal dues payments were to begin); thirdly, the principals of such arrears were to be repaid in proportional, 10% amounts; and finally (when the arrears and interest due on the annuities had been discharged), the Company's other creditors (including, of course, the bond creditors) were to be repaid by means of the coal dues surplus in such manner as a further Act of Parliament should stipulate. The Company had to make its accounts available for inspection by the annuitants and creditors, and indeed were obliged to lay summaries before Parliament each year. There was also a section, apparently introduced (or at least modified) at a comparatively late stage in the bill's passage,[M] which concerned the way in which the Company could deal with its London property. The general rule was that leases were to be granted in possession and not reversion (i.e. to take effect straight away and not at some future date),[N] for rack rents not fines, and for terms not exceeding twenty-one years. However, in the case of Long Acre and other property in need of rebuilding or repair, terms not exceeding sixty-one years (for rebuilding) and forty-one years (repairing) could be granted, taking whatever fines and rent were thought fit. As for Ireland, the new lease had to be in possession and not reversion, was not to exceed sixty-one years, or the longest of any three nominated lives, and could impose such fine and rent as could reasonably be obtained, provided the rent was no less than the current one. Only two further provisions deserve attention: the statement that the deeds of settlement were to remain in full force and effect, and the referral of Dr Shaw's claim for expenses to the Court of Exchequer for assessment, with a direction that payment be made out of the £3,000 per annum.[92]

THE IRISH ESTATE

Whether the Act of 1748 would prove an answer to the Company's financial problems remained to be seen, but it certainly gave the Company the opportunity to make a fresh, constructive assault on those problems. It is true that hand-to-mouth expedients were not entirely abandoned, as witness the hiring of the Hall to an oculist for lectures (1748),[93] the resurrection of a claim to £2,166 due on the City loan of 1643 (1749)[94] and the leasing of

[M] *The Royal Exchange Extracts. Extracts from the Records of the City of London* (n.d.), p. 43. The mere reference to a section 'impowering the Company to let leases and take fines' makes it impossible to be certain that it was the section itself rather than the Long Acre and Ireland provisos which was introduced.

[N] How this is consistent with a proviso limiting grants to within three years of the expiry of current leases is not clear. This appears to have been one of the defects the amending Act of 1751 (see below, p. 107) sought to remedy.

the bargehouse to the Coopers' Company (1751);[95] but at the same time long-term solutions were being sought. With the help of a clerk from the Bank of England, arrangements for 'methodising' the accounts were made,[96] a survey of the Company's lands ordered[97] and a review of the state of at least some of the charities undertaken.[98] More importantly still, attention was directed towards the potentially lucrative Long Acre and Irish estates. As far as the former was concerned, the General Committee was content to have a rental made and wait patiently for the £6,648 per annum thus revealed to come to hand.[99] As for Ireland, it might be thought that the Act's stipulation that leases be in possession, not reversion, would have had a similar effect on the desire to renew the Irish lease (which was not due to lapse until 1755). Nevertheless, the General Committee were evidently so anxious to secure a large entry fine on the grant of a reversionary lease and thus afford 'an immediate relief to the Company's annuitants' that they ignored Parliament's small print and invited proposals.[100] Three thousand 'particulars' and 6,000 handbills[101] led eventually to the acceptance of Alexander Stewart's offer of £16,500 for a lease for three nominated lives at the former rent of £420 per annum.[102] The Committee must have felt that at last the end of the Company's troubles was in sight, and there is indeed more than a hint of relief in their praise for the endeavours of their lawyer, Nathaniel Cole:[103]

> Your Committee also beg leave to inform this [General] Court of the sense they have of a great ability and application of Mr. Cole on this and many other occasions where the interest of the Company and its creditors was concerned. And that by his advice and assistance your Committee has been enabled to put themselves in a fair way to extricate the Company from the difficulties it has laboured under. They therefore hope you will permit them to recommend such eminent services to your consideration and that you will think them worthy your grateful acknowledgement and reward.

They spoke too soon. The legal experts to whom the proposed lease was submitted noticed various 'defects' in the Act (most notably the bar on reversionary grants) and advised that an amending Act would have to be procured.[104] The Committee acknowleged the problem and decided to make the best of it, by seeking not merely permission to grant the lease to Stewart on the agreed terms, but also 'confirmation' of its powers over the rest of its property and sanction to reimburse itself for its charges and expenses.[105] The resulting Act, obtained in May 1751, does not seem to have aroused much controversy and in most respects the Company got what it wanted.[106] It was empowered to grant a reversionary (i.e. future) lease of its Irish estate; it was expressly permitted to grant building and repairing leases of its London and Middlesex property (though fines were still only permitted in Long Acre); and it was enabled to discharge its necessary expenditure from settled estate income. There was, however, a price to be paid: namely, the requirement that the annuitants and other creditors, by majority in public meeting, should consent to both the granting of leases of the settled estate and the deduction of charges.

Meanwhile Stewart, the prospective lessee, was behaving with what the General Committee acknowledged to be 'great honour and candour',[107] qualities which were to be further tested when it was discovered that the amending Act was itself deficient ('and' had become 'or' in a vital phrase)![108] This time, however, it was sufficient for the Company's Parliamentary agent to offer his apologies and promise to put matters right in the next session of Parliament for the lease to be sealed on 22 August 1751.[109] Some £12,000 was paid immediately and the balance promised after the rectifying Act had been obtained.[110] Even after the deduction of the dividends totalling £1,500 due to the Cooks, Masons and Broderers, and expenses of £1,115, there was a good deal of money left to relieve the plight of the Mercers and their annuitants.[111] With the £3,000 per annum now available and Long Acre's renewal drawing near, the Company was indeed close to extricating itself from 'the difficulties it has laboured under'. It is a mystery why Parliament, earlier in 1748 or more especially in 1751, did not more rigorously

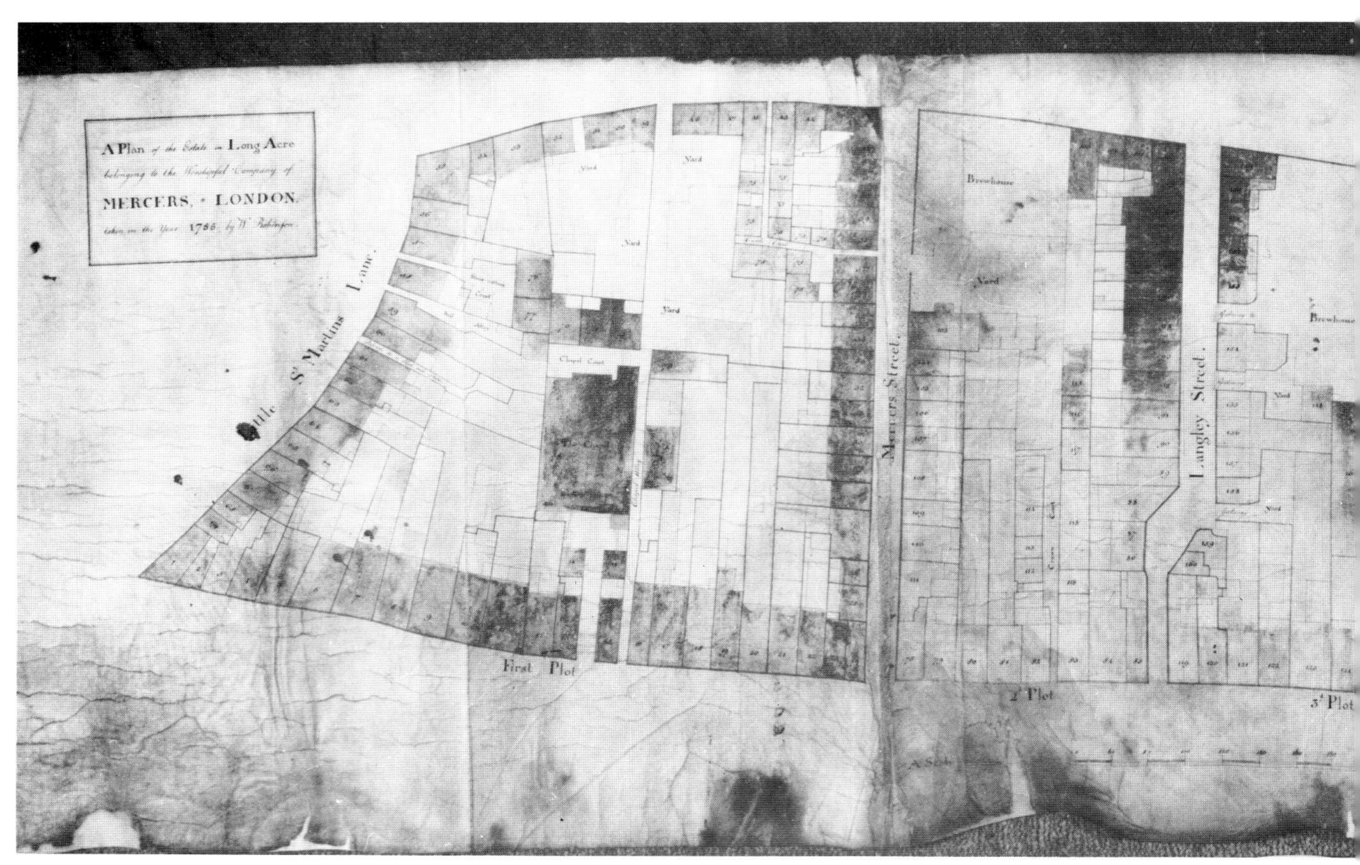

FIG. 46. Lady Bradbury's estate. Plan of Long Acre in Covent Garden by William Robinson, Company Surveyor, 1755.
Mercers' Company

investigate the Irish and Long Acre windfalls. A happy mystery, perhaps, from the Company's point of view, but a mystery none the less.

LONG ACRE

The years immediately following the passage of the 1751 Act were largely devoted to administrative matters: the drafting of a model lease for its London and Middlesex property,[112] the appointment of an accountant to ease the burden on the Clerk,[113] and another way of 'methodising' the Company's records (this time with the help of an official from the South Sea Company).[114] Then, in 1754, came a more progressive step: an 'informal' view of the Long Acre estate by the Master and other members, followed by a resolution to commission a professional investigation in preparation for a general invitation for offers for leases of individual lots.[115] The result, a survey and valuation by the Company's own William Robinson, formed the basis for the grant of leases of the western part of the estate (between Little St Martin's Lane and Mercers Street) in 1756–8 and the rest in 1760–1.[116] The effect on income was startling. At last the Company could turn its thoughts to ridding itself, not merely of the annuity debt, but its other debts as well.

These latter fell into three groups: first, the simple contract debts to workmen and other general 'trade' creditors who had been caught out by the 'stop' in 1745; secondly, payments charged on money legacies and suspended after the Fire; and thirdly, the bond debts themselves, amounting, in principal alone, to £84,700. There was an

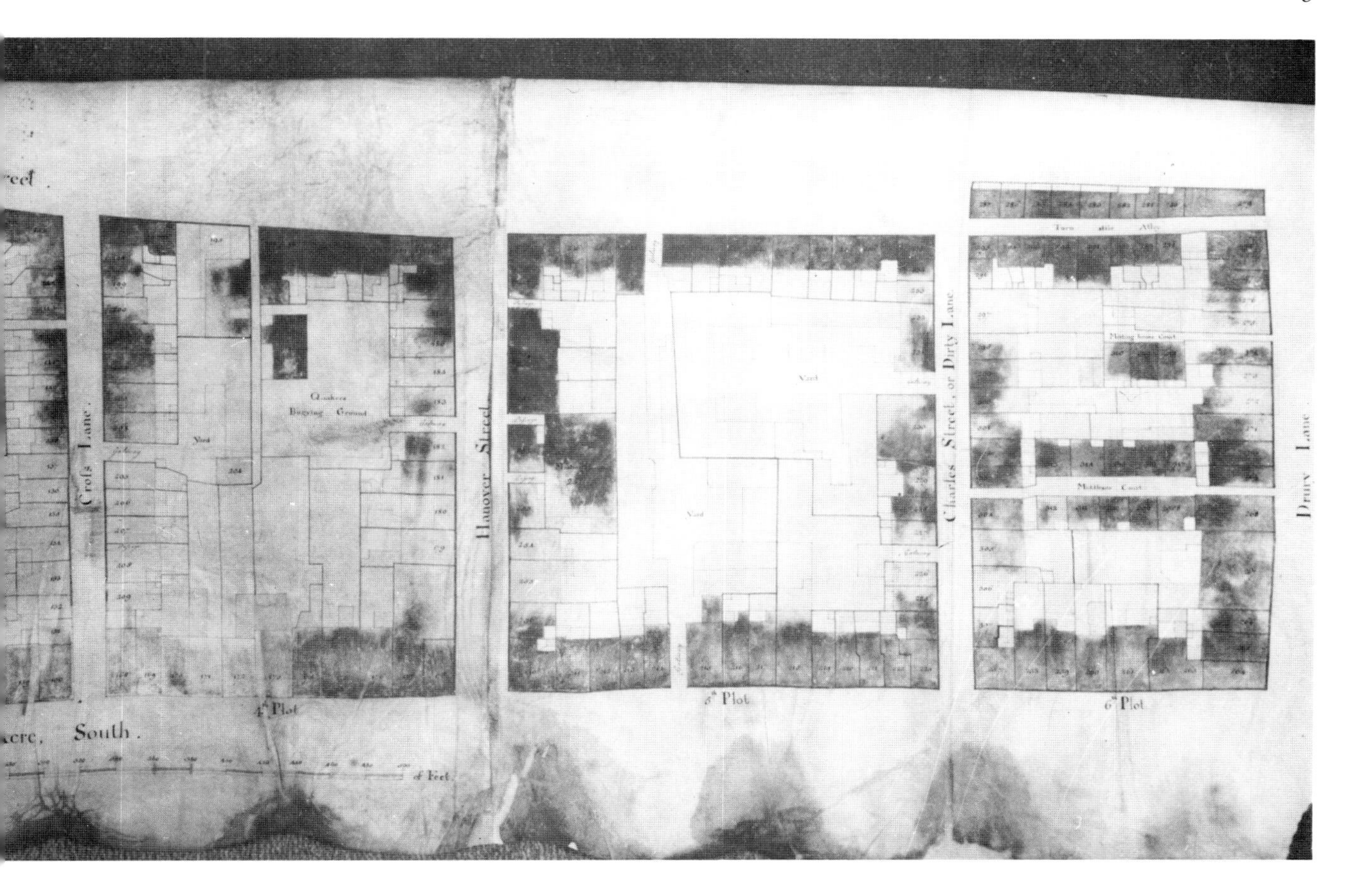

understanding, apparently, among such creditors that they would all 'wait for payment of their debts till the Company, by the death of their annuitants, should be able to pay them', and certainly when the late Clerk's administrator tried to set off a debt against monies owed to the Company he found the Company unwilling to accept any preferential repayment.[117] Long Acre now released the Company from such constraints and permitted the satisfaction of the creditors' demands before the annuity scheme expired. It was in September 1762, shortly after the second batch of Long Acre leases, that the question of applying to Parliament for the relief of the Company's creditors was first raised.[118] After due consideration of the accounts it was evidently accepted that the finances were healthy enough and eventually, in January 1763, a petition was presented to the House of Commons.[119]

The resulting Act of Parliament[120] passed into law with evidently little difficulty, partly no doubt because the 1748 Act expressly required that the Company return for directions for the discharge of the bond and other debts, and partly because it was palpably desirable that the Company's creditors be released from their difficulties as quickly and equitably as possible. The preamble recited that the Company had managed to meet its obligations to the annuitants and still generate a surplus of over £4,600. It was quite clear that further surpluses would accumulate in future. The enacting sections provided in the first place for the payment of arrears owed on the money legacy charities[O] and the contract debts. Once

[O] For the disregard of (or at least an unwillingness to acknowledge) this obligation see below, p. 128.

these obligations had been met, then (subject to the continuing responsibility to make the money legacy payments) the bond debts were to be tackled in the following way. The £84,700 principal was to be consolidated with the interest thereon and new bonds of £100 each[P] issued for that amount. Surplus revenue arising from the coal dues or the settled estate was to be used to pay 3% interest on these bonds, save that when £1,000 was available a lottery for the repayment of the bonds themselves was to be held. The Company subsequently discovered that more than 1,400 £100 bonds had to go into the 'box or wheel',[121] but at least it could see a way out of the morass of debt. The coal dues, Mr Stewart and the Long Acre tenants were likely to produce enough income to keep the annuitants and the bond creditors happy. The Acts of Court for 1766 contain the remark that 'the affairs of the Company are in a much better condition' than they were fifteen years earlier.[122] The Company would have been excused had it used rather more colourful language. Dr Assheton's incubus had finally been shaken off.

[P] There was of course provision for smaller sums and the repayment of odd amounts.

CHAPTER VIII
THE EIGHTEENTH CENTURY

The financial crisis engendered by the annuity scheme had such a profound effect on the Company that it required separate treatment. This Chapter considers other aspects of Company life in the eighteenth century.

It was a period that saw great changes in the size and commercial fortune of London. By the turn of the century, there were more than a million people living in the London area. At the heart of this expanding metropolis, the City was ceasing to be a place in which people both worked and lived. Residence as a qualification for office was quietly forgotten and the community of the City began to decline. London beyond the Square Mile was left to grow, without any contribution from the City's experience and civic organisation.

Even before the Industrial Revolution, new discoveries and processes began to stimulate production and commerce, and by the end of the century Britain had become the centre of world trade. The long periods of war were dislocating, of course, but the compelling need to pay for the armies and support allies also had a catalytic effect. The celebrated experiments and discoveries that suffused agriculture and industry had their parallels in trade and finance. There were countless schemes — Dr Assheton's was typical in its daring but atypical in its failure. For the most part, the wide-ranging attempts to create the sinews of expansion were remarkably successful.

GRESHAM COLLEGE

The post-Restoration period was a sorry time for the Gresham Trust. Neither the revenues of the Royal Exchange nor the academic achievements of the College were such as to excite much interest from hard-pressed corporations. (The City's position was scarcely more comfortable than the Company's.[1]) The Company indeed expressly disavowed at least some of Gresham's legacies. In 1699 the £100 per annum for Company dinners and 'other charges' was ordered to be omitted from the widows' settlement, 'the Company not thinking themselves liable to pay the same, his gift being all burnt to ashes and nothing left to pay the same withal'.[2] Similar sentiments were entertained of more important elements of the Gresham bequest, but the remedy had to be rather different. Gresham College could not simply be abandoned because, without it, the Company would not be entitled to any rent from the Royal Exchange. Indeed, because the income from the Exchange was so low, it was the College itself (or rather its desirable site) which offered a more realistic means of generating sufficient surplus revenue to reduce the mountainous Royal Exchange debt. Instead, therefore, of washing its hands of the Gresham Trust in its entirety, the Company (with the City) was left to struggle with the task of making the College 'pay'.

The first scheme took shape at the very beginning of the century. It involved demolishing the existing College, rebuilding it on a smaller site and letting out the rest of the land for development. Three attempts to secure Parliamentary approval were made, but the opposition of the celebrated Robert Hooke (who was Geometry lecturer), and the Royal Society (which had accommodation in the College), together with a simple shortage of session time, combined to frustrate them.[3] In 1717 the idea was revived, and for the same reason, namely that 'the Company are great losers by Sir Thomas Gresham's gift'.[4] There was a 'great decay of trade at the Royal Exchange . . . several pawns are shut up and other

FIG. 47. William Hogarth's *Industrious Apprentice*, 1747. The final plate (No. 12) from this moral series shows the Industrious Apprentice reaching the City's highest office as he rides in the mayoral coach at his election. Cheering crowds pack the streets and throng the balconies. The Mercers' Maiden is on the flag attached to the stand on the left.
By courtesy of Guildhall Library, Corporation of London

shops there untenanted'. This time, however, the General Court declined to endorse the committee's recommendation.[5] It decided that the expense of a rebuilt College was so great that it would absorb all the additional revenue generated by the redeveloped site. Instead the committee was asked to explore the possibility of securing coal due relief from the Royal Exchange debt.

No such relief was forthcoming and the problem simply grew. On the one hand, the Royal Exchange continued to lose its shopkeepers, though to some extent this was offset by the arrival of commercial tenants such as the Royal Exchange Assurance Company in 1719.[6] On the other hand, the College continued to decay, in every sense. To an institution that was crumbling physically, the lecturers gave no compensating intellectual vigour. Instead there was a depressing, if by now familiar, catalogue of sinecurist misdemeanours. A great deal more effort went into defending legal rights, whether in full-blown Chancery lawsuits,[7] pricklish quarrels with the Gresham Committee,[8] or in heated pamphleteering,[9] than into the furtherance of education. It is an indication of the nature of relations between the trustees and the lecturers that there was required of each newly admitted lecturer not only a £500 performance bond, but also a promise that he would by 'no ways or means whatsoever obstruct but further to the best of his power any

The Colet estate: the Hyde, Weston Turville, Buckinghamshire, surveyed by Thomas Tampon, 1654. The Company no longer owns the estate.
Mercers' Company

PLATE XIV

A. The Maiden's head: detail from a survey of Covent Garden by Thomas Lediard, 1742. (For the whole survey, see Fig. 45).
Mercers' Company

B. Ann Fanshawe's dress. She was the daughter of Sir Crisp Gascoyne, Lord Mayor of London, 1752–3, and the first to reside in the newly-built Mansion House. Since he was a widower, his daughter served as Lady Mayoress. Perhaps she wore this dress, made of sumptuous Spitalfields silk, with its enormously wide skirt — the very height of formal mid-eighteenth-century fashion — for receptions and balls during that year of office. Though Sir Crisp was a Brewer, not a Mercer, the dress is shown here to convey some idea of the top-quality fabrics in which the Mercers dealt.
By courtesy of the Museum of London

petition, bill or bills that shall be thought convenient to be brought to Parliament for rebuilding and improving Gresham College'.[10] Hooke's behaviour had convinced the Company that the lecturers were no more than tiresome obstacles in the path of a resolution of the trust's financial problems.

The final phase of the story began in 1759 when, faced with a repair bill of £2,000, the Gresham Committee again looked at the idea of redeveloping the site.[11] However, there was a new element in the plan. Instead of rebuilding the College on a smaller scale, the committee proposed merely to provide the lecturers with a public reading room and library, either in Bishopsgate or elsewhere, and to make monetary compensation for the loss of accommodation the lecturers would thus suffer. This presented a more attractive solution to the problem than the previous schemes; and, given the lecturers' likely acceptance, provided the additional salary was adequate, it is curious that it had not been considered earlier. The first attempts in 1761 and 1762 to secure the necessary Act of Parliament ended in failure,[12] but the plan was not allowed to lapse. In 1767 it was resurrected, albeit in slightly modified form, and this time it was pushed through to a successful conclusion. The modification arose from the need of the Excise Office for larger premises in place of Frederick House in Old Jewry. As noticed earlier, the Commissioners at one stage had contemplated moving into Mercers' Hall next door, but eventually stayed put for a further term.[A] When they renewed their search, their thoughts initially centred on Ely House in Holborn, but the Mercers countered with the proposal of the Gresham College site.[13] In due course it was agreed that in return for £1,800 (the estimated difference in cost between the Ely House and College options) the Crown would take the Bishopsgate site for £500 per annum in perpetuity. Future generations of Mercers might reflect ruefully on the failure to develop the site independently, but a certain income of £500 in non-inflationary times had understandable attractions for two indebted corporations.[B]

The Crown's interest in the matter meant that there were no Parliamentary mishaps on this occasion, and the Act received the Royal Assent on 10 March 1768.[14] The revisions not only recorded the consideration passing between the Gresham Committee and the Crown, but also the arrangements for the College. A 'sufficient and proper place' was to be found for the reading of lectures, the lecturers would receive an additional £50 per annum in lieu of accommodation (with special provision for the aged Professor of Physic, Dr Pemberton) and, because 'the collegiate life of the said lecturers, intended by the said Sir Thomas Gresham, will by the pulling down of the said College be put an end to', the lecturers succeeded in their last-minute petition and were allowed to marry. In due course, a 'sufficient and proper' lecture room was set up in the Royal Exchange[15] and there the now rather episodic life of Gresham College was continued for a further seventy years. There is nothing to suggest that the move affected the quality of the lecturing, either for better or worse, but from the Company's point of view at least the trust was now on a somewhat more sensible financial basis.

THE SCHOOLS

At least two of the Company's Schools, Collyer's and Mercers' own Chapel School, went through depressing times in the eighteenth century. At Horsham there is very little of merit to report after the resignation of Headmaster Wickliffe in 1669.[16] Only a Chancery quarrel over surplus estate income enlivens the mid-century record,[C][17] and

[A] See above, p. 103.

[B] For a similar verdict by Walter Scarborough early in the present century, see AC, 15 January 1909.

[C] The decree itself (in 1758) managed to avoid any pronouncement on the crucial question of entitlement to the surplus income, but the Company did obtain in 1751 opinions from the Solicitor and Attorney-Generals stating that the Company had no legal obligation to devote the surplus to the School: Collyer's School Papers, 4/39/10 and 4/39/117.

FIG. 48. Gresham College in Bishopsgate shortly before its demolition in 1768.
Mercers' Company

by the end of the period under Headmaster Jameson, there were simply no pupils at all.[18] The Mercers' School seems to have fared only a little better: not once during the long Headmastership of John Browne (1738–71) was there a full complement of twenty-five foundation scholars.[19]

The historians of these institutions have no hesitation in ascribing this 'Georgian decay',[20] in part at least, to the neglect of the Company. Certainly there is no doubt that the Company put little real effort into supervising the Schools; but criticism must be tempered by proper comprehension of a number of extenuating circumstances. As far as Collyer's is concerned, the Company's role was a distinctly limited one, confined to 'confirming' the local election of the headmaster and passing on a fixed sum from the Cheapside property appropriated to the School's purposes. At a time when it was itself facing financial disaster, the Company's reluctance to pay for additional building work,[21] or highly charged litigation,[22] can be readily understood. The Company's complaint that 'the town of Horsham have the sole benefit of the ... schoolhouse and ... the same never was any advantage to the Company'[23] may not have been entirely worthy of charitable trustees, but as a *cri de cœur* of a harassed corporation it deserves some respect.

The Chapel School's problems were rather different, but Company neglect was by no means the most important. The destruction of the Company's own corporate revenues, of course, ensured that no expansion could be contemplated; and the demolition of the School in 1784 to accommodate a widening of Old Jewry, together with the destruction by fire of the School's next premises in Budge Row, added to the difficulties.[24] To be sure, no Company scholars were presented to the School between 1764 and 1804,[25] but this may well be simply a reflection of the School's sad condition rather than a symptom of Company indifference.

Certainly the history of St Paul's School in the eighteenth century suggests that when the Company had sufficient resources at its disposal, it brought energy and determination to bear on its educational responsibilities. The Colet estate was excepted from the widows' settlement and so, when High Master Charles's 'bad temper and brutal violence' brought the School to its knees in 1748, the Company, notwithstanding its desperate difficulties elsewhere, was able to intervene decisively. Charles was removed, the School's merits (and its valuable exhibitions) were widely advertised, the estate was thoroughly reorganised, and the stage set for the largely successful High Masterships of Thicknesse (1748–69) and Roberts (1769–1814).[26]

FIG. 49. Benjamin Morland, High Master of St Paul's School, 1721–33, by an unknown artist, 1722.
Mercers' Company

There is, in fact, only one direct *contemporary* indictment of the Company's supervision of its charities. In the course of a heated quarrel, the almsmen of Trinity Hospital Greenwich alleged that their Warden was 'pleased to say he values the Mercers' Company no more than the dust under his feet, for he says what your worships have to say to him is over in half an hour and he can do what he pleases all the year after'.[27] This may or may not have been true of Trinity Hospital for which the Company had been given a limited and perhaps unexciting role, but certainly the evidence from the Schools (for which the Company had a more immediate and challenging responsibility) indicates that the complaint did not have wide application. Whether it reflected a high sense of duty or simply a fear that the charity might 'be taken out of the Company's hands' by a Commission of Charitable Uses,[28] the Company was always conscious of a potential breach of trust. The Mercers' Company's schools may not have been in bountiful hands in the eighteenth century, but they were not in negligent ones.

OLIGARCHY

The oligarchical tendencies noticed in earlier Chapters continued in the eighteenth century, in the Company as in the City generally. Relations between the General Court and the Court of Assistants, the best barometer of such matters, were disturbed on very few occasions. In 1747 the General Court asked for a justification of the Court of Assistants' supervision of Trinity Hospital Greenwich (and subsequent investigation established that the benefaction had indeed been given to the Wardens and *Commonalty*);[29] while in 1771 there was a full-scale row over the Master's use of a casting vote in the election of a Gresham College lecturer (though two years later the Master's right was affirmed by reference to precedent).[30] Otherwise the record is silent. Indeed, on

FIG. 50. Robert White's bird's-eye view of the second, post-Fire Royal Exchange, 1717.
By courtesy of Guildhall Library, Corporation of London

at least two occasions the General Court showed itself ready to relinquish power to its executive officers. In 1715 the patronage of an apprenticeship charity was expressly conceded to the Master and Wardens,[31] and from 1768 onwards the Master was allowed to appoint preachers under one of the Company's 'sermon' bequests.[32] Certainly, by the time the Company framed a new set of by-laws in 1808 the General Court did not feel emboldened to assume much authority itself.[33] Apart from the approval of the use of the Company's seal,[34] power lay in other hands. The Wardens and Assistants were to elect the Livery and new Assistants, and the Assistants the Wardens; only present and former Wardens could serve on the General Committee;[D] and the Master (or Chairman) kept his casting vote.[35]

It might be countered that these arrangements were no more 'oligarchic' than those in 1579, and that these years merely witnessed a failure by the General Court to assert itself. However, it should be appreciated that beneath these constitutional

[D] The by-laws refer simply to 'the Committee' but, as explained below, this was the former General Committee and is perhaps more helpfully described as such.

formalities there were developments of an undeniably significant kind. There had been long-lived committees before (notably in the post-Fire years[E]), but the *standing* committee is an eighteenth-century phenomenon. When the annuity crisis first arose, an Accounts Committee and a Tenants Committee were appointed.[36] Then in 1745, the General Committee appeared and, as already seen, it rapidly took over the management of the Company's financial affairs. Between November 1745 and April 1748 it met on no fewer than seventy-four occasions[37] and, though its work inevitably became less frenetic as the crisis abated, it established itself as a permanent feature of Company government. In 1767 it was allowed to subsume all save the Gresham and Bank Committees and was even empowered to appoint a standing sub-committee.[38] For this period the enquirer turns first to the General Committee minutes and only afterwards examines the Acts of Court. Such was the executive control of what came to be known as simply *the* Committee.

If the growth of the committee system represented the triumph of professionalism, then the abandonment of any pretence that members had *personally* to serve in the offices to which they were elected represents the demise of amateurism. The acceptance of fines in lieu of service became more and more common. Indeed they began to assume rather the character of impositions than compositions, and at least two members objected.[39] Neither was successful in their challenges, but the complaints of Mark Winn deserve attention if only for the rare insight they afford into the attitudes of 'ordinary' Company members. In 1756, after a request for another £20 for a Wardenship, Winn wrote to the Clerk that he

> made no use of my freedom and doubt not that the intention of being liable to offices either by serving or fining must be the advantage had by my freedom, else in all reason only bearly [?barely] my taking my freedom any other person might as well fine as one of the Company, a person not using his freedom or not being free in reason and equity being all one, and would be paying for nothing. As for being an Assistant, I believe after having paid a fine I might be chose, but knew nothing of it nor ever was at one Court at all. I believe for a great number of years I was not summoned to any Court at all. I know one of the Companies chose a member who had been in trade long and being retired were very well satisfied with one £20, excused him all offices as though he had served them. I am sure I can do the Company no benefit by serving any office in it and think except by form of words my being a member any one else has the same reason to be deemed one.
>
> Yours etc.
>
> P.S. The £20 I have paid and I am sure was paid for no value received whatsoever.[40]

It is clear that many others appreciated the logic buried in Winn's rather incoherent outburst. What was the point of belonging to a bankrupt Company which dunned you for office fines and could afford little in the way of compensatory entertainment? Only a trader who needed to be free of the City had reason to join a Company, and even he might spurn the Mercers, in favour of lower fines and more lavish feasts elsewhere.[41] The total membership declined inexorably:[42]

1739	274
1757	256
1761	252
1763	236
1771	199

The admission figures demonstrate that it was both the failure to attract apprentices and the annuity disaster which caused the decline. The efficacy of the City's freedom was certainly waning,[43] but it is hard to believe that without the Company's bankruptcy the fall in apprentice numbers would have been so dramatic. By 1745, the year of the 'crash', apprentices were scarcely more numerous than those entering by patrimony.

The consequences hardly require explication. The Company became more and more to comprise the sons of the existing freemen, and family dynasties quickly emerged (Tottons, Newnhams, Palmers, Watneys, and others). This in turn

[E] A committee 'for the letting of the Company's foundations' met from 1667 to 1672.

FIG. 51. Flagons presented in 1719 by the Corporation of the Mines Royal, later the Royal Exchange Assurance Company, in gratitude for the use of Mercers' Hall to take subscriptions.
Mercers' Company

encouraged exclusivity, and doubtless explains the decision in 1792–4 first to restrict,[44] and then in the 1808 by-laws to prohibit,[45] entry by redemption, which of course in turn accelerated the trend. The Company became, if not actually oligarchic, then at least self-regarding and was therefore more vulnerable to critical attention from those outside its high walls.

OCCUPATIONS

Cloth and silk traders continued to be well represented. Of 135 members' occupations recorded for the years 1732 to 1808, forty-three may be so categorised.[46] Some indeed were wealthy men, such as Sir Thomas Lombe, 'inventor' of England's first silk throwing machine.[47] Others were much less prosperous. A full study has not yet been undertaken, but these years, at least until the 1780s, seem to have been marked by an unusually large number of female apprentices and 'freemen', and it would be surprising if these women were not generally engaged in the cloth, particularly the silk, trade.[48]

However, the Company's most notable members were undoubtedly those who called themselves simply 'merchants' (numbering twenty in the list) or 'Turkey merchants' (seven). Sir William Joliffe, Sir John Williams ('the greatest exporter of cloth in England'), Richard Lockwood and Chauncy Townsend, all cut considerable figures in the commercial world of the day.[49] It is significant that Townsend was first described as a 'linen draper' but later became a 'merchant' when he developed his mineral extraction and Government contracting activities.

The Company indeed mirrors the growing role of the City of London in the provision of financial and other 'services'. That great burgeoning of a system of credit, stimulated by the long wars against Louis XIV and known as the Financial Revolution, is well reflected here. On a corporate level, the Company put its Hall at the disposal, first of the new and homeless Bank of England (during the latter part of 1694) and then, for subscription-raising purposes, of (successively) the ill-fated Land Bank, the new East India Company, the Royal Exchange Assurance Company and finally the South Sea Company.[50] As individuals, Mercers played their part too.[F] Michael Godfrey was one of the promoters and first Deputy Governor of the Bank of England (hence, presumably the invitation to use the Hall);[51] James Colebrooke, whose part in the annuity scheme was described in the last Chapter, was the founder of a bank first recorded as early as 1706, and which survived until his son's speculations killed it in the 1770s;[52] while Nathaniel Newnham (*c.* 1741–1809), after a few years helping to run the family grocery business and sugar bakery, set up a banking firm under his own name and others' in 1785.[53] Insurance too attracted attention. William Dunster, for example, was one of the main driving forces in the Royal Exchange Assurance Company from its inception until 1756;[54] while, somewhat more prosaically, Joseph Godfrey was the Secretary of the Sun Fire office from 1751 till shortly before his death in 1765.[55]

CIVIC LIFE

Despite all the humiliations of the eighteenth century, the Company retained its civic pride. It remained ready to play its part at Guildhall, and any threat to its position as the premier Livery Company was warmly countered. In 1697, for example, there was a suggestion that, instead of being the first company to greet William III on his ceremonial entry into the City in celebration of the Peace of Ryswick, members should for 'greater ease' stand outside the Hall; but 'upon consideration that their place was to sit on the right hand first to receive his Majesty before all other corporations within the City, it was unanimously carried in the Court of Assistants that the Company would take their place of precedency accordingly'.[56] When, on the same occasion, the Skinners, as the Lord Mayor's company, tried to oust the Mercers from their 'pride of place' they were firmly, and successfully, resisted.[57] In 1728 the Grocers, as the senior Sheriff's company, raised the same claim as the Skinners and again the Mercers maintained their entitlement to 'the right hand of fellowship upon all occasions in London', notwithstanding their member's lower rank.[58] The series was neatly concluded in 1760–1 when the Coronation of George III gave rise to another challenge from the Grocers, this time as the Lord Mayor's company. The Mercers' Assistants considered the 1728 precedent and instructed their Clerk to tell the Lord Mayor that 'as this Company is the chief of all the Companies in London this Court doth insist that the Master of the Company of right ought to take precedence of all other Companies of this City upon all public occasions of their meeting'.[59] The ensuing silence indicates that the message had the desired effect.

The Company's contribution to civic pageantry was necessarily limited by its indebtedness, but at least until bankruptcy loomed large a valiant effort was made to maintain tradition. Sir William Gore (1701–2) was the first Mercer Lord Mayor of this period, and when the question of a show was initially considered caution prevailed:[60]

> the Court considering whether it might be proper to mount any great Show on the ensuing Lord Mayor's Day were of the opinion that the present probability of the nation being speedily engaged [in war against Louis XIV], together with the ill state of the Company's affairs by reason of the great debt contracted and yet altogether unsatisified by rebuilding the Exchange, were sufficient grounds to obstruct any great expense on that occasion and thereupon the Court resolved that no other preparations be made for a Show ... than was [*sic*] in the Mayoralty of Sir John Chapman [in 1688–9] ...

Less than a week later, however, it was decided that there should be 'the addition of a chariot and a virgin to ride thereon and all other requisites';

[F] It will cause no surprise that in the bitter party-political contests of Walpole's time the Mercers polled strongly in favour of the Whigs. In the City parliamentary election of 1727 there were 85 'plumpers' for the Whigs and only 42 for the Tories, notwithstanding the fact that Sir John Williams and Richard Lockwood were standing as Tories. (There is a copy of the poll-book in Guildhall Library.)

FIG. 52. The swearing-in of Nathaniel Newnham, Mercer, Lord Mayor of London, 1782–3. Mezzotint after the oil painting by William Miller. The ceremony takes place in Guildhall. In the background, to the right, we can see John Bacon's enormous memorial to William Pitt, Earl of Chatham, commissioned by the Corporation of London in 1779; in the far distance, to the left, is John Francis Moore's statue of William Beckford, Lord Mayor in 1762. Both of them still stand in Guildhall.
By courtesy of Guildhall Art Gallery, Corporation of London

and what transpired was a full-scale pageant to which the Company, as well as the Rich Bachelors, contributed substantially.[61] Even as late as 1718 the Company commissioned an elaborate and expensive barge for future Thames 'triumphs'.[62]

Then the need for retrenchment really did begin to impress itself. Lord Mayor Williams's Show in 1735 was obviously a modest affair;[63] not long afterwards, when bankruptcy had to be formally acknowledged, even the yearly £100–£150 entertainments on Lord Mayor's Day were stopped and the barge sold;[64] while in 1761 the General Committee declined Common Council's general request for Companies to provide pageants on Lord Mayor's Day on the grounds that it would be 'improper' to do so 'in the light of the present circumstances of the Company'.[65] By the time the Company had begun to lift itself out of debt, the fashion for elaborate shows had fallen away and the Company contented itself with somewhat restrained support for Nathaniel Newnham in 1782.[66]

The Company's evident consciousness of City traditions is in marked contrast to the attitude of individual Mercers. Indifference is perhaps too strong a term, but it is remarkable how few members of the 'chief of all the Companies in London'

FIG. 53. Interior of the Royal Exchange, 1788. Building drawn by John Chapman, figures by Philip de Loutherburg, engraved by Bartolozzi. Issued with a dedication to the Prime Minister, William Pitt. Notice the robed and turbanned Asiatic figure on the bench to the right; beyond him, in the arcade, is a Jewish merchant. In the centre, his back turned to us, is another turbanned figure, this one possibly a Hungarian, with a Pole just beyond him, and a Dutchman with padded breeches towards the left. The dog in the centre is muzzled.
By courtesy of Guildhall Library, Corporation of London

troubled to take on office in Guildhall. Three Lord Mayors (Gore, Williams and Newnham) were supplemented by only eight other Aldermen and a mere dozen or so Common Councilmen throughout these years.[67] What is more, the figures, already low, were themselves declining. There were no Mercer Aldermen or Common Councilmen at all in 1800; and, with the contraction of the Company resulting from the fall in apprentice admissions and the prohibition on entry by redemption, the situation was likely only to get worse. It was only to be expected that relations between the City Corporation and the foremost Livery Company became more distant, and less predictable, than in the past.

FINANCIAL RECOVERY

The progress towards solvency was slow but sure. The first lottery for the repayment of £1,000 worth of bond debt was held in 1770. The Company could be excused for spending £13 on a modest dinner to mark the occasion because this truly was the turning point.[68] Further lotteries were held at yearly intervals, for larger and larger sums, as the years went by, and surplus revenue mounted.[69] By 1798 the settled estates were producing a clear £7,400 per annum.[70] The Company began to take a somewhat more relaxed view on 'unnecessary' expenditure. Applications for charity continued to receive a cold response,[71] but domestic needs were treated more warmly. In 1793 the Assistants' annual dinner to mark the election of the Master and Wardens, not held since the bankruptcy, was revived with the stipulation, adhered to for a mere six years, that expenditure should not exceed £40.[72] Four years later it was resolved to hold a Livery Dinner each year, with the cost of well over £100 plainly no deterrent.[73]

The last bond debt lottery was held in 1803 and this time, instead of a £13 dinner, the Company indulged the committee members concerned with plate worth £25 each.[74] The extravagance reflected a mixture of relief and confidence: relief that the century of humiliation and debt was at last over, and confidence that, with the slate now clean and revenues buoyant, the Company could adopt a much more expansive attitude towards its charitable and corporate endeavours. Money, 'the only engine that can give vigorous motion to the great and needful work',[G] had returned.

[G] See above, p. 80.

CHAPTER IX

THE EARLY NINETEENTH CENTURY

In 1803, when the final elimination of the bond debt was in sight, the Company instigated a full-scale review of its financial position.[1] Each estate and trust was examined to establish the amount of income being generated, the extent of any surplus, whether such surplus was available for the Company's own use or only for the trusts, and the need to make good any past mistakes or omissions. The result was not merely a spate of suggestions as to how better fulfil its charitable obligations, but also a thorough overhaul of the Company's administrative arrangements.

INTERNAL REFORMS

The appearance of a series of detailed reports on the charities was bound to raise questions about Company management. In December 1804 a member of the General Committee endeavoured, without success, to have the following resolutions adopted:[2]

> that the estates under the direction of the Company amounting to about £20,000 per annum, and occupied by about 450 tenants, are capable of much improvement and that it is expedient that a proper person be appointed to give particular information to the Committee respecting the condition thereof previous to any renewal of leases

and

> that the accounts of the Company should be more immediately under the inspection of some proper person previous to their being laid before the Court of Assistants for their examination and sanction.

This initiative was evidently considered premature or presumptuous, but the essence of it was soon given official blessing. In May of the following year William Palmer was thanked for his 'assiduity' in investigating and explaining the accounts of the Company, and was asked to advise the Clerk on improvements.[3] Palmer, in fact, went on to devise an entirely 'new mode' of accounts, involving the removal of personal responsibility from the Wardens and the centralisation of control under the Clerk and his staff, and this was duly, and gratefully, adopted in December 1806.[A4]

As far as the estates were concerned, these came under consideration in December 1805 and March 1806. The main concern was insurance, and after a report by another of its members, W. E. Ward, the General Committee instituted a number of provisions designed to make sure that premises were always adequately covered. However, there were also other measures and these included the revision of the Company's model lease, the granting of leases to tenants-at-will, a report by the Surveyor on the condition of the property, and improvements to the tenants' ledger and rental book.[5]

More general reforms were also put in hand. For example, directions were given for the taking of minutes at Court and Committee meetings so as to ensure that outstanding points were followed up.[6] Still more importantly, William Palmer was asked to make a review of the 'by-laws, rules and orders of the Company' to enable the Committee to 'make such selection therefrom and give such directions for the observance thereof as may tend to the better regulation of the Company's affairs'.[7]

[A] William Palmer made an important contribution to the Company's affairs at this time, as witness also his revision of the by-laws (see below) and involvement in the Hall debate (see p. 143 below). He was an East India Merchant. One of his sons, J. H. Palmer, became Governor of the Bank of England, and one of his grandsons was the William Palmer who defended the rights of the Gresham lecturers in the 1830s (see p. 133).

FIG. 54. William Palmer, Master of the Mercers' Company, 1795–6. The portrait has been made from a miniature by Paul Fischer, which was itself after a portrait, taken from life, by James Northcote, RA. Today it hangs in the Reception area outside the Livery Hall.
Mercers' Company

Palmer's careful work formed the basis of the 1808 code to which reference has already been made; but, of course, the 'better regulation of the Company's affairs' could not really be achieved by these domestic changes but rather by reforms in the trusts themselves.

ST PAUL'S SCHOOL

The most controversial and startling conclusion of the Select Committee's work concerned an alleged debt owed by the Company to the Colet estate. Surpluses had been drawn off over the years, accounts blended and some money simply misapplied. The total sum involved was no less than £34,000.[8] Despite the objection of some members,[9] the Company was sufficiently persuaded of the need to investigate its responsibility for the missing money to prepare a Case for counsel.[10] Unfortunately, the two eminent lawyers consulted took different views. The first one, Sir Samuel Romilly, advised that the debt *was* still owed, notwithstanding the passage of time;[11] while the second, Sir Vicary Gibbs, thought the Company could assume the debt had been extinguished and need only wait for a claim to arise.[12] Nevertheless a joint opinion that the £34,000 could not be safely used for any other purpose for fear of future proceedings for restitution,[13] in effect, meant that caution, and Romilly, prevailed; and, eventually, the Company made provision for repayment.

The decision, in June 1808, to set aside an initial £5,000 roused the opponents of restitution to new heights of indignation. Not only was the debt imaginary, or if real then dead, but its repayment constituted a fraud on the funds from which the money was being taken.[14] Even the House Warden, whose authority was needed to release the £5,000, adopted this argument.[15] But at length, and despite one very narrow vote,[16] the repayment fund was instituted. The actual liquidation of the debt did not begin until 1814, and thus gave the opportunity for further protest to be raised. A denial of the Company's right to use surplus revenue as it pleased may well be connected with the St Paul's School debt (it involved two of the earlier dissentients)[17] and the actual decision to set aside £1,000 twice a year was opposed by five Assistants.[18] By the time the debt was finally eliminated in 1824 there had been yet another flurry of discontent. A resolution was proposed for the appointment of a committee to revise all the accounts and reports relating to the presumed 'debt', but consideration of it was postponed (*sine die*, as it transpired).[19]

Another major debate about St Paul's School arose from the second of the 1803 Committee's conclusions. It was generally recognised that the post-Fire School building was in need of repair or reconstruction, and one obvious solution was to sell the valuable site and use the proceeds to establish the School in quieter, healthier surroundings outside London. The Select Committee sketched out a possible plan of action,[20] but the subsequent years were largely devoted to the question of the debt, and it was not until 1809 that the future of the School was considered in any detail. It is clear that the Assistants cared as deeply about this issue as the debt, and it was not without a warm debate that a committee was appointed even to review the possible options.[21] The committee had no difficulty in agreeing that alterations to the building were needed, and they were certainly prepared to obtain Counsel's opinion on the legality of taking the School out of London and creating at least a number of boarding places. But when they were told that they would have to obtain the sanction of the Court of Chancery for such changes, they were split seven votes to seven in authorising the preparation of such proceedings until the Chairman placed his casting vote in favour.[22] Their divisions were mirrored in the Court of Assistants where, after the initial adoption of the report, a resolution that 'the business of St. Paul's School shall in future be carried on in the usual manner' produced another equal vote, though on this occasion the Master declined to vote again.[23] Technically, therefore, the Court had plumped for change, but it seems clear that the absence of a clear majority dissuaded the proponents of reform from pressing the issue.

Certainly nothing further was said for over four years and then, in June 1814, a motion for the removal of St Paul's School was decisively defeated by eleven votes to seven.[24] The matter was again raised in 1816 but, although there was a vote in favour of the general principle of removal if inexpensive boarding thereby resulted, the more significant resolution concerned an inspection of the state of the buildings by the Surveyor with a brief to suggest improvements.[25] This set in train, first the passage of a private Act of Parliament enabling the Company to enlarge the School site,[26] secondly the decision to rebuild (and not merely enlarge) the existing building at an estimated cost of £16,000,[27] and finally in 1824 the completion of the new School for an actual cost of £23,000.[28]

The beneficiary of these improved premises was John Sleath (High Master, 1814–37) and he certainly appears to have done them justice: his time in office was a successful one, exemplified best perhaps by the career of Benjamin Jowett, the celebrated Master of Balliol, who was a pupil between 1829 and 1836.[29] However, as far as the Company was concerned, Sleath was associated less with his pedagogic achievements than with his attempts to change the terms of his appointment. In 1817 Sleath first raised an objection to his annual re-election, but he was told that 'the trustees in no respect considered the proceeding a mere form; on the contrary it is a control which they are justified by high legal authority in insisting on as a necessary guarantee for the safety of their own rights'.[30] Despite this firm rebuff, Sleath repeated his challenge in 1820, and this time with more persistence. He described the process of yearly 'dismissal' as 'degrading' but at the same time purely a matter of form, 'more honoured in the breach than in the observance'.[31] This immediately produced a threat of *real* dismissal unless Sleath acknowledged the Company's right. Almost as quickly Sleath withdrew his objection and asked to be reinstated.[32] The condescending tone of the response may be imagined. The Company did not merely reaffirm its constitutional position but also took the opportunity to impose

FIG. 55. St Paul's School, shortly after its third rebuilding. By Thomas Hosmer Shepherd for James Elmes's *Metropolitan Improvements*, 1827.
Mercers' Company

some other limitations on the High Master's power.[33] Sleath thus paid a price for his stand, though it was not a heavy one, and the effect on the educational progress of the School seems to have been negligible.

Meanwhile the revenues of the Colet estate continued to rise. Stepney, for example, was extensively developed during this period and an income of £863 in 1813 became £4,000 and more by 1840.[34] The Company trustees must have begun to question the wisdom of rebuilding the School on the existing site in 1822–4. Would it not have been better to have waited for still more money to become available and then taken the School out of London (which itself would have released additional funds)? Common sense, quite apart from the promptings of High Master Roberts,[B] should have dictated this course. As it was, the School made the best of its new and expensive building for a mere sixty years before the inevitable removal took place. By then a rather different social and political climate prevailed and the future development of St Paul's School was discussed in a much more critical, and much more public, manner.

HORSHAM[35]

In the case of Collyer's School, the Company's review of its charities at the beginning of the

[B] In August 1809 Roberts had written at length to the Assistants lamenting 'the perpetual vociferation in the streets and the noises of all sorts of carriages rapidly and incessantly rolling by the School'. AC, 25 January 1810.

century was less a case of accountancy or archival investigation than simple observation. When Thomas and William Palmer visited the School in 1807, after the resignation of Headmaster Jameson, they found no pupils whatsoever and, what was worse, the Usher, James Thornton, was the son of the proprietor of the rival academy in the town and was determined to thwart the Company's efforts at reform. However, undeterred by threats that they would suffer the same fate as the Merchant Taylors who had lost control of a Wolverhampton School, the Mercers demanded that the parish make adequate proposals for the better regulation of the School. Otherwise, the Company warned, the entirely gratuitous additions to the original sixteenth-century salaries would be withdrawn. Eventually a plan acceptable to both sides (and giving the Company considerable safeguards and powers, including the right to re-elect the Master and Usher in the manner of St Paul's School) was adopted and William Palmer went down to obtain the signatures of the Master and Usher. This was Thornton's opportunity, and he seized it. His refusal to sign at the behest of those whom he dubbed 'little tyrants' necessitated the appointment of a temporary Usher and, more importantly, an application to the Court of Chancery for confirmation of the trustees' authority. It was not until 1813 that the Lord Chancellor made the necessary decree, and by then Thornton, the cause of all the difficulty, had resigned both his office and his claims in return for £100 towards his legal costs. However, the decree did serve the useful purpose of minimising the scope for those disagreements which were always likely to arise, with or without obstreperous Ushers, in Collyer's rather curious constitutional arrangements. The decree, in fact, largely confirmed the plan rejected by Thornton, with the exception of the re-election provision, and appears to have worked quite well. Another Master–Usher quarrel occurred in 1821 but, when the former resigned, his successor, William Pirie, was able to bring a long period of tranquillity and scholastic achievement to the School. In 1839 it was reported that the School was 'exceedingly well conducted, extremely useful to the town of Horsham and reflecting great credit on the memory of its benevolent founder', and the Company readily authorised the rebuilding of the schoolhouse, at the eventual cost of over £2,600. The encomium was deserved, but perhaps too modest. The Company too deserves praise for putting the School back on its feet in 1807–13 and standing firm against Thornton's legalistic obstructionism.

MERCERS' SCHOOL[36]

The Chapel School was a voluntary commitment, funded out of the Company's own 'Henry VIII' estate (i.e. the property, including the Hall site, acquired at the Reformation). There was no obligation on the Company to do so, but when the Cheapside rents increased, it was thought that some of the extra money should be spent on Mercers' School. Accordingly, when the review of Company commitments at the beginning of the nineteenth century coincided with the death (in March 1804) of the School's Headmaster, the General Committee was ready to recommend quite radical reforms. On the constitutional side, the School at long last acquired a 'governing body': the Master and Wardens were to 'take upon themselves the management of the School and to attend to the well ordering of the same'; while on the educational side, there was to be a new 'Writing, Arithmetic and Accounts' Master at £80 per annum (a post admirably filled in due course by John Wills).[37] The next major development occurred in 1825 and again sprang from healthy finances. Indeed, the Assistants explicitly asked the Committee to 'take into consideration the state of funds of the Henry VIII estate and [give its] opinion [as to] any and what improvement can be made in respect of Mercers' Chapel School'. A surplus of £8,000 prompted the Committee to suggest not merely an increase in the number of scholars on the foundation but also a new schoolroom on the site of the recently vacated Whittington College.[38] As it transpired, legal rights claimed by the parish thwarted that scheme, but there were three houses nearby on

College Hill which could be used instead and, after the expenditure of £4,760, the new school building was ready for use in 1832. By the time Wills and his equally estimable Headmaster, the Revd Isaac Hill, retired from their respective positions later in the 1830s, the School was able to forget its unhappy experiences in the previous century and could look forward with confidence.

WHITTINGTON COLLEGE[39]

When the Select Committee looked at the Whittington estate in 1803–4, it recommended that the former practice of using the surplus revenue for general corporate purposes be discontinued. Apart from £63 per annum due to the Company in respect of a rent charge purchased in 1549, the property had been entrusted for *charitable* uses only. The immediate consequence of this decision was to charge the Whittington estate with various pensions and gifts to needy Company members. Later the College itself began to benefit. In the early 1820s, plans were formulated to increase the number of resident almswomen and create an equal number of outpensions. Eventually the figure of thirty was decided on and the question of enlarged accommodation at once raised itself. The College Hill site was deemed too small to permit a simple rebuilding, and so attention was turned to Highgate, and more especially the spot where Whittington was alleged to have heard Bow Bells. A site was acquired and the new College built in 1824 at a cost of £13,500. Fresh rules were passed for the occasion and their detailed concern with the residents' moral welfare and discipline might be taken to indicate either Christian rectitude or at least a deference to the founder's intentions on the Company's part. However, the wholesale neglect of the rules revealed by subsequent visitations suggests that not merely were the rules ill-framed, but that they were not systematically implemented either. Nevertheless, the mere existence of the Highgate College (whatever its administrative failings) and the enlarged scope of the charity's activities did the Company much credit; and with the Whittington Estate's City rents steadily increasing there was every prospect that Whittington's largesse would become still more bountiful in the years to come.

THE MONEY LEGACY CHARITIES

The so-called money legacy charities also benefited from the tidying-up process in these years. In this case, however, it was not the Mercers' own initiative, in the shape of the Select Committee reports of 1803–4, which led to change, but rather the possibility of a hostile Court action.

It will be recalled that the Company had received, in the sixteenth and early seventeenth centuries, a number of bequests of money to be used for loans to young members of the Company starting up in trade, subject to the requirement that the recipients pay interest on their loans in support of the poor or needy. These sums had been early casualties of the Company's desperate need for money in the Restoration period, and in most cases no loans were made after the Great Fire. When the bankruptcy occurred eighty years later, the General Committee decided to write off these debts, the rationale evidently being that since the legacies had been given to the Company for the benefit of members they 'ought not to be made a charge upon the Company to the prejudice of their creditors'.[40] Accordingly the sums were removed from the books and were thus apparently deemed not to qualify as 'arrears' for the purposes of the Act of 1764 which provided for repayment of such arrears before the discharge of the bond debts. For presumably the same reasons, the arrears do not even seem to have nagged at the conscience of the extremely thorough Select Committee in 1803–4. It was not until Lady Campden's equally neglected loan scheme[C] became the subject of a successful Chancery lawsuit (and eventually a formal 'scheme') that the Company looked again at its other forgotten money legacies.

[C] See above, p. 92.

PLATE XV

A. (above) Mercers' School, College Hill; watercolour by an unknown artist, as rebuilt in 1832.
Mercers' Company

B. (left) The entrance to Mercers' Hall in Cheapside, watercolour by George Shepherd, 1811. The magnificent porch was taken down during the restoration of the Hall in 1880, and was re-erected as the entrance to Swanage Town Hall, which it still adorns.
Mercers' Company

A. Whittington College, Highgate, painted by George Smith, Company Surveyor, *c.* 1824. Founded in 1424, it was first located at College Hill; it moved to Highgate in 1824; the modern Whittington College is at East Grinstead, Sussex. The ambitious edifice shown here should be compared with the building as erected (Fig. 57).
Mercers' Company

B. The Mercers' arms, engraved and hand-coloured by Charles Cope, *c.* 1850.
Mercers' Company

Fig. 56. Mercers' School, College Hill, 1829.
Mercers' Company

Fig. 57 (below). Whittington College, Highgate, by Thomas Hosmer Shepherd, engraved by T. Dale, for James Elmes's *Metropolitan Improvements*, 1827.
Mercers' Company

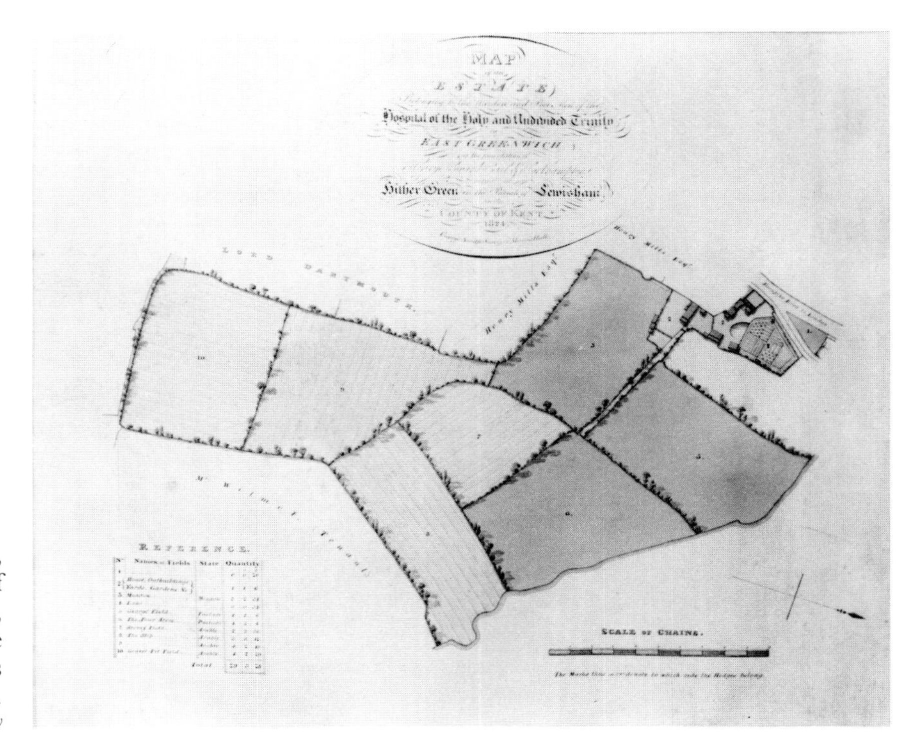

FIG. 58. Hither Green, Lewisham, Earl of Northampton's estate, surveyed and drawn by George Smith, the Company's Surveyor, 1824.
Mercers' Company

The first result was a long committee report in May 1831 which concluded that:[41]

[this] Committee concurs in the opinion of the [General] Committee in 1745 that these legacies being for the benefit of the Company ought not to be considered as a charge to the Company's creditors, but it by no means follows that when these debts were paid that these legacies should not be again appropriated to the original purpose and looking again at the Vice-Chancellor's decision in the case of Lady Campden's legacy they cannot conceive any reason why the same principle should not be applied to the [other] bequests . . .

There followed a voluntary application to the Court and this led in turn to a scheme which amalgamated other money legacies (including Fishborne's £1,000[D]) and imposed one simple set of terms in accordance with which loans were to be made.[42] At long last, and not without some 'encouragement', the Company had set the record straight. No doubt it should have happened much earlier, but to its credit, when the principles of its trusteeship were directly challenged, the Company made amends.

D See above, p. [80].

THE GRESHAM LECTURES[43]

The resolution of the Company's financial problems made little difference to Gresham College. The Select Committee recognised, of course, that the Company was under no obligation to devote any surpluses to the trust,[44] but even if the opportunity for generosity arose from an increase in Royal Exchange rents, the Company was more likely to recoup past losses than devote more money to its unhappy charity. The College's problems were not fundamentally financial. The stipends may have been modest and the premises unsatisfactory, but these were peripheral issues. The heart of the difficulty lay in devising a format for the lectures which would adhere to the spirit of the founder's wishes, reconcile the conflicting interests of the Joint Committee and the lecturers, yet also capture the imagination of a largely indifferent public.

By selling the College itself to the Customs and Excise, the trustees had removed the lectures' separate identity and, though the performance of the lectures before 1768 gave precious little justification for optimism, it was generally recognised that the rather anonymous accommodation the 'College' enjoyed in the Royal Exchange was an impediment to rejuvenation. Efforts *were* made in 1799 and 1815 to give the lectures held in the Exchange more publicity, but these evidently had little effect. Attendances averaging twenty or so were scarcely satisfactory, and alternative schemes came up for consideration. The first serious suggestion concerned the London Institution for the Advancement of Literature and the Diffusion of Useful Knowledge, founded in 1805 and soon to establish itself at Moorfields. An initial proposal in 1815, however, was regarded as too radical, amounting effectively to a merger of the two schemes and thus arousing fears of a destruction of Gresham's Trust. A second plan, in 1820, was more tactfully presented but failed to remove all the earlier concern and met with a similar rebuff. Then in 1829 Common Council took the initiative and, after obtaining encouragement from the Attorney-General on its power to alter the lectures, the Gresham Committee reopened negotiations with the London Institution and agreed on a comfortably vague arrangement for a trial period. Now it was the turn of the lecturers to become involved and, by their refusal to allow the lectures to become an appendage to the London Institution, they forced the Committee to abandon the plans.

FIG. 59. Edward Taylor, Gresham Professor of Music, 1837–63. He established the Gresham Music Library, now at Guildhall Library.
By courtesy of Guildhall Library, Corporation of London

The lecturers were in fact to drive the City and the Company close to distraction over the coming years. Angered by what they had come to see as a fundamental weakening of the College's position in the sell-out of 1768, the lecturers were in no mood to co-operate. They were determined to retain their independence and, though they were prepared to move from the Exchange (for all their professed pleasure at being in the heart of Gresham's City they realised how tucked away they were), they had no desire to cohabit, still less to 'merge', with another institution interested only in Gresham's money and prestige. Ironically, since this same obstinacy extended also to attempts to alter the conduct of lectures (not merely their venue), the lecturers proved unable to reduce the pressure for change by judicious concessions on less fundamental matters. Thus an objection even to the advance distribution of syllabuses, as proposed in 1832, led the Committee to abandon any hope of 'securing the will of the liberal donor being executed in an effectual manner': despair which in fact not only caused them to renounce measures which the lecturers could have accepted but also spurred them on in their search for an alternative to the Royal Exchange.

In 1833 it was Guildhall which came under scrutiny and was quickly rejected by the lecturers; and then in the following year the City of London School, just being established, was given prolonged consideration. At first both 'sides' of the Gresham Committee appear to have been equally

FIG. 60. The new Gresham College in Basinghall Street. Drawn by Thomas Hosmer Shepherd, engraved by J. Taylor, 1842.
Mercers' Company

interested in the idea, but after a while it became clear that the Mercers were a good deal less enthusiastic than the City. When in 1836 Common Council refused to accept the Committee's admission of defeat in the face of the lecturers' opposition and called for a reconsideration, the Mercers began to side with the lecturers. In March 1837 the Court of Assistants gave a robust response to a challenge to its attitude.[45] It acknowledged as axiomatic that it was 'highly desirable to give effect to any well arranged plan for rendering the lectures founded by Sir Thomas Gresham of more general and permanent utility'. The problem was not whether, but how, the lectures should be reformed. So far as the City of London School plan was concerned:

> this Court is of the opinion that such removal would be highly inexpedient as the lectures were not founded for the purposes of delivering to youth the elementary principles of the sciences, forming the subjects of the lectures, but for the benefit of those of maturer judgement, and for the advancement of the sciences in the higher departments. And moreover that if it were thought right to annex the lectures to such an institution, the claims of St. Paul's School must be generally admitted to be prior to that of any other in the City of London.[E]

The Assistants also pointed out that:

> a mere change of place for the delivery of the lectures, either by appropriating any existing building or by erecting any new building exclusively for that purpose, without such other changes as the times and circumstances seem to require, will fail to secure the objects avowed in the first resolution.

[E] The possibility of combining the Colet and Gresham trusts in some way had been the subject of discussion on at least two previous occasions. See an anonymous letter in 1816 when it was suggested that a lecture room could be constructed adjacent to a rebuilt School (W.P.P. 1/35/292) and Jean Imray's draft typescript Memoir on the history of the Gresham lectures for a proposal in 1833 (which the High Master scotched as likely to cause too much disruption).

The Court concluded with an interesting, and almost prophetic,[F] reference to the recently incorporated University of London as a possible means of reforming the lectures in a way which would 'at once preserve the integrity of the institution and promote the desired end of general and permanent utility'.

It is difficult not to associate this change of mind with the influence of the newly-appointed Gresham Professor of Law, William Palmer, who staunchly opposed attaching the lectures to any other institution.[46] Palmer was also a Mercer and, as a scholarly barrister, his opinions carried considerable weight in the Company. His success in persuading fellow members to reassess their position came at a critical juncture, for the City had just lost patience with the lecturers' obstructionism and had taken legal advice on pressing on without their consent. The result was encouraging, but the City was told that it had to act jointly with the Mercers. Palmer, if Palmer it was, had managed to forestall the move in the nick of time.

Meanwhile outsiders had not given up hope of grafting the Gresham benefaction on to their own ventures. One of the most persistent was Maria Hackett, sponsor of the attempt to restore and preserve the dilapidated Crosby Hall,[G] then still situated in Bishopsgate.[47] Nothing seemed more appropriate to her than that the lifeless Gresham lectures should be reinvigorated in Gresham's old parish. She enlisted a number of influential supporters, including J. W. Burgon, prize-winning author of *The Life and Times of Sir Thomas Gresham* (1839).[48] However, even her powers of persuasion were insufficient to convince the City and Mercers. Burgon was outraged:[49]

> I am quite disgusted with the Gresham Committee. The preponderance of crooked fellows among them, however, explains every crooked proceeding. Radicals are always crooked fellows in everything.[H]

Miss Hackett was left to see her project founder (the Hall's rescue being postponed until 1908 when it was taken off to Chelsea) and Burgon took his Tory indignation to Oxford where he became a leading High Churchman.

In a few hours during the night of 10 January 1838, the long-drawn-out debate on the future of the Gresham lectures was quite literally overtaken by events. The effects of the fire which destroyed the Royal Exchange are more fully described below,[I] but the loss of the lecture room and library made at least an interim decision on the Gresham lectures essential. Although the move was expressly stated to be 'without prejudice', the decision to have the lectures delivered, pro tem, in the City of London School caused Palmer and his fellow lecturers much concern and prompted them to press for the express reservation of their right to be reinstated either in the Royal Exchange or in another separate building in the rebuilding Act for which the Committee applied to Parliament. The lecturers thought that this was the least the legislature should do 'to redress the evil and unequal bargain effected in the alienation of Gresham College [in 1768]'. The Committee opposed the lecturers' petition, but the influence of certain MPs ensured that the Act for 'Improving the Site of the Royal Exchange' clearly stated that the principal purpose of the Gresham Trust was to support Gresham College (not the Royal Exchange, as was generally supposed) and that the Gresham Committee remained bound to support the College, notwithstanding the passage of the Act.[50]

Mindful of this warning and conscious of the lecturers' capacity for opposition, the Committee at least intended to incorporate the Gresham lecture room and library in the rebuilt Exchange. Then in 1841 they received an attractive offer for the proposed accommodation, and resolved that 'it will be expedient to appropriate that portion of the new building at present allotted for the Gresham lectures to other purposes, provided the

[F] See below, p. 188.

[G] Crosby Hall had started life as a rich merchant's mansion, but was later used for religious and commercial purposes. By this time it was a warehouse.

[H] The City Corporation at least was at this time renowned for its Whiggery.

[I] See below, pp. 134–40.

FIG. 61. The disastrous fire at the Royal Exchange, 10 January 1838. A popular print showing the blaze which could be seen twenty-four miles away at Windsor to the south-west, and at Roydon Mount near Epping, eighteen miles to the east.
By courtesy of Guildhall Library, Corporation of London

same can be effected satisfactorily to all parties interested'.[51] This was a weighty proviso in the light of past events, but this time the lecturers were eventually persuaded to move. Not, of course, to another institution, but to a separate purpose-built establishment on the corner of Basinghall Street and Cateaton (later Gresham) Street. There in November 1843 the lecturers were installed, with a library, committee room, lecture room and gallery, and private rooms in the attic. All at a cost of £14,000.[52] The lecturers' long campaign had won the day. Whether they would make proper use of their new surroundings remained to be seen. The Committee at least would have been aware that a 'mere change of place ... without such other changes as the times and circumstances seem to require' would fail to render the lectures founded by Sir Thomas Gresham 'of more general and permanent utility'. The price of continued failure would be that outsiders with less charitable intentions than the London Institution and Maria Hackett would start taking an interest in Gresham College and try to force the City, Mercers and lecturers alike to adopt less palatable remedies for the College's ills than those mooted in the 1820s and 1830s.

THE ROYAL EXCHANGE

The Select Committee's solemn pronouncement in 1804 that the Company could use the surplus revenue from the Gresham Trust for its own purposes must have provoked a good deal of hollow laughter. The prospect of the Royal

Exchange offering any recompense for the financial disasters of the past was remote indeed. Instead it retained all the potential of a monstrous liability should decay, or still worse destruction, strike again. In fact a few years later the building's tower was found to be in need of reconstruction and further investigation revealed a host of other problems caused partly by old age and partly by the scarcity of good materials after the Great Fire. Between 1819 and 1825, a small matter of £46,500 had to be spent shoring up the second Exchange.[53] That seemed to have effectively exorcised the malignant Gresham spirit for the foreseeable future, but worse was to follow. The 1838 fire gutted the second Exchange as thoroughly as its 1666 counterpart had gutted the first, and the Joint Committee of the City and the Mercers was once again faced with the task of starting all over again. This time there was at least some assistance from the insurers; but the £45,000 from (appropriately enough) the Royal Exchange Assurance Company[54] fell well short of the £150,000 which soon emerged as the likely cost of rebuilding on the same scale.

It would be easy to assume therefore that both the City and the Company approached their task with something bordering on despair; but certainly as far as the City was concerned this was emphatically not the case. From the start the City side of the Joint Gresham Committee took the initiative in the discussions and argued warmly for an open-handed approach to the problem. At the first informal meeting the City Committee chairman, R. L. Jones, said that the City believed that 'the Exchange should be enlarged and a building erected that should be an ornament to the City and worthy of the metropolis of this country'. When reminded that the Gresham Trust was 'considerably indebted' to the City and the Company, Jones replied that 'it would be quite useless now to think of these debts and they had better be thrown overboard altogether . . . the two Corporations should now take an enlarged view of the matter and erect a building that would do them credit'. He then outlined a scheme for an open, oblong structure in place of the present hemmed-in, square site. Jones expressed his confidence that the Government would afford the Gresham trustees 'such necessary assistance as would enable them to purchase and clear the additional ground . . .'. The claim on the Government's generosity was twofold: first, the advantages the public would gain from the street improvements (particularly 'a good, open street' from Bank to Bishopsgate) which would be part and parcel of the scheme, and secondly the Excise Office 'bargain'. The money to build the new Exchange itself would come from the City and the Company 'so as to preserve the Gresham Trust entire'.[55]

The Company was much less sanguine than Jones and his colleagues. At first the Company Side responded that 'they do not consider it to be within their province to incur any material excess of charge beyond that which will appertain to their proportion upon the reinstatement of the former building, unless a reasonable prospect be held out of an adequate return for such increased expenditure'.[56] When they had conceded the principle of enlarging the site, the Company Side still had expense uppermost in their minds. Should it eventually prove necessary to rebuild on the present site, might some of the old building be retained? The surveyors gave a firm negative to the suggestion.[57]

By early March the Company Side was able to place the City's 'suggestions' formally before the Company. These were:[58]

1st. That the Royal Exchange be rebuilt upon an enlarged scale in such manner as to afford increased accommodation to the mercantile interests, to improve contiguous approaches, and to render the building in all respects worthy of this great metropolis, and in order to effect this it will be necessary to take down the whole of Bank Buildings and a considerable number of houses between Cornhill and Threadneedle Street at the eastern end of the present site of the Exchange.

2nd. That such new Exchange may be erected for the sum of £150,000 which should be paid by the Corporation of London and the Mercers' Company in equal moieties, they being reimbursed (after paying the Gresham lecturers etc.) out of the future surplus income of the Gresham estate.

3rd. That the Gresham trustees give up to the public so much of the ground now forming part of the Royal Exchange as should be required for the public convenience and in lieu thereof the site of the ground on which the proposed Exchange and buildings shall be erected shall become part of the Gresham trust.

4th. In as much as all the outlay beyond the said sum of £150,000 will be rendered necessary for the public convenience and not for the benefit of the Gresham Trust, an application be made by the Corporation and the Mercers' Company to Her Majesty's Government for a grant of a sum of money sufficient for that purpose, which it is apprehended will not exceed £200,000.

The Committee recommended that the Company concur with the City's plan, but subject to the following conditions:

1st. That the proposed new ground for the Exchange be obtained and conveyed to the Gresham Trust in lieu of the ground taken from that trust for public improvement.

2nd. That the design, plan, elevation and arrangements for the Royal Exchange be mutually agreed by the City and Company under condition that the cost shall not exceed £150,000.

3rd. That the sum of £45,000 to be received from the Royal Exchange Fire Assurance office be first applied toward the expense of rebuilding and the difference to be supplied by the City and the Company in equal proportions to make up £150,000 if required.

4th. That the Gresham [Trust] be in no way mixed up with any other City improvements than that of building the Royal Exchange in a manner that shall be creditable to the City and Company.

Even these careful stipulations did not pass entirely without demur. An interesting amendment was moved:

1st. That the Committee be requested to ascertain whether there are any persons desirous of taking the site upon which the Royal Exchange stood on a building lease and upon what terms.

2nd. If such terms be advantageous then the Committee is hereby instructed to apply to Parliament for powers to enable trustees to receive such terms for benefit of a trust.

Although it was defeated, the amendment reinforces the general impression that the Company was much more suspicious of the rebuilding scheme than the City. Doubtless this was partly because the City regarded the fire as an opportunity to carry out some municipal improvements in its role as local authority, a point of view which the Company did not share. Perhaps also the City could afford to be more relaxed about the financial commitment which the proposals entailed. It was certainly already adept at raising large sums for such projects,[59] whereas the Company had no equivalent experience. Even after the decision to concur with the City's scheme had been taken, the Company remained vigilant to ensure that its obligations, particularly the financial obligations, were kept within bounds. Enforcing the £150,000 maximum, limiting the compensation payable to the former tenants of the Exchange and ensuring adequate rent from the new buildings, all received close attention,[60] and the City's Act for 'Improving the Site of the Royal Exchange and the City of London and the Avenues adjoining thereto' was appropriately amended.[61] When the Company came to approve the ground plan the following resolution was adopted:[62]

this [General] Court feeling it necessary that in any plans which may be produced for the rebuilding of the Royal Exchange due consideration should be paid to reducing the claims for compensation on the part of the old tenants as much as possible [i.e. by making sure they could be offered very similar premises in the new building] and securing an adequate rent from new tenants to repay the Company for the advance which they will be called upon to make as their moiety of the expense of the new building, feel confident that the Committee, on the Mercers' Side, will take every means in their power to provide for the same and to prevent the Company being directly or indirectly committed in regard to any plan having a different tendency, due regard being paid to the character of the building.

'Due regard' was a conveniently vague expression and there can be little doubt that the Mercers wished to subordinate architecture to economics.

As late as October 1839 when a Case was submitted to Counsel, the Company thought fit to include in its questions 'whether they are now bound to rebuild [the Royal Exchange]' and also 'whether the trustees can let the site of the Royal

FIG. 62. The third Royal Exchange: one of a series of contract plans by George Smith, Company Surveyor, 1841.
Mercers' Company

FIG. 63. Prince Albert laying the foundation stone of the third Royal Exchange, 17 January 1842. Lithograph by Thomas Allom.
By courtesy of Guildhall Library, Corporation of London

Exchange on a building lease, reserving [merely] sufficient rents to satisfy the annuities given by Sir Thomas Gresham's will and having regard to the other trusts thereof'. Sir William Follett's brisk replies in the affirmative and negative respectively should not obscure the significance of the questions having been asked in the first place.[63]

The long and rather embarrassing rigmarole to select a suitable architect, resulting eventually in the choice of William Tite and his elaborate classical design, is an object lesson in how not to conduct such competitions, but it is not of any real relevance to this Chapter's theme.[J] [64] Of more interest is the Company's reaction when finally confronted with drawings requiring its approval. Not only did it ask the Mercers' Side to report on certain architectural features it found disquieting, but it also asked for further information on the probable rental to be obtained from the proposed building.[65] Its subsequent approval of the plan was given only after some determined resistance by a minority of Assistants who were unimpressed by the argument that changes in detail should be discussed after this initial formal step.[66] One of the dissentients, the former Governor of the Bank of England, J. H. Palmer,[K] subsequently felt obliged to resign from the Joint Grand Committee, explaining that the suggested alterations, far from being points of detail, were 'indispensable to ensure the construction of an appropriate edifice and at the same time to secure an adequate revenue to the trust . . .'.[67]

The foundation stone of the third Royal Exchange was laid, with much ceremony, by Prince Albert on 17 January 1842 and the building was opened, with even greater ceremony, by Queen Victoria on 28 October 1844.[68] The eventual cost, with the £150,000 maximum inevitably

Fig. 64. Statue of Queen Victoria by William Hamo Thornycroft, RA, 1896, for the Royal Exchange.
Mercers' Company

[J] It is generally believed that the Committee should not have allowed Tite, originally appointed as an assessor only, to enter the re-run competition, and that they should have chosen C. R. Cockerell's superior design. The propriety of Tite's involvement and the deficiencies of his work caused a good deal of controversy at the time. Cockerell was deeply hurt by the affair.

[K] For whom see above, p. 123 n.]. He was of course the uncle of the Gresham lecturer, William Palmer.

Fig. 65. Irish estate plan: Kilrea, by Daniel Watney, the Company Surveyor, 1876. The Company no longer owns the Irish estate.
Mercers' Company

exceeded, though not by much, was no great burden to the Company. A loan facility of £50,000 was easily arranged with the Bank of England, and the Master and Wardens were disarmingly confident about the Company's ability to repay:[69]

> The annual surplus revenue of the Company will in all probability be more than sufficient to pay the interest while the Company's moiety calculated at £5,000 per annum of the rents expected from the new Royal Exchange will suffice for the yearly extinction of the debt.

In a sense, therefore, the Company's recurrent anxiety about the financial aspects of the rebuilding had been misplaced. The Mercers had failed to realise that they were living in times quite removed from those of the last rebuilding. Substantially increased property revenues made the 'crash' of 1745 nothing worse than a dark memory. 'Surpluses' were now commonplace. Nevertheless it is also easy to appreciate why the Company had been so cautious. The Gresham Trust had been a main cause, if not the only one, of the Company's bankruptcy, and the fear that the consequences of 1666 would be repeated in 1838 must have been very real. When this trepidation is placed alongside the suspicions of a fiercely independent corporation obliged to co-operate with another, still richer, corporation, with a significantly different view of the débâcle, the Mercers' attitude towards the third Royal Exchange is readily understood.

IRELAND

The Select Committee's reminder in 1804 that the Company could use the revenue from its Irish estates for whatever purpose it chose was as theoretical as the pronouncement on Gresham's 'surpluses'. Until the lease to Stewart expired, the Company had to content itself with its modest £420 per annum. The Stewart children proved to be unhelpfully sturdy, and it was not until 1831 that the last of the three nominated back in 1751 finally died. In the meantime the Company could do no more than listen, with mounting impatience, to the depressing accounts of the condition of its property. It was not merely local philanthropists and agitators but also the Company's own representatives who told of short-sighted exploitation on the part of the Stewarts and resentful listlessness on the part of the tenants.[70]

As soon as the last nominee died, the Company sent a deputation to Ireland to take possession and make the necessary arrangements for future management. The most pressing problem concerned the substantial arrears of rent owed by the tenants. If Stewart's executors took action to recover the arrears, there was a real risk that the many impoverished tenants would be brought to 'entire ruin'. Even the better-off might be seriously affected. The Company therefore decided to purchase the right to the arrears for £12,000.[71] The motives were not entirely altruistic. The heavy-handed enforcement of arrears by persons no longer interested in the long-term well-being of the estate was clearly against the Company's material as well as moral interests; and the assignment of forfeiture rights for non-payment of rent gave the Company the chance to remove undesirable tenants and enlarge the often uneconomically small landholdings. Nevertheless it would seem that the main concern was to ensure that the tenants could recover from their sad plight without undue harassment from their landlords.

Implicit in the method adopted for the problem of arrears was the understanding that the Company would itself manage the estate, though it was not until December 1831 that the Assistants, 'with the example before them of what the Drapers [in 1817] and other Companies [the Fishmongers in 1820 and the Grocers in 1821, for example] have done with their estates in Ireland', resolved that 'it will be most for the advantage of the Mercers' Company and other Companies associated with them, and also of the tenantry themselves, to retain the management of their estate, late under lease to Stewart, in their own hands'.[L] [72] Later in the same month a member of the Court (and one of the deputation which had visited Ireland some weeks earlier), W. H. Holmes, was appointed Company agent with the brief to 'be especially careful to hold an unbiased judgement and conduct towards the different religions and political parties upon the estate', and with remuneration fixed at the outset and not dependent upon rental income, an arrangement which was deemed not likely to be more expensive for the Company but would at the same time be 'more agreeable to the tenantry'.[73]

Even more important to the 'tenantry' was the Company's revaluation of their holdings. This was the task entrusted to another deputation which visited the estate in the middle of 1834.[74] The overall result was a 19% reduction in rents,

[L] This decision was duly communicated to the Cooks, Broderers and Masons a week or so later. It is interesting to note that the Company obtained a legal opinion on its right to deal with the estate without reference to its associates and even on the possibility of purchasing the other Companies' interests. The matter was taken no further and in fact the original resolution (which prompted the review) was rescinded. AC, 16 November 1831, 11 January and 3 February 1832.

and the deputation's claim that 'the tenantry entertain very grateful feelings towards the Company for the relief afforded them' certainly gained support from an address received a few weeks later:[75]

We the undersigned on behalf of ourselves and others, tenants of your estate . . . , beg leave to express our grateful acknowledgements for the kind and liberal feelings you have displayed in the valuation and setting of our farms. Guided by the maxim of a wise and generous proprietory 'live and let live' you appear to have satisfied the just expectations of a wise and industrious tenantry. To us a new era has indeed commenced. Bog fees, leet-money and other feudal exactions abolished, tithe merged in rent, lime quarries opened to furnish cheaply fertility to our fields, comfort and cleanliness to our dwellings, roads laid out to facilitate intercourse and provide employment, medical aid liberally and promptly administered to the indigent sick, education fostered to meet the wants of a rising generation, all under your paternal counsels already in execution, or auspiciously commenced by a gentleman [Holmes] whose vigilant solicitude to diffuse comfort and improvement throughout your estate fully justifies your happy choice of an agent and whose courteous deportment is well calculated to preserve that affectionate relation which should ever subsist between the owners and the occupiers of the soil, and which in our case we hope may continue unimpaired.

Whether such a gushing address was the gratuitous response of a representative number of tenants might be doubted, but the Company did provide its tenants with a good deal more than lower rents. Spending on the other benefits mentioned in the address was substantial, as witness not only the contemporary details in the Court records,[76] but also a later summary by the Company for the years 1831 to 1873:[77]

		£	s	d
1.	Compulsory payments of rates, taxes, and tithes	£35,212	15	6
2.	Buildings yielding some rental	13,491	5	2
	Buildings yielding no rental, viz.			
3.	Churches and chapels	11,999	11	10
4.	Agent's residence	5,894	7	3
5.	Schools	4,611	2	8
6.	Waterworks, market houses, etc.	7,651	12	1
7.	Expended in improvement of estate, viz. drainage, roads, planting etc.	18,779	16	0
8.	Salaries to agents and officers	55,087	16	9
9.	Dispensaries	8,093	2	1
10.	Maintenance of schools	13,140	7	11
11.	Donations to ministers and places of worship	5,561	19	1
12.	Repairs and expenses connected with bathing, infirmary, markets, etc.	4,504	2	4
13.	Incidental expenses, including donations, insurance, stationery etc.	13,581	12	9
14.	Mapping and valuing, expenses of deputations, compensation for houses pulled down, etc.	12,075	7	11
15.	Lough Neagh drainage assessment £1,406 5 1 less received for land taken 1,093 6 7	312	18	6
16.	Loans	5,181	0	10
		£215,178	18	8

During the same period gross receipts amounted to £338,658, so expenditure in Ireland on the estate amounted to 55%. Not a poor record, it might be thought, for a landlord entitled to do as he pleased with his income, and who had paid very heavily in the days of James I and Charles I for the 'privilege' of owning land in one of the least prosperous parts of the kingdom. But in the eyes of many the percentage was not high enough. The very fact that the summary was prepared is indicative of the pressure on the Company to justify its conduct.[78] As the century wore on, the political climate in both Ireland and England became more and more antipathetic towards absentee landlords, and privileged corporations (as the Livery Companies came to be regarded) were particularly vulnerable. Before considering the ensuing attacks in the next Chapter, it is important here to appreciate the extent of the Mercers' achievements after 1831. At considerable cost to themselves, they removed the spectre of landlord caprice, relieved the burden of rent and made considerable improvements to the land

FIG. 66. Mercers' Hall, new Cheapside frontage, from *The Illustrated London News*, 16 April 1881.
Mercers' Company

and local facilities. If they were unable to do more, it was because the prevailing economic conditions and stubborn historic factors (notably the hopelessly small landholdings which not even subsidised emigration to America could cure[M]) proved too much.[79] But as 'moderate and progressive' landlords[80] they deserve credit for trying.

THE HALL[81]

The Company's own buildings in Cheapside and Ironmonger Lane were not specifically considered by the Select Committee in 1803–4, but members were well aware that the condition of the Hall in particular left much to be desired. The difficult circumstances of construction after the Great Fire and the simple passage of time had combined to render the Hall structure unstable, even dangerous. The Company's financial problems, however, precluded any thorough investigation and encouraged the adoption of temporary expedients. For example, when a large stone fell off the front of the Hall in 1783, the General Committee acknowledged the defects revealed by subsequent inspection but declined to spend more than £30 remedying them. They postponed serious consideration of the question until after the watershed

[M] In 1838 the agent Holmes was authorised to spend £300 per annum in assisting poor tenants to leave the country and to purchase unwanted houses. AC, 25 May 1838.

year of 1804, and even then focused on it only when the leases of the premises fronting Cheapside came up for renewal. In 1805 the Surveyor, James Lewis, gave cautious sanction for the extension of the existing terms for a further five or seven years. Then in 1811, with the additional terms close to expiry, Lewis presented a full-scale report on the state of the Hall buildings. He painted a very gloomy picture indeed and concluded that the most economic course of action would be demolition. The General Committee found it difficult to accept this and, having failed to persuade Lewis to prepare a less drastic plan, they turned to another surveyor for a second opinion. Thomas Hardwick proved to be even more pessimistic than Lewis and the General Committee had to bow to the experts. On 14 November 1811 the General Court formally agreed that the Hall would have to be pulled down.

Various rebuilding schemes had been suggested by Lewis. The three most favoured ones, ranging in cost from £18,000 to £23,000, involved using the existing site, but two meant taking the Hall to King's Arms Yard (owned by the Whittington estate), leaving the Chapel alongside new rent-producing premises in Cheapside. These latter schemes, or at least the principle which lay behind them, found an influential proponent in William Palmer.[N] He thought that rebuilding the Hall on its present site was as extravagant as repairing it. Much better to take the Hall off to less valuable ground and leave Cheapside and Ironmonger Lane to produce the attractive rental he was confident that it could command:[82]

> this spot [is] most desirable for such a purpose [i.e. counting houses with sleeping accommodation above], far more so than any other thereabouts, being more convenient either for business or pleasure, whether the family residences of the tenants are either at the West End of the town or at a short distance from it . . . The demand and value of such buildings must be known to everyone and I am sure I do not over-rate them when I say [that] every counting house with a sleeping room over it would be worth more than £50 per annum and a very large ground rent would be therefore produced . . .

Palmer's commercial argument, prophetic almost of the solutions adopted later by his own and many other Companies, did not carry the day. The more conventional schemes were always the most likely to be endorsed and eventually Plan C, leaving the Chapel intact but rebuilding the Hall and other buildings to face Ironmonger Lane, was chosen. Lewis himself had preferred Plan B (£18,000) but clearly the Committee thought that the greater elaboration in Plan C, giving the Hall 'more the character of a public edifice', outweighed the additional £4,000.

There, it might be thought, the debate would have ended. But the 'repair' lobby kept up the struggle with much persistence and continued, even after the adoption of Plan C, to tug at the financial consciences of their colleagues. Nothing was done to implement Plan C. Instead, when faced with the obvious dilapidation of the Chapel Porch or a warning 'hint' from the District Surveyor,[O] they exasperated Lewis by asking him to suggest short-term remedies. Eventually, almost a year after the adoption of Plan C, it was decided to seek a *third* opinion. This produced a quite remarkable contradiction of the earlier report. One of the authors thought that repairs costing no more than £1,000 were feasible and the other, George Smith, put his estimate no higher than £740.

The result can be imagined. Despite Lewis's warnings of 'the danger of attempting to botch up old premises even when arrived to a far less state of ruin than your Hall and its appendages', the General Court on 12 August 1813 rescinded its resolution passed in November 1811 and Smith was instructed to oversee the work. Not long

[N] For whom see above, p. 123.

[O] One of the proponents of repair (as opposed to rebuilding) contrived to characterise the District Surveyor's low-key intervention as 'the interference of an officer of the Corporation of London with the concerns of the independent Company of Mercers'. Sutton Papers, no. 4 (an undated memorandum).

afterwards Lewis tendered his resignation and in May 1814 Smith was appointed Surveyor in his place.

Whether the Company was right to side with Smith rather than Lewis is hard to tell. Certainly the eventual cost of the repair work, £926,[83] was not so very much more than Smith had estimated, and the buildings did manage to survive the ravages of old age and further alterations for many more years. However, the total bill was by no means limited to the £926. Not all the additional money can be attributed to deficiencies in Smith's report (though a proportion of the £850 for repairing the Chapel certainly comes into this category): at least £3,500 was spent on refurbishments which the Company decided to make while the repair works were in progress. Nevertheless the total bill of over £7,000[84] must have given Lewis cause for rueful reflection. Was this really a better deal than £22,000 and an income of £891 per annum?

Of course, as far as the Company was concerned what mattered was the size of the initial capital payment, and in this respect at least they had been prudent to the point of shortsightedness. Why was this? An explanation for this somewhat muddle-headed behaviour has to be sought in the corporate consciousness of these curious post-bankruptcy years. The tidying up of the trust accounts, and in particular the settlement of the St Paul's School debt, both reflected and contributed to an acute fastidiousness. Integrity and caution were the watchwords. It is significant that the prevarication over Plan C coincided with the warm quarrel over the Company's power to use trust surpluses already mentioned.[P] In December 1811, when it was proposed to put aside £5,000 as a fund for rebuilding the Hall, the contrary claims of the St Paul's School debt were immediately advanced.[85] In the following month, two Assistants were fiercely criticised by some of their colleagues for claiming that the Company's accounting methods amounted to a breach of trust.[86] Such views, or at least the sensitivity which they had revealed by way of reaction, are also reflected in a draft letter written by Robert Sutton to the Clerk in June 1812.

Sutton objected to 'this enormous expense in the present situation of our affairs which if conducted prudently for some few years might put us in a state to bear this expenditure without appearing in the character of a spendthrift exhausting his resources by anticipating his receipts'. In view of a recent Charities Act, Sutton thought 'this a very improper season (when on our books we appear largely indebted to St Paul's School) to launch out into so lavish an expenditure ...'. He was also anxious to leave the Company free to help those 'many private and public charities which of late have so frequently [asked] for relief'. Sutton believed that a decision in favour of rebuilding the Hall would only add to the ill-will and dissension created by the St Paul's School debt.

> First let us be just, then let us be generous, but till our riches are superabundant, let us not be extravagant . . .

It was, Sutton declared, 'better to be rich in a cottage than poor in a palace'.[87]

Sutton's attitude goes a long way towards explaining why the relief generated by the final banishment of bankruptcy in 1804 did not lead to euphoria. The Select Committee's investigations may certainly have indicated that there were surpluses at the disposal of the Company, but the lessons of 1745 were too deeply entrenched for it to feel emboldened to take major steps forward. However healthy the balance sheet or however shrewd the investment, rebuilding the Hall, still less the erection of a Cheapside office block, unnerved the Company's sensitive members. The ghost of Dr Assheton ensured that it would be some while before the Company could get used to the idea of regarding surpluses as a challenge, rather than a snare.

[P] See above, pp. 124–5.

CHAPTER X
PARLIAMENT AND PUBLIC OPINION

If the main theme of the first half of the nineteenth century was post-bankruptcy recovery and reorganisation, the chief feature of the second half was undoubtedly the role of the legislature. After a century and a half of constitutional calm, chartered corporations found themselves once again subject to public scrutiny. The Mercers were thrust into the political arena, and for at least the last three decades of the century had to fight hard to maintain their property and privileges.

MUNICIPAL CORPORATIONS

The first signs of political intervention came in the 1830s when the great Whig reformers enacted a series of fundamental changes to some of the country's most important institutions. From the Great Reform Act of 1832, which dealt with the parliamentary system, it was only a short, and logical, step to an assault on local politics. The Municipal Corporations Commission of 1833 naturally included London in its investigations, albeit as a rather special case. The clever radicals who dominated the Commission allocated London to their most assiduous member, Sir Francis Palgrave, later to become Deputy Keeper of the Public Records. Palgrave proceeded to immerse himself in the City Corporation's voluminous records and, on the premise that the Livery was an important element in the City's constitution, he extended his enquiries to the Companies as well.[1]

When the Mercers received Palgrave's request for information, in September 1833, they took Counsel's opinion before responding.[2] One of the lawyers (Sir James Scarlett) thought the Commission had no right to compel production of documents and advised that any co-operation be accompanied by a protective protest. The other (C. C. Pepys) took the opposite view and thought refusal pointless. Not surprisingly the former advice was adopted and a duly qualified willingness to assist was conveyed by letter to the Commission together with the information requested.[3]

In late October, Palgrave came back for more, and after the Company had taken the precaution of giving a general retainer to eminent Counsel (though not Pepys this time!) and had asked one of them to check the validity of the by-laws now exposed to scrutiny, three Company representatives had a meeting with Palgrave on 11 November.[4] Despite the guarded nature of the exchanges, two points emerged quite clearly. The first was that, in Palgrave's opinion, the Mercers (and the other Companies) 'were a municipal body — as being an integral part of the [City] Corporation and were one of the doors through which all parties entered the Corporation of the City of London. Consequently that all property we had was *municipal* and that this Commission gave him full power to enquire into any particular relating to the property of the Corporation'. The second point was that the Mercers could expect to find its Clerk and its members subpoenaed to appear before the Commission for 'a viva-voce examination in open court on any subject connected with the Company that they [the Commissioners] may think proper to enquire into and compel him to bring all papers and records that they may require'.[5] All this was reported at the next Court meeting and a resolution adopted that all witnesses summoned before the Commissioners should refuse to be sworn and should not give any information on the Company's property.[6]

This Indenture witnesseth That

doth put himself Apprentice to Citizen and MERCER of LONDON to learn his Art, and with him (after the manner of an Apprentice) to serve from unto the full end and term of Years from thence next following to be fully complete and ended. During which Term the said Apprentice his said Master faithfully shall serve, his Secrets keep, his lawful Commandments every where gladly do. He shall do no damage to his said Master nor see to be done of others, but that he to his power shall let or forthwith give warning to his said Master of the same. He shall not waste the Goods of his said Master, nor lend them unlawfully to any. He shall not commit Fornication nor contract Matrimony within the said Term. He shall not play at Cards, Dice, Tables, or any other unlawful Games whereby his said Master may have any loss. With his own goods, or others during the said Term without licence of his said Master he shall neither buy nor sell. He shall not haunt Taverns or Play-houses, nor absent himself from his said Masters service day nor night unlawfully, But in all things as a faithful Apprentice he shall behave himself towards his said Master and all his during the said term. And the said Master (for and in Consideration of the

in the same Art which he useth by the best means that he can shall teach and instruct, or cause to be taught & instructed finding unto his said Apprentice meat, drink, apparel lodging and all other Necessaries, according to the Custom of the City of LONDON during the said Term: And to the true performance of all and every the said Covenants and Agreements either of the said parties binds himself unto the other by these presents. In Witness whereof the parties abovenamed to these Indentures interchangeably have put their Hands and Seals the day of in the Year of the Reign of our Sovereign QUEEN VICTORIA of Great Britain &c. A.D. 18

Witness

Note The Indenture, Covenant, Article or Contract must bear Date the Day it is Executed and what Money or other thing is given or Contracted for with the Clerk or Apprentice must be Inserted in Words at Length and the Duty paid to the Stamp Office if in London or within the Weekly Bills of Mortality within one Month after the Execution, and if in the Country and out of the said Bills of Mortality within Two Months to a Distributor of the Stamps or his Substitute otherwise the Indenture will be Void the Master or Mistress Forfeit Fifty Pounds and another Penalty and the Apprentice be disabled to follow his Trade, or be made Free.

FIG. 67. Apprenticeship indenture, *c.* 1850s.
Mercers' Company

In the event, the Company escaped quite lightly. No subpoenas were received and the request for further information (despite subsequent pressure) was successfully resisted. The Commissioners had to be content with copies of the Charters and a statement covering such matters as the Mercers believed related to their connection with the 'Municipal Corporation of London'.[7] The risk, of course, was that this reluctance left the way open for critics and busybodies to have their own unchallenged say about the Company, and certainly the Commissioners' report made mention of two complainants who had been refused full details of the Company's membership on certain occasions.[8] There was also some brief questioning of one of the City's officials which touched on the state of the Gresham accounts.[9] Generally speaking, however, the Company incurred little by way of serious criticism in the report.

In fact, the whole report proved to be yet another wasted exercise. By the time it appeared, in 1837, municipal reform for the rest of the country had already been achieved in the Municipal Corporations Act of 1835, and there was no desire to mount another campaign simply to draw London into the same regime. (Indeed it seemed that Palgrave had been encouraged to treat the City as a separate issue in order to absorb his antiquarian energies and ensure that the powerful interests in the Square Mile did not thwart all legislation on the 'municipal' question.) None the less, the need to reform the City Corporation's increasingly anomalous franchise remained and, since any scheme was likely to involve a curtailment of their Liverymen's right to vote in Common Hall (whether in parliamentary or civic elections), the Companies could not avoid involvement in the City's 'municipal' difficulties.[10] In 1843, when proposals got no further than Common Council,[11] and again in 1852, when a bill was actually presented to Parliament,[12] the Mercers were constrained to protest against the City Corporation's own plans to enlarge the electorate; while in 1856, when a Royal Commission had prompted the formulation by the Liberal ministry of a root-and-branch London Corporation bill which provided, among other things, for the abolition of the Livery's civic franchise, the Company again expressed its opposition, though this time on the side of the Corporation.[13] By dint of determined resistance, the City managed to avoid major changes and certainly the Livery's rights were left intact.[14]

The most important feature of the aftermath of 1833 is that the Livery Companies were not criticised *qua* Companies. Only because they provided the Liverymen for the municipal elections at Guildhall did they really attract the radicals' attentions. One or two of the pamphleteers referred to 'snug family nests' of Palmers, Suttons and Watneys, but most took little interest in the Mercers or their fellow Companies.[15] The early reformers were preoccupied with the electoral system, national and local, and the nature of the franchise. Only later would they begin to

Fig. 68. The silver-gilt Rosewater Dish of 1836, which is often used today as a table centrepiece.
Mercers' Company

concern themselves with social as well as political matters.

THE CHARITY COMMISSIONERS

If the Livery Companies had little difficulty in deflecting the critical attention paid to their purported municipal role, they had a much harder task dealing with investigations of their charitable functions. Indeed many reformers were more interested in the Companies as the custodians of ancient trusts than as anomalous elements in the electoral system. As the so-called Age of Reform arrived, there was pressure for 'abuses' to be rectified and for 'surplus' revenue to be identified, all in the cause of utilitarianism. The Mercers, in common with many of their fellow Companies, found themselves subject to a series of actions in the Courts, with the Attorney-General acting on behalf of individual 'interested' applicants. The effects varied enormously. On occasion the Company managed to have the proceedings struck out on the grounds that the individuals (who were often conducting a number of similar actions against various Companies) had no real interest in the charity concerned or could not provide sufficient security for costs. Success of this kind was achieved in 1834 when the conduct of Dauntsey's benefaction came under scrutiny.[16] On the other hand, an action could lead, directly or indirectly, to significant changes. In 1830 the Court's attention was drawn to the fact that none of Lady Campden's loans for young men had been made since 1669.[17] The Company realised that the mere fact that it had been unable to assist 'freemen' for the simple reason that all (or at least most)[A] freemen now became Liverymen (and were thus ineligible) was an insufficient defence and, having failed to prove that the relator had no *locus standi*, it had to accept the inevitable retribution, which duly arrived in the form of a Vice-Chancellor's decree in May 1831.[18] At once the Company investigated its obligations to the other money legacy charities and, as noticed above,[B] made arrangements to obtain a scheme of general application. The Court proceedings were successfully concluded early in 1833.[19]

More significant, however, than this litigation by individuals was the creation of a Royal Commission of Enquiry into charities in 1818. Effectively lasting until 1837, the Commission was not merely a 'legal research unit' assembling information about the nation's charitable trusts, but also an 'agency of reform', advising, cajoling and, as a last resort, threatening to encourage a suit in Chancery against the trustees.[20] The Mercers experienced the effects of these powers in two particular instances. In 1821 the Company was told that the Commission had come to the view that the charities of both Sir Thomas Bennett[C] and John Banks[D] should benefit from the whole of the income derived from the benefactions. Five years later, the Court of Exchequer endorsed the Commissioners' opinion and, after an unsuccessful appeal to the House of Lords in 1828, the Company had to resign itself to negotiating a scheme which incorporated the legal verdict.[21] The second instance concerned the Elizabethan bequest of Peter Symonds. The trust included payments of £4 2*s.* per annum for the City of Winchester and £2 12*s.* for Christ's Hospital. No such payments had been made since 1772, and the Charity Commission superintended (but probably did not instigate) the fulfilment of the Company's offer to make full reparation.[22]

The Charity Commission, despite its longevity, was no more than a Commission of Inquiry, and it took many years of campaigning before a permanent Board of Commissioners was established. A series of Charitable Trust bills was proposed, and the early ones at least contained stringent judicial powers.[23] The Mercers were vehement in their opposition: the provisions were 'arbitrary' and 'oppressive', and indeed

[A] For the figures, see below, p. 179.

[B] See above, pp. 128–30.

[C] For whom see above, p. 91.

[D] In 1619 Banks had left land in north London in trust for Christ's Hospital and the Barber-Surgeons' Company, as well as the Mercers.

most of their valuable charities would never have been endowed had the donors contemplated the possibility of the corporation of which they were members being interfered with in the management of their bounty or deprived of its control.[24]

The Company found itself attacked in Parliament for the liberality of its Trinity Hospital visitation. The Lord Chancellor, in a withering exposé, used the extravagant menus to deride the Livery Companies' claim to exemption from the provisions of the bill.[25] The final series of bills was much less worrying from the Company's point of view, chiefly because the Board was to have no judicial power. The Mercers, at least publicly, remained opposed to the measure,[26] but they cannot have been too dismayed by the Charitable Trusts Act of 1853. Nevertheless, the mere fact that it now existed and did so in permanent form, gave the Charity Commission considerable influence and, with some additions to its powers in 1860 and, more importantly, with a gradual shift in public opinion, it began to play an effective role in reforming and modernising trust administration.

The first Company trust that received the Charity Commission's attention was Gresham College. In 1856–7 a report was published which concluded that the College should either become an affiliated member of London University or seek some form of union with one of those old suitors, the London Institution, the City of London School or the Association of Evening Classes at Crosby Hall. The lecturers, smarting under some rather unkind remarks about their work, refused to contemplate any of the latter alternatives, but were prepared to consider affiliation. The Gresham Committee was simply adamant that, whatever scheme was adopted, no additional expenditure could be contemplated. Another characteristic stalemate thus transpired.[27]

In 1859 it was the turn of Lady Campden's trust. The impropriation or rectorial rent charge to support the Grantham lectureship had still not been purchased, and the Charity Commissioners duly noted the omission. This was sufficiently unnerving for the Company to put an immediate end to more than two centuries of procrastination and defiance of at least one specific judicial injunction. Perhaps it was just as well that the transaction was carried out through agents rather than 'giving unnecessary publicity' by advertising.[28] Two years later the Commission wrote to the Company on the subject of the Bennett charity. Suggestions emanating from the Wallingford trustees involved the sale of the Kirton advowson. On this occasion, but only after taking Counsel's opinion, the Company stood firm, emphasising its readiness to help with the proposals but professing its inability as a matter of law to sanction the sale.[29] The Charity Commission were unwilling to accept the validity of the Company's stand but evidently did not press the point.[30]

Thus far the relations between the Commission and the Mercers were fairly amicable, if only because the proposed changes were not fundamental, or at least not pressed to the issue. However, in the 1860s the Commissioners involved themselves in the status of St Paul's School, and they soon found that the Company's readiness to co-operate had its limits, particularly when one of its most prestigious and valuable trusts was at stake.

ST PAUL'S SCHOOL AND THE PUBLIC SCHOOLS ACT 1868

The first stage in what proved to be a long drawn-out struggle with the Charity Commission over the status of St Paul's School began with a seemingly unimportant transaction. The Company had almost concluded an agreement with Lord Rothschild for an exchange of land involving some of the Colet property in Buckinghamshire when it decided to withdraw. In an attempt to secure the performance of the purported contract, Rothschild (with the support of the Charity Commission) advanced a claim in the Courts that the exchange was advantageous to the Colet charity and that, since the Company was a mere trustee, it had a duty to carry it through. The Company, needless to say, firmly denied the Charity Commissioners' right to intervene, and fought Rothschild's claim in the Courts.[31] Eventually a

FIG. 69 (left). Dick Whittington, the most celebrated Mercer of all, is represented as an urchin, cocking a snook at an unreformed City. Cartoon from *Punch*, 3 December 1853.
By courtesy of Guildhall Library, Corporation of London

FIG. 70 (below). A more respectful representation of London's most famous Lord Mayor and one of the Company's most generous benefactors. An illustration from *The Story of Sir Richard Whittington* by Gabrielle Carr (Longmans, 1871).
Mercers' Company

measure of success was achieved. In May 1862 Vice-Chancellor Wood decided that there had not been a concluded agreement and accordingly, only if the bargain had been extremely beneficial for the trust *and* the Company were a simple trustee, would he give an order for specific performance. Since the exchange was not significantly advantageous, the Vice-Chancellor was able to refuse the application without pronouncing on the question of the Company's status as custodian of the Colet benefaction.[32]

This omission was of immediate practical importance because, even as the Vice-Chancellor spoke, a Royal Commission was investigating the country's nine 'public schools', including St Paul's. Faced with the Company's insistence that it was beneficially entitled to the Colet estate subject only to the requirements of the original ordinances for the School,[E] [33] the Commissioners, in the light of the Rothschild decree, adopted an understandably cautious approach and (albeit reluctantly) decided that St Paul's should be excluded from the proposed Public Schools bill, pending resolution of the legal argument. The Company must have felt that the threat had been scotched, and even began discussing the intrinsic merits of the Royal Commission's proposals to see whether they should be adopted on a purely voluntary basis until the Solicitor warned of the danger that this could be construed as a tacit acceptance of the 'trust' argument.[34] As it transpired, the relief was premature. Notwithstanding the Commissioners' report, the Public Schools bill *did* include St Paul's School and provided not only for the inclusion of two Crown nominees on the new governing body, but also empowered the governors to prepare for approval by the Privy Council a scheme dealing with the removal of the School from its present site. No one in the Company denied that St Paul's School would have to leave sooner or later, but for the decision to be pre-empted in this way was a shock for a corporation still unused to legislative intervention. For the petition against the bill to describe the appointment of the two outsiders as interference 'both arbitary and unprecedented' may suggest exaggeration or special pleading,[35] but the Company was certainly prepared to fight hard for its independence, and there ensued much powerful lobbying of friendly politicians and persistent advocacy before the House of Lords Select Committee to secure the exclusion of the School from the bill.[36] Even the reinstatement of the Assistants as the School's governors, failed to calm the Company's fears. The main concern remained the denial of any suggestion that the surplus income was subject to a charitable trust:[37]

> to subject us to the operation of the bill would be a positive divesting of all our rights of property without . . . having an opportunity of having our claims determined by any of the regular tribunals of the country.

The argument succeeded, though only just, with the Select Committee dividing equally on the point. Even when the bill reached the Commons, there were attempts to restore the School to it. A leading London reformer, A. S. Ayrton, poured scorn on what he regarded as the pusillanimous decision to omit St Paul's:[38]

> The right honourable gentleman [the Home Secretary, Spencer Walpole] had said that Parliament would have to leave St Paul's untouched because it belonged to an influential City Company, who might set up claims of its own. Now, he never knew any City Company that was not willing to set up claims of its own and the City Companies were always fond of perverting the charities which came under their control . . .

[E] There was a good deal of unreality attached to this stance. In practice the Company had devoted the entire Colet income to the School and notwithstanding warm objections from some members (who perhaps deserved more credit for perspicacity than they received) it had repaid the £34,000 'debt' on the basis of a moral, if not legal, obligation (see above, pp. 124–5). When the School's accounts were submitted to the Charity Commissioners in 1863, the Company had to acknowledge that 'for a long time [they] considered that they held the estate and property of Dean Colet as trustees for the maintenance of St. Paul's School but they now claim to be beneficially entitled to such estate and property subject only to a charge thereon created by Dean Colet for the maintenance of the School' (AC, 12 June 1863). The Company's position was made still more delicate by the desire to protect the 'trust' from the payment of income tax.

Despite the vituperation, the Minister had his way and the Public Schools Act 1868 did not deal with St Paul's.

Of course, matters did not rest there. The Charity Commission was firm in its resolve to have the legal status of the Colet benefaction finally determined and when the Company, in fulfilment of an understanding with the Privy Council Committee on Education, formulated plans for an Act of Parliament to move the School and to make other changes,[39] the Commissioners immediately intervened. After some ineffectual sparring, the Company was obliged to drop its bill and await the outcome of the Court proceedings instituted by the Commissioners.[F] [40]

It took nearly four years for Chancery procedures to be exhausted, and there was more than sufficient time in the interim to put in hand a thorough review of the accounts, establishing that no unwarranted 'trusts' were being inadvertently acknowledged.[41] If the Company was indeed fearing the worst, its fears were justified because in February 1870 Vice-Chancellor James gave judgment that the Mercers held the Colet estate and property entirely for the use and benefit of the School as a charity.[42] As leading Counsel in the Rothschild case (a fact which gave the Company some cause for concern),[43] it was appropriate that it was James who now completed Vice-Chancellor Wood's unfinished business.

With the Charity Commissioners now satisfied (and no doubt ready to enforce the Company's charitable obligations as soon as occasion arose), the Company was in a position to give renewed consideration to a scheme for the School.

The crucial question now to be determined was under whose aegis would the scheme be devised and accepted. With nothing to lose following the post-Rothschild decree, the obvious stratagem was to apply for the inclusion of St Paul's in the Public Schools Act of 1868. However, in 1869, Parliament had passed a supplementary measure, the Endowed Schools Act, and it was generally (though perhaps fallaciously) accepted that, since St Paul's had not been included in the 1868 Act, it fell within the provisions of the 1869 Act. This brought the Company under the zealous and inquisitive eyes of the Endowed Schools Commissioners and, though the Mercers did their best to obtain an Act of Parliament to escape this daunting prospect and secure separate public school status, they did not succeed.[44] With some degree of rough justice, therefore, the Company had to live with the consequences of its misguided obstinacy back in 1865.

The Company's readiness to propose a scheme of reform abated suddenly, and it was left to the Endowed Schools Commissioners to take the initiative.[45] It was not until the end of 1873 that the two sides began to exchange firm ideas and meet face to face.[46] When the Commissioners' 'Heads' eventually emerged, they contained the following key proposals:[47]

1. The relocation of the School elsewhere in the metropolitan area and its subdivision into two boys' schools dealing with 'classical' and 'modern' subjects (either separately or by departments in the same school) and one (possibly two) girls' school(s).
2. The allocation of two-thirds of the endowment to the boys' schools and one third to the girls' school(s).
3. A governing body numbering twenty, of whom eleven would be Mercers.
4. Provision for fee-payers and boarders, but retaining the 153 'foundation scholars' who would be chosen by competitive examination and comprise 102 boys and 51 girls.

The Company's response was to take issue with:

1. The allocation of income. It wanted this left to the discretion of the governing body, but with no more than one-quarter going to the girls' school(s). There was a keen desire not to jeopardise Colet's original benefaction for

[F] The Attorney-General who had to give the necessary fiat was none other than Roundell Palmer, later Lord Selborne. Palmer's letter to the Company informing it of his action was a model of delicate courtesy: AC, 23 February 1866.

the sake of these later additions. The Charity Commissioners had admitted that the girls' school(s) were to 'a certain extent experimental'.[48]

2. The constitution of the governing body. An earlier meeting with one of the Commissioners had led the Company to expect 'a decided preponderance'[49] among the governors and a bare majority was thought unreasonable. Thirteen out of twenty was offered instead, with vacancies filled by co-option.
3. The selection of foundation scholars. Merit and not examination performance was proposed as an alternative criterion. The Company also wanted the distribution of such scholars between the schools to be a matter for the governing body.

It might also be mentioned, if only because it is of interest in the light of subsequent developments, that the Company favoured separate *schools* rather than departments for the boys studying 'classical' and 'modern' subjects.

These formal exchanges were followed by somewhat less formal discussions and it became clear that, while the Commissioners were ready to limit the income of the girls' school(s) in some appropriate manner, they were much less accommodating on the other two points. The constitution of the governing body was the subject of a good deal of argument and, although the Company was eventually offered twelve out of twenty-one, there was no mention of co-option. The selection of foundation scholars caused only slightly fewer difficulties, with the Commissioners striving to bring 'new blood', particularly from lower grade schools, into the schools and to reduce what was termed the 'aristocratic element' by means of competitive examinations and fixed quotas. The Company was resigned to losing the right of nomination enjoyed by the Assistants, but opposed the requirement for open competition in all cases, and wanted at least to be able to fill vacancies from existing pupils on the basis of 'merit' alone.[50]

Eventually the negotiations came to an end and the *Charity* Commissioners (who by now had taken over from their Endowed Schools counterparts) prepared their formal scheme. When some old Paulines asked for support for an Act of Parliament to bring St Paul's within the Public Schools Act, the Company felt obliged to accept the settlement thrashed out with the Commissioners[51] and thus in March 1876 the scheme came into force.[52] So far as finance was concerned, there was merely a requirement that the girls' school(s) would receive no less than one-quarter of the trust's net income. The governing body for the boys' schools was to comprise thirteen Mercers and three nominees from each of the Universities of Oxford, Cambridge and London, with four additional co-opted women for the girls' school(s). There were to be 153 foundation scholars in the boys' schools, divided between the Classical department/school (seventy-seven) and the Modern (seventy-six). A third of the scholarships were to be reserved for those between twelve and fourteen (whether already at the school or not) and awarded on the basis of competitive examination. The remaining two-thirds were also to be the subject of competitive examination, but were otherwise to be awarded in accordance with the governing body's own regulations. The girls' foundation scholarships were to total thirty-nine and were to be granted on the same basis as the boys, save that 'some like test of merit . . . prescribed by the Governors' was offered as an alternative to the competitive examination for the twelve- to fourteen-year-olds. The final point to note is that, while the scheme provided for the establishment of Classical and Modern schools (with about 500 boys in each), it did give the governing body the option of establishing two separate *departments* within one school.

It was, in fact, this last provision which gave rise to a postscript to this phase in the School's history. In 1879, as one of a number of amendments to 1876 scheme, the governors exercised their option and thus created one boys' school only.[53] It is tempting to associate this change of plan with the arrival of a new High

Master in 1876. The remarkable F. W. Walker, an astonishing compound of academic rigour and worldly determination, openly championed the Classics, and he may well have encouraged a move which increased his own power and offered the possibility of affording less than equal status to Modern subjects. However, it is clear that Walker did not make the exercise of the option a precondition of his appointment: a real debate continued after his arrival;[54] and, on Walker's testimony at least, it was the influential member Lord Selborne who was responsible for the ultimate decision.[G] [55] Of course, the decision would not have been necessary at all had not the time come for the boys' school to leave its Cathedral home. After more than 350 years, and at least fifty years too late, the School was obliged to look for another site. Eventually sixteen rather controversially overpriced acres were found in West Kensington, and Waterhouse was commissioned to design his red-brick pile. Walker's enormously successful High Mastership had begun, and the first phase of the School's stormy dealings with the Charity Commissioners was over.

TECHNICAL EDUCATION

Towards the end of the 1870s the Livery Companies found themselves subject to intense public and party-political scrutiny. As pressure for social and, in particular, educational reform mounted, the Companies' fierce independence and their obvious wealth excited covetous attention. The St Paul's School schemes were negotiated in largely legalistic and at least apolitical terms. The Charity Commissioners were concerned more with administrative efficiency than political utilitarianism. However, even as the 1876 scheme was settled, there were demands in the Press and in the Commons for a more radical approach. If the Livery Companies' charitable trusts were administered with scrupulous care, what about the unencumbered corporate funds? Should not these be deployed for 'public' purposes? It was generally acknowledged that the country was failing to

[G] The evidence is certainly unequivocal, though it is to be noted that a few years earlier Selborne had declared himself firmly opposed to the proposal: AC, 6 December 1872.

Roundell Palmer, 1st Earl of Selborne (1812–95), was a major figure in national politics and a highly influential force in the Company over a long period. He was the second son of W. J. Palmer, and was educated first at Rugby and then Winchester. He had a brilliant undergraduate career at Oxford, winning a clutch of major University prizes, and became a Fellow of Magdalen College in 1835. He was called to the Bar, from Lincoln's Inn, in 1837, took silk in 1849 and rose rapidly in the equity bar, which was then very strong and full of talent. He had the reputation for being very subtle, learned and masterful, with a prodigious memory and an impressive presence, which was not carried through to his advocacy in court, where his delivery was said to be rather monotonous. He was a devout High Churchman, and an equally dedicated naturalist. He first entered the House of Commons in 1847, in the Peelite interest; in 1850 he was a determined opponent of the Commission of Inquiry into the Universities, and of the Ecclesiastical Titles Bill. He was out of Parliament from 1857 to 1861, but became Solicitor-General in Palmerston's ministry in 1861, and was returned as member for Richmond in Yorkshire. He was Attorney-General from 1863 to 1866. In 1868 he declined the Lord Chancellorship and a peerage, because Gladstone was pledged to disestablish the Church in Ireland. In 1870–1, he was the British Counsel in Geneva when the Alabama case went to international arbitration. In 1872, however, he was appointed Lord Chancellor, as a Baron, and was responsible for planning and carrying through the major reforms of the judiciary that were codified in 1873 in the Supreme Court of Act. He went out of office after the General Election on 1874, but became Lord Chancellor again in 1880. When, in 1885–6, Gladstone's conversion to the cause of Irish Home Rule split the Liberal Party, Selborne followed the Unionist group of the party which, eventually, coalesced with the Conservative Party.

He was a man of wide interests; the countryside, natural history and, on the other hand, the history and literature of the Church of England, were all followed actively and skilfully. He became a Fellow of the Royal Society in 1860, and was given an honorary doctorate by Oxford, where he served as University Counsel from 1861 to 1863. He was also elected Rector of St Andrew's University in 1878, and became High Steward of Oxford in 1891.

He was an enormously distinguished public servant, whose skill and concerns became available to the Company at a difficult and threatening time; his family connection only partly explains his long and active involvement, in the same way that his great professional reputation only partly explains the extent of his influence within the Company. It was his personal qualities and his deep commitment which added to the weight of his opinions. (*Peter Nailor*)

FIG. 71 (above). The third St Paul's School, drawn by Paul Holden. The artist shows the main schoolroom just prior to demolition. The bust of Dean Colet is on the wall, above the High Master's chair. If we could look through the double-sashed windows to the left, we would see St Paul's Cathedral.
Mercers' Company

FIG. 72 (right). Frederick William Walker, High Master of St Paul's School, 1876–1905. Cartoon by 'Spy' from *Vanity Fair*, 1901.
Mercers' Company

FIG. 73. The Central Institution. Established as part of the drive by the London Livery Companies to provide technical education, the Prince of Wales laid the foundation stone in 1881, as shown here in *The Graphic Magazine*, 23 July. The building, by Alfred Waterhouse, who also designed the new St Paul's School (see Pl. XVIIA), opened in 1884; it was demolished in the 1960s.
By courtesy of Guildhall Library, Corporation of London

keep up with its industrial competitors in the field of technical education, and nothing seemed more appropriate than that guilds formed for the purpose of fostering now-obsolete crafts should encourage the development of new ones.[56]

The Companies were certainly receptive to the suggestion, and indeed there were one or two initiatives before any kind of public pressure arose. Nevertheless, it really took a direct appeal by no less a politician than W. E. Gladstone in 1875 to prompt united practical action. The Mercers did not play a leading role in the initial formation of the City and Guilds of London Institute in 1878 (the Clothworkers and the Drapers were evidently more active), but they did lend influential support. Any doubts which the Company may have had were allayed by Lord Selborne's warm advocacy.[57] Selborne became Chairman of the Institute's Council and clearly played an important part in ensuring that the Mercers were one of the founding Companies, contributing not merely £2,000 per annum,[58] but also the services of the Clerk, John Watney, as one of the two Honorary Secretaries.

Selborne was also responsible for keeping the Company committed to the task even when the Institute's expenditure rose and contributions had to increase. When a proposal to raise income

FIG. 74. Roundell Palmer, 1st Earl of Selborne, Master of the Mercers' Company, 1875–6, by Henry Tanworth Wells, 1872. This splendid portrait hangs today in the Reception area, outside the Livery Hall. Lord Selborne is shown in his robes as Lord Chancellor.
Mercers' Company

from £24,000 to £40,000 was made late in 1885, Selborne wrote a powerful letter in support to the Master of the Mercers' Company:[59]

whether I look to the special wants of our country at the present time or to [the] special position, history and opportunities of the Corporation and Guilds of the City of London, I am persuaded that the Corporation and Guilds have never undertaken and could not possibly undertake a work more useful or more worthy of themselves than this. As a member of the Mercers' Company I have rejoiced to see them associated with it and to be able myself to take a prominent part in it. The name which it bears ought, I think, to stimulate us all to make it worthy of that name and I am confident that, if what has been so well begun is worthily completed and developed, by a continuance of the same wise liberality and public spirit by which it has been brought to its present stage of progress, the Corporation and Guilds will have established for themselves a lasting and imperishable title to be held in honour not [only] by this generation but by all posterity.

The Times looked behind this rhetoric and shrewdly linked Selborne's campaign with the threat of radical legislative reform:

The Livery Companies apprehend interference with the management of their funds and Lord Selborne, who shares their antipathy to it, points to the Institute as a lightning conductor. He promises them the sense of a right to national gratitude and a probability of its fruition if they will declare his Institute a first charge on their revenues.[60]

Despite Selborne's eloquence and the political threat, the proposed increase in expenditure provoked much heart-searching among City Liverymen, not least at Mercers' Hall where Daniel Watney was moved to circulate a trenchant letter of opposition. Watney poured scorn on Selborne's subtle 'extortion':[61]

Shall we be induced by threats and cajolery to go on throwing our money into this professional gulf? The doing so will only strengthen the combination leagued against us. If we are to succumb, let it be at least in a noble cause, not in supporting one of the greatest shams of modern times. Will a censorious world pity us in our misfortune? Rather will they say 'Imbeciles', who could spend your £40,000 a year pretending to benefit artisans, but really benefiting everyone else. 'You deserve your fate which calls not for pity but contempt!'

Watney's fellow Mercers, however, remained unmoved and heeded Selborne's call with an additional £1,000 per annum, thus helping to resolve the Institute's first real crisis.[62] The Company was certainly not ready to allow increased expenditure to pass without challenge,[63] but there was no question of withdrawal.

The next intervention by the ex-Master and Lord Chancellor came in 1888 when the Drapers' withdrawal from the Institute occasioned a further period of uncertainty. According at least to one partial witness, Selborne's 'patience and counsels saved the Institute from possible dissolution'[64] and, though there is no direct evidence of an appeal to his own Company, the Mercers gave no hint of wavering in their support and indeed even urged their Clerk, John Watney, to resume the Honorary Secretaryship he had resigned.[65]

The Company remained somewhat sceptical of the Institute's achievements (it pressed regularly for information on the practical benefits accruing to trade and manufacture) and motions were raised, though defeated, for the reduction of the subscription to £2,500 per annum.[66] Then in 1896 the Company resolved to ask for a review of the expenditure of the Central Institution in Kensington, 'especially as compared with results', and, although this may reflect the Company's misgivings about the controversial decision to set up an establishment so far from the City (which had prompted the Drapers' severance of support[H]),

[H] The Company were always more comfortable with the smaller, more practical and more obviously cost-effective Finsbury Technical College than the larger, more scientific and more expensive Central Institution. The latter occupied a site in Kensington granted by the 1851 Commission which, though certainly not central either to London or to the Companies, had been accepted and occupied in 1884. The Companies put a good deal of pressure on the Institute's first Organising Secretary and Director, Philip Magnus, to spend more time in the City, and when he refused, he was effectively demoted. The more spacious Central Institution eventually came into its own and Magnus had to be restored to his former status. The Institute survived the 'Kensington versus the City' tension and it proved to be more a symptom than a cause of the Companies' misgivings about their technical education initiative. See J. Lang, *City and Guilds of London Institute* (1978), ch. 4.

there appears to have been also a certain amount of general disenchantment.[67] In the opening years of the new century the annual contribution came under serious scrutiny, though there were certainly special circumstances which called for a reconsideration. The newly-formed University of London had begun to absorb the Central Institution, and the Education Act of 1902 (*inter alia*) gave local authorities at least the power to encourage technical education. Given also the waning of any political threat to the Companies it should hardly cause surprise if the Mercers felt that their task was done, or at least less pressing. In 1898 the contribution was reduced to £2,000, and in 1904 it was resolved either to reduce it to £1,000 or (on the basis that it was undignified to fail to match other Companies' contributions) to cease payment altogether. In fact, the decision was taken to give £1,000 to the Central Institution and the other £1,000 to the newly extended technical college in Finsbury.[68] In 1905 the Assistants did actually resolve to give only £1,000 in total, but when Selborne's successor as Chairman, Lord Chancellor Halsbury, appealed for continued support, the General Court responded and reinstated the £2,000 per annum.[69] Mercers were treated to a reminder of the political benefits of supporting the Institute ('I can imagine no work more calculated to bring kudos to the City Companies in the day of their trial ...'), the wishes of the late Lord Selborne ('it is well known that he hoped the Mercers' Company would continue to carry out the work they had taken up'), and the obligations of Company service ('are we who may one day be called upon to render an account of our stewardship to run the risk of being told that once, many years ago, a very great man pointed out to us the policy we should pursue and that for no sufficient reason we departed from it?').[70]

All told, it was a creditable record. Whether through fear or altruism, it was the sentiments of Selborne, not those of Daniel Watney, that prevailed and the City and Guilds of London Institute derived great benefit from the support of the Company. As Sir Philip Magnus, effective head of the Central Institution, was only too well aware, where 'the premier and most conservative guild' led, other Companies would follow.[71] Selborne's Company did not let him down.

THE LIVERY COMPANIES' COMMISSION

The Companies' support for technical education did not in fact defuse the reformers' agitation, and the pressure for some form of public inquiry into the Livery Companies continued to mount. The prime mover was a formidable lawyer-polemicist, J. F. B. Firth, and no sooner had a Liberal Government taken office again in 1880 than Firth persuaded Gladstone to appoint a Royal Commission. The terms of reference for the Commission were extremely broad and there was no doubt that the Companies' very survival was at risk.[72]

How were the Mercers to respond? Within a matter of days of the formal announcement, the Company was treated to a lengthy letter of robust advice from a prominent barrister (and Company member), G. H. Blakesley.[73] There were two quite distinct courses of action according to Blakesley:

> that we should either meet the proposed inquiry with a generous readiness, relying on the complete vindication of our conduct which will be the result of any investigation to justify in the eyes of the country our continued existence; or on the other hand that we should pull up our drawbridge, sit upon our muniment boxes and adopt a plainly declared and unmistakably defensive attitude.

He had no doubt that the latter was the better choice. If the Companies were to give an inch, the politicians would take a mile. Binding compromises were based on strength, not weakness.

> The fact is that the Companies have been too public spirited for their own safety; and through their munificence the idea has grown up that they are more or less national, and are to some (as yet undefined) extent trustees of their private property for some (as yet undefined) public purposes ... One thing is plain from nineteenth century history, that nothing is to be permanently saved, unless the idea of 'public purposes' can be got rid of ... Once let the public get hold of the idea that there are any duties attaching to our position, except in the conventional sense in which we say that all property has its duties, and the end is at hand ...

The Mercers should make life as difficult as possible for the Commissioners, and oblige the Government to *prove* its case. Co-operation would only put ammunition in the hands of the assailants:

If the Companies give all information which may be required of them, it will be impossible to prevent the most milk-white innocence from being twisted into a party debate into quite enough resemblance to red-handed guilt to ground a demand for further powers. Any material of this sort would enable the Government to evade the difference between guilt in the eye of the law and guilt in the eye of the Liberal Party, between breach of trust and breach of duty, and by generalities, mixing up the motives of the founders with the duties of the foundations, to avoid the admission to which they might otherwise be driven.

Blakesley concluded with a suggestion that legal obstructionism be augmented by some practical pre-emptive measures:

... the greater the prize in view is, the greater will be the keenness of the confiscators. It is therefore expedient to use all the means which ingenuity can devise in the way of investments, so as to keep our property in a readily available form and to defeat as far as possible the effect of a general confiscating Act. If land cannot be sold, it may be mortgaged. No doubt our next General Court will with the utmost readiness give full powers to effect anything of this kind.

This advice became all the more significant when, in October 1880, Blakesley was one of three Counsel appointed by the Company to advise them.[74] Certainly in the early stages the position adopted, if not quite as uncompromising as Blakesley's personal recommendation, was reasonably firm. The Commissioners would be given information only in so far as this was not incompatible with the Company's corporate property rights.[75] Subsequently it was corporate expenditure rather than property rights in general which seemed to cause difficulty,[76] and eventually it was decided to provide full information and simply attach a formal Protest reserving the Company's legal position.[77] The reason for this 'retreat', if it may be so construed, was spelt out plainly in the opening words of the Opinion which Blakesley and two QCs gave in January 1882:[78]

whatever might have been advisable if the rest or a larger majority of the principal Livery Companies had adopted a different line to that which we understand them to have taken, yet as matters stand and in face of the fact that the Mercers would find themselves in a position of almost complete isolation, we cannot advise them as a matter of policy to act to the full extent of what is their clear legal right to refuse to answer any enquiries as to their private property.

All the Company withheld was evidence as to its legal title to its corporate property, and in all other respects relied upon its Protest to shield itself from the consequences of full disclosure.[79] In formal terms, the Protest was no doubt effective, but in practical, political terms, it was hopelessly inadequate. No amount of learned phraseology could disguise the fact that the Mercers' affairs were now public knowledge.

In March 1882 the Commissioners began their oral hearings and, despite the presentation of evidence with which they disagreed, the Mercers adhered firmly to their resolve not to submit themselves to the uncertainties of cross-examination.[80] All they permitted themselves was a short letter in December 1882 offering to help on specific points but otherwise declining to add anything to their return.[81] Only one substantive statement was made and this concerned the controversial question of expenditure:

the Company trust that the same sense of the duties attaching to the possession of property, which has hitherto guided them in the administration of their own, will continue to do so; and they venture to think that in this respect they have no reason to fear a comparison with the most liberal among the wealthy gentry and nobility of the realm; but considering this point to be one affecting themselves only, they decline to notice either the censure or the commendation which may have been expressed by others in reference to it.

Elsewhere in the letter the Clerk referred to the Company's Protest with regard to its private property and expressed the Company's pleasure derived from the 'unqualified confirmation [of its position] in the oral testimony of a legal authority of the highest rank ...'. This was an allusion to some almost incidental remarks made by Lord

Selborne, who had appeared before the Commission on behalf of the City and Guilds Technical Institute. Selborne was careful to distinguish between legality and morality and he was certainly not suggesting that the Companies should neglect their public obligations, but he did emphasise the crucial distinction between corporate and trust property:[82]

Are we to take it from you that the City Companies are entitled to their property in the same manner and as fully as a private owner would be? — In point of law they are in my opinion absolutely entitled to it and under no trust whatever. It will of course be understood that I do not speak of estates which have been given to them on any special trusts. Morally I do not think that I as a member of a City Company should choose to be a party to using it in exactly the same way as I should use what was my own as an individual.

You acknowledge a greater moral responsibility to the public than in the case of private property, but not any greater legal right? — That is my impression. I do not know that I can express it much better. They are ancient institutions; the funds which I call their own property were derived, as far as my knowledge extends, from their own subscriptions, and gifts by their own members and others, intended to be for their absolute use; and although I do not think the present generation ought to put those gifts into their pockets, yet on the other hand I cannot admit for a moment that they are upon the footing of public trusts.

From a Lord Chancellor these were indeed reassuring words, and it is hardly surprising that his own Company should have exulted a little.

When they came to frame their report, the Commissioners found it difficult to agree and, despite many months of deliberation, it was only a Majority Report which appeared. Such divisions on the Commission must have given the Companies some satisfaction, but the Report itself was not at all to their liking. A standing commission was to be appointed in order to supervise a major redistribution of Company income. Ancient trusts would be refashioned and a certain amount of corporate property applied to public purposes. If the Companies could not devise such schemes themselves, then the Commission would impose schemes of its own. In the interim, steps should be taken to prevent the alienation of corporate property by Companies anxious to pre-empt State 'redistribution'.

The Company did not respond immediately. A proposal that the Queen be petitioned was quite briskly rejected and the Company settled down to consider how best to 'protect its interests and secure its corporate property'.[83] Various proposals were made. The most obvious was to publish vigorous defences of the Companies' position.[84] Less obvious, and more controversial, were schemes to absorb the Company's surplus cash and otherwise hypothecate spare income.[85] Business loans to new Liverymen, a £20,000 church in Covent Garden, endowments for the London Hospital, an asylum for members and the relocation of Mercers' School were all proposed, though only the two last were actually adopted.[86] The next stage was for the Assistants to report to the General Court, and it was at this point that caution began to prevail. The General Court asked the Assistants to obtain Counsel's opinion. Horace Davey QC, R. E. Webster QC and G. H. Blakesley (again) told the Company that if an Act embodying the Commissioners' recommendations were passed, there was nothing the Company could do to escape its effects.[87] This did not, of course, preclude pre-emptive measures of the kind proposed, but it seems to have been sufficiently discouraging in general terms to dissuade the Company from proceeding. One Liveryman declared that if the General Court accepted the opinion 'they would be signing their death warrant',[88] but his was a minority, if not singular, view and caution did indeed prevail. The Company confined itself to an honorarium for G. H. Blakesley whose *Comment on the Majority Report* may not have been exactly uncontroversial in tone ('illogical, superficial, unjust, unconstitutional and discreditable to the signatories' was the verdict), but it was assuredly so in method.[89] The Company would fight openly in the Press and not secretly in the Hall.

Whether shrewd calculation as well as honest sobriety played a part is hard to say. It is certainly the case that the pressure of other issues (the Franchise, Ireland, Egypt and Afghanistan) made early legislation by Gladstone's Government extremely unlikely. The President of the Local Government Board, Sir Charles Dilke, certainly wanted to pursue the Livery Companies question, but he was opposed in Cabinet by the Mercers' own Lord Selborne.[90] All that was achieved before the Liberals lost power in July 1885 was a Corporate Property Security bill (i.e. a suspensory measure pending substantive legislation), but even this was dropped on the second reading. A brief return to office for Gladstone late in the year proved no real opportunity for the Livery Companies legislation, and in 1886 Salisbury's Conservatives started a six-year period in power. Radical reform of the Companies was shelved.

What should the Mercers do now? Four Liverymen at least thought the opportunity should be seized to make the Company's corporate property 'safe' from future depredations. The Revd Canon R. Sutton, G.H. Palmer, A.R. Rayden and (yet again) G. H. Blakesley suggested borrowing as much money as possible and investing it in securities.[91] With the Company's wealth in realisable form 'the Company would be in a much more favourable position for making terms with their enemies ...'. The reply by the Master (Daniel Watney) merits a full quotation:[92]

I have submitted your letter ... to my Wardens and also to the Court of Assistants and am desired to say that they are quite unable to agree with the policy you appear to contemplate and regret that the course of action anticipated by our opponents on the Livery Companies Commission and so strongly deprecated by Lord Selborne in his evidence before the Commissioners should now be suggested by members of our own Company.[1]

The Court of Assistants after the discussion in General Court some years ago since [curiously enough, a reference, it transpired, to the debates at the end of 1884 and beginning of 1885] thoroughly considered (among other suggestions) the advisability of raising money on the security of the Company's property and came to the conclusion that such a course was not expedient even if it were practicable and would in all probability be fraught with disastrous consequences to the Company and they have again since the receipt of your letter given their best attention to the matter with the same result. The Court are convinced that no considerable sum of money could be raised without the subject becoming a matter of public notoriety and if such should be the case the passing of a suspensory bill as recommended by the Majority of the Livery Companies Commission would in their opinion be inevitable whatever Government might be in power at the time.

It must be remembered that before the Royal Commission the Companies were accused of an intention to divide their property among their members, a charge which was distinctly repudiated by the Commissioners who signed the Minority Report ... It would in the judgement of the Court of Assistants be impossible if the Mercers' Company should borrow to any extent on their corporate property to satisfy any tribunal that such borrowing was not effected with a view to ultimate division; and further the Court of Assistants consider that it would be most discreditable to the premier Company to have initiated a policy which might involve all the Companies in one common disaster.

In conclusion it is submitted that at the present juncture when the country generally appears to have veered round to the Conservative principles or when at any rate there is a strong reaction against the crude revolutionary theories recently put forward by extreme speculative radicals it does not seem desirable that the Mercers' Company or the Companies generally should draw on themselves the attention of the country or the legislature by a course which while it would most likely alienate their best friends would stir up their enemies to renewed exertions with a very much greater probability of success than has hitherto attended their efforts.

It was not until late October that the four Liverymen managed to respond to this rebuke.[93] Their main aim was to emphasise that they were not in fact advocating division or alienation, but merely protection. The former may have been deprecated by Lord Selborne and the Minority Commissioners, but not the latter. They also gave a vivid description of the way in which their plan would work. The aim was to 'shift the battlefield from Parliament, the ground chosen by our enemies, into the law courts'.

[1] In addition to the remarks quoted above (p. 161) Selborne had denied any knowledge of 'a dividend being made of the property of the Company; it may be so in some cases for anything I know, but I never have heard of it and certainly it is not so in the only Company with which I am well acquainted'. *Report on the Livery Companies*, I, p. 190 (Question 1695).

If our scheme were carried out, any [Parliamentary] bill would have to be made retrospective, i.e. to annul transactions entered into before the date of its passing into law, because otherwise it would not be sure of attaching anything. For example, a Company with its property in negotiable securities might say to the Government upon a suspensory bill being brought in, If you will try the question of law, and succeed, the property of the Company shall be duly forthcoming but if you persist in endeavouring to override the law and to take away by a special Act of Parliament what by the existing law belongs to us, your efforts shall be vain; we will put a light to the whole or otherwise make away with it before your bill becomes law. The Government would thereby be forced either to comply with the very reasonable demand to have the question settled in the law courts first ... or else to make the bill retrospective. Now to make it retrospective, to undo transactions perfectly lawful at the time they took place, would be so palpably unjust and so unusual and strange a piece of legislation that the difficulty of passing the Act would be enormously increased thereby. Moreover the banks and insurance offices from whom money might have been borrowed would raise a considerable outcry, and an outcry that would be attended to, at the impeachment of their securities by retrospective legislation. It is practically certain therefore that, if we could carry out such a scheme, we need never fear any suspensory Act.

With legislation thus prevented, the struggle would be taken into the Courts, and there was every prospect of success if that were to happen. Hence, claimed the Liverymen, the determination to foist legislation upon the Companies. The letter concluded thus:

We conceive that the policy we have suggested ... might and ought to be so conducted as not to alienate a single wellwisher. And we think that the premier Company could do nothing more worthy of its position among the guilds of London than to initiate ... such a policy which would in our opinion be more likely than anything else to confirm all the Companies in their raison d'être as against all unrighteous attacks and to preserve them in the exercise of those moral trusts which they have held and discharged so honourably in the past and in the present generations.

The Assistants were still unpersuaded. The Master told the four Liverymen that:[94]

there is an element of great danger to the Company if the property should be dealt with in any other manner than that in which a prudent landowner would deal with his estates, altering his investments from time to time as might in his judgement seem expedient, but declining under the influence of caprice or panic to sell or mortgage merely for the purpose of raising a large sum of ready money.

Moreover, 'it is in the highest degree undesirable that any steps should be taken by the Livery Companies which would, to say the least, savour of defiance of Parliament and would alienate the many friends on whom they might rely in both Houses'. The Master finished his letter with an inevitable reference to Blakesley's rather different advice two years earlier, and made it clear that Selborne himself had endorsed the reply. There the dispute ended. Early in March 1887 the four Liverymen expressed themselves 'quite content to be corrected, even though not perhaps convinced' by so eminent an authority as Lord Selborne, merely adding (with just a hint of mischief) that they hoped he was right.[95]

The significance of the episode attaches not so much to the proposals themselves (for there was really little likelihood of their adoption) as to the response they evoked. The Assistants showed a keen sense of the need for caution and responsibility. In the aftermath of the Report, they had been quite ready to contemplate drastic measures not really dissimilar to (and in some respects more suspect than) the four Liverymen's proposals. After time for reflection and in the absence of any immediate political threat, the Assistants recovered their nerve and judgement. It is tempting to detect the influence of Lord Selborne here, but quite why he should have been able to intervene so effectively in 1886 yet failed to do so in 1884 is hard to explain. Apart from the brief allusion in the Master's last letter, there is no real information on Selborne's interventions. Nevertheless, Selborne's prestige was enormous and, if only as an unimpeachable referee in all legal and political matters, he was invaluable to the hard-pressed Assistants. The four Liverymen may have been ready to question many Company shibboleths, but they declined to take issue with Selborne. Selborne performed many important

FIG. 75. Dauntsey's School, 1895. This early photograph shows the School most clearly; the saplings are now fully grown trees.
By courtesy of Dauntsey's School

the Company in these difficult years, but his role during and in the aftermath of the Livery Companies Commission may have been the most valuable of all.

DAUNTSEY'S SCHOOL[96]

If the brief references in the Company's records are any guide, Alderman William Dauntsey's School at West Lavington in Wiltshire led a singularly uneventful existence for at least the first 300 years. It was probably undistinguished too. Certainly by the 1870s the School had little to recommend it, and when the Charity Commissioners proposed a scheme they met with no opposition at all from the Company and a positive barrage of 'grievances' and 'claims' from the local inhabitants. After formulating their ideas, the Commissioners approached the Mercers to see how much money would be available as a permanent endowment.[97] The benefaction itself (or more particularly a supplemental decree of 1633) merely required the Company to contribute £60 per annum to both the School and the associated almshouses, and, though this sum was regularly and amply exceeded, there was no legal obligation to do so.

It is interesting to note how the Company reacted. Instead of offering simply to increase the annual outlay, the Mercers proposed a once-and-for-all payment of £20,000.[98] It is possible that this was nothing more than a shrewd negotiation, but its coincidence with the appointment of the Livery Companies Commission suggests the possibility that it was also a device to put some surplus cash out of the reach of the State and claim the Dauntsey estate (which was situated in the City of London) as unencumbered corporate property. The Company was certainly keen to pursue the idea. The Commissioners' insistence on £30,000 did not make it flinch,[99] and it was even ready to ignore advice from Counsel that any commutation of this kind might not 'work'.[J] It was sufficient that the plan apparently gave the Company *practical* relief from future liabilites, and the lawyers were told to swallow their doubts and

[J] The advice had been obtained in relation to the proposed Collyer's School scheme (for which see below, pp. 167–8).

make the arrangements as efficacious as possible.[100] It may also be significant that, when the negotiations on the details of the scheme became protracted and slipped into 1884, the Company's Clerk, John Watney, was at least alleged to have emphasised the need for a rapid settlement in case a Suspensory Act was passed precluding such 'disposals'.[101]

The proposals involved the allocation of £14,000 to an elementary school and some almshouses in West Lavington itself and the remaining £16,000 to a county school (probably at Devizes). This caused the local inhabitants great anguish: the village appeared to be losing a good proportion of its benefaction.[102] Committees were formed and the support of politicians enlisted. A strident campaign got under way to prevent the adoption of the Charity Commissioners' scheme.[103] There were questions in the House of Commons from Joseph Chamberlain and Jesse Collings, articles and letters in the Press and even a full-length pamphlet. William Saunders' *History of the Dauntsey Charity showing how the Charity Commissioners and the City Companies Rob the Poor* was as vivid in its text as in its title. The scheme was denounced as a betrayal of both West Lavington and its poor, and the £30,000 composition was dismissed as akin to robbery. The former assertion was supported by antiquarian researches, the latter by some tendentious calculations:[104]

Assuming that the income of this magnificent charity [i.e. from its City property] is £5,500 a year, the disposition thereof by the Charity Commissioners is as follows:—

	£
School at West Lavington, the primary object of the charity	85.00
Scholarships and Exhibitions [at the county school] 'for sons of farmers'	85.00
Almshouses	250.00
To be put in a napkin for future use	480.00
To the Mercers' Company, for Turtle Soup	4,600.00
	£5,500.00

The publicity had its desired effect. At the end of March 1887 the House of Lords formally asked the Queen to withhold her consent and the scheme was dropped.

Whether the Company was glad of an opportunity to escape from a commitment rendered less pressing now by the return of a Conservative Government, or whether it was intimidated by the blaze of publicity (and in particular the intervention of Chamberlain and Collings) is difficult to say; but it certainly showed itself willing to listen sympathetically to the campaigners' proposals.[105] There were in fact two committees, one pressing for effectively a middle-class 'secondary' school (catering for would-be clerks) in addition to the elementary school, and the other advocating a technical agricultural school for the working-classes. Chamberlain and Collings sided emphatically with the latter: indeed it might be more accurate to say that they manœuvred the 'working-class' committee (chaired by Samuel Saunders, brother of the pamphleteer) into adopting their own long-nurtured plans for agricultural reform.[106] Needless to say, it was to Chamberlain and Collings that the Company paid closest attention, and the two politicians set to work on a rather worried Company. In an interview with Chamberlain in July 1887 the Renter Warden was treated to a chilling warning:[107]

everyone must be aware that the tendency of recent legislation was to examine the right of the City Companies to administer their charity money and it was inevitable that if the Mercers' Company elect to stand upon their legal rights in this case the larger question involving the very existence of the City Companies will be raised in the House of Commons and that it would be wiser for the Mercers' Company to adopt a reasonable view of the situation and by so doing defer the larger question being raised and gain for themselves a good name with the public.

Chamberlain went on to say that:

[he would require] that a sufficient sum of money be advanced to carry out a scheme for establishing an agricultural school at West Lavington. The New Allotments bill [which became the Allotments Act 1887] is a very great boon to the poor and a good farm education will enable them to reap the benefits of it. There are no agricultural schools though there are colleges and schools where gardeners' work, dairy work and work of other departments of farm labour are taught. This would be the first school of the kind and it would be followed by a number of others in other counties. Such an opportunity would probably never occur again for the Mercers' Company would undoubtedly get a vast amount of credit for initiating the system of agricultural schools. He said [he] was empowered [by the Saunders Committee] to state that if an adequate sum were offered for this purpose the account would be closed. The claim for the whole [of the Dauntsey property] would not be made . . . 'It is one of those opportunities', he added, 'which unfortunately rich men often fail to avail themselves of in time.' Agree with thine adversary quickly whilst thou art in the way with him.

Despite the fact that he was inviting the Company to finance an avowed experiment, Chamberlain won the day. Selborne urged his fellow Assistants 'not to sacrifice anything to revolutionary ideas'. 'Do what is right and don't be frightened by Chamberlain into doing what is wrong'.[108] His colleagues, however, were evidently not so robust and decided to elicit further information on the agricultural school at another interview. In October, Chamberlain gave a second exposition of the merits of this scheme in a tone which brooked no argument. A brief reference to the views of the 'middle-class' committee provoked a warm response:[109]

He said that West Lavington, which he knew well, was not a suitable place for a middle class school and he could not consent to the establishment of one of these as the money was left for the benefit of the poor [and] that any scheme for a middle class school would be rejected by the present House of Commons and *a fortiori* by a more Liberal House. Mr Chamberlain said he did not wish to argue the question of the right of the Company to the estates left to them by Alderman Dauntsey but he thought that it would be for their interest to come to terms even though a Conservative government was in power at the time; that Mr [William not Samuel presumably] Saunders had induced a large number of Members of Parliament on all sides of the House to take his view; that in a year or two there might be a strong demand for reform and that it was quite on the cards that Parliament might demand an investigation into the matter and the result of the investigation might be that the whole of the property might be taken away from the Company. On the other hand, if the Company came to terms the matter would be settled and Parliament could not then interfere.

Chamberlain persuaded the Assistants to agree to commit £600 per annum towards the free elementary school (and the almshouses) and £1,400 per annum towards the agricultural school. A protest in General Court against the Company assuming responsibility for 'this new experiment in technical education' was defeated and the decision was endorsed.[110] All that remained was to convince the Charity Commissioners and frame a suitable scheme. This took nearly three years and caused much disquiet in the process. On the one hand Collings and Chamberlain were simply irritated by what they saw as pettifogging officialdom. On the other the Company had to balance their desire to co-operate with powerful politicians against the continuing need for amicable relations with the Commissioners.[111]

When the scheme was finally approved, there were complaints from Collings and Saunders that the agricultural school was likely to take boys from middle-class, not working-class, homes.[112] They were careful, however, to lay the blame at the door of the Charity Commission, not the Company. At the end of 1888 Collings had stated that the Mercers 'have acted in a manner the most enlightened and liberal in the interests of the people of West Lavington and the district and in offering to supply the greatest educational want which exists in England'.[113] He did not alter his view.

Whether the historian should be quite as charitable is doubtful. The Company's conduct seems to have been as influenced by expediency as enlightenment. When the commutation scheme foundered in the face of local opposition, the Mercers fell into the embrace of Joseph Chamberlain and surrendered rather too readily. These were, of course, difficult times and Chamberlain was a powerful politician, but it may be doubted whether these are sufficient excuses. After all, the agricultural school itself had a faltering start to its new life, with much uncertainty as to the best curriculum and system to adopt.[114] Any 'experiment' will have its problems, but the signs are that there were more than there should have been. Had the Company steered a steadier course between the lobbyists on the one hand and the Charity Commission on the other, Dauntsey's School might have had a more successful 'refoundation'.[K]

COLLYER'S SCHOOL[115]

The capitalisation or commutation plan so nearly adopted for Dauntsey's School was actually carried out for Collyer's. After a brief exploration of the Company's entitlement to the 'surplus' Cheapside income in 1876,[116] the Charity Commissioners acknowledged the weakness of the legal position and effectively invited the Company to endow its proposed new scheme as generously as it could. This led to a certain amount of horse-trading in 1881–2 and eventually produced an agreed capital sum of £3,000 and an annual contribution of £600.[117] More interestingly, it was made clear that this would be a final settlement of the Company's liability to the trust. As in the case of Dauntsey's School, there was some legal agonising over the efficacy of the arrangement and, as before, the Company decided to tell the lawyers simply to do the best they could.[118] Again, the influence of the Royal Commission has to be considered and again it is difficult to deny the connection. The Commission certainly figured largely when the Company came to decide how to secure the £600 annual contribution. The general view was that £20,000 worth of stock should be lodged with the Official Trustees of Charitable Funds: there was plenty of spare cash available and the alternative of a mortgage was undesirable. The Renter Warden, however, thought otherwise:[119]

> seeing that our corporate income is threatened by the proceedings of the Royal Commission, it would appear to me to be wiser to charge this income with such payments rather than to pay them off by advancing a capital sum out of the corporate property of the Company, thereby giving the public an interest in maintaining our income rather than destroying it. Again by paying off the charge we leave the Government free scope for making other demands and despoiling us by degrees of all our property and it might well be that a time might come when it would be advantageous to us to have a charge on our property.

It was in fact not until 1889 that the scheme was finally adopted. The delay was caused by a vigorous local campaign against the introduction of fees and in favour of a *free* school. Much of the agitation passed the Company by, but it did have the effect of drawing into the dispute the formidable persuasive powers of Jesse Collings. The compromise orchestrated by Collings in 1887–9 involved an increase in the annual payment to £700 and the introduction of an evening technical school. Four more years elapsed before the 'refounded' School really got under way, on a new site and in a new building; but it was the scheme of 1889 which was crucial. The Company certainly deserves some credit for accepting that, notwithstanding its strict legal rights (as evidenced in the

[K] There is perhaps another criticism to be made, though a more charitable one. It was naïve of the Company to imagine that it could simply turn its back on the School. The scheme may have been expensive or generous, but there was no guarantee that the School would not be tempted to apply to the Company for assistance in years to come. After the First World War, the Headmaster and a potential benefactor made such approaches and they met with firm resistance. The Clerk, Sir Frank Watney, was determined not to allow any tampering with the clean break negotiated by his father. A dangerous precedent would be set. Voluntary gifts might suggest that 'we either had a guilty conscience or had more money than we knew what to do with'. After the Second World War this dogmatism became less acceptable. In urging the merits of responding to a School appeal in 1954, one member declared that even a small sum would 'show that we are not going to be forever more wrapped up in a spotless white sheet of self-righteousness. I am far more interested in supporting an excellent cause with four centuries of Mercer ancestry than in keeping open a sore caused by a rather sordid quarrel in which the Company may have had all the right and justificiation on their side. I think the perpetuation of it only harms our good name. A small gesture would do much good'. The School's general progress during these years (largely the result of the energy of the Headmaster, G. W. Olive, and the generosity of S. W. Farmer and his trustees) is traced in Olive's *A School's Adventure* (1954). The Company's involvement is mentioned only briefly and then in extremely bland terms.

FIG. 76. Collyer's School, Horsham, from *The Building News*, 21 July 1893.
By courtesy of Guildhall Library, Corporation of London

eminent opinions given in 1751 and reaffirmed by the 'scheme' of 1811–13), it did have further obligations to the School. Nevertheless, there is more than a hint of opportunism in the readiness to secure a discharge of its future commitments. The Company did not *have* to do as much; but it *could* have done more.

ST PAUL'S SCHOOL (1890–1900)[120]

It will be recalled that, under the revised scheme of 1879, provision had been made for the establishment of Classical and Modern departments (each comprising 500 boys) at St Paul's School. The move to West Kensington in 1884 made early implementation of the changes difficult, but even when he had settled down in his new School, Walker showed no inclination to imperil the Classical emphasis of his teaching. He made much of the 'Modern' elements in the curriculum and pointed to the achievements of old Paulines who had specialised in 'Modern' subjects (especially mathematics),[121] but there could be no denying that more had to be done if the scheme was to be properly observed. Would anything, or anyone, force the High Master's hand?

Walker did in fact make matters more difficult than they might have been by his own success. The number of boys rose rapidly when the School moved to West Kensington and was eventually held at 600. This, of course, turned a potential breach of the 1879 scheme into an actual one. It was also the case that the School was beginning to receive the critical attention of the radicals. In 1887 James Beal, a veteran campaigner for London reform, first revealed the 'scandals' of West Kensington.[122] The charges ranged from the general (the exclusivity of a foundation intended to benefit the poor) to the specific (the success of the neighbouring preparatory school run by the bursar's brother[L]) and gained important 'local' support from the Fulham Vestry and (from its inception in 1889) the London County Council. However, these factors might not have been sufficient had it not been for the intervention of Colonel Montagu Clementi. Clementi was an old Pauline and governor who cared deeply for the welfare of his School. He was staunchly opposed to the establishment of a girls' school and, perhaps for this reason or simply because he disliked Walker's concentration on the Classics, he also championed the cause of the separate Modern department. In 1890 he proposed to his fellow governors that the Modern department be established and the girls' school be postponed. The motion was lost by thirteen votes to two and consideration of another motion, either to restrict the Classical scholarships to seventy-seven or ask the Charity Commissioners for their specific sanction for the allocation of all 153 scholarships to the Classical department pending the creation of the Modern department, was postponed.[123]

Clementi refused to accept his fellow governors' verdict and took his grievance directly to the Charity Commissioners. In due course the governors received a copy of his communication and for the first time they had formally to take notice of the problem.[124] Lord Selborne and another distinguished lawyer, Sir James Hannen, were asked to prepare a report, and in March 1891 they did so. Selborne and Hannen (by then Lord Hannen) were clearly anxious to do what they could to preserve Walker's achievements and they avoided an over-literal interpretation of the 1879 scheme.[125] Nevertheless, they were obliged to accept that an application to the Charity Commissioners would have to be made, not only to ensure a proper division of scholarships between 'Classical' and 'Modern' candidates but also to obtain sanction for the admission of 600 boys to the Classical department pending the creation of the Modern department. In June the governors were treated to a long review of the lawyers' report, stressing the importance of 'unity' and agreeing on the need to apply to the Charity Commissioners for their 'opinion and advice'.[126] This, of course, was a portentous move. In asking the Commissioners to make some formal modification to the existing scheme, the governors ran the risk of reopening a host of sensitive and difficult issues. Once the wheels of the Charity Commission had been set in motion there was no telling how far they might turn. What was worse, the involvement of the Charity Commission turned a private debate into a public one and gave the reformers every incentive to increase their agitation. The early months of 1891 saw a series of articles in the Press, the publication of Beal's *St Paul's School and its Scandals*[M] and a number of questions in the House of Commons. The Governors might try to maintain the confidentiality of their proceedings,[127] but Clementi was more than ready to air his views in the Press,[128] and in any event the main issues were already well known. Any disposition the Charity Commissioners might have had to deal comprehensively with the School would only be encouraged by the public concern.

Discussions (or negotiations) got under way in February 1892, and the result was a draft scheme which, after first appearing in December, was

[L] Whether the connection between Bewsher's and St Paul's School itself was so close as to lead to impropriety is hard to say. The fact that the bursar of the main school, Samuel Bewsher, started the prep. school and appointed his brother James as Headmaster was certainly unfortunate and gave critics ample scope for denigration. Bewsher's could hardly be blamed for its excellent results, but its success was so great as to *appear* monopolistic. The self-justificatory comments in J. Bewsher (and others), *The Story of Colet Court* (1963) are not convincing (see p. 5). The figures cited make the denial of a monopoly seem somewhat over-anxious.

[M] Beal had left his restrained correspondence with individual governors far behind. Wit and malice were enthusiastically combined: 'There is no greater mystery in the world than the Mercers' Company, a body which has repeatedly set Royal Commissions of Inquiry at defiance and refused to give information as to its existence. I am not aware that this association does good to anybody; all that is known of them is that they meet periodically in the City of London and end their proceedings with inordinate festivities' (p. 12).

FIG. 77. The Roysse Room, Abingdon School, Abingdon, Oxfordshire. A nineteenth-century engraving by Thomas G. Owen. The school was re-founded by John Roysse, Mercer, in 1563; it still flourishes today, encouraged by the Mercers' Company.
By courtesy of Abingdon School

actually published in March 1893.[129] To a certain extent it confirmed the governors' worst fears. The Commissioners had seen fit to make wholesale changes in the foundation. The provision for the establishment of separate Modern boys' and girls' schools of an inferior grade may not have caused much anguish. Indeed there is some evidence to suggest that, so far as the boys' school was concerned, this had been supported by the governors as a device to maintain the unity of St Paul's School itself.[N] However, the requirement that one-third of the 153 scholarships be reserved for candidates from endowed or public elementary schools and the £8,000 per annum limit on the Colet estate income which could be applied to the main School did arouse indignation.[130] The former seemed to endanger intellectual (and perhaps also social[O]) standards and the latter seemed both imprudent and unfair. Both struck at the integrity of Colet's foundation. It was one thing to accept that additional elements should be grafted on to a bountiful benefaction; it was another to allow those additional elements to jeopardise what the Chief Commissioner conceded was 'magnificent work'.[131]

Lobbying began in earnest. The fierce utterances of Colonel Clementi could perhaps be disregarded as unrepresentative,[132] despite his position as Master of the Company (and thus chairman of the governors), and perhaps the opposition of various old Paulines (including Benjamin Jowett) was only to be expected;[133] but when *The Times* too inveighed against 'novel and unpromising experiments'[134] the Charity Commissioners knew that concessions would be needed. The more important of these involved the omission of the preference for boys from endowed or public elementary schools in favour of a simple requirement that for one-third of the scholarships special weight would be given to 'Modern' subjects (i.e. excluding Greek). The assistance for public elementary schoolchildren would be transferred to the inferior grade schools where half the scholarships would be available for them. The other concession was merely an acknowledgement that the £8,000 per annum (and the £2,500 per

[N] This would explain the governors' readiness to reconsider their preference for first establisning the girls' school: SPS GM, 21 May 1892.

[O] Much was and has been been made of this point. The views of J. G. Fitch were probably as objective as anyone's and he acknowledged that 'much of the objection [to the scholarship Clause 75] was founded rather on a feeling of social exclusiveness than on educational standards': SPS GM, 19 January 1894.

FIG. 78. Sir Cecil Clementi-Smith, Master of the Mercers' Company, 1897–8, by Reginald Granville Eves, 1912. Today, this painting hangs in the Reception area, outside the Livery Hall. Sir Cecil wears the Order of a Knight Grand Commander of St Michael and St George.
Mercers' Company

annum allocated to each of the other two schools) was to exclude the cost of structural repairs. One further alteration deserves notice and this was certainly no concession. In place of the three Company Wardens acting as governors to St Paul's School ex officio, three representatives of the LCC were to be appointed.[135]

By the time the governors responded, a Royal Commission on Intermediate and Secondary Education had been announced and they used this as a pretext for suggesting that the proceedings be suspended until the Commission reported.[136] At the same time they made it clear that they thought that the 'inferior grade' boys' and girls' schools were more appropriately supported from other sources.[137] There is more than a hint of opportunism here. The Commission's appointment, of course, was extremely convenient and the sudden opposition to the 'inferior grade' schools was quite new. It seems quite possible that the concessions made by the Commissioners had encouraged the governors to believe that their

FIG. 79. St Paul's Girls' School opened in 1904. Miss Frances Gray, the first High Mistress (1903–27), is seen here with the first VIIIth Form, 1907–8.
By courtesy of St Paul's Girls' School

position was stronger than they had believed it to be. They might after all manage to secure the minor modifications to the 1879 scheme for which they had first applied and avoid the new scheme to which they had recently become resigned.

The Commissioners' reaction in large measure justified the governors' stand. Consideration of the separate boys' and girls' schools was duly postponed. However, the Commissioners saw no reason to hold back the provisions for St Paul's School itself and, since they were ready to reinstate the Wardens as governors ex officio (though retaining the three LCC representatives), they sent the scheme to the Committee of the Privy Council on Education for the final stage of approval.[138] If the Commissioners genuinely thought that the governors would now acquiesce then they were unduly optimistic; and if this was merely a ploy to encourage acquiescence then they were naïve. Certain serious objections of the governors had still to be addressed. For example, the financial arrangements for St Paul's School remained a source of real disquiet and merely allowing additional expenditure on 'structural repairs' was unlikely to be regarded as affording adequate flexibility. It should have come, therefore, as no surprise when the governors made their opposition plain to the Committee. More surprising, perhaps, was the scope of the criticisms. Quite apart from the financial argument and some other detailed points, the governors reopened the entire girls' school issue.[139] For some reason they woke up, or at least claimed to wake up, to the fact that the girls' school in the

1876 scheme had become the inferior grade school in the 1893 scheme. The governors now asserted that they had only wanted the establishment of an inferior grade girls' school to be postponed and that they had always wanted to proceed with a girls' school of the highest rank.[P]

Quite how the governors can have failed to appreciate that the girls' school had changed its form is difficult to comprehend, and some special pleading before a new tribunal may perhaps be the real explanation. Suspicion is further aroused by the fact that the governors also chose the occasion to advance the striking proposition that 'no part of the estates bequeathed by Dean Colet should be devoted to education other than that of the highest possible kind'.[Q] If the Charity Commissioners had tried to outmanœuvre the governors, they had certainly met their match. Instead of simply accepting the postponement of the boys' and girls' schools as the best that could be achieved (and it was after all a considerable concession), the governors had taken the opportunity of their 'appeal' to the Committee to attempt to prevent the revival of such plans. They could scarcely refuse to establish a girls' school at all: it had been an important part of the 1876 scheme and any attempt to evade the commitment would have been doomed to failure; and so the governors appear to have felt obliged to reintroduce the girls' school as first conceived before closing the door on the inferior grade schools with the claim that they were inappropriate objects for the Colet bequest.[R] This is surmise, but it does seem the interpretation which best accords with the evidence.

Before criticising the governors' conduct it is important to take into account the sense of betrayal which the Commissioners' decision to formulate a full-blown scheme engendered. When the Assistants, as the managers of the Colet estate, offered the Committee their own objections to the scheme, they included the following complaint:[140]

> The only modification in the Scheme now in force, which was concurred in by the Court [of Assistants], was that as to the establishment of a Modern School and it came upon the Court as a complete surprise that proposals should be made for introducing great and radical changes into all that relates to St. Paul's School, which is in the highest possible state of efficiency and which the Chief [Charity] Commissioner has declared to be doing 'magnificent work'.

It is also only fair to recognise that the dispute had now dragged on for over four years and the governors at least were always changing. Complete consistency was perhaps impossible and indeed, in the eyes of the zealots, might not even be desirable. Nevertheless the tergiversations in the governors' approach to the proposed reforms cannot be wholly excused and certainly did not enhance their reputation as educational trustees.

The 'appeal' to the Committee, and subsequent discussions, had limited success. The higher grade girls' school was duly included in the scheme and £9,000, not £8,000, was allowed for expenditure on St Paul's School each year. The governors, however, were still unhappy with the financial provisions: at least £10,000 was deemed essential; and they still objected to LCC representation.[141] When the Committee refused to make any further concessions, the governors decided to petition the Privy Council against the scheme.[142] It was not in fact until June 1896 that the Judicial Committee of the Privy Council heard the case

[P] The first hint that the governors would adopt this position came in February 1894 in the course of the governors' request for a postponement of the 'inferior grade' schools scheme. A draft resolution that 'the existing [i.e. 1876/1879] scheme is intended to provide education of the highest grade both for boys and girls and that in the interests of the higher education in London it is important that this object be fulfilled' was incorporated in a covering letter as a declaration that 'the Governors have always desired to maintain for St. Paul's School a position of the highest educational rank and the terms of the Scheme under which they are now acting indicate that the Schools, for both boys and for girls, shall possess this character'. SPS GM, 26 January, 23 February 1894.

[Q] Again there had been an indication of this view earlier in the year, as a pretext for postponement, but a suggestion that 'the provision of intermediate and secondary education ... may be more appropriately made by other endowments ...' was diffident in comparison.

[R] A governor later told the first High Mistress, Frances Gray, that he and his colleagues had had to fight the Charity Commissioners to ensure equal status for the girls' school: F. R. Gray, *And gladly wolde he lerne and gladly teche* (1931), p. 82. This may not be the whole of the story.

and, after a good deal of legalistic rather than substantive argument, judgment was reserved. In fact, the judgment was never delivered because the governors and Charity Commissioners reopened negotiations and eventually managed to reach agreement. In one sense it is possible to credit this breakthrough to one of the governors' retained Counsel who, late in 1896, prepared the memorandum which formed the basis of the fresh round of discussions.[143] However, the terms of the memorandum were so vague and indeed so unlike the eventual settlement that the real explanation must lie elsewhere.

Much of the learned debate before the Privy Council had centred on the so-called Boarding School Conscience clause of the Endowed Schools Act 1869. The provision was not important in itself and the technicalities can be ignored here, but questions of great moment and complexity arose. In effect, the issue was whether the Church of England had any pre-Reformation existence. This was evidently the reason for their Lordships refusing to make any immediate pronouncement, and the prospect of years of contention and controversy is believed to have induced the Commissioners to adopt a much more conciliatory attitude.[144] At first sight, this seems rather fanciful, but in default of any other explanation it has to be accorded some respect. Certainly there is no other apparent reason for the Charity Commissioners' decision early in 1897 to accept the memorandum as the basis for reopened negotiations.[145] After some hesitation, the governors decided to take the initiative and offer their own detailed proposals.[146]

It might be imagined that these called for no more than a modification of the 1879 scheme. Nevertheless, the Charity Commissioners proved willing to accept most of the proposals, save in one important respect. They were still insistent that St Paul's School should be limited to a specified income.[147] They were certainly ready to be more liberal than heretofore. A maximum of £21,000 per annum (with two-thirds for St Paul's School and one-third for the girls' school) could now be spent, but any income over and above that figure had to be the subject of further schemes for higher educational purposes in or near London.[148] There are indications that the governors were uncertain as to how far to press the point (they accepted that surplus, though *properly* surplus, income should be available for the purposes suggested by the Commissioners[149]) and it was only on the chairman's casting vote that they resolved formally to inform the Commissioners that St Paul's School must not be 'shut out' from surplus income if need arose for additional money in the future.[150] The Assistants, however, were quite adamant and the Commissioners were made all too aware of their views in a long and indignant letter. The kernel of the argument was expressed thus:[151]

> The Court find it difficult to believe that the Commissioners have fully considered that their proposals involve the abolition of all connection between the prosperity of St Paul's School and the advantageous management of the Colet estate. After 400 years of honourable and successful management of that estate in the interest of St Paul's School in accordance with the conditions under which the Company accepted the trust, the Court are now asked to disregard the obligations imposed by the trust and to agree to hold and manage the estate for schools not on the foundation, with which they are to have no official connection beyond paying over to them some part of the income. The proposal of the Commissioners is to limit St Paul's School to a fixed maximum sum per annum. That sum may be adequate or inadequate, but the result evidently will be that the Mercers' Company will be liable to lose their full interest in the management of the estate, because St Paul's School is not to benefit by any surplus over that maximum. The proposal treats the Mercers' Company as a body to whom it is a matter of entire indifference what may be the institution interested in their management of the estate. The Court of Assistants conceive that such a change is both unnecessary and unwise in the best interests of the charity. They consider that the Company is bound by its obligations under Dean Colet's will and cannot prospectively shut out St. Paul's School (which was, and is, the sole beneficiary thereunder) from its existing right to profit by future increment of the funds in trust if and when the school requires it.

This was a powerful argument, but it should not cause surprise that the Commissioners, having conceded almost all the other major points,

FIG. 80. Silhouette of St Paul's Girls' School senior orchestra, being conducted by Gustav Holst, July 1926. Holst (1874–1934) was Music Master at St Paul's Girls' School from 1905 to 1934. He wrote his well-known *St Paul's Suite* and *Brook Green Suite* for the orchestra to play.
By courtesy of St Paul's Girls' School

refused to give ground and indicated that they were prepared to recommence proceedings to implement the 1893–4 scheme.[152] The governors, a good deal less committed to the principle than the Assistants, were so impressed by the apparent vigour of the Commissioners' response that they suggested that the 'surplus' issue be held over for the present in order to avoid jeopardising 'so promising a settlement'.[S] The Commissioners acknowledged the proposal with due courtesy, but said that it could not work for two reasons: the Company would have to agree (and there was no indication from the tone of its latest submission that it would) and the Committee of the Privy Council on Education would only agree to the formal withdrawal of the draft scheme, the subject of the Privy Council appeal, if definite alternative arrangements had been settled.[153] The impasse thus remained.

Towards the end of 1898 the Assistants tried to resolve the difficulty. They suggested that two-thirds of the Colet estate income (subject to a minimum of £14,000 per annum) be devoted to St Paul's School and the remaining third to the girls' school. Any money not required would be accumulated and new schemes devised, provided that in the formulation of such schemes the interests of the two schools should be given first consideration. The governors were more than ready to endorse the proposals and a joint application to the Charity Commissioners was duly made.[154] In December the Commissioners replied to both the Assistants and the governors, and it was at once clear that at long last agreement had been reached. In all essentials, the Assistants' formula had been approved.[155] Why? The Assistants had certainly not made any significant concessions. The provision for dealing with 'surplus' income had every prospect of remaining a dead letter. The chances of the governors deciding that the schools did not need all the available money were slim indeed. The formula almost seems to have been designed to enable the Commissioners to save face; and the question is therefore why the Commissioners decided to accept the offered 'escape route'. It may simply be that, having effectively abandoned hope of enforcing the 1894 scheme and being now committed to a negotiated settlement (and perhaps also because the Tories

[S] It is significant that the proposers of the successful motion were two of the University Governors, the Bishop of Bristol and Fitch (now Sir Joshua), and the proposers of an amendment were two Mercers, George Palmer and W. Lane-Claypon. *The Times* on 7 July 1898 noticed these differences and they undoubtedly help to explain why the governors were more conciliatory than the Assistants.

were now in power), time was not on the Commissioners' side. The governors could hold out indefinitely and, if the Commissioners were to achieve anything, they would have to accept the limited amount on offer. A rather pragmatic attitude perhaps for a public body to adopt, but after nine years of trial and tribulation, pragmatism was essential.

There remained only some detailed textual work on the proposals before the scheme was finally adopted and published in June 1900.[156] It might be worth repeating that this was not a *new* scheme (as its abortive predecessor in 1894 had been) but a modification of the 1879 scheme. There were three principal amendments:

1. The new financial arangements just described.
2. The establishment of a Modern *department* at St Paul's School.
3. Preference for Modern subjects (excluding Greek) in examinations for one-third of the 153 foundation scholarships at St Paul's School.

When these provisions are compared with the position in 1890 the extent of the governors', or perhaps the Assistants', 'achievement' becomes clear. The allocation of income may have represented a concession (at least so far as the substitution of a fixed quarter for a possible one-third was concerned), but the other regulations were certainly no more than those acknowledged to be necessary in 1890, and in the case of scholarships, better than the 1879 scheme (where a division of 77/76 had been made). The governors of course would have retorted that their 'achievement' had been merely to persuade the Commissioners to treat their application in the spirit in which it had been made. They had asked only for a regularisation of what they regarded as unavoidable difficulties, and after a long struggle 'justice' had been done.

There were two postscripts. The first came in 1904 when St Paul's Girls' School began life at Brook Green (though not before Colonel Clementi had fought a last battle against the expenditure involved[157]). Then in 1905 F. W. Walker retired as High Master of St Paul's School. His advocacy, the loyalty he inspired in his own and former old Paulines and the outstanding successes of his scholars, all contributed powerfully to the successful resistance of the 1890s. The St Paul's School reflected in the scheme of 1900 was very much Walker's school. For advocates of 'Modern' education, in both the educational and the social sense, this was a matter of regret; but for those who saw in the rigorous study of the Classics the best hope of preserving civilised values and enhancing educational standards, it was a source of pleasure and pride.

IRELAND

The Company's political vulnerability in Ireland as an absentee landlord has already been noticed.[T] It was during the latter part of the nineteenth century that tenants began to campaign for what were called their three Fs, namely fair rent, fixity of tenure and free sale. The tenant-right movement, as it was known, took a deep hold and it mattered little how benevolent a landlord might be. 'Moderate and progressive Companies like the Mercers did not escape the outcome.' So remarks the historian of Lot 8.[158] For thirty years the Company fought a rather weary rearguard action and then bowed to the inevitable.

This last phase of the Irish plantation began in 1874 with a revaluation of a patently more prosperous estate. The increases in rent which followed caused much resentment and a deputation led by Lord Selborne was sent to negotiate a settlement. Selborne commented later:[159]

> I learnt then more than I had known before of the relations between owners and occupiers of land in Ireland, and the friction arising out of them, and the dangers of agrarian agitation ... A disposition was growing up to look upon any substantial increase of rents, under whatever circumstances, as an encroachment on ... [legal] rights.

Even a substantial reduction in the proposed figure of £14,000 per annum was insufficient to

[T] See above, p. 141.

quell opposition, and another deputation followed by a further reduction (to £11,769 per annum) was necessary before a semblance of contentment was restored.

It was not long, however, before there was further trouble. Poor harvests in the late 1870s led to rent arrears which in turn led to evictions. Tenant-right pressure became more intense and a lively meeting was held at Kilrea at the end of 1880. The ensuing Press coverage included the following comment in a letter to the *Coleraine Chronicle*:[160]

It is a pity that the amicable relationship between the tenants and their landlords ever had been shattered and war between them the consequence — and all about £2,000 a year, a trifling sum to a rich and powerful corporation like the Mercers, but a matter of life and death to the poor tiller of the soil on their Irish estate.

FIG. 81. The Associated Companies' Cup, presented to the Mercers by the Cooks', Broderers' and Masons' Companies in memory of their Irish estate association, 1909.
Mercers' Company

In fact, relief for the 'poor tiller' was almost to hand. The Land Act of 1881 gave the tenants two of their goals: the right to a 'fair' rent and the right to purchase their holdings. The latter was not of immediate value since the Company was prepared only to consider a sale of the entire estate, and an offer of £150,000 in 1885 was declined as inadequate.[161] The former had a more direct impact, with the Mercers agreeing to reduce the rent from £11,769 to £9,700 per annum.[162]

The Royal Commission of 1880–4 drew Parliament's attention to the Livery Companies' role in Ireland, and a House of Commons Select Committee in 1889–91 recommended that the Companies should be allowed to sell their estates but stated that the proceeds should be applied to specifically Irish purposes. No legislation ensued, but the Livery Companies fully appreciated that it was time to sell, and in view of the possibility that they might not be allowed free use of their money, the sooner this was done the better. The Mercers, in fact, hung on longer than their fellow 'planters', but pressure to leave became irresistible. In 1898 the Swatragh Tenants Defence Association was treated to a fierce anti-Mercers harangue which included the following reflection:[163]

All the other Companies have cleared out of Derry County and I think it would do no harm if we saw the 12th one on the other side of the Irish Sea.

The Irish Land Act of 1903 differed from its 1881 predecessor in the sense that an application to purchase their holdings from three-quarters of the tenants would 'trigger' the sale of the whole estate. Whether it was this difference or the simple passage of time which led to the change of mind is hard to say, but early in 1904 the decision was taken to 'clear out of Ireland altogether'.[164] By 1906 most of the properties had been sold, though some ground rents were retained to finance a few continuing obligations. The proceeds at one stage were expected to total £190,000 but in the event amounted to £150,000, precisely the sum rejected in 1885.[165] After the deduction of £9,000 for the Cooks, £7,000 for the Broderers and £4,500 for the Masons, the Mercers were left with £129,500 to show for their prolonged Irish adventure. Browbeaten at the outset by James I and Charles I and pilloried at the end by tenant-right campaigners, the Company gained little from Lot 8.

CONCLUSION

The late Victorian period was a difficult time for the Company, but it emerged relatively unscathed. Some of the trusts, notably Colet's and Dauntsey's, were radically altered; but the Company itself was unchanged. The Charity Commissioners managed to make administrative reforms but the Royal Commissions of 1833–7 and 1880–4 were much less successful with their essentially political plans. Why was this? Factors outside the Company's control, of course, played a very large part. Party-political changes in fortune, a shortage of Parliamentary time for secondary legislation, and a deep-seated reluctance to undermine property rights, all contributed to the Company's 'survival'.

However, the role of the Company itself deserves some attention. To some extent, the Mercers relied on the City Guilds Defence Association to do its lobbying for it,[166] but the importance of the Association's work is hard to assess;[U] and in any event the Company seems to have been careful to maintain its independence of the Association.[V] To a large extent the Company was its own advocate, and the vigour, tempered always by discretion, which characterised the Company's campaigns is impressive. How far this achievement is to be attributed to the qualities of Lord Selborne (and no doubt also the long-serving Clerk, Sir John Watney) and how far to the collective wisdom of a battle-hardened Court of Assistants is hard to say; but the effects were plain enough. The Company managed to avoid most of the traps which awaited a threatened corporation in the Gladstone years without making many political sacrifices (though Dauntsey's School is an obvious exception). It emerged not merely intact, but also (due to its support for technical education in particular) better able to win the battle for public opinion in the years to come.

[U] The Association's papers are preserved at Goldsmiths' Hall. Although they have been used by Dr Nicholson in his valuable thesis, 'The Politics of Metropolitan Reform: the background to the establishment of the London County Council, 1876–89' (Toronto Univ. PhD, 1972), they await full investigation.

[V] In 1885 the Clerk resigned as Secretary of the Association because the policies of the Company and the Association were 'not identical': AC, 1 May 1885.

CHAPTER XI

THE COMPANY AT THE ONSET OF THE FIRST WORLD WAR

STRUCTURE

At the beginning of the nineteenth century, the total membership of the Company stood at no more than 110 or so. Then there ensued a gentle increase to 150 by the 1870s, with a more rapid expansion at the end of the century.[1] By 1892, the membership stood at 201, and by 1910, 211. No doubt the Company's improved financial position explains a part of the reversal of the eighteenth-century decline, though the extent to which the modesty of the initial recovery is attributable simply to the prohibition on entry by redemption or also reflects the general malaise in Livery Company fortunes is uncertain. The surge in numbers at the end of the century might simply be demographic in origin, but it would be surprising if it were not also related to the renewed interest in the Company, and the Company's fresh sense of purpose, engendered by 'political' attacks. There were similar increases in most of the other Companies.[2]

Entry to the Company was usually by patrimony. Fifty-three of the seventy-two freemen admitted between 1813 and 1833 fell into this category.[3] The qualifications were strictly enforced. In 1809 William Whateley's freedom was revoked when it was discovered that his father had not been free of the City when Whateley junior had been born;[4] while in 1849–50 Nathaniel Collyer failed in his application for the same reason.[5] A freeman by patrimony had to be the son of a citizen and a Mercer *at birth*. Apprentices were a good deal less numerous, comprising only eighteen of the seventy-two admissions above and decreasing gradually, in relative if not absolute terms, as the century progressed.[6] Again admission was by no means automatic. A case in 1839–40, involving misconduct, dubious 'turnings-over' to different Masters and an apparently 'colourable' (or sham) apprenticeship, was perhaps unremarkable;[7] but another one in 1894 was distinctly 'hard'.[8] Redemption was, and (despite a motion in 1850[9]) remained, impossible; while 'honorary' freedoms were extremely rare. When a descendant of Sir Lionel Duckett promised to leave the great man's portrait to the Company in 1863 and asked to be made a freeman in return, he was told that admission had to be either by patrimony or apprenticeship.[A] [10] The overwhelming impression is that the Company was making it as difficult as decently possible for new members to join its ranks.

During the first half of the century there were still a number of freemen who had not been 'called' to the Livery. In 1833, for example, there were eleven such out of the total of 122 members.[11] It was thus premature for the Company in 1830 to attempt to justify its failure to make any Lady Campden loans with the 'explanation' that all freemen were now Liverymen.[B] Nevertheless the numbers of freemen *semple* were certainly dwindling and in 1849 most of the existing freemen were made Liverymen and a decision apparently made to eliminate the separate 'freemen' category (save perhaps for a brief

[A] The portrait was later (after some hesitation and doubts as to its attribution) purchased fom the erstwhile applicant for £525 (AC, 28 March and 4 April 1879), and remains in the Company's possession (see Fig. 3).

[B] See above, p. 148.

probationary period[12]) in future.[C] The Livery and the membership thus became effectively synonymous. The reason for the change is not readily fathomed, though it is difficult not to believe that it formed a part of the increasing exclusivity discernible in the admission process. The benefits of membership were now entirely social, not economic, and entrants were presumably deemed entitled to the Livery's entertainments from the outset. Whatever the explanation, and however inevitable it may have been, the decision produced a radical alteration in the traditional structure of the Company. 'Freemen', 'bachelors' and (at least in their proper sense) 'calls on the Livery' were no more.

The Court of Assistants began the century with a rival, the General Committee, but it soon made sure that, with the bankruptcy well and truly over, the General Committee would no longer wield executive power. In 1811 William Palmer declared that 'no General Committee is now necessary' and it was the Assistants who 'ought to digest all the affairs of the Company'.[13] Two years later a motion that the General Committee be continued was only just carried[14] and it was clear that the Committee's days of influence were over. It became little more than a clearing-house for licences to assign and sublet, and even in that capacity more of a hindrance than a help.[15]

'Elections' to the Court of Assistants seem to have been governed by the same principles as admissions to the Company itself. The personal standing of 'candidates' was closely scrutinised and any suggestion of an inability to discharge debts was fatal.[D] If a member's relatives were in receipt of monetary assistance from the Company (particularly if he was also an employee and not an independent businessman) then the prospects of election were slim.[16] The frustration, even bitterness, felt by those excluded was heightened by the fact that selection was usually by seniority, or at least collective will, rather than by ballot. It is true that in 1814–15, when there was a full-scale quarrel about the St Paul's School debt,[E] the Assistants decided to choose three additional members by ballot.[17] However, 'ancient practice' (as it was called) seems to have prevailed on other occasions.[F] There was also a complaint that Assistants stayed in their posts too long, blocking the advancement of Liverymen; but the suggestion of a superannuation scheme came to nothing.[18]

Before 1808, at least the junior Wardenships were filled by senior Liverymen. The new by-laws then adopted limited the selection to Assistants, and in fact for the first few years it was the *senior* Assistants who served as Master and Upper Warden in order (evidently) to shield newly-elected members from the demands of the highest offices.[19] In 1833 the Municipal Corporations Commission prompted a review of the by-laws and Counsel advised that the Assistants should be directed simply to choose those who were 'most proper' and the wording was altered accordingly.[20] There is no indication, however, that this had any effect on the selection of Assistants rather than Liverymen. Indeed there is at least some evidence to the contrary. In the early 1850s a litigant-member, trying to curtail the Assistants' power, claimed that it was the invariable practice for the Assistants to choose the Master and Wardens from their own number. The Company denied that this was a rule, but conceded that as a

[C] There was certainly a large 'call' of 18 freemen in November 1849 (AC, 16 November 1849, 17 May 1850), and thereafter freemen appear to have progressed quickly to the Livery. The call comprised simply those who 'are qualified and have been admitted into the freedom of the Company in or before this day' (e.g. AC, 25 December 1859). 'Qualified' was a usefully vague expression, but in practice meant anyone who had been 'admitted'.

[D] Hence Scarborough's protest at being passed by for Assistant in 1904: 'my record both socially and commercially is stainless' (Charter Box 1–2). The real reason, of course, may have been Scarborough's warm advocacy of Livery rights (see below, p. 193).

[E] See above, pp. 124–5.

[F] It was certainly for long regarded as inappropriate for the Assistants to vote as individuals rather than accept a collective 'view'. In 1898 it was resolved that subsequent reference to the actual numbers of any vote taken in the Court was 'out of order' (AC, 15 July 1898) and it was not until 1908 that two of the Court's committees were chosen by ballot and not seniority (AC, 13 March 1908).

matter of 'practice' Assistants had been chosen 'of late years', for the simple reason that members of the Court had 'more knowledge and experience of the affairs of the Company than others not upon the Court'.[21] Further evidence of this practice occurred in 1871 when an Assistant, the Revd Robert Sutton, was chosen Renter Warden.[22] When he attempted to follow the time-honoured course of Liverymen in similar circumstances before 1808 and fine off for £20 (on grounds of insufficient time to devote to the office), he was told by the Master that he had an obligation to serve and that if he could not do so he should resign from the Court. This caused much disquiet among Sutton's fellow Assistants and, though it was resolved that future Assistants would have to give a binding undertaking to serve as Wardens and Master,[G] Sutton's tendered resignation was not accepted. A third example dates from 1917 when Reginald Watney wanted to know how he could be elected Warden. The Clerk played a thoroughly defensive bat in reply and emphasised that the choice lay entirely with the Assistants, but he did make it clear that Watney would not even be eligible until he had been called on to the Court.[23] Only Assistants therefore appear to have been regarded as 'most proper' for service as Masters and Wardens.

FIG. 82. Walter Scarborough, Master of the Mercers' Company, 1909–10, by his daughter. He wears the Master's robes, and round his neck is the Master's badge. The painting hangs in the Reception area.
Mercers' Company

TENSIONS

The exclusivity which characterised the Company's constitution in the nineteenth century might have been expected to produce discontent. Liverymen denied access to the Company's accounts and given only a brief glance at the by-laws certainly had reason to feel aggrieved;[24] and in 1894 members were treated to the following remarks from Walter Scarborough:[25]

> We cannot shut our eyes to the fact that there is a growing feeling amongst our Liverymen that they do not receive that consideration from the Governing Body, to which, as members of and partners in a great and wealthy Company, they are entitled. It is only of late years they have begun to apprehend that they have inalienable rights and to understand that they are all-powerful if they choose to assert them. For this we have to thank the Royal Commission, which, while enlightening the public who had no just claim to the information, enlightened us who had, and who, up to that time, had been kept in utter ignorance of our own concerns. We can see symptoms of what I mean in the various notices of motion which have been lately and are still agitating our hitherto placid existence: we are waking up from the lethargy of centuries and to our Governing Body I would say, '*verb. sap.*'.

It is important, however, that the writer felt constrained to emphasise that the proposals, of which

[G] The new rule was broken almost at once, in the case of Roundell Palmer. Selborne, as he became in 1872, was excused service as Renter Warden during his first period as Lord Chancellor (1872–4), and he was allowed to serve as Master in 1875–6, without prior service as a Warden. AC, 13 September 1872, 12 September 1873, 17 June, 10 September 1875.

these observations formed part, involved '*no constitutional question*':

> *The privileges of the Governing Body will not be curtailed* and I for one, although I cannot regard with equanimity any infringement of the rights of the Livery, am not prepared, so long as those rights are freely conceded and observed, to abate one whit of the prerogatives of the Governing Body.

Such caution or deference was typical and in a sense speaks more eloquently than the message itself. It is also significant that, despite Scarborough's soothing presentation, his motion (involving the provision of common room facilities at the Hall) was defeated[26] and it only achieved some eventual and limited success (in the form of a reading and writing room) by reason of an unconstrained decision by the Assistants.[27]

The Assistants also found themselves under attack from individual Liverymen disappointed of their hopes of election to the 'Governing Body'. In 1852–3 Henry Newnham obtained a writ of Quo Warranto to establish that the choice of Master and Warden lay with the membership at large and not the Assistants alone, but he failed in his case.[28] Newnham later resorted to circulating his fellow Liverymen with *Observations and Suggestions* on the Assistants' 'arbitrary functions'.[29] However, despite diligent historical research and emotive prose, Newnham failed to persuade the 'Commonalty' to instigate an inquiry into the Assistants' authority or turn the General Court into an effective debating chamber which would review rather than rubber-stamp the Assistants' resolutions.[30] Shortly after the turn of the century in 1908, Richard Collyer was tempted to 'bring the conduct of a section of the Mercers' Company under the critical envious eye of the public through the medium of the Law Courts',[31] but eventually confined himself to a lengthy, if sometimes bitter, correspondence.

Before 1808 the Wardens may well also have felt themselves at the mercy of the all-powerful Assistants, but thereafter their feelings were no doubt rather different. It is therefore significant that the only *cri de cœur* of this kind arose before the new by-laws took effect. House Warden Hillier was one of those opposed to the controversial repayment of the St Paul's School debt, but he did not know whether he was entitled or empowered to act independently. 'If the Wardens are merely cash-keepers to the Company I feel myself bound to obey this resolution; but if the Wardens have a discretionary power I must decline complying with it'.[32]

For the most part tensions were conspicuous by their absence. There are signs that as numbers rose at the end of the century the Livery did indeed raise the occasional murmur of discontent, but, apart from one or two invocations of Livery 'rights' in order to advance a particular cause or course of action,[H] there was scarcely any *constitutional* element in the protest. The Scarborough episode in 1894, for example, merely concerned the provision of better social facilities at the Hall. It was on such issues that Liverymen chose to disturb the Company's 'placid existence'. The Assistants' exclusive control aroused little real resentment.

THE MEMBERSHIP

The Company in fact took on an unmistakably exclusive air in the nineteenth century. The 'old families' became more and more preponderant and the 'snug family nests' still cosier, as the effects of admission by patrimony made themselves felt. These are the numbers of Liverymen in four of the Company's most numerous families:

	Watney	*Palmer*	*Collyer*	*Hodson*
1815	3	7	4	2
1870	15	14	8	8
1914	43	17	13	14

[H] The four Liverymen who in 1887 suggested some form of pre-emptive action in the face of the worst effects of State intervention concluded their campaign by thanking the Master for the courteous tone of his final letter, 'specially as we may infer from it that though some members of the Court of Assistants may and do we know think otherwise the majority of them consider as we certainly do ourselves that the Liverymen of the Company are not precluded from feeling an interest in its welfare or in matters of corporate significance in a respectful and constitutional manner from offering suggestions to its head [i.e. the Master]'. AC, 4 March 1887.

Gibes at 'Watney, Palmer & Co' from the radical Press during the debate aroused by the Royal Commission of 1880–4 were exaggerated and opportunistic,[33] but they were not easily rebutted. Even members unconnected by blood were sometimes associated in business or trade.[I] Exclusivity, even introspection, were features of many Companies of this time (especially the Great Twelve), but the Mercers displayed a particularly acute form of the 'disease' and it made them vulnerable.

Occupations are not easily assessed, but there are signs of a further shift away from 'trade' to the professions. There were some genuine tradesmen, including even a manufacturer of lace and hosiery,[34] at the beginning of the century, but they appear to have had few counterparts at the end of the period.[35] By then stockbrokers had taken their place. Again this trend simply reflected a general social change, but it still had the effect of making the task of justifying the Company's existence more difficult. A society composed of clerics, lawyers, bankers and brokers drawn from a handful of families was an easy target for the radicals. How could such men be relied upon to discharge their charitable 'duties' to the poor and needy?

PRIVILEGES

The benefits of Company membership took various forms. For outside observers the most important were the feasts. 'Turtle soup' became the symbol of City decadence for the polemicists.[J] Certainly for most Liverymen the dinners were the only obvious reason for membership. The occasions were clearly given, even by Livery Company standards, careful and expensive treatment.[36] In 1903, for example, nearly £4,900 out of a gross corporate (i.e. unencumbered) income of £53,000 was spent on dinners. Mercers' School received only £4,100.[37] When a Liveryman found he was too late to secure a place at table he made a great fuss and spoke warmly of constitutional 'rights'.[38] In fact, considerable care was taken to prevent such outbursts. When the increase in Livery numbers made it necessary to make new arrangements, the matter was exhaustively discussed.[39] Whether the hospitality was 'excessive' is difficult to establish. On the one hand, the Liverymen were invited to dine at the Hall only twice a year, and one of them saw fit to make a full-scale complaint.[40] On the other hand, there would certainly have been more Livery Dinners had there been more space at the Hall, and there were plenty of other smaller or special feasts.[41] A diner in 1899 described his Mercers' feast as 'important enough to be styled a banquet' but 'not so long as to be wearying'. The eight-course menu might seem long enough by modern standards, but it was evidently fairly restrained by contemporary ones.[42]

The Company's critics were also much exercised by the question of patronage. Some of the Church livings, it has to be acknowledged, went to Mercers or their relations. A notable example occurred in 1891 when the Clerk, John Watney, managed to secure the replacement of his late brother James at Canwick with his nephew Henry, thus ensuring proper provision for the widow and the rest of her children. It is significant that the complainant was another member who thought he was better qualified![K] [43] The Company's Gresham lectureships were occasionally awarded to members (though William Palmer's conduct shows that this did not guarantee meek compliance).[44] Offices, too, were largely the preserve of Company men. The example of two

[I] The 1814–15 Livery list (which unlike later compilations gives a good number of business addresses) and contemporary trade directories reveal that Messrs Barker, Britton, Helm and Plater were all silversmiths at the same address in Hatton Garden; Delafosse and Archdale Palmer were tea-dealers in Fenchurch Street; Barnes and Newton were merchants and insurance brokers in Copthall Court; and Clarke and Yellowley were stationers in Gracechurch Street.

[J] See above, p. 165 for Saunders' description of the Dauntsey 'surplus'.

[K] Nine benefices or lecturerships were in the gift of the Company in 1880. Two, including Canwick, were held by members, though six years later, when the Company had its first opportunity to present to the combined parish of St Andrew by the Wardrobe and St Anne's Blackfriars, another member was chosen.

FIG. 83. Sir John Watney (1834–1923). Solicitor to the Mercers' Company, 1870–5, and then Clerk, 1875–1906.
Mercers' Company

Clerks will suffice.[45] H. E. Barnes was the son of the previous Clerk and served as both Irish or Junior Office Clerk (in succession to his brother) and Accountant before his election. John Watney was Accountant and then Solicitor prior to his Clerkship. Indeed it is hard to find a principal officer who had *not* been a Liveryman when elected and, though there was some private concern that 'the Company was getting too close a corporation',[46] personal or family ties prevailed. Candidates were always anxious to stress their Company 'lineage'.[47] On the other hand, surprisingly few tenants of Company property were Mercers. A full list supplied to the Royal Commissioners in 1882 affords very few examples indeed.[48] There was certainly no suggestion that Company property, whether trust or corporate, was let on favourable terms.

'Pensions' or doles were also the subject of the Commissioners' scrutiny, and a total of £4,400 was stated to have been spent in this way in 1880.[49] Virtually all the recipients were members of the Company, or their widows and families. £3,000 came from the burgeoning Whittington fund,[50] but, although the nomination of a growing number of pensioners by Assistants constituted a technical breach of trust, there was no question of malpractice.[L] The Company was more than ready to revise its arrangements so as to ensure that the *Court* of Assistants voted on all nominations. Sir John Watney's selection of one of his domestic servants in 1905 may have caused a minor stir in the Press (following a 'leak' by an antagonistic member[M])[51] and led in due course to a new scheme, but the Charity Commissioners went out of their way to emphasise that they did 'not question the good faith of the Company as trustees of the Charity ...'.[52] All the Company had done had been to extend the charity beyond its own ranks and had indeed eventually dispensed with any kind of residential qualification. This, it was acknowledged, went beyond the terms of the Whittington foundation charter.[53]

The Whittington nomination system apart, applications for assistance were treated with considerable care and caution. The precise financial and personal circumstances were established with exemplary, if sometimes rather chilling, thoroughness and the awards were hard-headed almost to a fault.[54] Refusals were by no means uncommon, even for members.[55] Pensioners found that the eighth by-law, prohibiting those in receipt of financial aid from attending General Courts, was strictly enforced. At one stage there was doubt as to whether loans as well as pensions were cause for disqualification,[56] but from 1883, following Lord Selborne's intervention, it was

[L] In 1881 the Revd A. E. Clementi-Smith successfully defended himself against the charge that he had nominated to an out-pension in return for a sale of property at an undervalue. AC, 18 February, 11 and 18 March 1881. A year or so earlier a fellow Assistant had complained of Clementi-Smith's conduct for an unspecified reason. It may be surmised that the Whittington nomination was the cause. AC, 7, 13 and 28 November, 5 and 12 December 1879, 6 and 12 February 1880.

[M] This was Colonel M. Clementi, whose penchant for direct communication with the Charity Commissioners in relation to St Paul's School has already been noticed (see above, p. 169). See AC, 14 April, 7 July 1905. Clementi declined to confirm that he was responsible for the Press comments, but it hardly admits of doubt.

established that anyone who defaulted in his repayments was included.[57] The number of 'non-voting' Liverymen in various years was as follows:[58]

1860	27 out of	140
1868	22	151
1879	18	157
1892	27	201
1900	25	212
1910	32	211

The totals might perhaps be used as evidence of the extent to which the Company looked after its own. On the other hand, their existence shows that the Company regarded its franchise and its largesse as quite incompatible. A Liveryman had to choose.[N]

There was, however, one aspect of the Commissioners' review which did reveal unequivocably disturbing evidence. In 1870 the Assistants decided to double their attendance fee. Henceforward they were to be paid four guineas for appearing at either General Courts or their own meetings, and two guineas for committees. It would appear that the intention was to absorb some of the surplus yearly income and prevent it accumulating as a bait for political predators.[59] Even the strenuously expressed doubts of the Solicitor, John Watney, as to the power of the Assistants to vote money to themselves without the consent of the General Court were insufficient to deter them.[60] By the time of the Royal Commission a considerable sum was being paid in this way,[61] and the more partisan Commissioners made sure they mentioned this during Selborne's otherwise fairly comfortable appearance on behalf of the City and Guilds Institute.[62] Sir Arthur Hobhouse alluded to the fees in a considered article in the influential *Contemporary Review*,[63] while the more popular Press thoroughly enjoyed itself on the point. The *Spectator* commented: 'when the other Companies compare themselves

FIG. 84. Bronze medallion of the Maiden by W. Bainbridge Reynolds, made in 1909. This originally adorned the gates at the old Frederick's Place entrance to the Company's offices, but is now at the Ironmonger Lane entrance.
Mercers' Company

with the Mercers they must indeed stand astonished at their own moderation';[64] while *Truth* was characteristically crude and direct: 'the Court of the Mercers is a particularly happy family and I should much like to know how much money passed . . . out of the corporate exchequer into the pockets of the two great Mercer families [of Palmer and Watney presumably]'.[65]

Even when the *parti pris* had been discounted, there remained much force in the allegations. The Assistants ensured that they were properly remunerated for their efforts. When Walter Scarborough tried to obtain better facilities for the Livery at the Hall in 1894,[O] he pointed out:[66]

It must not be overlooked — and I say this with all due respect — that the services rendered by those who manage our affairs are not voluntary; substantial fees are paid out of the Company's funds for every individual attendance . . .

[N] Indeed, he chose on behalf of himself *and* his relatives. As indicated above (p. 180), a family could find itself debarred from office if any of its members accepted assistance from the Company.

[O] See below, p. 193.

The Assistants may have worked hard to prevent abuse of the privileges enjoyed by the membership as a whole, but they could not accept that they should not be rewarded for that work. Their lack of judgement in this matter jeopardised their other achievements and indeed tarred all members with the same brush:[67]

> The common rumour [is] that this company is so rich that they do not know what to do with their money and that when a young man comes on the Company he commences not by paying but by receiving money.

In a sense this was right: most members were now admitted through patrimony rather than redemption or apprenticeship, and all those attending General Court did receive an attendance fee; but the cause of this mischievous exaggeration was undoubtedly the *Assistants'* Court fees. The entire membership had reason to regret the decision of 1870.

ADMINISTRATION

The two preceding Chapters will have indicated the extent to which the Company's work increased in the nineteenth century. The new-found surpluses, the resumption of control over the Irish estate, the regular (and complex) dealings with the Charity Commissioners, and the welter of legislation (potential and actual), all placed a heavy burden on the Company's administrative resources. In 1871 John Watney, then the Accountant, pointed out that since 1840 the number of Court and committee meetings held each year had almost doubled, rising from seventy-one to 138. Four years later Watney became Clerk, and in 1888 he estimated that business had increased by 25% during his Clerkship alone. He also contrasted the combined total of income and expenditure in 1887 (£104,000) with its equivalent in 1833 (£46,000).[68]

Part of the burden, of course, was shouldered by the Master, Wardens and Assistants. The demands on their time and energy might in fact explain why the Assistants distanced themselves from the Livery. A hard-pressed executive tends to be impatient of constitutional niceties. Nevertheless there remained a great deal of day-to-day or otherwise routine work to be undertaken by the Company's officers and staff.[69] The employees included an Accountant, Receiver (of rents), Irish or Junior Office Clerk, Copying or Conveyancing Clerk, Beadle, Under-Beadle (who also had clerical duties), porters and a labourer (or maintenance man). More or less independent retainers were the Surveyors, Solicitor and Land Agent. The key figure however, remained the Clerk himself. The remuneration may have been substantial (John Watney enjoyed a composite income well in excess of £2,000),[70] but so was the responsibility. In 1879 there was talk of relieving the Clerk of at least some tasks,[71] and no doubt if Watney had not been such a robust, able man the suggestion would have borne fruit. As it was, Watney continued unaided to discharge his many tasks (which included the Clerkships of the Gresham Committee and the Governing Body of St Paul's School and the Joint Secretaryship of the City and Guilds Institute, as well as his obvious Company duties) until his retirement in 1906. His pension reflected his remuneration and it aroused some criticism in the Press,[72] but the Company had every reason to be grateful to Watney for coping so effectively for so long (and during such perilous times) with the heavy demands of the Clerk's office.

The increase in business necessarily also created a need for better facilities in Ironmonger Lane. Alterations in the office accommodation following the expiration of the Stewart lease in Ireland in 1831 were related expressly to the 'increased' business of the Company.[73] These were only one of a series of such changes in the nineteenth century. Most were of a minor nature, but in 1907 the offices were entirely and expensively reconstructed.[74]

THE CITY AND GRESHAM COLLEGE

The Company's relations with the City Corporation deteriorated still further in the nineteenth century. Scarcely any members held civic office: there were only two Common Councilmen and no Aldermen.[75] A disgruntled outsider spoke of the

FIG. 85. William Waldegrave Palmer, 2nd Earl of Selborne, Master of the Mercers' Company, 1910–11 and 1933–4, by Philip de Laszlo. This handsome oil painting now hangs in the Reception area, outside the Livery Hall; Lord Selborne wears court dress under his mantle as a Knight of the Garter.
Mercers' Company

Company standing 'ostentatiously aloof'.[76] Indifference would be a more accurate term. The Mercer families were more than content to reserve their energies for the premier Company. The Company's recent experiences were bound to have fostered a cautious and introspective attitude on the part of its members. Mercers saw little point in involving themselves in the Corporation's work when it had ceased to be municipally irrelevant or obstructive (as it certainly was in the first half of the century), and became highly contentious and party-political.[77] It was not, it would seem, merely the absence of a Mercer Lord Mayor which led to a distinct lack of interest in the Lord Mayor's Show. The decision in the 1820s not to join in the procession from Westminster to Guildhall[78] probably reflected the show's descent from spectacle to pantomime.[79] It is true that the Company remained sensitive on the question of precedence, but it is interesting to note that it was on a royal rather than strictly civic occasion that the Company made a stand. When George IV went by river to Trinity Hospital at Greenwich the Goldsmiths' barge preceded the Mercers'. The Company had to accept that this was simply a temporary aberration by way of courtesy to the King's own Company, but it took the matter very seriously and did what it could to protect its position for the future.[80]

In the absence of civic ties, the most important contact between the City and the Company occurred in relation to the administration of the Gresham benefaction.[81] The difference of attitude during the building of the Royal Exchange has already been noticed. It remains here to trace the tensions arising from the work of Gresham College itself. The construction of the new building in 1843 did nothing to increase attendances at lectures or generally revitalise the College. The Charity Commission suggested approaching the old suitors (for example, the London Institution and the Association of Evening Classes at Crosby Hall) but, in the face of the customary warm opposition from the lecturers,[P] the City seemed no more inclined to do so than the Company. Then, in 1875, the City began to show signs of

[P] It is difficult to resist the opportunity to quote Music Professor Edward Taylor's riposte to the charge that his lectures were merely free concerts. 'If my lecture is styled a free concert, with equal accuracy and equal propriety might a lecture on one branch of chemistry be called a display of fireworks or a lecture on botany a horticultural show.' Taylor is quoted by Jean Imray, in her typescript 'Memoir on the Gresham Lectures'.

impatience. It decided to require candidates for its chairs to give 'trial' lectures and to restrict appointments to one year only. Ten years later came a more important step. The City or, to be more precise, Common Council pressed for the sale of the College building and the distribution of the proceeds in accordance with Gresham's will. This would have meant the end of the College as an institution but offered the opportunity of a much more flexible, and utilitarian, application of the fund. However, the City Side of the Joint Gresham Committee resisted Common Council's pressure and in conjunction with the Company's representatives was able to ensure that the proposals came to nothing. The next few years were taken up by the College's peripheral involvement in the heated struggle to establish a University of London which would not merely examine but also teach.[82] The appointment at one stage of a 'Gresham University Commission' might suggest that the College came close to a glorious transmogrification, but the reformers based their hopes on the quite false assumption that there was not merely a name on offer but money as well. In fact, the City no less than the Company made it perfectly plain that any form of endowment was out of the question. The Commission took the hint and 'Gresham' was conspicuously absent from its recommendations. The University of London was reconstituted without any help from the Square Mile.

Differences between the City and the Company over the College re-emerged in 1907–9. The prosaic question of a fire escape led to a full-scale assessment of the viability of the College buildings, and then to the utility of the College itself. The issue of removal and amalgamation was revived. Again the lead came from the City, with its special committee urging the merits of the London Institution, the City of London School or even London University. The City's attitude may well have been fashioned by its anxiety to avoid Corporation duty and its willingness to allow the Gresham benefaction to become subject to at least a *de facto* trust. The Mercers had decided to keep a free hand and pay the duty, and they had in fact only just managed to stop the City pressing its case for exemption to the House of Lords.[83] There may well have been also a simple reluctance to spend any more money on the unloved College. The Company was plainly less than keen for the City to encourage expensive new schemes to which it would find itself obliged to contribute half the cost. The Mercers were ready to contemplate selling the College building and allocating the present £700 expenditure elsewhere, but, in Walter Scarborough's words,[84] they were

not prepared to abdicate their rights at the bidding of irresponsible persons, unacquainted with the facts, who pose in the Press as philanthropists on the strength of their efforts to regulate the administration of other people's property.

As the rather strident tone indicates, the Company was conscious of its vulnerability to public criticism. It was difficult to refute the superficial cogency of one newspaper's suggestion that, if the Mercers did not want to co-operate in the City's plan, it should sever its links with the trust and make a grant from its half-share in the surplus, thus leaving the City to 'work out the salvation of this all-but moribund institution'.[85] It was Scarborough (a former board member of the London Institution) who appears to have been chiefly responsible for ensuring that the Company successfully parried the attack, partly by emphasising the Company's 'public-spirited and self-sacrificing' conduct from the outset ('the trust, so far as it is a trust, has entailed a very serious strain upon their own private resources'), and partly by urging his fellow Assistants to be ready to countenance at least modest changes to the College regime.[86] In the event the Company permitted an experimental relocation of the lectures at the City of London School and, when this produced no cure, the decision was taken to rebuild the College on an enlarged site and with some paying tenants. On balance the Company had won the argument, though it was not a success which can have given it much pleasure.

It would be easy to suggest that the differences over Gresham College were a symptom, or perhaps even the cause, of the estrangement between the Company and the City. No doubt the presence of a Mercer Alderman or two would have helped to bridge the obvious gap in attitudes, and perhaps a flourishing College would have eroded some of the mutual indifference, but the divide between Company and Corporation had much deeper causes. It was the product of an economic and social process which, as Chapter I indicated, began as early as the late sixteenth century. Only the dramatic political events of the late nineteenth century reversed the trend, and even then a good deal of mistrust remained. The Corporation felt that the Companies were not doing enough to meet their civic obligations, while the Companies (particularly the Great Twelve), if they did not actually disapprove of the City's conduct, certainly wanted to distance themselves from the party-political dangers attendant on municipal affairs. The Mercers exemplified this process. Newnham's Mayoralty in 1782 became not so much a distant memory as a curious fact in Company history.

Fig. 86. 1911 Grant of Arms to the Mercers' Company. Hereafter, the Maiden is frozen in time, no longer following the fashion.
Mercers' Company

CONCLUSION

Any general assessment of the nineteenth century Company has to acknowledge the considerable loyalty and pride it inspired. The lengthy service of so many of the Mercers' officers and servants reflected much more than the comfort and security of their posts.[87] There was a genuine affection for the Company. When James Barnes left his son an inkstand given in recognition of James's service to the Gresham Committee, he was clearly gratified by his son's promise that the gift would never leave the Hall; and in due course the pledge was fulfilled.[88] The Company's traditions also received respectful attention, particularly after the self-assessment which arose as a result of the political pressures towards the end of the century. The introduction of stained-glass representations of benefactors and other important figures from the Company's past during the refurbishment of the Livery Hall in 1880 may be more than a conventional response in such circumstances (and in any event the initiative appears to have come from the contractor and not the Assistants);[89] but the lavish celebrations of the 500th anniversary of the first Charter in January 1894 were perhaps more significant. A service in the Chapel was followed by dinner and the presentation to members of 181 reproductions of the Sydenham monteith (costing a total of more than £2,000).[90]

Even more significant was the determination to keep Mercers' School alive. By the end of the century the School was finding the competition from the new London County Council schools increasingly difficult to withstand.[91] Despite the efforts of an able and scholarly Headmaster (the Revd Dr D. L. Scott), numbers began to decline quickly. Even an expensive move in 1894 to Barnards Inn did not arrest the trend (indeed, by

FIG. 87 (right). Lord Baden-Powell, Master of the Mercers' Company, 1913–14, by David Jagger, 1929. This portrait of the hero of Mafeking and founder of the Boy Scouts' movement hangs in the Reception area, opposite the entrance to the Livery Hall.
Mercers' Company

FIG. 88 (opposite page). Doodles on the back of minutes of meetings, *c.* 1918, by Lord Baden-Powell, who was an enthusiastic and witty cartoonist.
Mercers' Company

confining the School to the City in a physical and educational sense, it made matters worse[Q]) and it was not long before the House Warden was complaining that 'we get nothing from this School except the reputation of extravagant liberality'.[92] The House Warden's remedy was to try to balance the books by raising fees or reducing salaries, albeit with the important proviso that any changes must do the Company no discredit. Ten years later, in 1909, the situation had deteriorated and there was talk of closure. Notice was given of the following motion:[93]

that in view of the serious and continued falling off of numbers in Mercers' School owing to the competition of Government schools it is undesirable to continue Mercers' School under existing conditions and that the Master and Wardens be instructed to consult the Board of Education informally as to the advisability of applying to the Board for a scheme for appropriating the endowment of the School to some more efficient educational object.

[Q] See below, p. 209 *et seq.*

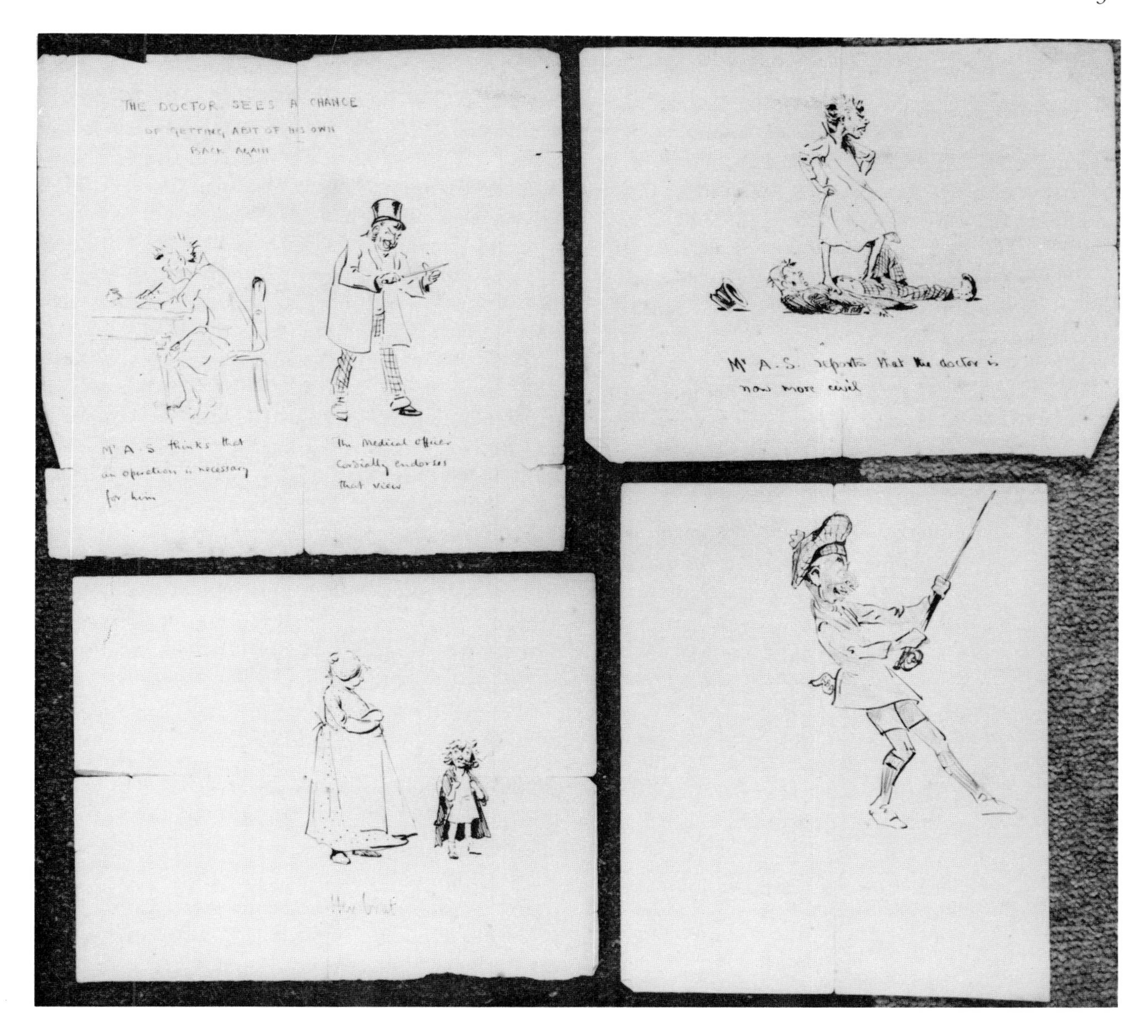

Although the motion (together with amended versions) was eventually withdrawn, a warm debate was provoked. It is interesting to see how vigorously the proposal was opposed. One Assistant thought closure 'would be almost a sin'; another advocated reducing the fees, 'never mind what it costs'.[94] All manner of expedients were discussed and some (including better facilities, further awards and more assertive advertising) were adopted.[95]

Closure, however, was ruled out. It evidently mattered little that no Mercers sent their sons to the School any more; it was sufficient that the reputation of the Company was at stake. The School had been part of the Henrician settlement and as such formed an important element in the Company's past. It would not be jettisoned for the sake of 'some more efficient educational object'.

By 1912, with the political storms largely quelled, the Company was prepared to consider the publication of a brief history compiled from the returns to the Royal Commission in 1880–2. However, the proposal gave rise to considerable concern and debate.[96] Opponents tried to substitute an annual almanac and pocket diary, or a mere statement of affairs, and although the original proposal was eventually adopted, it is noteworthy that a reference to bringing the returns up to date was omitted (and indeed also that the Charter's ordinances and by-laws which were to accompany the 'History' were to be *extracts* only). The result was *An Account of the Mistery of Mercers*, compiled by Sir John Watney and published in 1914. The former Clerk was certainly faithful to his brief. The book was slim and the text bland. It may have been pride which prompted the initial idea of publication, but it was caution which ultimately prevailed. Watney's 'compilation' was indeed an *Account*, more an historical handbook than a 'History'. The Company had no intention of giving its critics any ammunition. Sir John Watney could be relied on to give a version of events which, while not inaccurate, was certainly 'authorised'. Other investigators, even those with impeccable scholarly credentials, were less welcome. In the year before Watney's volume appeared, the Company was fiercely rebuked by the learned historian of *The Aldermen of the City of London*:[97]

> The most important of all the Companies, once the most closely connected of all with the Aldermen of London . . . , has done singularly little towards opening to the historical student the treasures of its ancient records and, instead of welcoming, does its best to repel with a frigid non possumus those who would willingly, at no cost to that guild's not very slender financial resources, do some small portion of the work which a more adequate conception of the moral duty of those who have important historical material in their charge, would impel its officials to undertake themselves or entrust to capable hands.

The Revd A. B. Beaven's experience was not unique.[98]

The Company's cautious, even secretive, attitude was closely associated with a general feeling of self-sufficiency. In a very real sense the Company was a closed community. There was quite literally a family atmosphere in Ironmonger Lane, as the recollections of someone who spent her childhood there in the 1890s make plain.[99] Her father, J. W. Parker (the Under-Beadle), had friends and relations not merely among fellow employees and retainers but also in more elevated positions. One summer the Parker family looked after a Clementi-Smith riverside home at Staines. The Company's generous treatment of staff in times of personal difficulty reflected a great deal more than calculating paternalism: a real intimacy is evident.[100] When the Accountant, Nathaniel Clark, died in 1861 the Master offered much more than the usual condolences. The Company, he said, had lost 'a most faithful servant and a most kind and assiduous friend'. It is important to appreciate that Clark, and indeed J. W. Parker, were Liverymen as well as officers or employees. It was commonplace for Liverymen who lacked independent means to find a niche at Ironmonger Lane.[101] Hence, of course, part of the explanation for the large number of non-voting Liverymen noticed earlier.[R]

It is tempting to deduce from all this that the Company was degenerating from guild to club. It is certainly true that the extensive rebuilding and refurbishment works carried out at Cheapside between 1877 and 1883, which cost over £71,000, created a luxurious, if still rather dangerous, setting for the Company's entertainments;[S] but the original motivation at least was simply to accommodate the increasing number of Liverymen diners, and the subsequent redecoration and embellishment reflected straightforward

[R] See above, p. 185. Officers and employees were disqualified under by-law 18, pensioners and debtors under by-law 8.

[S] The shored-up old building remained far from stable. When the future Clerk, Frank Watney, was still a schoolboy 'he attended a Ball [at the Hall] and during the first waltz it became apparent that the building was swaying in time with the music. His father, Sir John, rushed on to the floor shouting to the band to stop and the terrified dancers were able to feel the quaking building slowly settle back on its foundation. After that Ladies' Nights were held elswhere'. From the transcript of a talk given by Dr Roger Lane to the General Court, September 1974.

A. St Paul's School: north elevation of the fourth school building, at Hammersmith, which opened in 1884, by Sir Alfred Waterhouse, 29 October 1880. Coloured lithograph. Waterhouse also designed the Central Institution (see Fig. 73); his most famous building is the Natural History Museum.

Mercers' Company

B. The Livery Hall by John Crowther, 1901.

By courtesy of Guildhall Library, Corporation of London: Chadwyck-Healey Collection/Bridgeman Art Library Ltd

PLATE XVIII

First World War memorial window from the Chapel. Dedicated on 23 January 1923 to the twenty-five Mercers who lost their lives. The window survived the destruction of Mercers' Hall in 1941, and was sent to Dauntsey's School in 1973.

Mercers' Company

Company pride rather than clubbish self-indulgence.[102] It is also true that Walter Scarborough in 1894 called expressly for a 'centre for social communion' for the young Liverymen. However, he emphasised that his plan did 'not mean turning Mercers' Hall into a clubhouse', and it was certainly clear that Scarborough did not believe that the Company had become a mere club, still less did he wish to encourage the process. His aim was merely to give those Members who had only spasmodic contact with the Company an opportunity to 'belong'. If there *was* a club, it was one formed out of the Master, Wardens and Assistants, and Scarborough's proposals were designed to throw open its doors to a wider membership.[103]

To deny that the Company had become a club is not to suggest that it was still, in any worthwhile sense, a guild. The Assistants were unlikely to have given much consideration to the Company's original *raison d'être*: a sense of duty to benefactors and previous generations of Mercers was sufficient motivation to fight for the preservation and proper use of the wealth entrusted to them. For the first half of the nineteenth century there was little reason, and certainly no social pressure, for the Mercers to consider how they should be contributing to the lives of their fellow citizens. In the second half of the century they were certainly asked to consider such questions, but at a time of such political threat that they were usually responding in haste to events or demands, rather than making their own positive plans for the future. Hence the pricklish, defensive air of a Company which, in truth, had little, except its wealth, to hide.

CHAPTER XII

RECENT TIMES, 1914–59

In many respects, the recent history of the Company falls into two parts. Both were shaped by the effects of the two World Wars.

It is difficult to over-emphasise what a watershed the outbreak of the First World War was to contemporaries. The war was quite unlike any other great war in British experience. The effort and the sacrifices were unprecedented. The Second World War, though traumatic, not least because it came so soon after the war to end all wars, did not involve the same carnage.

For Londoners, however, the conflict of the 1939–45 war proved to have a longer-lasting impact than that of 1914–18. In the First World War, fewer than 600 people were killed in air raids on London, whereas in the Second World War 20,000 were killed during the Blitz alone. The City suffered 715 air-raid alarms; 164 acres out of 460 were totally razed. Eighteen churches, and sixteen Livery Halls, were destroyed. It was a catastrophe that could only be compared with the destruction caused by the Great Fire, and it called for resolve and imagination to deal with the consequences.

PART I. 1914 to 1941

CONSTITUTIONAL PRESSURE

In May 1918 seven senior Liverymen sent a circular to their fellow members suggesting that they attend a meeting to consider how to reassert the Livery's rights and privileges.[1] At present the General Court was merely rubber-stamping the 'arbitrary' rule of that 'self-elected Executive Body', the Court of Assistants. Such a state of affairs was 'not in keeping with the powers permitted by the internal constitutions of the principal institutions and corporations existing in this country' and (in a significant end-of-War sentiment) was 'not in accord with the spirit of these times'. The meeting would appoint a committee to consider how 'the rules and regulations of the Company can be altered so as to improve the internal administration of the Company and more effectually safeguard the interests of the Livery'. The product of the ensuing debates was the following notice of a motion to be placed before the General Court:[2]

> That the Livery having been from time to time deprived of certain of the rights and privileges formerly enjoyed by them, a Committee be now formed with power to enquire fully into the circumstances and at the next General Court to submit a report as to the best method of restoring to the Livery their ancient rights and privileges [and] that the Committee shall consist of the Master, Wardens, three members of the Court of Assistants and seven members of the Livery, the latter to be selected by the Commonalty [who could thus determine the Committee's 'complexion'].

The Master and Wardens stalled, denying any knowledge of the alleged loss of rights and privileges, and asking for details of any 'irregularities or wrongful acts'.[3] The Livery Committee persisted and duly provided the following 'details':[4]

- the discrepancy between the by-laws and the original charters and ordinances
- the election to positions of profit and grants of money without consent of the General Body
- the removal of the administration of the Whittington Charity from the General Body to the Court of Assistants.

FIG. 89. The Royal Exchange by Sydney B. Jones, *c.* 1920. Note the line of omnibuses.
By courtesy of Guardian Royal Exchange Collection

The Committee could have been more specific (the election of H. R. Wilson in October 1917 as Acting Clerk was almost certainly the reason for the reference to elections without consent), but these extremely vague 'details' were sufficient to satisfy the Master and Wardens' request and they left the Committee with a free hand.

The motion was heard at a General Court held on 27 September 1918. There is an account of the debate in a letter from the Master, Archdale Palmer, to the future Clerk, F. D. Watney, then serving as a Colonel with the Egyptian Expeditionary Force. It is most unusual to be given such an insider's view and, notwithstanding the obvious *parti pris*, it deserves lengthy quotation:[5]

The Meeting was one of no little importance because of a certain Bolshevist tendency that, during some little time, has been simmering over here among a certain section in the Company. You have probably heard of meetings convened by Richard Collyer, Reginald Watney, Wilfred Powell and others, for the purpose of raising questions affecting — as they allege — the rights and privileges of the Livery. These meetings culminated in a Notice of Motion given by Wilfred Powell at the General Court in June last, for discussion to-day, in something like the following terms: 'That the Livery, having been deprived of certain of their rights and privileges, hitherto enjoyed by them, a Committee be appointed with full powers to examine the same and report to the next General Court as to the best methods to be adopted to secure their restoration'. We had asked for particulars to the alleged deprivations, in order to investigate the same before this Court, but they refused to disclose them and we went into Court in complete [*sic*] ignorance of what they were going to say; but we had a clear conscience, and some indication of some of their grievances had reached us, and all these were prepared for. Your cousin, [T]. Savile Watney, had the answering of the case, and while his case to answer was not difficult, seeing that the proposer admitted that he had no particulars to furnish, and therefore was asking for a more or less roving Commission of Inquiry, Savile did the work extraordinarily well. I prefaced the whole proceedings by an announcement to the Court of the steps that we had taken to apprise ourselves of what their complaint was, and of our failure to elicit anything [*sic*], and then called upon Mr. Powell to propose his motion. His method was not effective. He was seconded by Mr.

[C.F.P.] Hodson ... and he too made an ineffective speech. [A.E.] Rayden spoke quite nicely, also in support of the proposal to appoint a Committee. I then asked if there was anybody else anxious to disclose any further alleged deprivations and this brought Mr. [Richard] Collyer to his legs, but he did not say very much. The result of the whole thing was that their case, as presented, was not very clear. After the complete answering of the four points that they alleged by the Upper Warden [T. S. Watney],[A] Lord Selborne spoke very effectively and urged that nothing could be more unfortunate for the Company at the present moment than the appointment of a Committee of this kind after the answer that had been so completely given by the Upper Warden. Basil Watson put the final nail into their coffin, and nobody else spoke. Selborne having moved an amendment that we should proceed to the next business, I put it to the Court and 47 Members held up their hands in support. The contrary secured 29 votes only. The second portion of their motion, which was as to the constitution of the proposed Committee, therefore fell to the ground and I think everybody feels relieved at the matter having been thus disposed of. The measure of applause that greeted the speeches was entirely on their side, as very often happens in public meetings those who are in favour of the existing order of things not perhaps gaining so much applause as the party that felt that they had a weak cause and wished to bolster up their supporters. Thank you many times for your warm congratulations upon my assumption of the Mastership. I am no end relieved at what has taken place today as I have been thinking about it almost incessantly for the last three months.

The margin of the Livery Committee's defeat, though conclusive, was not emphatic. To have gathered twenty-nine votes in favour of a direct attack on the Assistants was something of an achievement and there was obviously ground for hope that, if the rest of the membership could be roused to attend, success was possible. It is not surprising therefore that it was not long before there were further signs of the 'Bolshevist tendency'. The General Court held in December 1918 was asked to consider a motion that 'the Master and Wardens be requested to consider and report to the next Quarterly General Court as to the means by which the usefulness of the Company as the Premier Guild of the City of London may be extended and enhanced'.[6] This seems to have emanated from the Livery Committee or at least its supporters. The committee's first circular had declared that 'during this Great War the executive of the Company has shown a want of initiative and has taken no opportunity of discussing with the Livery by what means the individual effort and material resources of the Company could be best employed'.[7] Whether the dissatisfaction was merely a general one, a feeling that the spirit of the times (or indeed the prospect of a Labour Government) called for greater efforts, or whether there were specific grievances (perhaps, for example, the recent deferment of proposals to found a Mercers' Scholarship in Commerce at London University[8]) cannot be established; but it was the obvious corollary to a *constitutional* assault on the Court of Assistants.

The motion in December was withdrawn following an undertaking from the Master and Wardens that they would submit the requested report in due course.[9] Six months later, with the June General Court imminent and no sign of the Master and Wardens' report, the cause was taken up by Colonel T. C. Hodson (C. F. P. Hodson's cousin), then serving in France. Hodson offered a resolution which would have had the effect of imposing close Livery control over the Court of Assistants.[10] There were to be only twelve Assistants in all, six elected by former Masters from former Masters and six by the General Court from those who had not served and were not serving as Wardens, and all were to serve for one year only (though there was nothing to prevent their reelection). The Master and Wardens were to receive only two guineas for their weekly meetings, and the Assistants the same amount for their monthly Courts.[B] The Master refused to accept these proposals for discussion, believing them 'quite out of order'.[11] Hodson evidently accepted

[A] Three of the points, as summarised by Palmer in a marginal note, were much as the prior 'details' suggested they would be. The fourth was evidently the rather theoretical possibility of 'impending trouble from a possible Labour Government'.

[B] It will be recalled that fees were increased to *four* guineas in 1870 (see above, p. 185).

FIGS 90–3. Between 1926 and 1930, an extensive restoration of the Hall was carried out under the supervision of Sir Frank Baines. A. E. Rayden was Master, 1926–7, and served on the Hall Committee, 1926–30. He commissioned a series of 'before and after' photographs, four of which are given here.
Mercers' Company

FIG. 90. The Ambulatory, before restoration.

FIG. 91. The Ambulatory, after restoration.

the position and framed an alternative proposal. The second notice of motion, handed to the Master at the General Court meeting on 27 June, ran thus:[12]

> that in the interests of economy and efficiency it is desirable *firstly* that the number of members of the Court of Assistants should not exceed that laid down in the ordinances of the Company, *secondly* that the General Court should participate more directly and more intimately than heretofore in the administration of the Company's business, and that the Master and Wardens be requested to prepare and present to the Court at its meeting to be held in March 1920 a scheme for the reorganisation of the administration of the Company's business based on the principles set forth above.

Again the Master found the notice unacceptable, though he did say that if Hodson wished to move that the present number of Assistants was contrary to a particular by-law or ordinance or was otherwise illegal there could be no objection to that.[13] This resulted, not in a more specific attack on the number of Assistants, but in an amalgam of the December 1918 and June 1919 proposals:[14]

> that in order to enable the Company, being the first of all the Companies, to extend its charities and its support to schemes of public interest, By-Law 20 [which dealt with fees] be and hereby is rescinded and that no fees be paid to members of the Company for attending meetings of the General Court, the Court of Assistants and Committees.

Hodson had clearly decided that the Master and Wardens were unlikely to fulfil their undertaking in relation to the December 1918 motion, and he was now ready to press his fee reductions in the June 1919 motion to their logical extreme. The result did at least find favour with the Master (who affected to regard the amendments to the notice as somehow in accordance with his advice) and the notice was duly accepted for appearance on the agenda. Hodson was unable to attend the October Court and the motion was held over, but when a vote was finally taken in December the motion was lost.[15] In the absence of another eye-witness account it is impossible to say how much support Hodson received, but it is significant that this was the last sign of Livery disquiet for a number of years. The impatience with the oligarchic status quo was so obviously a product of the end-of-War desire for change that it is not surprising that, as peace-time disillusion (or realism) set in, the pressure for reform waned.

'NEW BLOOD'

The 'Bolshevist tendency' did not re-emerge until the mid-1920s, and then only briefly and unthreateningly. The occasion was the first real attempt to broaden the Company's membership. In April 1924 the Assistants were reminded of the Company's domination by an uncomfortably small number of families. Whereas in 1802 the Company's 106 members came from sixty-eight families, in 1924 235 members represented only forty-four families. With admission now almost totally by patrimony the position was likely only to worsen.[16] 'New blood' was obviously required. It is probable that the intention was not simply to effect a general leavening of Company ranks but also to attract potential Assistants, since a member's acceptance of Company largesse could disqualify all his close relations and since also it was becoming increasingly difficult to persuade hard-pressed businessmen to spare the time required for the Wardenships. The Master and Wardens in their report to the Court of Assistants did not advocate a formal amendment to by-law 19 which prohibited redemption, but urged the consideration of individual cases on their merits, subject always to the consent of the General Court. The fate of this recommendation is not clear. In October the General Court endorsed a rather different proposal, namely an amendment to by-law 19 to enable the Master and Wardens, with the Livery's consent, to admit as £100 redemptioners' sons and grandsons (in the male line) who did not qualify for entry by patrimony.[17] It may well be that the General Court objected to the prospect of 'outsiders' securing admission and would only accommodate those sons and grandsons who were excluded by technical rules. Certainly subsequent developments made plain the

FIG. 92. The Livery Hall, before restoration.

FIG. 93. The Livery Hall, after restoration.

Livery's disquiet at any general relaxation of restrictions.

The Assistants addressed the membership problem again in April 1927. The amendment to by-law 19 had resulted in the admission of only three redemptioners, and the number of families had in fact fallen from forty-four to forty-one. The Master and Wardens recommended that the Court consider the need for 'a plan for the resuscitation of admission by redemption on a limited scale'. It was agreed to present to the General Court a new by-law which would enable the Master and Wardens (subject in every case to the consent of the Livery) to admit ten 300-guinea redemptioners (aged twenty-one to thirty-four) between 1928 and 1938 (with no more than two in any one year).[18] A report embodying these principles was placed before the General Court in July 1927 and it was at this point that the 'simmering' unrest among the Livery manifested itself again. Even before the Court convened, the Assistants were made aware of opposition by notice of an amendment. C. T. Watney's motion expressed approval for the 'underlying principle' of the Master and Warden's report but asked for a reconsideration of the methods proposed.[19] At the Court itself one of those who organised the 1918 campaign, Wilfred Powell, evidently posed some questions clearly born of a desire to protect the existing Liverymen's rights:[20]

— will the redemptioners' sons be able take advantage of the recent amendment of by-law 19?
— what seniority will the redemptioners enjoy?
— are there likely to be more redemptioners after these initial ten (bearing in mind that all ten could be admitted within five years)?

The prospect of an influx of new members who might be given early 'promotion' was sufficient to make the Liverymen pause, and Watney's amendment was carried.[21] In March 1928 the General Court agreed with the suggested appointment of a committee, comprising the Master and Wardens, four Assistants and eight Liverymen.[22]

With the Company now fully engaged in a debate on the freedom issue, T. C. Hodson, by now a Cambridge academic, decided to offer his own contribution in the form of two memoranda, one in April 1928 and the other just before the June General Court. The first consisted of a fairly brief review of the methods for broadening Company membership and, perhaps predictably, rejected admission by 'purchase' as either too cheap or as savouring of 'the traffic in honours' and thus 'unworthy of the best traditions of the Company', and favoured a carefully controlled extension of admission by 'redemption' to certain sons and grandsons of freemen.[23] Hodson emphasised the need for the fullest possible review by the Livery of any applications for the admission of 'strangers': all due measures 'can be and must be devised to protect the Livery against diminution of their permanent interests as still an integral, and formerly an important, element in the administration of the Company'. The second memorandum was a lengthier document and included a complete revision of the by-laws, incorporating not merely his proposals for redemptioners but also his older ideas for curtailing the power of the executive.[24] The Livery were to be given extensive control over the selection of the Wardens and, through the Wardens, the Assistants as well. The requirement that nominees for the Wardenships be of at least twenty-five years standing as Liverymen is of particular interest. Hodson was determined to ensure that seniority on the Livery roll received its proper reward.

Hodson's efforts met with little success. The attempt to revise the by-laws was perhaps bound to fail: it is indeed doubtful whether his second memorandum was given any serious consideration; but even his opposition to a formal intake of 'strangers' proved to be fruitless. On 22 March 1929 a 'freedom' committee presented to the General Court certain recommendations which in fact went somewhat further than the 1927 proposals:[25]

— a maximum of 20 new members with no more than 4 in any one year
— those presented to the Court to be chosen by the Master and Wardens (with the consent of the Assistants)

— nominees to be between 21 and 30 years of age
— no priority to be given to sons of daughters of Mercers
— a fee of 300 guineas, save in the case of sons of daughters of Mercers who were to pay 150 guineas.

The committee was advised, if it was not already aware, that a new by-law would be required, and in June the changes were incorporated in by-law 19a.[26]

There was no great influx of 'new blood' redemptioners in the years which followed. The full yearly quota of four was never achieved, and in 1935 there were no admissions at all. It was only in 1945 that the total of twenty was reached.[27] No doubt some realistic and clear-thinking members recognised that this could only be regarded as the start of the infusion process. More than twenty redemptioners would be needed not only to offset the effects of patrimony, but also to broaden the range of expertise at the Company's disposal. The difficulty was, of course, that many members were unable or unwilling to accept this, and as the experiment of 1929–45 showed, any changes had to be gradual in the extreme. The conservatism characteristic of an ancient corporation, and the jealousy of those waiting for promotion, combined powerfully to make wholesale reforms impossible. It was ironic that the pressure for 'democracy' after the First World War had the effect of ensuring that the Company remained, if not oligarchic, then certainly exclusive. When pressure for change reappeared after the Second World War it took a rather different form and proved much harder to resist.

PART II. 1941 to 1959

THE BLITZ AND ITS AFTERMATH

The post-Fire Hall stood for 265 years. It was extensively altered and refurbished, as noticed earlier, in the early 1810s and late 1870s, and there was further major shoring-up work, costing over £80,000,[C] in the late 1920s. The post-restoration photographs reveal a building exuding Victorian opulence but still adhering to the post-Fire, indeed pre-Fire, plan with an entrance on Cheapside leading to the ambulatory which supported the Hall and adjoining rooms at the first-floor level.[28]

The Hall's long life came to an end not, as the early nineteenth-century experts had predicted, through natural decrepitude, but as a result of enemy action. The Acts of Court for 11 May 1941 record, with impressive simplicity, that:

> On the night of 10th–11th May 1941 the buildings of Mercers' Hall, including the Hall, Ambulatory, Chapel, Drawing Room and Grand Staircase, were destroyed by a fire, which was started by incendiary bombs, and only the offices and cellars were left undamaged.

The fire-fighting squad fought hard to prevent the destruction and it was their efforts which saved the offices; but the bombing of one of the City's water mains prevented them using their hoses and they had to use stirrup-pumps instead. They could do little with the flames which 'spread with great rapidity on account of the polished and waxed panelling and old timbers', and it was fortunate that most of the Company's treasures, including the archives and plate, had already been removed for safe-keeping. There was time only to rescue a few effects (including the gowns, the Master's chair, the Master's and Wardens' papers and 'the Dick Whittington model') before the building was consumed.[D] [29]

The Assistants were given an account of the destruction on 16 May and the General Court on

[C] For the details, see Imray, *Mercers' Hall*, ch. 7.

[D] A former Master recalls opening his door at School on the morning of the 11th and finding 'an elderly weeping figure [the recently-retired Clerk], Sir Frank Watney, who could only mumble over and over again, "It's all gone".' (Talk given by Dr Roger Lane to the General Court, September 1974.) Emotion also overcame Norman Collyer who, after informing his uncle (the Warden of Trinity Hospital Greenwich) of the Hall's fate, added: 'I am too upset to write any more': Imray, *Mercers' Hall*, p. 406.

FIG. 94. Sir Winston Churchill's Admission to the Freedom of the Mercers' Company, 25 April 1945. The ceremony took place among the ruins of the Hall.
Mercers' Company

20 June. It can be imagined that by the latter date the Company had had time to collect its thoughts. After praising the fire-fighters for their selfless work, the Master declared that:

the example of these men will illustrate how vain is Hitler's hope that by German frightfulness he can undermine the courage of our Londoners. The only effect of his brutality is to harden our resolve to destroy him and all his works. We are also resolved that after this War, as after the Great Fire of 1666, there shall arise a new Mercers' Hall to embody the splendid traditions of our past and transmit them to future generations.

The parallel with 1666 was to prove more appropriate than the Master appreciated. The financial difficulties which attended the post-Fire rebuilding were evident again after the Blitz. The destruction of the Hall was only the most serious of the bombings which the Company's property suffered, and it was not long before the resultant fall in rents made itself felt.[30] For the rest of the War, of course, the Company dealt with problems as they arose, and it was not in fact until 1949 that a considered review of its financial position was undertaken. By this stage payments for most of the war damage had been received and repairs effected.[E] It was thus possible to predict the Company's likely income. Likewise the recovery of

[E] Save of course for the Hall itself (for which see below, pp. 205–9).

schools from war-time dislocation made it feasible to assess future levels of expenditure.

The results of the Master's and Wardens' analysis were not at all comforting, particularly in relation to the corporate and Colet estates.[31] Even without an allowance for any 'temporary reduction' in revenue attendant on the rebuilding of the Hall (and events were to show the optimism or naïvety of this assumption), annual income from the corporate estate was placed no higher than £80,000. Expenditure was expected to reach £92,500. 'While the Company's Corporate funds are large enough to support a deficit of some £12,500 a year for a long period it must be pointed out that such a deficit will not be able to be met for more than four years without resort to the sale of property'.

As far as the Colet estate was concerned, the main source of income was no longer the property in Stepney. The effects of rent controls and the rising cost of repairs to the old and rudimentary houses (quite apart from war damage) meant that a net income of no more than £26,000 could be relied on. This figure was exceeded in some measure by the dividends from the Maintenance Fund of some £1 million which the Company trustees had prudently been accumulating in anticipation of the deterioration of the Stepney houses. Such prudence became providential as post-Fire expenditure on the Colet Schools (particularly St Paul's School itself) rose rapidly. The allowances of £30,000 (to St Paul's School) and £10,000 (to St Paul's School for Girls) were overspent, as the Master and Wardens put it, 'on a generous scale', and, had it not been for the Maintenance Fund dividends of £31,000 per annum, 'it is not an exaggeration to say that ... St Paul's Schools would already be facing bankruptcy'. The capital of the fund would certainly have to be used to meet the deficit in 1949 and, though it was hoped that the heavy expenditure was born of unusual post-war circumstances,[32] this was a dangerous precedent.

The Master and Wardens described the situation as 'grave' and one 'that ought not to be allowed to drift'. In the absence of any likelihood of an increase in income, their recommendations concentrated on outgoings. 'A proper system of forward budgeting and control of expenditure' must be adopted. The co-operation of all concerned was essential. It was, in fact, doubtful whether

> some of the officials, particularly the Headmaster of Mercers' School and the High Master and High Mistress of St. Paul's Schools, have any real conception of the seriousness of the situation which faces the Company and Dean Colet's estate unless some corrective action is taken.

The following pages show how the Company tried to tackle its Colet and corporate expenditure. The Colet excesses may have seemed more pressing in 1949 but the fund's bounty proved to be a more than adequate cushion, and in any event there was, of course, no chance of the financial problems spreading beyond the trust itself. The corporate deficit, less obviously a problem in 1949, became more serious (particularly when the cost of rebuilding the Hall rose dramatically), and the reference to Mercers' School in the Master's and Wardens' summary acquired a new significance.

THE COLET ESTATE

Not long after the general review of the Company's finances, the Assistants, as trustees of the Colet estate, gave the governors a blunt analysis of the problems they were facing.[33] The combined income from property and the fund, amounting to £63,000 per annum, only just exceeded the anticipated requirements of St Paul's School (£47,500) and St Paul's School for Girls (£15,000). This effectively left no reserve for any extraordinary expenditure, however modest. The trustees decided to increase the annual allowances from £30,000 and £10,000 to £40,000 and £12,000 respectively, but they made it perfectly clear that the deficit (i.e. £7,500 and £3,000) which would result would have to be met by the Schools themselves. The governors, together with the High Master and High Mistress (who hitherto had been relieved of 'all financial distraction' but whose 'intelligent co-operation' was now 'indispensable'), would have to increase fees or reduce expenditure, or both. The trustees concluded by warning that if these measures were not adopted the independence of the Schools would be at risk. The price of State assistance would be Government control.

The plan was not entirely successful. Three years later the Schools were still overspending, despite the increased allowances.[34] Nevertheless the deficit totalled only £6,000 (as opposed to £10,500 in 1949) and an increase in the estate's income to £72,000 resulted in a healthy balance of £14,000. There was, it is true, one cause for concern. £24,000 of the £72,000 derived from the Stepney properties and, although the figure was decreasing, it was still significant. As parts of the Stepney estate were compulsorily purchased by the local authority, the already dwindling rent-roll fell further still. Fortunately the fund and the other Colet properties more than compensated for Stepney's difficulties. By 1955 net income had almost reached £80,000 and even an increased deficit of £11,000 (comprising no less than £10,000 at St Paul's School and a mere £1,000 at St Paul's School for Girls) could be readily absorbed.[35] A memorandum by the Clerk did express real concern at the level of the St Paul's School expenditure, particularly since there were costly future plans (including playing fields at Osterley Park) and he stressed the need to keep the fund inviolate. Nevertheless £80,000 was a handsome income (acknowledged by the Clerk to be evidently 'far and away' higher than for any other school foundation) and it was clear that provided the Schools were kept on a fairly tight rein there was no reason why the Colet estate should not be able to meet the demands made on it. The gloomy prognosis in 1949 thus proved over-pessimistic.

CORPORATE ESTATE

The Company first began to appreciate that the deficits on their corporate account might be more serious than the Colet 'deficits' in March 1950. The Master and Wardens were obliged to report that the likely deficit of £12,500 had proved to be an actual one of almost £14,000.[36] Income amounted to £82,250 but expenditure exceeded £96,000. As war-time difficulties disappeared there was hope of an increase in income, but this could not be guaranteed. Taking into account the effects of taxation, an additional £25,500 was needed to bridge the present gap. The best that could in practice be expected was £13,000. Little wonder therefore that Master and Wardens did 'not consider that this situation is a healthy one'. So far as expenditure was concerned, modest benefits were anticipated from a tightening of procedures, but the only possibility of substantial reductions seemed to lie in the avoidance of part of the Company's liability for income tax (then amounting to £31,500) and a review of the tax position was recommended.

No further steps were taken before the fear of a new world war, sparked by the conflict in Korea, distracted the Company's attention from its longer term problems. The prospect of air attacks on London made the Company realise how much of its wealth was invested in property and how much of that property was situated in the capital. In February 1951 the Master and Wardens declared that:[37]

> the Company's property is . . . concentrated in one very small area and that area perhaps the most vulnerable to enemy action in the whole world. It is not inconceivable that one concentrated bombing might obliterate nine-tenths of the Company's corporate income. The experience of the last War shows that when an income-producing property is obliterated many years must pass before it can be reinstated. The Company is still deriving no income from its properties in Bread Street and Cheapside, although it is now ten years since they were destroyed, which fact is partly responsible for the difficulty which we find at the present moment in arriving at a balance between income and expenditure.

The obvious solution was to sell some of the central London property and either re-invest in property (agricultural and urban) elsewhere or invest the cash in securities.

After a review of the financial implications the Master and Wardens did indeed so recommend, but it is doubtful whether any practical results would have followed had it not been for the Company's worsening financial position. For some months the Company had been aware of a liquidity problem and various proposals for realising or releasing capital had been considered.[38] This new fear was the spur the Company needed, and it was not long before the sale of central London property to the value of no less than £1 million and the re-investment of that sum in Stock Exchange securities was put in hand.[39]

Dramatic though this decision was, it did not have any immediate bearing on the problem of corporate deficits. Nor indeed was it influenced by those deficits (save, of course, that the current low rental income reminded the Company of the perils of war). The Company was not primarily trying to increase its income but merely make its assets available in a more accessible and less vulnerable form. The struggle to balance the books was not resumed until May 1951 when the Wardens reviewed the accounts of 1950.[40] It was revealed that the £14,000 deficit in the previous year had been reduced to £9,500. Savings of £2,000 or so may not have been remarkable (and they certainly did not include the hoped-for reduction in income tax liability), but when taken with an increase in income of £2,500 they made for a reassuring trend. Some further means of reducing expenditure were under consideration, and the Master and Wardens warned that Court and committee fees would almost certainly have to be included. Nevertheless the figures were deemed sufficiently encouraging to warrant a postponement of the question of fees for a further two years. By the time fees were reconsidered, in June 1953, the Company's corporate funds were almost in balance.[41] The deficit was down to £2,200 and had it not been for a war damage contribution (for which prior provision should have been made) there would even have been a small surplus. All this justified a further postponement of the question of fees, but the Master and Wardens made clear the need for vigilance:

Although the date of redevelopment of the Hall site cannot be foreseen, it is of paramount importance that the Company shall have sufficient resources to carry out the scheme as soon as it is permitted to do so and we believe that we should be failing in our duty if we did not stress again the vital necessity to scrutinize every item of expenditure and to be satisfied that it is essential (rather than desirable) to the Company's status before giving approval.[F] As for the income from rents, we appreciate that it has been the Company's policy in the past to charge only moderate rents but, having regard to the Company's financial needs and to the present demand for accommodation, we recommend that the Surveyor should be instructed that, when negotiating new leases on behalf of the Company, the best possible rent should be obtained.

Leaving aside the interesting acknowledgement towards the end of this passage, this is significant in that, for the first time, the cost of the new Hall (and adjacent office block) was brought into consideration. The Master and Wardens were obviously anxious to ensure that with a contingent liability of unknown proportions looming large, the Company should not be caught unprepared. Nevertheless it was clearly a matter of commercial prudence rather than real concern. The Company evidently had no reason to believe that it would not be able to find the necessary money. It was not, in fact, until early in 1956 that the Company realised that the cost of redeveloping the Hall site was likely to exceed all previous estimates by 40%.[G] The Company's corporate estate was then faced with a financial crisis of daunting proportions.

THE HALL AND BECKET HOUSE

The fulfilment of the Master's promise in 1941 was a slow and, in the latter stages at least,

[F] An early instance occurred in October 1953 when the Company resolved to limit its subscription to the City and Guilds Institute to £2,000 rather than £2,500 (to which it had been increased under the then current deed of covenant). The Master and Wardens were conscious of 'the demands that are likely to be made upon the Company's strained resources during the next few years, particularly in respect of the rebuilding of the Hall and of Mercers' School. . .'. 'We have not arrived at this decision without much thought having regard to the close affinity between the Company and the Institute, but we feel that the Company's private affairs must receive priority of consideration', AC, 8 October 1953.

[G] See below, p. 207.

FIG. 95. Her Majesty Queen Mary receiving the Freedom of the Mercers' Company, 26 July 1949, and is pictured here in the ruins of the Hall with members of the Company.
Mercers' Company

agonising process. Post-war restrictions may have been inevitable but they were still frustrating. It was not until 1949–50 that the Company felt able to give serious consideration to the way in which the Hall site should be redeveloped. The Hall and the Company's other 'personal' accommodation did of course only form part of the site. There were also offices and shops which took advantage of Cheapside's commercial popularity. In the light of the Company's financial problems discussed earlier, it will not cause surprise that the Company, from the outset, attached great importance to the latter. The original architect employed in the scheme, Austin Blomfield, remarked in his first report in October 1950:[42]

I am advised that it is most important that there should be sufficient income from the commercial use of the Cheapside frontage to pay for the upkeep of that part of the whole block ... which will be occupied by the Company for its own use, i.e. the Hall, Court Room, Drawing Room, Chapel etc. If this income is not available, the Company's premises when rebuilt might financially be an impossible burden. If the premises fronting to Cheapside are to be usable and to be capable of economic rent they must be adequate and sufficiently deep for their purpose. The former shops were barely sufficient in depth and with the set-back [resulting from a widening of Cheapside] they would have an average depth of only about 15 feet, which commercially is hopeless. I give as my considered opinion that they should have a depth of 30 feet. This can only be obtained by putting the rear wall of these shops roughly flush with the south wall of the Chapel. Proceeding westwards this would entail in the case of shops encroaching some 12 feet upon the southern portion of the ambulatory. I regard this as a matter of prime importance which requires the Company's decision before I can proceed further ...

The Company had little hesitation in giving its approval to the 'encroachments'. Mindful of 'the vital need to obtain as much revenue as possible by way of rent so as to make the rebuilding and normal maintenance of the Hall itself an economical proposition', the Company duly endorsed the report.[43]

It was in fact not long before the Company terminated Blomfield's retainer, and it is interesting to note that one of the reasons was the alleged inadequacy of the 'commercial' provisions in Blomfield's plans. The appointment of Blomfield's successor, E. N. Clifton of Gunton & Gunton, was undoubtedly influenced by the need to maximise rental income from what became known as Becket House;[H] and throughout the remainder of the project Clifton and the Hall Committee were always conscious of this consideration. In January 1954, for example, encroachments on, and alterations to, the former Chapel area were justified or at least counterbalanced by reference to the enhanced 'letting value of the commercial portion [of the new building]'.[44]

It took an inordinately long time for the likely cost of the new Hall and Becket House to emerge. There were fairly casual references to a Company liability of some £200,000 in 1952 and 1953,[45] but it was not until December 1954 that a total sum was actually ventured.[46] At £665,000 it was in rough accord with the earlier estimates, since two-thirds was deemed recoverable from the War Damage Commission.[47] Unfortunately the Company did not appreciate the uncertainties attached to the 'approximation', and when an authoritative figure finally transpired in 1956 it was clear that the final bill was likely to be in excess of £1 million.[48] This caused nothing short of consternation and the Finance Committee immediately considered the implications as part of a long-term review of the Company's corporate finances. In its report to the Court of Assistants in June 1956 the committee was reasonably sanguine that there were sufficient realisable assets to deal with the simple liquidity problem caused by the unexpected demand for further money for the rebuilding.[49] The real problem, of course, was that the realisation of these assets would reduce income and, as the second part of the report made plain, this was something the Company could ill afford. An estimate for 1959 indicated that income (taking into account the rents from Becket House, but deducting the anticipated loss of dividends) would amount to £139,000. This barely exceeded the anticipated expenditure of £138,532. Bearing in mind the possibility of substantial additional expenditure on Mercers' School, the need for a sinking fund for the Hall and Becket House, and a depreciation fund for the rack-rented properties, not to mention the Company's desire to

> contribute to appeals and make charitable donations more in keeping with its premier position as it used to do in the past and as it has not been able to do in more recent times,

it was clear that remedial action was essential.

Economies were considered under four heads. The first was taxation, but the Company was obliged to defer to the accountants' advice that no worthwhile savings were possible. The second was administration. Economies in the strict sense were deemed impracticable: 'the volume of work in the office grows greater and not less and no increase has been made in the number of the staff for many years'. However, two-thirds of the cost of the office was incurred in administering the Company's charitable trusts, and there seemed no reason why the Company should not charge the trusts for services rendered.[I] A figure of £12,000 per annum was suggested, though only part of this sum would be charged to begin with. The third head was connected with the second. If charges were to be made for the administration of trusts then 'it would not look well' if the Company did not also reduce its expenditure on Court and

[H] As witness the Master's draft memorandum prepared for the Hall Committee, 27 June 1951: Hall Rebuilding Papers, Box 1, Clerk's file 3 (Negotiations with Noel Clifton). Another architect was considered 'the right man to do the artistic side of the work', but the Master at least was 'not fully convinced that he would be equally successful in getting the maximum amount of rental in the layout of the commercial space'.

[I] In the course of a reference to the charges made by other of the Great Twelve Companies, the committee made the interesting assertion that the Mercers' trusts accounted for £240,000 of the £360,000 combined income arising from the Great Twelve's trusts. This became £260,000 of £320,000 *charitable* trust income in the report to the General Court. AC, 15 June, 14 September 1956.

committee fees 'which are on a far higher scale than those paid by any other Livery Company'. A good deal of money could be saved each year if Courts of Assistants were held every fortnight (not every week) and General Courts every six months (not every quarter), and if no fees were paid for committees meeting on the same days as Courts of Assistants. The last head was Mercers' School. However,

we regret to report that no economy seems possible there; on the contrary there is every prospect of the cost of the School rising indefinitely and to a point beyond the Company's means to support it.

The committee recommended that the Company's subsidy be fixed at £22,500 per annum and the Headmaster be told to budget accordingly. The committee was conscious that there was a limit to the Headmaster's ability to remedy the shortfall through increased fees, having regard to 'the class of parent for whom Mercers' School caters'. The financial regime might thus lead to 'drastic changes in the form of Mercers' School as it is today but the alternative seems to be a cost beyond the powers of the Company to meet'. The committee concluded their report first with a summary of the financial effect of their proposals and this suggested a saving of some £11,500 per annum. They then urged that the General Court should be informed of the Company's financial position since 'it is clear that the Livery have little idea of the difficulties that beset the Company both now and in the future'. The committee's final remarks seemed to transform the parallel between the Great Fire and the Blitz from a rhetorical conceit (as surely it had been in 1941[J]) into practicality.

Over the centuries when the Company has been in straitened circumstances, the Livery have bent their efforts towards restoring its fortunes and we feel that it would be an error not to give them an opportunity to do so yet again.

The Master's and Wardens' report to the General Court in September 1956 followed the Finance Committee's report in general terms, though there were some additional introductory remarks and a marked absence of figures.[50] It is also interesting to note that the section on Mercers' School contained no grim warning of the effects of the new financial constraints. The only proposal which the General Court was actually asked to approve was the reduction in expenditure on attendance fees. The Livery's sacrifice this time was thus scarcely equal to that nearly three centuries earlier. Then the Liverymen had contributed their own money to the rebuilding work;[K] now they were merely faced with the loss of half their usual Court fees, either by a straightforward reduction or by meeting only twice a year.[L]

The immediate cause of all this heart-searching was, of course, the inflated cost of the Hall and Becket House. It should not be imagined that the Company accepted the estimate without demur. Quite the contrary, in fact. The architect and the quantity surveyors were asked the most searching questions and were left in no doubt of the Company's grave concern. The recriminations were perhaps expressed in over-sombre terms and perhaps also Counsel were guilty of hyperbole or gullibility when they alluded in a joint opinion to 'financial implications so grave as to endanger the future of this ancient Livery'.[51] Nevertheless the Clerk was certainly not exaggerating when he told the architect in a letter in June 1956 that 'the position is extremely serious'[52] and it certainly warranted the effort that was made to reduce the final bill from £1 million or more to £800,000.[53] When it became clear that there was little chance of savings on this scale, and since the outcome of public dispute or litigation was uncertain (and indeed might even be counter-productive since it could jeopardise the compensation from the War Damage Commission), the Company could only snipe at the building costs and professional fees. For a real solution to its difficulties it was forced to look elsewhere. The proposals placed before the

J See above, p. 202.

K For the Livery's not entirely enthusiastic efforts after the Great Fire, see above, p. 75.

L They plumped for the former: GCM, 14 December 1956.

A. Trinity Hospital, Shotesham, Norfolk; late nineteenth-century watercolour by an unknown artist. Built in 1885 to complement Trinity Hospital, Greenwich, this saved those recipients of the Earl of Northampton's charity who were native to his birthplace from having to travel south to Greenwich.
Mercers' Company

B. Perspective watercolour drawing of proposed Cheapside elevation of Mercers' Hall and Becket House, by Noel Clifton, 1952.
Mercers' Company

A. St Thomas Becket: stained glass from the staircase window in the present Mercers' Hall, to commemorate his birthplace which stood on the Mercers' Hall site. This glass was made by H. L. Pawle for the third Mercers' Hall.
Mercers' Company

B. The Mercers' coat of arms: stained-glass window, also by H. L. Pawle, from the Livery Hall, with the Maiden as regulated in the 1911 Grant of Arms (see Fig. 86).
Mercers' Company

General Court in September 1956 would undoubtedly have assisted, but they were based on the assumption that there would be no additional expenditure. When the Headmaster of Mercers' School made it plain that he could not keep expenditure within the limits imposed by the Finance Committee, and indeed needed further money merely to keep pace with educational change,[M] the Company had to reconsider its commitment to the School. The cost of rebuilding the Chapel School's former home began to threaten the School's future.

MERCERS' SCHOOL

The move to new premises in Barnards Inn in 1894 had not altered Mercers' School's modest character. The Headmastership of the scholarly Dr D. L. Scott (1879–1914) may have given the School a certain academic reputation, but the succeeding regimes of C. H. Bicknell (1914–29) and R. W. Jepson (1929–46), both more robust and more practical men than Scott, ensured that the School continued to cater essentially for would-be City clerks.[54] The advertisement for Scott's successor declared that:[55]

> the intention of the school work has been to give a good general education to boys who are intending to take commercial posts or who wish to enter one of the professions . . .

In 1947 the Company decided to change Mercers' School into an avowedly *public* school, catering not so much for vocational training as for university entrance.[56] The occasion of this change of tack was the appointment of an able 'progressive' Headmaster, W. D. Haden, but the underlying cause was the change in social and educational policy after the Second World War. When in 1952 Haden himself attempted to explain the 'change in the character of the School' to the Clerk he wrote thus:[57]

> This has come about, I think, for two main reasons, that the demand for places in the School fell away when secondary education was provided free of charge for all boys up to the age of 15 by local authorities and, on the other hand, that the opportunity offered to a boy leaving school at 16 and taking up a clerkship in a business in London diminished as typewriters and calculating machines came increasingly to be used and young women came increasingly to be employed. Before the War boys were sent here either by City clerks, policemen, firemen, caretakers and other workers in the City or by business men living in the Southgate area. These parents after 1947 either were inclined or were forced to send their sons to the schools of the LCC or Middlesex which provided a secondary education free of charge. On the other hand, parents who were willing and able to pay school fees looked for an education which would take their sons further and offer them a better launching into a career than the State secondary schools. It became necessary to provide an education for which parents would pay without detriment to the character of the School.

The ensuing decision 'that Mercers' School should become of the Public School type' was, of course, a costly one and with Haden's energetic guidance the Company made a good deal of additional money available to improve facilities. However, as Haden's regular memoranda on 'policy' made clear, this left the long-term development of the School unresolved. By committing the School to a 'public school' character the Company had started a process which was fraught with difficulty and uncertainty. The Barnards Inn site was really quite unsuitable for a school. The playing fields at Grove Park near Mottingham may have been handsomely equipped but they were too distant to be of proper value. In their report in 1949 the School Inspectors described the Holborn buildings as being 'tucked away . . . in this corner of the City among veritable cliffs of bricks and mortar'.[58] Viewed with hindsight the move to Barnards Inn was clearly a mistake. The Company had been transfixed by the School's association with the City or perhaps, more charitably, over-anxious to comply with the letter of its agreement with Henry VIII.[N] It is certainly easy to see

[M] See below, p. 211.

[N] After the decision to close the School had been taken the Company (rather belatedly, it might be thought) took legal advice from the Ministry of Education on this point. Any action for breach of covenant was considered most unlikely. AC, 7 November 1958.

Fig. 96. Mercers' School: Form I with master, 1895–6. Note the Mercers' Maiden on the schoolboys' caps.
Mercers' Company

Fig. 97. Mercers' School: obstacle race, Sports Day, 1899.
Mercers' Company

Fig. 98. Mercers' School: rifle team, *c.* 1901.
Mercers' Company

why it is argued that if Mercers' School had followed the example of Charterhouse, Christ's Hospital and indeed St Paul's and moved out of the City, it 'would be flourishing today'.[59] Of course, the Company never saw Mercers' School in the same terms as St Paul's and the capital expenditure involved (with only *corporate* funds to draw on) would not have been acceptable. The Company could also be forgiven for failing to anticipate the post-war changes which left the School without its original *raison d'être*.

Nevertheless the 1894 decision was a mistake and the Company was left with a serious handicap when it tried to meet the School's new aspirations after 1947. The Headmaster's clear preference was for relocation outside London. This was 'the surest course ... if the object is to assure the long-term future of Mercers as an independent school ...'.[60] Haden appreciated, however, that this might not be a practical possibility. He must have been aware that the Company's corporate finances were causing concern and that the cost of relocation (even allowing for the value of the Holborn site) would make the Company blench. In default of a new site entirely, Haden naturally favoured the large-scale development of the existing site and (if possible) adjoining land. There was certainly scope for a new block fronting on to Norwich Street, but the financial implications were such as to make it necessary to combine the new schoolrooms with commercial premises and it seemed doubtful whether the result would be satisfactory (particularly since it would preclude any future expansion).[61] Haden was thus obliged to advocate piecemeal improvements to the present premises and make do as best he could. Even on this basis expenditure on the School rose considerably. Between 1947 and 1953 some £22,000 was spent on 'improvements', and this appears to have been over and above the annual 'subsidy' of £15,000 (itself an increase from £10,000 following the 1947 decision).[62]

At one stage there was a possibility that there would be assistance from a wealthy old Mercer, but the proposed benefaction proved to be less attractive than first supposed and it was declined.[63] The Company came to realise that it alone would have to finance the revitalised School and its voracious needs. By June 1956 the 'subsidy' had risen to £18,250 (excluding a pensions covenant of £6,750) and there seemed no limit to future expenditure.[64] The Finance Committee's allusion to costs 'rising ... to a point beyond the Company's means to support [the School]', and the acknowledgement that the formal limitation of the 'subsidy' to £22,500 could lead to 'drastic changes' might be regarded as portentous, but in fact the first serious consideration of the future of the School did not occur until October 1956. It was then that the Master and Wardens asked the Headmaster for a report on the School's 'dilemma'. Haden summarised the problem thus:[65]

> Mercers' School cannot continue to compete as an independent fee-charging grammar school with the well-known independent fee-charging schools and with the free grammar schools unless the School's offer to the public is solid and continues to be solid. On the other hand, the cost of maintaining the School at the present level of efficiency and of the minimum necessary development outruns the resources available to it from the Company and from fees.

Haden tackled the question of closure first. He was thoroughly realistic:

> A break with this continuous history [of over 400 years] would be a tragedy, but it must be said that there is some weakness inherent in the School's very gradual and limited growth and dependence upon the Mercers' Company ... our strength is very limited ... numbers [even] when the School is full are dangerously small ...

Haden acknowledged that costs would continue to rise and that, unless some kind of 'reinvestment' were possible following relocation or unless financial liability could be shared with the taxpayer or ratepayer, the Company would have to consider closing the School.

This took the Headmaster on to the possibility of moving the School. He did not know what the financial consequences would be, but he wondered whether it would be possible for the School through this 're-investment' to release itself from its present strait-jacket. He also discussed what he termed the 're-establishment' of the School and concluded that a great deal depended on the reaction of the local education authority and indeed also the headmasters of the local preparatory schools.

The last two sections of Haden's report were devoted to financial assistance. He urged the Company to make sure that the School did not lose the opportunity to obtain 'direct grant' status, though he implied that this would be impossible unless the School acquired a new site. Local authority assistance would involve a loss of independence which the Company might find unacceptable. 'However, reporting as I do from the School side, I am bound to make the point that continuance under partial or even complete control of the LCC would be more acceptable to a majority of the Old Boys and Masters than closure'.

The Headmaster's conclusion was scrupulously objective. On the assumption the School could not be continued in its present form, Haden reviewed the options thus:

> to move the School would be a considerable undertaking about which one can perhaps only say this further that, finance apart, there may be a moment now for moving which would be unlikely to recur. However, we have nothing like the strength of a Merchant Taylors' School or a Haberdashers' School for such a move and all would depend on our having the Mercers themselves and substantial funds behind the enterprise up to the time when the School could stand on its own feet and in the end be strong enough, if necessary, to attract public funds in the form of the direct grant. Short of that, there is much to be said for coming to an arrangement with the London County Council, if that is possible, whereby the School and the Old Boys might be saved from the negation of closure.

It was clear that Haden favoured relocation (on another occasion he remarked, 'I wish it were possible for us to summon the strength to make a move, given the chance'),[66] but he was certainly well aware of the difficulties involved and had no intention of making a stand on the point. His discretion and realism made the Company's task much easier than it might have been. A Headmaster prepared to fight blindly for the School to the last would have been a serious embarrassment.

Haden's report formed only one part of a general review by the Master and Wardens on the future of the School. Officials from the Ministry of Education were also consulted and assistance obtained from co-opted members of the Court of Assistants and General Court. The Master and Wardens made their first formal report in June 1957.[67] In the light of Haden's remarks it will cause no surprise that the report reduced the issue to straightforward alternatives:

> whether Mercers' School should be moved to a new site somewhere in the London dormitory area where there is a need for a new Grammar School and where its presence would be welcome to the local Education Authority and rebuilt to modern standards in such a way as to be eligible for a public grant; or whether it should be eventually closed down.

The first option meant, of course, either aided or direct grant status. The former simply involved finding a local education authority ready to assume responsibility, but the Company would effectively lose control over the School. The latter would leave the Company still in charge (perhaps on a Dauntsey-type basis), but it carried with it the risk that by the end of the four or five years it would take to gain acceptance there might have been a change of Government and the direct grant list closed. Relocation was thus characterised as a 'tremendous gamble':

> at the best the Mercers' Company would still retain a school in which they would have about the same interest as they have today in Dauntsey's, but with this difference, that whereas Dauntsey's still remains in its original place and its tradition continues to be bound up with the locality, Mercers would be an immigrant school with no traditional connections with its locality while, at the worst, the Mercers' Company would in substance merely have made a gift of some £150,000 [being the estimated capital cost involved] to a local education authority.

Even if relocation were deemed a sensible option, financial considerations seemed to preclude it. The Master and Wardens failed to see how the Company could find the bridging finance needed to maintain continuity in the School's life.

They concluded therefore that the Company had no choice but to close the School. This was a decision 'which no Mercer could view with other than infinite regret', but it was the only realistic one. An attempt should be made to prolong the School's present existence for as long as possible by at least applying for a direct grant or (if refused) aided status. If there was little chance of success, then at least 'no blame can attach to the Company if it is compelled to close the School down because it cannot afford to continue supporting it'.

It is difficult to resist the conclusion that the Master and Wardens had decided that the School would have to be closed and that they were now seeking to implement that decision in the least painful way. The possibility of relocation had not been fully explored, or at least not presented as a worthwhile option, for no better reason than the alleged impossibility of purchasing the new site and building prior to the sale of Barnards Inn and the playing fields. Credit restrictions notwithstanding, it should have been possible to release the value of the existing sites before the School's actual departure. The truth was probably that the enormously inflated cost of the new Hall and Becket House had so shaken the Assistants that they felt it imperative to make a permanent and

FIG. 99. Mercers' School: Field Marshal Viscount Montgomery visits the School, 11 June 1948; here he is accompanied by the Headmaster Mr W. D. Haden.
Mercers' Company

material cut in expenditure.[O] It is possible, of course, that for some this was a pretext rather than a reason (and it is worth recalling that by now few members sent their sons to Mercers' School), but the absence of any hint of closure before 1956 suggests that for most the response was genuine enough. A school using only corporate funds to match its endowed or State-funded competitors was a responsibility the Company could not afford in its post-war difficulties. An old Mercer remarked epigrammatically that 'the bombs missed the School buildings but they destroyed the source of its life . . .'.[68] This over-simplified matters, particularly since it suggested that the Company had no option save closure. Nevertheless there was a direct link between the Blitz and the decision in 1957.

There were only two significant developments between the interim report of June 1957 and the final one in March 1958. The first took the form of proposals from the School's masters to improve the finances.[69] They suggested that there was scope for some increase in both fees and numbers. They were also prepared to accept that their salaries be no longer tied to the State Burnham scale and that they did not 'overlook the possibility of having to work with a reduced staff as resignations and retirements occur'.

Other significant economies would be difficult to make without changing something of the character, administration and activities of the School; but we recognise that all these might have to be reviewed if there were to be no other way of preserving the life of the School, now threatened by the 'bloodless revolution' being brought about by taxation and inflation.

The Headmaster, however, could not support his staff. He did not agree that fees and numbers could be increased, and so far as the cutbacks and economies were concerned these represented 'a gradual run-down of the School'. Moreover, he did not believe that the proposals tackled the main problem, namely 'the survival of the School in any satisfactory form in its present buildings, having regard to the operation of the Education Act 1944 and the trend of education generally'. Needless to say, the Master and Wardens appreciated Haden's realism, declaring in their report that 'we support the Headmaster's view to the full'.

Later in the year came the second development, namely the application for the admission of the School to the direct grant list. Two months later, in February 1958, came the Ministry's refusal.[70] The message was bald enough but it was evident that, as anticipated, it was the School's buildings that were the cause of the difficulty. The Company was also aware that before making his decision the Minister had taken the views of the local authorities in whose areas the boys lived, and the Company deduced that the response cannot have been encouraging. This suggested that the likelihood of aided status was slim, whether or not the Company was ready to 'offer a local authority a gift of a very large sum of money which it would otherwise have had to raise from its ratepayers'.

The manner in which the Company dealt with the masters' proposals and the application to the Ministry is surely confirmation that it could see no alternative to closure. The masters' faintly desperate self-denial could perhaps be regarded as naïve, but the mere assumption that aided status was impossible, together with the bald assertion that if conferred it was unacceptable, was less than convincing. Certainly, in their report to the Court of Assistants on 14 March 1958,[71] the Master and Wardens moved rapidly from a brief account of the masters' proposals and the application for a direct grant to the unanimous recommendation, 'made with the greatest reluctance',

[O] It is significant that what appears to be the first indication of a decision to close the School occurs in the context of negotiations on the cost of the Hall and Becket House. In February 1957 the Surveyor (or possibly the Clerk) made the following jottings for a meeting with the architect and quantity surveyor: 'Jeopardy of place in the City. No alternative but to close Mercers' School. After 450 years can't afford School and [the projected £300,000] loan'. (Enclosed with Surveyor's letter to W. Yates (consultant architect), 25 February 1957: Hall Rebuilding Papers, Box 2, Clerk's file 15 (Mercers' Hall Rebuilding Papers, December 1956 to October 1957.)). As evidence of a formal decision this is obviously suspect: it was all too convenient for the Company to characterise the *possibility* of closure in this way; but as a sign of the close connection between the School and the reconstruction of the Hall it is revealing.

that a date be fixed for the closure of Mercers' School.

While it would be our natural inclination to postpone the date for closure over a number of years, we fully realise that such a course would be unrealistic and would only postpone the problem, in so far as it would lead only to the School's future being of a very restricted kind with a gradual disintegration of pupils and staff. Accordingly we recommend that no further boys be admitted to the School from now on and that the School be closed on the conclusion of the Summer Term 1959.

The remainder of the report was largely devoted to the practical aspects of the closure (transfer of boys, provision for staff and so forth), though there was one section which expressed the Company's determination to continue to make a contribution to education (albeit with a significant qualification: 'within the limits of its resources') and a conclusion describing the closure as 'little short of a tragedy'.

No more than a few days later a letter was sent to all parents explaining the decision.[72] For the most part it was a judicious summary of the Master's and Wardens' report, making the Company's regret quite plain but taking care to give no encouragement to hopes of a reprieve. Needless to say there were parents who would or could not accept the decision, and both the Headmaster and the Clerk had to cope with a good deal of well-intentioned harassment.[73] The Clerk, of course, stuck firmly though politely to the Court's decision. Haden was in a more exposed position, but his resolve did not weaken either. On 27 March 1958 he summarised his views to the Clerk in the following way:[74]

I accept the necessity that the School in Holborn must be closed for the reason that it has no future here. Some parents and friends and, of course, some Mercers too, look at short-term expedients and hope at least that the School's existence can be protracted. It will not do. Anyone who is interested in the long-term future of the School is looking at the possibility of the Mercers' School [being] established in say Cuffley, Orpington or Richmond three or four years from now. I doubt whether many of those who expressed their interest in the possibility of a fund to save Mercers' School really understand that or are interested in it, for of course it could not mean much to them unless the School were built in their part of London. It is difficult for me to dismiss the possibility altogether because I am bound in my position to cling to any hope that the School may be continued. However, since I have not the slightest doubt that it has no future here in the City and I have the gravest doubts whether the financial problems could be overcome and if so the political horizon would be clear, I regard the possibility as too remote to take seriously or to offer to anybody at all. It is accepted here that the School is being closed and we are proceeding with the practical problem . . .

The Headmaster's attitude was crucial: a glimmer of encouragement from him would have given great support to the opponents of closure. As it was, pressure for a reprieve remained powerful for at least another month and on 25 April it was felt necessary to reaffirm the closure decision and for the Master to write to *The Times* explaining why the Company could not accept offers of help.[75] Increasing fees by a suggested 50% could well prove unacceptable to future parents in view of the facilities on offer, and rebuilding the School on the 'London fringe' with the aid of the promised 'substantial contributions' would not be possible unless either direct grant or aided status could be obtained, and the former was impracticable and the latter unattractive for the reasons rehearsed elsewhere. Whether it was the letter or, more likely, the simple passage of time is not clear, but the pressure on the Company abated and the School's fate came generally to be accepted.

The School was indeed closed at the end of the summer term 1959, with its boys placed elsewhere, its masters retired or re-employed and its Headmaster, William Haden, bound (eventually) for the Royal Grammar School in Newcastle. The School's legacy might conventionally be described as its 400-year existence, and this longevity was the subject of pious and rather anguished comment in all the Company's pronouncements. Nevertheless it has to be recognised that, for much of that time, and certainly until the arrival of Dr Scott in 1879, the School was modest in scale and fairly undistinguished in achievement. The School's real legacy was the loyalty it inspired in the parents and former pupils who

FIG. 100. Rebuilding Mercers' Hall: the site cleared, 2 February 1955. *Mercers' Company*

benefited from the improvements before and especially after the Second World War. It is one of the many ironies of the School's closure that the loyalty which made closure so painful was the Company's 'reward' for increasing its expenditure on the School. It is hard to explain why a school should be closed for becoming too successful, and the Company never really convinced its critics. It probably *was* the correct decision, given the financial difficulties faced in Cheapside and given the open-ended commitment the School required. Nevertheless it has to be asked why the Company in 1947 decided to allow Haden to take the School into direct competition with the State sector. Might it not have been wiser to consider closure then? This may be hindsight at its worst, but even without the unexpected expenditure on the Hall and Becket House, the Company would have found the additional cost of the School (including its inevitable relocation) hard to justify. Those who still question the decision taken in 1958 should perhaps turn their attention to the decision that was avoided in 1947.

CONCLUSION

The new Hall was opened in May 1958. A relatively small reduction in cost had been effected, a somewhat larger sum than expected had been

FIG. 101. Rebuilding Mercers' Hall: the Lord Mayor, the Master (N. C. Watney), the Clerk (Geoffrey Logsdon), the Bishop of Stepney, the Chaplain and the Court of Assistants await the arrival of the Duke of Gloucester, to open the new Hall, on 13 May 1958.
By courtesy of The Times Newspapers Ltd

FIG. 102. Rebuilding Mercers' Hall: the new Hall from Cheapside, 8 January 1958.
Mercers' Company

received from the War Damage Commission and a loan had been arranged to bridge the 'liquidity' gap. The Company's corporate finances may have been dented, but they had survived. There was therefore cause for relief as well as celebration at the opening ceremony. There was a service of dedication and blessing followed by appropriate speeches from the Master, the Duke of Gloucester (a freeman since 1921) and the Lord Mayor.[76] It was a predictable and soothing conclusion to a thoroughly unpredictable and unnerving episode.

The opening of the Hall was inevitably characterised by the Master as a 'new chapter' in the Company's history. What was this likely to bring? The Company in 1958–9 was faced with two problems. The first was the recurrent one of membership. In an egalitarian age suspicious of exclusivity, the Company would find it more and more difficult to explain why it adhered so strictly to patrimony. The admission of redemptioners was only having a limited effect,[P] and more 'new blood' would be needed to bring not only ability but also credibility to the Hall. The second problem, of course, was financial. The closure of Mercers' School would no doubt help a good deal but the recovery of the corporate revenues would depend on the state of the property market. The experience of both the war of 1939–45 and the post-War Labour Government made it clear that the Company would have to exploit its properties much more actively in the future. A docile landlord would find his income eroded by taxation. The task, indeed, was not simply to protect income but also increase it. The Company was well aware that it was not doing as much as it would have liked for public and charitable causes. It will be recalled that in June 1956 the Finance Committee drew attention to the need to make contributions and donations 'more in keeping with [the Company's] premier position as it used to do in the past and as it has not been able to do in more recent times'. Public pressure for such contributions and donations was bound to increase and the prudence, as well as the altruism, of such a policy was self-evident. An obviously 'anomalous' and 'privileged' society might survive astringent democratic scrutiny provided it was of equally obvious public value. Unless the Company became less exclusive and more expansive, it would find that a long, interesting and largely meritorious history would count for nothing.

[P] In September 1959 the Master noted that there were representatives of 54 families among the 212 members. This was a significant improvement on the 1920s (see above, p. 198), but the Master thought it obvious that 'serious consideration' would have to be given to further recruitment. He described the admission of the twenty new members rather vaguely as 'not an unqualified success' (GCM, 25 September 1959). This last remark was something of an understatement. Only two of the twenty became Assistants, and neither brought sons into the Company (ex. inf. Dr Roger Lane).

ENVOI

This account of the fortunes of the Mercers' Company began in the sixteenth century which was a time of great and violent change. We leave it in the mid-course of the twentieth century, which has been even more violent and certainly no less arduous. The two World Wars and their aftermaths had profound effects upon British society and prosperity; and the pace of change, which was challenging enough in the days of the Renaissance and the Reformation, has accelerated markedly, not least under the pressures of scientific and technological innovation.

The completion of the new Mercers' Hall and the closure of Mercers' School together provide a significant staging-point in the Company's history at which to stop — for the time being. It is certainly not the end of the story, nor anything other than a convenient point at which to pause, in providing a suitably detailed account of the fortunes of the Company. There will be another volume to carry the story forward at some time, when we are able to see, in a broader historical perspective, what the twentieth century leads on to.

But, as a foretaste of what will need to be told, let us note that the Mercers' Company tackled the problems with which it was faced in 1959 with a vigour and determination which showed that the Company understood very well that it must adapt or decline.

The administration of the Company's affairs was substantially re-organised in the 1960s and 1970s, and the Company began to develop its property interests directly, rather than to share the equity with development partners. This innovatory policy called for a considerable enlargement of the Company's staff; but it enabled the Company to take advantage of the general growth in prosperity which occurred during the period, and of the benefits which followed from the development of the City of London's international position in banking, insurance and financial services.

These changes, above all else, enabled the Mercers' Company to enlarge its charitable and educational activities, which once again became the core, and the heart, of its public services.

In 1966, the Company moved Whittington College, which had been located in Highgate for 140 years, to East Grinstead where the new buildings now provide 60 homes for elderly ladies and some married couples. In addition the Whittington estate provides some 300 out-pensions. Trinity Hospital, founded at Greenwich by the Earl of Northampton, has been completely modernised within the seventeenth-century shell, and provides 21 self-contained flats for elderly men. Under the same trust, almshouses for married couples are provided at Shotesham in Norfolk: and a number of out-pensions and allowances are paid. Lady Mico's almshouses in Stepney have also been moved and enlarged.

St Paul's School was moved from Hammersmith to a new site at Barnes in 1968, and the Company's connections with Dauntsey's School, Abingdon School and Collyer's School (which is now a Sixth Form College) have all been maintained and strengthened.

The Educational Trust Fund, which was established after the closure of Mercers' School, has been able to provide funds and support to a variety of individuals and institutions, and remains a significant part of the Company's educational interests.

Tne Mercers' Charitable Foundation, which was created in 1983, has enabled an expansion of funds to be made available for charitable purposes, and the scope of the Company's grant-making has been widened to include scientific and medical research, the environment and the performing arts as well as additional educational purposes. The most significant of these include the creation of a new City Technology College at Telford (the Thomas Telford School), and the funding of new developments at Dauntsey's and Abingdon Schools. At the same time, an extension of the Company's church patronage has been achieved, with an increase both in the number of livings and in the number of parishes. The Gresham professorships (raised to eight by the endowment of a Mercers' School Memorial Chair of Commerce) have been raised in status and activity, and given something of the collegiate character that they enjoyed at the College's start in the College's new home in Barnards Inn Hall.

Also during the period, membership of the Mercers' Company has been extended by the admission of new freemen by redemption, including in the 1970s freemen who, because of their professional or business standing, were recruited with a view to early admission to the Court of Assistants and to serving the offices. These policies have been more successful in their consequences than earlier attempts to extend the range of active and useful Liverymen, and have melded well with the service of new generations of Liverymen from the old families. One particular example should be noted; Alderman Sir Alexander Graham, after serving as Master of the Company, also went on to civic office, as Sheriff in 1986–7 and as Lord Mayor in 1990–1.

Membership of the Company now stands at 250.

PETER NAILOR

REFERENCES

CHAPTER I
THE ELIZABETHAN COMPANY

1. The classic accounts of the Livery Companies by George Unwin are now somewhat dated. For a more recent introduction to the subject, which specifically deals with the theme touched on here, see T. F. Reddaway, 'The Livery Companies of Tudor London', *History*, LI (1966), pp. 287–99.
2. For Duckett's copper-smelting activities, see M. B. Donald, *Elizabethan Copper: A History of the Mines Royal 1568–1605* (1955), pp. 43–7.
3. Expert use of John Isham's business papers has been made by G. D. Ramsay in *John Isham, Mercer and Merchant Adventurer* (Norhamptonshire Record Society, 1962). John Isham's 'retirement' activities are analysed in M. E. Finch, *The Wealth of Five Northamptonshire Families 1540–1640* (Northamptonshire Record Society, 1956), ch. 2.
4. Attention was first drawn to Dee's membership of the Company by Dr J. H. Appleby in 'Dr Arthur Dee: Merchant and Litigant', *The Slavonic and East European Review*, LVII (1979), pp. 32–4.
5. AC, 1560–95, f. 7v. Appleby transcribes the entry in 'Dr Arthur Dee', p. 34. There is a substantial secondary literature on Jenkinson's adventures.
6. See G. D. Ramsay's introduction to 'A letter to the earls of East Friesland', in *The politics of a Tudor Merchant Adventurer* (1979).
7. Copley's letters were edited by R. C. Christie in 1897.
8. AC, 1560–95, f. 240.
9. The 1562 list is to be found in AC, 1560–95; the 1581 revision in the 'Black Book' (or 'Assessments on the Livery').
10. J. W. Burgon, *The Life and Times of Sir Thomas Gresham* (1839), I, pp. 46–7.
11. Ramsay, *Isham*, pp. xiv–xv.
12. AC, 1560–95, ff. 288–91v.
13. This was one of the penalties suffered by debtor-members entered in the Black Book (see p. 22). For another instance, in 1593, see AC, 1560–75, f. 463.
14. Ibid., f. 307.
15. Ibid., f. 33–v.
16. Ibid., ff. 232v, 234v.
17. Ibid., ff. 230v, 327v, 348, 430, 434–v.
18. Ibid., ff. 246v, 372, 399v.
19. Ibid., ff. 199v, 323v, 327.
20. Ibid., ff. 204v, 223v.
21. Ibid., f. 317.
22. Ibid., f. 13v.
23. Ibid., f. 301.
24. Ibid., ff. 113v (a Customs official) and 294 (the 'traveller' Michael Lock).
25. J. M. Parker, 'The Ordinance Book of the Mercers' Company of London' (London University M.Phil. thesis, 1980), p. 82. Dr Parker's work chiefly concerns the years before this book begins, but it contains much useful background information.
26. See William Quarles' complaint in 1588: AC, 1560–95, f. 438–v.
27. Ibid., f. 3–v.
28. Ibid., f. 78.
29. Ibid., f. 63–v.
30. Ibid., f. 245.
31. Ibid., f. 236v.
32. Barefoot's selection as a Master Bachelor is recorded at ibid., ff. 67v–8. His premature death is suggested by the absence of any further references in the Acts after 1573.
33. Ibid., ff. 237, 298, 308.
34. Ibid., f. 186v.
35. Ibid., ff. 91–v, 101–v, 108, 112–v, 133v.
36. Ibid., ff. 9, 14, 83.
37. Ibid., ff. 80, 94.
38. Ibid., ff. 204, 255.
39. Ibid., ff. 430, 451, 461, 468, 473.
40. Ibid., f. 297v.
41. Ibid., ff. 342, 343, 349–50. Similar provisions were applied to the St Paul's School estate: SPS AC, 1513–1622, f. 192–v.
42. AC, 1560–95, f. 283.
43. Ibid., ff. 313v–14.
44. Ibid., f. 315–v.
45. Cheke, 'Register of Lands 1578'.
46. Renter Wardens' Accounts, 1577–1603.
47. AC, 1560–95, ff. 15v–17v.
48. Ibid., ff. 18, 19v, 22v, 25–v, 29.
49. Ibid., f. 348v. The provisions were also applied to St Paul's School: SPS AC, 1513–1622, ff. 192–v, 196.
50. AC, 1560–95, ff. 349v–50.
51. Ibid., ff. 360v, 363, 366, 367v, 379v.
52. Ibid., f. 8.
53. Ibid., ff. 126–v, 130, 134–v.
54. Ibid., ff. 380–1; SPS AC, 1513–1622, ff. 203v, 204v.
55. *The Life of Dean Colet by Erasmus*, trans. William Palmer (1851), p. 10. For William Palmer, see further p. 133.
56. AC, 1560–95, f. 335–v.
57. Ibid., f. 350.
58. Ibid., f. 373–v.
59. Ibid., ff. 57–v, 64–v. See also, M. F. J. McDonnell, *The Annals of St Paul's School* (1959), pp. 85–6, 102.

60. AC, 1560–95, ff. 147, 339v.
61. Ibid., ff. 98–v, 215, 453v, 472.
62. Ibid., f. 122v. In the following year, however, and again in 1570 Lodge was given the sum of £20: ibid., ff. 139v, 162.
63. Ibid., f. 143v.
64. See J. Imray, *The Charity of Richard Whittington* (1968), pp. 53–6.
65. McDonnell, *Annals*, pp. 109–63.
66. A. N. Willson, *A History of Collyer's School* (1965), pp. 38–46.
67. G. D. Ramsay has discussed this relationship in a number of his definitive studies of the mid-sixteenth-century English economy, most notably in *Isham*, ch. VI.
68. J. Imray, 'The Merchant Adventurers and their Records', *Journal of the Society of Archivists*, II (1962), pp. 457–67.
69. Ramsay. *Isham*, pp. xxxi–ii.
70. AC, 1560–95, ff. 23–5v, 26v.
71. Ibid., ff. 184, 192v–3v.
72. Ibid., f. 225.
73. Ibid., ff. 194v–6.
74. Ibid., ff. 244v–5v.
75. Ibid., f. 287v.
76. Ibid., ff. 288–91v. There has plainly been a mistake in the transcription of the provisions relating to redemptioners, and the text gives the only intelligible version permitted by the Acts.
77. Ibid., f. 439.
78. Ibid., ff. 185v, 214.
79. Ibid., f. 233v.
80. Ibid., ff. 4v, 103v, 116v, 284v.
81. Ibid., ff. 18, 245v, 274–5.
82. Ibid., ff. 157, 158, 159, 475v–6.
83. Ibid., f. 306.
84. Ibid., ff. 306, 455.
85. R. R. Sharpe, *London and the Kingdom* (1895), I, p. 495.
86. AC, 1560–95, f. 192v.
87. Leigh, Martin, Alleyn and Duckett.
88. 1579: Alleyn and Duckett; 1603: Bennett and Rowe.
89. AC, 1560–95, f. 313v.
90. Ibid., ff. 350v–60.
91. The volume is actually entitled 'Assessments on the Livery towards hiring troops to go to Ireland . . .'.
92. AC, 1560–95, ff. 263–v, 264v, 265–9, 274v, 276. Derek Keene sets out the rather complicated details in K&H, 105/16, pp. 194–7.
93. AC, 1560–95, ff. 313, 318–v, 326v.
94. SPS AC, f. 202v.
95. AC, 1560–95, ff. 429–30.
96. See K&H, 105/18.
97. This was certainly true of 1582–3 and 1585: ibid., ff. 372, 386, 410; and the reduction in the normal £50 allowance to £10 suggests it was also true of 1586–9: ibid., ff. 419v, 425v, 435v–6, 442. For 1578 see p. 13.
98. Ibid., f. 467.
99. Ibid., f. 214. See K&H, 105/18, pp. 269–70.
100. AC, 1560–95, f. 308.
101. Ramsay, *Isham*, p. 171. (The italicised words are deleted but are presumably accurate and add to the sense.)
102. AC, 1560–95, ff. 61v–2v.
103. Ramsay, *Isham*, p. lxxi.
104. Register of Writings, II, ff. 119v–21v. See Keene's remarks on these 'elaborate distinctions' in K&H, 105/18, pp. 68–72.
105. Register of Writings, II, f. 118; AC, 1560–95, f. 237. For the Bachelors' other duties, see pp. 10–11.
106. Register of Writings, II, ff. 122v–3v. See also K&H, 105/18, p. 272.
107. AC, 1560–95, f. 450. For a general account, see J. L. Nevinson, 'Crowns and Garlands of the Livery Companies', *Guildhall Studies in London History*, I (1974), 68–81.
108. AC, 1560–95, ff. 102v, 127. See also McDonnell, *Annals*, p. 56. This dinner is still held at St Paul's School.
109. AC, 1560–95, ff. 160, 312v, 335–v, 346v, 471. See also above, p. 16.
110. Ibid., f. 295.
111. Ibid., ff. 129, 130–1, 159–v.
112. Ibid., f. 309.
113. AC, 1595–1629, f. 13.
114. Lord Mayors: Leigh, Mallory, Martin, Allen and Duckett; Sheriffs: Baskerfield, Duckett, Haydon, Elkin, Rowe and Bennett.
115. Bromley's argument is that while Watney relied simply on an absence of any express identification of the Maiden as the Virgin, there are some compelling points in favour of the identification:

1. The likelihood (in the absence of any secular, especially royal, alternative) that the Maidenhead has a religious significance.
2. The association of the Virgin Mary with the Hospital of St Thomas of Acre.
3. The conventional use of 'Maiden' as a term for the Virgin.
4. The possibility that the clouds surrounding the Maiden in the Company's arms symbolise the Assumption of the Virgin Mary.

116. There is much information in the Acts of Court, but the most useful source is the Register of Writings, II. See AC, 1560–95, ff. 146–50 for Lord Mayors and ff. 125v–7v and 138v for Sheriffs.
117. Ibid., f. 136.
118. Ibid., f. 99. See also K&H, 105/18, p. 273.
119. AC, 1560–95, f. 246v. See also ff. 131–v, 143, 151–v.

CHAPTER II
THE GRESHAM LEGACY

1. For the circumstances of publication, see S. T. Bindoff's Neale lecture, *The Fame of Sir Thomas Gresham* (1975).
2. Ibid., and I. Adamson, 'The Foundation and Early History of Gresham College London, 1596–1704' (Cambridge Univ. Ph.D. thesis, 1975), ch. I.
3. Burgon, *Gresham*, I, p. 409.
4. AC, 1560–95, f. 81v. The contributors are listed in 'A Book concerning the New Bourse', in *The Royal Exchange. Extracts from the Records of the City of London* (n.d.), pp. 16–17.
5. AC, 1560–95, f. 85v.
6. *Royal Exchange Extracts*, p. 26. See also A. Saunders, *The Royal Exchange* (1991).
7. Bindoff, *Thomas Gresham*, pp. 15–19.
8. The will is printed in full in J. Ward, *The Lives of the Professors of Gresham College* (1740), pp. 19–25.
9. Adamson, 'Gresham College', ch. I *passim.*
10. AC, 1560–95, ff. 344, 347v–8. For Hogan, see above, p. 7.
11. Again the Act is most conveniently consulted in Ward's *Lives of the Professors*, Appendix VI (pp. 16–27).
12. There are allusions to the Act in AC, 1560–95, ff. 345, 361v.
13. GR, 1596–1625, p. 210.
14. AC, 1560–95, ff. 418v, 419–v.
15. Ibid., ff. 442, 452–v, 464, 466.
16. Quoted by Ward, *The Lives of the Professors*, pp. 30–1.
17. AC, 1560–95, ff. 465v–6.
18. *Royal Exchange Extracts*, pp. 34–5.
19. GR, 1596–1625, p. 43.
20. AC, 1560–95, ff. 482v–4v, 488–v.
21. AC, 1595–1629, f. 14–v.
22. GR, 1596–1625, pp. 43–7.
23. Ibid., pp. 48–9.
24. Ibid., pp. 54–5.
25. Ibid., p. 56.
26. Ibid., pp. 58–60, 61–4.
27. Ibid., pp. 65–9.
28. Ibid., p. 70.
29. Ibid., pp. 72, 79.
30. Ibid., p. 81.
31. Ibid., pp. 81–3.
32. Ibid., pp. 128–31.
33. These are the 'Ordinances and Agreements', a contemporary copy of which is preserved in the Company's archives in a volume entitled 'Ordinances for the Government of Gresham College' and which was itself copied by Ward in the MS appendix to his annotated copy of *The Lives of the Professors* in the British Library. Dr Adamson reproduces Ward's copy in 'Gresham College' at pp. 267–75 as 'MS Ords II'. Adamson found another version, missing a small section, in the library of Trinity College, Cambridge. Ward's appendix also contains some 'Rules and Orders for the Readers in Gresham College', evidently an earlier version of 'Ordinances and Agreements' and reproduced by Adamson as 'MS Ords I' at pp. 255–62; 'Reasons why the lectures in Gresham College ought to be in the English tongue ...' (pp. 263–4); and 'Reasons why the Divinity lecture ought to be in the English tongue' (pp. 265–6). No other versions of these latter documents have been found and their provenance has to remain conjectural.
34. GR, 1596–1625, pp. 10, 16, 17.
35. Such disagreements as there may have been between the Mercers and the City were certainly over by January 1598 because MS Ords II were declared to have been sealed by all three parties (though they clearly were not). The delay of a year before formally requesting the lecturers to seal the ordinances is only readily explicable by reference to the inertia, disillusion or simple distraction resulting from the quarrel with the tenants.
36. GR, 1596–1625, p. 95.
37. Ibid., pp. 99, 103.
38. Ibid., pp. 107–8.
39. Ibid., pp. 112–13, 120–1.
40. Ibid., p. 124.
41. Ibid., pp. 132, 134.
42. Ibid., p. 136.
43. These and the figures which follow are taken from the Gresham Accounts, 1596–1625, and the Renter Wardens' Gresham Accounts, 1625–54.
44. Gresham Accounts, 1596–1625, p. 291. The repayment is recorded at p. 300.
45. Second Wardens' Accounts, 1617–29, f. 87v; Renter Wardens' Gresham Accounts, 1619–36 (y/e 1628).
46. Renter Wardens' Gresham Accounts, 1625–54, pp. 57–8. The repayment is recorded in Second Wardens' Accounts, 1617–29, f. 322.
47. Renter Wardens' Gresham Accounts, 1636–58 (y/e 1641). £50 was repaid in 1642/3.
48. GR, 1596–1625, p. 176.
49. GR, 1626–69, pp. 7, 20. The 20 marks payment was suspended briefly because of 'some unkindness and neglect used towards the [City and Mercers] Committees'.
50. Renter Wardens' Gresham Accounts, pp. 52, 184.
51. GR, 1596–1625, p. 219.
52. Ibid., p. 220.
53. Ibid., p. 250.
54. Ibid., pp. 183–5. Adamson gives full details of patronage in 'Gresham College': for a checklist see Appendix II, pp. 276–81.
55. GR, 1596–1625, pp. 203–4, 228, 230–1; GR, 1626–69, pp. 4–5, 61–2; and Adamson, 'Gresham College', pp. 83–5, 201–2.
56. Adamson, 'Gresham College', ch. V, gives a full analysis.
57. M. Feingold, *The Mathematician's Apprenticeship* (1984), ch. V.

CHAPTER III
TWO BENEFACTIONS

1. W. K. Jordan's *The Charities of London 1480–1660* (1960) is obviously of most relevance here. Whether charitable giving actually *increased* is another matter: see W. G. Bittle and R. T. Lane, 'Inflation and Philanthropy in England: a Re-assessment of W. K. Jordan's data', *Economic History Review*, 2nd ser., XXIX (1976), pp. 203–10 and the subsequent debate in the same journal, XXXI (1978), pp. 105–28.

2. L. L. Peck, *Northampton: Patronage and Policy at the Court of James I* (1982), p. 7.

3. Ibid., p. 21.

4. Peck gives a summary at p. 75.

5. This information is taken chiefly from two manuscripts both entitled 'A note of the lands and possessions of the Hospital...' (1/126/34 and 1/126/600).

6. See generally Peck, *Northampton*, ch. 7.

7. M. Prestwich, *Cranfield. Politics and Profit under the Early Stuarts* (1966), pp. 115–16.

8. R. H. Tawney, *Business and Politics under James I* (1958), 83 n.

9. Ibid., 123 n.

10. AC, 1595–1629, f. 139.

11. There are copies at 1/125/137–8.

12. For this and much of what follows, see J. Imray, 'The early days of Trinity Hospital', *Transactions of the Greenwich and Lewisham Antiquarian Society*, IX (1981), pp. 117–36.

13. AC, 1595–1629, f. 215.

14. Ibid., f. 217; Imray, 'Trinity Hospital', p. 127, and see the Ordinances.

15. See the detailed analysis in Imray, 'Trinity Hospital', pp. 127–32.

16. AC, 1619–25 (rough), f. 170.

17. AC, 1625–31 (rough), ff. 157v–8.

18. Imray, 'Trinity Hospital', p. 126.

19. AC, 1625–31 (rough), f. 158.

20. VCM for 1628, THG 1/125/615.

21. AC, 1631–7 (rough), f. 81.

22. Ibid., f. 167v.

23. AC, 1619–25 (rough), ff. 132, 170.

24. Ibid., ff. 131v–2.

25. 'Book of Entry of Corrections and Licences of Absence' 1621–57: transcript by C. W. Simpson, Misc. MS 7.27, p. 25.

26. THG 1/116/401.

27. There is a full set of documents, at THG 1/116/354–424.

28. Daccombe papers, THG nos 1, 4, 8 and 9.

29. AC, 1625–31 (rough), f. 210 and VCM for 1629, THG 1/125/605.

30. AC, 1625–31 (rough), f. 326v.

31. Ibid., f. 307 and VCM for 1630, THG 1/125/604.

32. AC, 1631–7 (rough), f. 24.

33. Ibid., f. 81.

34. AC, 1619–25 (rough), ff. 190–1 and 207 and VCM for 1626, THG 1/125/611.

35. AC, 1619–25 (rough), f. 208v.

36. VCM for 1626, THG 1/125/611.

37. AC, 1619–25 (rough), f. 206.

38. Daccombe papers, THG no. 1.

39. AC, 1637–41 (rough), f. 154v.

40. AC, 1631–7, ff. 34–5, 82, 125, 211v, 225; 1637–41 (rough), f. 105v.

41. The exiguous biographical information which follows is largely taken from Nathaniel Shute's funeral sermon, *Corona Charitatis* (1626). There is also an epitaph in verse by William Strode in *Poetical Works*, ed. B. Dobell (1907), p. 84.

42. For a plan and description of the Throgmorton Street property Fishborne rented from the Clothworkers' Company, see *The London Surveys of Ralph Treswell*, ed. J. Schofield (London Topographical Society, 1987), pp. 123–5.

43. Christopher Hill's celebrated essay on 'Puritans and the Dark Corners of the Land' in *Change and Continuity in Seventeenth-century England* (1974) makes brief reference to Fishborne (p. 17).

44. AC, 1595–1629, f. 270v.

45. Register of Benefactors' Wills, II, pp. 247–57. An interesting parallel is the equally generous bequest of William Jones to the Haberdashers' Company. See Ian W. Archer, *The History of the Haberdashers' Company* (1991), pp. 72–4.

46. For one example, involving the Manor of Orset in Essex, see AC, 1595–1629, ff. 306–9v, 316v. Even Sir Baptist Hicks was unable to persuade the vendor to reduce his price and, in the face of such 'stiff dealing', the Company withdrew.

47. Ibid., f. 298–v; AC, 1631–7 (rough), f. 6.

48. AC, 1595–1629, f. 299–v; 1625–31 (rough), ff. 248, 254, 260v, 267, 268–9.

49. AC, 1595–1629, f. 317.

50. Ibid., f. 339v.

51. AC, 1625–31 (rough), ff. 300v–1. Year-by-year legal expenses may be traced in the Fishborne Account Book, 1626–56.

52. AC, 1631–7 (rough), ff. 21, 80, 100.

53. Ibid., ff. 184, 190, 236, 239, 248, 252v, 258–v; AC, 1637–41 (rough), ff. 38v, 51v, 56–v, 216v. See also *Calendar of State Papers Domestic* (1637–8), p. 540.

54. AC, 1595–1629, ff. 306, 310; 1625–31 (rough), ff. 268–9.

55. See J. Morrill, 'The Making of Oliver Cromwell', *Oliver Cromwell and the English Revolution*, ed. Morrill (1990), ch. 2. Morrill not only throws new light on Beard's 'greedy' pluralism, but also gives an interesting account of the implementation of the benefaction from the Huntingdon standpoint (pp. 26–31).

56. AC, 1595–1629, ff. 275–7.

57. Ibid., f. 282–v.

58. Ibid., ff. 286v–7.

59. Ibid., ff. 296v, 309v, 317v, 322v.

60. *The Works of William Laud*, edd. W. Scot and J. Bliss (1847–60), VII, p. 321.

61. Ibid., VI, p. 349.

62. AC, 1631–7 (rough), ff. 115v, 131, 145; 1637–41 (rough), ff. 43, 66v, 115v–16, 121, 123, 190, 197; and *Calendar of State Papers Domestic* (1637–8), p. 426.
63. AC, 1637–41 (rough), f. 203; 1641–5 (rough), f. 116.
64. *Calendar of State Papers Domestic* (1641–3), pp. 540–1.
65. Ibid. (1636–7), p. 549.
66. Ibid. (1641–3), pp. 540–1.
67. Ibid. (1639–40), pp. 104–5.
68. AC, 1637–41 (rough), ff. 132v, 141v, 145; *Calendar of State Papers Domestic* (1637–8), p. 216.
69. AC, 1637–41 (rough), f. 203.
70. Ibid., ff. 212v–13, 216–v. The financial compensation given to Sydeserffe was perhaps less significant than a payment of £10 to Jemmat (f. 205).
71. Christopher Hill in *Economic Problems of the Church* (1956) emphasises the Puritanism of the Company and its appointees (pp. 59, 270–1).

CHAPTER IV
THE CROWN, PARLIAMENT, AND THE CIVIL WAR

1. For the best general analysis of the Livery Companies during this period, see Robert Ashton, *The City and the Court* (1979), ch. 2. For obvious reasons, the Mercers did not experience the trade/craft tensions, the inter-Company disputes and the Crown's support for rival Companies or monopolists which afflicted many other Companies.
2. Ashton's *The Crown and the Money Market 1603–1640* (1960) provides a definitive analysis of the subject in general, including a certain amount of Livery Company information.
3. The years covered by this Chapter are magisterially treated by T. W. Moody's *The Londonderry Plantation 1609–41* (1939). The entire history is tackled by J. S. Curl in *The Londonderry Plantation 1609–1909* (1986) and this includes a chapter on the Mercers' estate. Sister M. Cécile Diamond's unpublished M.Phil. thesis on 'The Irish Estates of the Mercers' Company, 1609–1906' (Coleraine University, 1974) looks at its subject largely from the Irish standpoint.
4. AC, 1595–1629, f. 97v.
5. Ibid., f. 101v.
6. Ibid., f. 102. The Company was not in fact the most heavily assessed; the Grocers and Merchant Taylors were required to pay more.
7. AC, 1595–1629, f. 102–v.
8. Ibid., f. 103.
9. Ibid., f. 104v.
10. Ibid.
11. Ibid., ff. 102v–3v.
12. Ibid., ff. 104v–5.
13. Ibid., ff. 105–6.
14. Ibid., f. 111v.
15. Ibid., f. 112.
16. Ibid., ff. 112v–13.
17. Ibid., f. 116v.
18. Ibid., ff. 117–v, 128.
19. Moody, *Londonderry Plantation*, pp. 154–6.
20. Ibid., pp. 156, 176–7.
21. The figures are set out in Appendices C and D in Moody's book.
22. AC, 1595–1629, f. 131v.
23. AC, 1619–25 (rough), ff. 95v–6, 106.
24. Ibid., f. 114–v.
25. AC, 1625–31 (rough), f. 332v.
26. Vernon's misdemeanours, revealed by Church himself, are referred to in AC, 1619–25 (rough), ff. 52, 86v, 93v, 100v, 107–v, 163–v. The quotation comes from f. 163–v.
27. These remarks summarise the findings of Moody, *Londonderry Plantation*, and Diamond, 'Irish Estates of the Mercers' Company'.
28. For various figures in this range, see AC, 1619–25 (rough), ff. 64v–5, 123 and Moody, *Londonderry Plantation*, p. 328.
29. AC, 1631–7 (rough), ff. 26–7, 149v.
30. Ibid., ff. 157v–9v, 189v, 190v, 243–v; 1637–41 (rough), f. 23.
31. Ibid., ff. 66v–7, 70. £24 was described as a gift since the Company believed that on the basis of the corn rate it should have been obliged to pay only £496.
32. Ibid., ff. 75–v, 85–8.
33. Ibid., ff. 194v–5.
34. Moody, *Londonderry Plantation*, p. 414.
35. AC, 1641–5 (rough), ff. 15–v, 23v–4, 25–v, 37v–8, 80v–1.
36. AC, 1657–63, ff. 21, 23, 24–v, 27–30, 51, 66.
37. AC, 1595–1629 (rough), ff. 57v–8.
38. Ibid., f. 111v.
39. Ibid., ff. 213–14.
40. Ibid., ff. 320v, 321v–4.
41. Ibid., f. 333–v.
42. Ibid., ff. 335–6, 339. Clegate's Case is the subject of an article of that name by J. R. Jones in *English Historical Review*, XC (1975), pp. 262–86. Brief reference to the Mercers' 'long rearguard action' is made by Ashton in *The Crown and the Money Market*, p. 141.
43. AC, 1595–1629 (rough), f. 337–v.
44. Ibid., ff. 357v–8v.
45. AC, 1625–31 (rough), ff. 259v–60.
46. AC, 1631–7 (rough), f. 248.
47. AC, 1637–41 (rough), ff. 91, 93–v, 94v.

48. Ibid., f. 164.
49. The Renter Wardens' accounts cover the entire period; the Second Wardens' accounts only commence in 1617.
50. AC, 1641–5 (rough), ff. 78v–9.
51. The calculation is based on the figures given in J. Watney, *Some Account of the Hospital of St Thomas of Acon in the Cheap, London, and of the Plate of the Mercers' Company* (1892), pp. 219–22.
52. AC, 1641–5 (rough), ff. 110, 119.
53. 'The account of the Company of Mercers London for monies and arms by them lent at the instance of the State and Parliament' (Chalgrave Estate Papers, 4/F1/1992); Second Wardens' Accounts, 1638–48, ff. 284v, 325.
54. AC, 1641–5, f. 237v.
55. Chalgrave Estate Papers, 4/F1/1992; Accounts, 19 May 1651, 10 November 1652, and 7 December 1652.
56. AC, 1641–5, f. 244.
57. AC, 1651–7, ff. 3v, 7.
58. Ibid., ff. 10–20.
59. Renter Wardens' Accounts, 1639–53, 1653–66.
60. Second Wardens' Accounts, 1648–58.
61. AC, 1657–63, f. 8.
62. Ibid., ff. 16v–17v.
63. Ibid., f. 18v.
64. V. Pearl, *London and the Outbreak of the Puritan Revolution* (1960).
65. Ashton, *The City and the Court*.
66. Pearl, *Puritan Revolution*, pp. 297–8.
67. Ibid., pp. 149–50.
68. For Russell as a money-lender to the Crown, see R. Ashton, 'The Disbursing Official under the Early Stuarts: the cases of Sir William Russell and Philip Burlamachi', *Bulletin of the Institute of Historical Research*, XXX (1957), pp. 162–74.
69. Pearl, *Puritan Revolution*, pp. 311–12.
70. Ibid., p. 75; D. A. Kirby, 'The Radicals of St Stephen's Coleman Street, London, 1624–42', *Guildhall Miscellany*, III (1970), pp. 98–119.
71. G. E. Aylmer, *The State's Servants* (1973), pp. 214–16.
72. See also D. Williams Whitney's brief remarks in 'London Puritanism: the Haberdashers' Company', *Church History*, XXXIII (1963), p. 22 n. 2.
73. Ibid., p. 21.
74. M. F. J. McDonnell, *The History of St Paul's School* (1909), pp. 182–91 and *Annals*, pp. 202–20.
75. Willson, *Collyer's School*, pp. 59–64.
76. McDonnell, *Annals*, p. 222.
77. AC, 1641–5 (rough), f. 51.
78. Adamson, 'Gresham College', p. 95.
79. Willson, *Collyer's School*, p. 63.
80. Adamson, 'Gresham College', pp. 186–7.
81. Ibid., pp. 95–6.
82. AC, 1641–5 (rough), f. 95v.
83. AC, 1657–63, ff. 95–101. 'Sumptuous' was the description in *Mercurius Politicus*, 7 March 1660.
84. AC, 1657–63, f. 105–v.
85. Ibid., f. 108–v.
86. Ibid., ff. 117v–18, 119v–20.
87. Ibid., ff. 142, 144, 148.
88. Sharpe, *London and the Kingdom*, II, p. 374.

CHAPTER V
THE GREAT FIRE AND ITS AFTERMATH

1. T. F. Reddaway, *The Rebuilding of London after the Great Fire* (1940).
2. The author has touched on this subject in 'The Government of the City of London, 1694–1767' (Oxford Univ. D.Phil. thesis, 1980), ch. VI and 'The City's West End Estate: a "Remarkable Omission"', *London Journal*, VII (1981), pp. 15–27.
3. For comments on the period after 1694, see the author's 'Government of the City of London', ch. VII.
4. This section owes much to Jean Imray, *The Mercers' Hall* (1991).
5. *The Diary of Samuel Pepys*, edd. R. Latham and W. Matthews (1970–83), VIII, pp. 276–7. See also W. G. Bell, *The Great Fire of London* (1923), p. 89.
6. AC, 1663–9, f. 68.
7. Ibid., f. 79–v.
8. Ibid., f. 94v.
9. Ibid., f. 79v *et seq.* See also Imray, *Mercers' Hall*, pp. 49–66.
10. The figures are taken from Imray, *Mercers' Hall*, p. 67.
11. Ibid., p. 49.
12. *The Fire Court*, ed. P. E. Jones (1966–70), I, p. xix; AC, 1663–9, f. 79–v.
13. Imray, *Mercers' Hall*, p. 43.
14. AC, 1663–9, ff. 75–6; Watney, *Hospital of St Thomas of Acon*, p. 177.
15. The first two figures are taken from Imray, *Mercers' Hall*, and the third is calculated from the 120 admissions in 1670 (AC, 1669–75, ff. 40v, 41v, 43v) and the 70 in 1679 (ibid., ff. 107v–8). There were slightly more redemptions than usual in these years, but not so many as to suggest deliberate revenue-raising, and in any event most of those admitted were given the benefit of the customary rebate of £10 or £15 on the £50 fee.
16. Imray, *Mercers' Hall*, pp. 45–6.
17. AC, 1669–75, f. 153v.
18. This section leans heavily on Jean Imray's *Charity of Richard Whittington* (1968), pp. 68–71.
19. AC, 1663–9, f. 75v.
20. See SPS Surveyors' Accounts, 1664–82, and A. C. Chibnall, *Sherrington: Fiefs and Fields of a Buckinghamshire Village* (1965), p. 234 (Table 40).

21. St Paul's Papers, 'Account of the Cost of Rebuilding [St Paul's] School, 1667–76' (1/226/7).
22. AC, 1663–9, f. 143v; 1669–75, f. 60v.
23. SPS Surveyors' Accounts, 1664–82.
24. There are general accounts of the rebuilding in McDonnell's *History*, pp. 234–7, and *Annals*, pp. 237–44.
25. *Diary of Samuel Pepys*, VIII, p. 218.
26. J. Stow, *A Survey of the Cities of London and Westminster* ... (ed. J. Strype, 1754 edn), I, p. 186.
27. Reddaway gives an account of the rebuilding of the Royal Exchange in his *Rebuilding of London*, pp. 266–70. Jean Imray's unpublished work (Misc. MS 2.12) has been of considerable assistance. See also Saunders, *Royal Exchange*.
28. T. Vincent, *God's Terrible Voice in the City* (1667), pp. 61–2.
29. GR, 1626–69, p. 232.
30. Ibid., p. 274.
31. Ibid., pp. 283, 285, 291–3.
32. Ibid., pp. 282, 298.
33. Ibid., p. 340.
34. Ibid., p. 303.
35. Ibid., p. 333.
36. Ibid., pp. 329–31.
37. Ibid., p. 331.
38. AC, 1663–9, f. 163.
39. AC, 1663–9, f. 163.
40. GR, 1626–69, pp. 360–5, 379–81, 380–1, 387–9.
41. GR, 1626–69, p. 395; Stow, *Survey* (1754 edn), I, p. 462.
42. The figure is taken from the Company's evidence presented to Parliament in 1747, when the Company was seeking relief from its debts. See *Royal Exchange Extracts*, p. 23 and Appendix 5. The figures rehearsed are from the Company's contemporary account books, and there is nothing to suggest that the figures are misleading. The Company's expenditure was no doubt fully recorded, but not exaggerated. Reddaway thought that the Company had double-counted the land costs of £7,000: *Rebuilding of London*, p. 269, n. 4. He may have been right, but there is no evidence of this.
43. GR, 1626–69, pp. 262–3.
44. Ibid., pp. 357–63. The figure results from the addition of £9,000 (for the additional land), £18,000 (for the 'outward' porticoes) and £22,000 (for the inner quadrangle), less a £1,400 saving for a wooden rather than stone cupola.
45. GR, 1626–69, p. 355.
46. Ibid., p. 278.
47. 'Account of money taken up at interest ... for the building of the Royal Exchange ...' in Renter Wardens' Gresham Accounts, 1675–83. The interest charges became still more burdensome later. By 1682 the outstanding principal debt amounted to £45,795. Even allowing for the reduction in interest to 5% this increased the annual charge to some £2,290.
48. GR, 1626–69, pp. 358–61.
49. This is Reddaway's figure: *Rebuilding of London*, p. 270. The eighteenth-century composite figures produced by the Company suggest that it was lower still, but these cover a longer period when rents were declining.
50. GR, 1678–1722, p. 118.
51. GR, 1669–76, p. 77.
52. GR, 1678–1722, p. 110.
53. AC, 1675–81, f. 135.
54. Renter Wardens' Gresham Accounts, 1676–83, 15 June 1683.
55. By 1687/8 the debt had been reduced to £41,838: Renter Wardens' Gresham Accounts, 1683–90.
56. AC, 1663–9, f. 89; 1669–75, f. 156v; 1675–81, f. 130v.
57. Ibid., ff. 86–v, 105v.
58. AC, 1669–75, f. 47v.
59. Into the former category falls Peter Symonds' gift of £10, part of which was still in arrears in 1681: AC, 1675–81, ff. 136–v, 137v. The latter category includes Lady Campden's lectureships (see p. 92), the salaries for which were reduced in November 1666: AC, 1663–9, f. 76v.
60. Renter and Second Wardens' Accounts, 1678–82, 1682–90.
61. AC, 1681–7, f. 169.
62. AC, 1663–9, f. 141. Dawnay's appointment is recorded at ibid., f. 88.
63. AC, 1675–81, f. 12v.
64. AC, 1681–7, f. 56v.
65. Ibid., ff. 59–v, 62–4.
66. Ibid., f. 66.
67. Ibid., ff. 79v, 84v, 87.
68. Cranfield's lease was for a term of 77 years from 1644 and Clarendon's reversionary lease was for a term of 39 years and thus would expire in 1760.

CHAPTER VI

THE COMPANY ON THE EVE OF THE GLORIOUS REVOLUTION

1. For a general account, albeit written from a legal point of view, see J. Levin, *The Charter Controversy in the City of London 1660–1688 and its Consequences* (1969).
2. There are no full-scale modern accounts of North, Papillon or Godfrey. The parliamentary careers of North and Papillon are set out in *The History of Parliament 1660–90*, ed. B. Henning (1983) and the Papillon papers (now in the Kent Record Office) have formed the basis of A. F. W. Papillon's *Memoirs of Thomas Papillon of London* (1887) and D. Ormrod's 'Puritanism and Patriarchy: the Career and Spiritual Writings of Thomas Papillon', *Studies in Modern Kentish History* (1983), pp. 123–37. I. Scouloudi's 'Thomas Papillon, Merchant and Whig, 1623–1702', *Proceedings of the Huguenot Society*, XVIII (1947), pp. 49–72, is based on printed sources.

3. Narcissus Luttrell, quoted by Sharpe, *London and the Kingdom*, II, p. 489.
4. AC, 1681–7, f. 50v. Whether there is any significance in the fact that usually such payments were made in advance is hard to tell.
5. Ibid., f. 53v.
6. Ibid., ff. 56–7.
7. Ibid., ff. 58–9.
8. Ibid., ff. 77–v, 80v.
9. See Orders respecting the Livery etc., 1681–5 (1/54/29) for (*inter alia*) a list of the 16 Assistants 'left out upon the surrender of the Charter'.
10. AC, 1681–7, ff. 83–4.
11. Ibid., ff. 89–92.
12. The new Liverymen are listed (with the Master, Wardens and Assistants), in Orders respecting the Livery etc., 1681–5 (at 1/54/30) and the 24 Liverymen 'not taken in again', ibid. (at 1/54/29).
13. AC, 1681–7, ff. 116v, 122v–3.
14. Ibid., ff. 156v–8v. Two of those rejected, John Archer and Richard Seale, were added to the Livery without apparent difficulty in June 1687: ibid., f. 172v.
15. AC, 1687–93, ff. 9v–18v.
16. Ibid., ff. 17v, 19–v. The Assistants decided not to record the address in the Acts. It was printed in the *London Gazette* on 31 October 1687, a copy of which is preserved under reference 1/63.
17. AC, 1687–93, ff. 24v–5v.
18. Ibid., f. 24.
19. Ibid., ff. 48–v, 53v–4v.
20. The figures are taken from pp. 59–89 of T. C. Dale's transcript of the returns. The typescript is kept at Guildhall Library.
21. Ibid., p. 89. The source is E179/272/50 (in the Public Record Office). The list is obviously incomplete: hence 'at least'.
22. Ibid., pp. 88–9. The source is also PRO E179/272/50 but it appears to be complete.
23. Ibid., pp. 87–8. The source is PRO E179/251/22. The list is obviously incomplete. The heading is simply 'the names of all such persons as are of the Livery . . . and have not been Wardens . . .'; but the existence of an additional list of other members designated 'Mr' but without reference to service as Warden suggests that these are *senior* Liverymen. It is tempting to assume they were Assistants, but as earlier pages have indicated (p. 11), Assistants had evidently to have served as at least junior Wardens before they could be selected.
24. Ibid., pp. 74–6. The source is State Papers (Domestic) 16/539 (in the Public Record Office), ff. 138–9v.
25. Ibid., pp. 59–73 (from the same source at ff. 115–36). The total may be somewhat too high (for the reasons discussed elsewhere): hence 'perhaps as many as'.
26. See p. 23.
27. Twenty-eight names are annotated with 'D' for dead, and the original total of 601 has been reduced accordingly.
28. AC, 1595–1629, f. 102v. See also p. 57.
29. The figures are compiled from the Acts of Court and the Register of Freemen.
30. AC, 1595–1629, f. 40 (1602). The order was waived in 1610 to allow apprentices then bound to masters in manual trades to assume the freedom (ibid., f. 110v), but it was confirmed in 1627 (ibid., f. 318v). For evidence of enforcement, see AC, 1631–7 (rough), f. 103v (1633, a joiner) and 1637–41 (rough), f. 63–v (1638, vintners generally). Categorising various trades inevitably caused difficulty. In 1638 the Company took legal advice as to whether 'a writing master who teacheth to keep accounts may be construed to be a handicraftsman' (ibid., f. 38-v). There certainly seems to have been an inclination to exclude rather than include doubtful trades, and indeed the bar on handicraftsmen may even have broadened into a vague rule of social or moral exclusivity. In 1672 a coffeehouse-keeper was refused permission to bind an apprentice because his trade was not one 'allowed by law wherein to educate and bring up youth' (AC, 1669–75, f. 78).
31. AC, 1631–7 (rough), ff. 230v, 233v, 235–6, 249v–50. The complainant, a brazier called William Thompson, was eventually 'bought off', but the principle was left intact.
32. Ibid., ff. 143v, 192 (1634–5); 1651–7, f. 93v (1654); 1675–81, f. 134 (1681). For applications of the rules, indicating that waivers were by no means easily obtained, see AC, 1657–63, f. 142 (1661); 1663–9, f. 126v (1668); 1675–8, ff. 63v–4 (1678), and f. 133v (1681).
33. T. C. Mendenhall, *The Shrewsbury Drapers and the Welsh Wool Trade in the 16th and 17th Centuries* (1953), pp. 65, 92.
34. Appleby, 'Dr Arthur Dee', pp. 35–8, 44.
35. R. G. Lang, 'London's Aldermen in Business, 1600–1625', *Guildhall Studies in London History*, III (1971), pp. 247–9. Hicks is the subject of ch. VII in Mrs William Hicks-Beach's *A Cotswold Family* (1909).
36. Corporation of London Record Office, MS Companies 3.24. Orders respecting the Livery etc., 1681–5, 1/54/38.
37. For one of a number of general summaries of the position, see D. C. Coleman's 'Textile Growth' in *Textile History and Economic History*, edd. N. Harte and K. G. Ponting (1973), pp. 8–9. For an estimate that the silk trade increased twenty-fold between 1664 and 1713, see G. B. Hertz, 'The English Silk Trade in the 18th Century', *English Historical Review*, XXIV (1909), pp. 710–27.
38. In 1670 the first 50 of the new Liverymen were ranked by the Court of Assistants and the second by 'antiquity': AC, 1669–75, ff. 39, 41. In 1659 the Assistants asked the Clerk for information on dates of enrolment and admission, but they do not appear to have adhered strictly to such 'antiquity' in giving each Liveryman what they called 'his due place': AC, 1657–63, f. 79.
39. For Rich Bachelors, see AC, 1651–7, f. 161; for Liverymen, see AC, 1675–81, ff. 107v–9; 1681–7, f. 158v.
40. AC, 1595–1629, ff. 263–v, 281–v.
41. AC, 1631–7 (rough), f. 144v.
42. Ibid., f. 266; 1663–9, f. 88; 1675–81, ff. 23, 107v.
43. AC, 1651–7, ff. 167–v, 175v–6, 177v.
44. For a Liveryman, see AC, 1631–7 (rough), f. 4–v; for a Warden, see 1637–41 (rough), f. 62.
45. AC, 1631–7 (rough), f. 137v. Sir Baptist Hicks accepted office in 1621 'at the earnest request' of the Court. Whether this was mere deference or genuine persuasion is hard to say. AC, 1619–25 (rough), f. 106.
46. For example, a case in 1678 ('lived out of town and had some affairs upon him which hinder his diligence') and two

cases in 1688 (country residence and a simple inability to serve): AC, 1675–81, f. 70; 1687–93, ff. 46–7.

47. AC, 1641–5 (rough), f. 124–v (£30 only); 1669–75, ff. 6v (fine left to the applicant's 'generosity' or discretion) and 27v–8 (no fine but a gift of plate as a 'return of respects').

48. AC, 1641–5 (rough), f. 124–v (a Renter Warden); 1651–7, ff. 202v–3, 219v (qualification for Mastership); 1687–93, f. 46 (fine for Renter Wardenship sufficient to secure selection as Assistant).

49. AC, 1595–1629, f. 128.

50. Ibid., f. 224.

51. Ibid., f. 139v.

52. AC, 1657–63, f. 131.

53. AC, 1645–51, f. 6; 1657–63, f. 18.

54. For Harrison's charges see the Chancery bill presented by Harrison and two others in 1596 (1/213). Nevertheless there is sufficient circumstantial detail amid the angry ravings to merit further research. For example, Harrison claimed that the Colet estate rents had doubled since the foundation of the School. McDonnell (*Annals*, p. 151) accepts that there had been an increase but denies it was as large as Harrison suggested. However, he overlooks the fact that the School's statutes as revised in 1602 actually refer to a doubling of rents (Ordinances and Orders, SPS Box 3.3). For Harrison's unhappy High Mastership see p. 17. Gill's claims are mentioned by McDonnell (*Annals*, p. 217). His dismissal is referred to at p. 69.

55. J. Imray, 'The Mercers' Company and East London: the first two hundred years', *East London Papers*, VI (1963), pp. 99–100.

56. AC, 1641–5 (rough), f. 121.

57. AC, 1657–63, f. 131. Suspension of half the payments was considered in 1657, but shelved: ibid., ff. 1v–2, 3v, 4v. The evidence belies the statement in Papillon's *Memoirs* (p. 14) that no further Fishborne loans for young men were made after 1646.

58. AC, 1663–9, f. 78v.

59. W. E. F. Ward, *A History of Mercers' School* (1971), pp. 12–13.

60. AC, 1669–75, f. 101v; 1681–7, f. 86v. See also McDonnell, *Annals*, pp. 246–7.

61. For a detailed account, see Adamson, 'Gresham College', ch. VII.

62. See Adamson, 'The Royal Society and Gresham College, 1660–1711', *Notes and Records of the Royal Society of London*, XXXIII (1978), pp. 1–21.

63. See McDonnell, *Annals*, chs VI–X.

64. See Imray, 'The Mercers' Company and East London: the first two hundred years', pp. 98–9.

65. AC, 1631–7 (rough), f. 204v; 1637–41 (rough), f. 13.

66. AC, 1669–75, ff. 59v, 77v, 81, 107v, 170v; 1675–81, ff. 131v–3, 134, 136–7; 1681–7, f. 14–v.

67. Jean Imray gives an account of the almshouses in 'The Mercers' Company and East London: the first two hundred years', pp. 99–101.

68. Letter dated 18 March 1692, Lady Mico's Almshouse papers, 1/30/317. The letter is quoted *in extenso* (though without the deletion) in Imray, 'The Mercers' Company and East London: the first two hundred years', pp. 100–1.

69. See Jean Imray's unpublished account of the Covent Garden estate.

70. The information is taken from A. B. Beaven, *The Aldermen of the City of London* (1908–13), I, pp. 336–7. The 1680s and 1690s are disregarded as exceptional.

71. Prestwich, *Cranfield*, p. 51.

72. Beaven, *Aldermen*, II, pp. xlii–iii and Hicks-Beach, *Cotswold Family*, pp. 86–7.

73. Papillon, *Memoirs*, p. 204.

74. Ibid., pp. 351–3.

75. AC, 1669–75, f. 41.

76. AC, 1687–93, f. 49.

77. AC, 1681–7, ff. 135v–6.

78. There is a good deal of information in AC, 1651–7, f. 160v *et seq.* (1655), and 1681–7, f. 135v *et seq.* (1686). See also Imray, *Mercers' Hall*, ch. 17.

79. Edmund Gayton, *Charity Triumphant or the Virgin Show* (1655) and Matthew Taubman, *London's Yearly Jubilee* (1686). (Both can be found in Guildhall Library.)

80. T. Murdoch, 'The Lord Mayor's Procession of 1686: the Chariot of the Virgin Queen', *Transactions of the London and Middlesex Archaeological Society*, XXXIV (1983), pp. 207–12.

CHAPTER VII
THE ANNUITY SCHEME

1. In one accounting year, 1693–4, £10,900 was borrowed (at 5% interest): AC, 1693–1700, f. 21v.

2. There is a contemporary 'life' of Assheton by Thomas Watts entitled *The Christian Indeed* (1714), and also an entry in the *Dictionary of National Biography*. Watts mentions the annuity scheme in bland and still optimistic terms at p. 85.

3. See N. Cox, *Bridging the Gap: a History of the Corporation of the Sons of the Clergy* (1978), pp. 34, 67–8.

4. Jean Imray gives us an account of the Annuity Scheme in *Mercers' Hall*, ch. 15.

5. AC, 1693–1700, f. 142v.

6. Ibid., f. 143–v.

7. Ibid., f. 144. The figures are given in the account of the negotiations at f. 149v.

8. Ibid., f. 145v. (The Report was first presented to the General Court on 23 December and then repeated on 13 January.)

9. Ibid.

10. Ibid., ff. 146v–7.

11. Ibid., f. 147–v.

12. Ibid., ff. 149–52.
13. There is a copy in the British Library at reference T. 1823(4). There were a number of subsequent editions published to incorporate changes in the scheme, the last one appearing in 1741. The title was altered to *A Full Account of the Rise, Progress and Advantages of Dr. Assheton's Proposal....*
14. AC, 1693–1700, f. 149v. The passage appears in *A Full Account* at p. 24.
15. The total for the years 1699–1716 (when the 30% rate still applied) was only £67,888: 'Computation showing what the Company might have made of the subscription money...', pp. 25–6 (1/157).
16. AC, 1693–1700, f. 159.
17. Ibid., f. 160.
18. Ibid., ff. 179v–81.
19. For the accounting arrangements, see ibid., f. 181v.
20. AC, 1707–14, ff. 55v–6.
21. Ibid., ff. 170v–1.
22. AC, 1714–21, ff. 56–7.
23. Ibid., f. 61.
24. Ibid., ff. 81v, 83–4v.
25. Ibid., f. 85–v.
26. Ibid., f. 92–v.
27. Ibid., ff. 204v–5, 218v, 245v–7v.
28. AC, 1721–8, ff. 48v, 51v–6.
29. Ibid., f. 110–v.
30. Ibid., ff. 114–15. For the committee's name see AC, 1742–7, f. 118.
31. AC, 1721–8, f. 137v.
32. Ibid., ff. 167v–8.
33. AC, 1735–42, ff. 29, 62v–3.
34. AC, 1721–8, f. 144v (1726); 1728–35, ff. 153–4 (1732); 1735–42, f. 111v (1737).
35. For evidence of such activity see AC, 1728–35, f. 254v; 1735–42, ff. 10, 17v, 45.
36. Ibid., f. 170.
37. Ibid., f. 202.
38. Ibid., ff. 249v, 273; 1742–7, ff. 25v, 120v.
39. AC, 1735–42, f. 274.
40. Ibid., ff. 278v–9, 287; 1742–7, ff. 20, 22v, 25v, 29, 57, 97v, 99v.
41. AC, 1735–42, ff. 274, 275, 276v.
42. AC, 1742–7, f. 27v.
43. AC, 1742–7, 1 November 1745.
44. Ibid., 4 November 1745.
45. Ibid., 8 November 1745.
46. The General Committee was formally created a *standing* committee in February 1746: AC, 1742–7, f. 202.
47. GC, 1745–7, pp. 1, 4–6.
48. Case and opinion Attorney-General, etc., November, December 1745: Misc. Papers, Annuity Scheme (1/34/418). There is a copy in the Shaw MSS in the Suffolk Record Office.
49. AC, 1742–7, ff. 27–172.
50. Ibid., f. 173.
51. GC, 1745–7, pp. 253–9; AC, 1742–7, ff. 203–5.
52. Ibid., f. 187.
53. GC, 1745–7, pp. 270–1.
54. AC, 1742–7, f. 224.
55. GC, 1745–7, p. 277.
56. GC, 1745–7, pp. 303, 316, 354; AC, 1742–7, ff. 2, 53.
57. Ibid., f. 247.
58. GC, 1745–7, pp. 280–1, 288; AC, 1742–7, f. 245. See also Imray, *Mercers' Hall*, pp. 266–9.
59. GC, 1745–7, pp. 302, 310–11.
60. Ibid., pp. 317–19.
61. Ibid., pp. 313, 320.
62. Ibid., pp. 321–3. (It has been assumed that the 'Master' referred to in the proposal is a *Chancery* Master.) See also 1/35/192.
63. GC, 1745–7, pp. 324–7. See also WPP, 1/35/196 and 197.
64. The schedule annexed to the 1764 Act of Parliament (for which see p. 109) shows that Shaw was owed a total of £3,500 on bonds sealed between March 1742 and June 1745.
65. GC, 1745, pp. 305–9.
66. See 'Drafts of an address...' and a printed invitation to the meeting in the Suffolk Record Office, Shaw MSS nos 2 and 12.
67. *Royal Exchange Extracts*, pp. 9–10.
68. Ibid., pp. 11–13. See also AC, 1742–7, ff. 12–15.
69. Ibid., ff. 33–5.
70. Suffolk Record Office, Shaw MSS nos 4, 6, 8, 9 and 11.
71. GC, 1745–7, p. 348.
72. For example, James Colebrooke, Sir William Joliffe and Thomas and Nathaniel Newnham.
73. *Royal Exchange Extracts*, p. 14.
74. GC, 1745–7, pp. 352–4.
75. AC, 1742–7, ff. 52–3. See also GC, 1745–7, pp. 345, 358.
76. Ibid., pp. 404–5.
77. Ibid., pp. 393–5.
78. Ibid., p. 400.
79. Ibid., 1745–7, pp. 9–10; AC, 1747–51, f. 21.
80. Ibid., pp. 23–4. As presented, or at least as printed in the *Commons' Journals*, the petition differed in some slight particulars from the version in the Acts.
81. See the author's remarks in 'The City's West End Estate', pp. 16, 22–3.
82. AC, 1747–51, pp. 24–5.
83. For the City's position see the author's 'The City of London's Debt to its Orphans, 1694–1767', *Bulletin of the Institute of Historical Research*, LVI (1983), pp. 46–59.
84. GC, 1747–9, pp. 22–36; AC, 1747–51, pp. 28–9; *Royal Exchange Extracts*, pp. 15–16; Mr Hunter's Collection, 1722–1955, 4/38/4 (a copy of the Company's Case).
85. *Royal Exchange Extracts*, pp. 16–26. The reference to Long Acre appears at p. 26.
86. Ibid., p. 39.
87. Ibid., p. 40.
88. Ibid., pp. 40–1.
89. AC, 1747–51, pp. 53–8. For the results of the investigations see pp. 72, 77–102, 110–11.
90. *Royal Exchange Extracts*, pp. 43–4.
91. 21 Geo. II c.32.
92. Shaw eventually received £603: AC, 1747–51, p. 86.
93. GC, 1747–9, p. 142.
94. AC, 1747–51, pp. 145–6, 1 (paginated by year). £2,167 was the balance remaining after the repayment of £1,083 of the £3,250 loan (see pp. 63, 64).
95. GC, 1751–2, p. 29; AC, 1747–51, pp. 84–6; W. Foster, *A Short History of the Worshipful Company of Coopers of London* (1944), p. 33.

96. GC, 1749–51, pp. 154, 203, 315. There had been a false start in December 1749: GC, 1747–9, p. 339.
97. Ibid., p. 265.
98. AC, 1747–51, pp. 21–88.
99. GC, 1747–9, pp. 336–7; 1749–51, p. 172.
100. AC, 1747–51, pp. 110–32. (The quoted remark appears at p. 113.)
101. GC, 1749–51, pp. 108–9.
102. Ibid., pp. 179–87.
103. Ibid., p. 195.
104. Ibid., pp. 242–5.
105. Ibid., pp. 278–90, 294–301.
106. 24 Geo. II c.14.
107. AC, 1747–51, p. 96.
108. GC, 1751–2, p. 59; AC, 1747–51, pp. 91–9.
109. GC, 1751–2, p. 67.
110. The Act passed without mishap as 25 Geo. II c.7.
111. GC, 1751–2, pp. 77–9, 85, 89.
112. GC, 1751–2, pp. 210–13; AC, 1751–6, pp. 84–5, 92.
113. GC, 1751–2, pp. 144, 151; 1752–4, pp. 9–10; AC, 1751–6, p. 93. The first appointee was William Cawne, the Clerk's assistant (and future Clerk).
114. GC, 1751–2, p. 193; GC, 11 January 1753.
115. GC, 18 October 1754; AC, 6 November 1754.
116. GC, 13 August, 20 October 1756; AC, 18 August 1756, 22 June 1758, 26 June, 2 October, 19 December 1760, 2 April, 23 October 1761. Robinson's survey is entitled 'Rent Roll etc of Lady Bradbury's Estate, 1757'.
117. GC, 28 July, 25 August, 8 September, 10 October 1756.
118. GC, 17 September 1762.
119. GC, 7 January, 16 December 1763, 27 January 1764; AC, 13 January 1764.
120. 4 Geo. III c.50.
121. AC, 24 August 1764. The total bond debt was £146,551 17*s.* 3*d.*
122. AC, 2 October 1766.

CHAPTER VIII
THE EIGHTEENTH CENTURY

1. The City's finances are examined in chs IV and V of the author's thesis on 'The Government of the City of London, 1694–1767'. Chapter IV forms the basis for his article on 'The City of London's debt to its Orphans'. Chapter V deals with the City's general income and expenditure.
2. AC, 1693–1700, f. 179.
3. For a summary see Adamson, 'Gresham College', pp. 233–42. Adamson published an account of this episode in 'The Royal Society and Gresham College', pp. 7–12.
4. AC, 1714–21, f. 90.
5. Ibid., f. 92–v.
6. B. E. Supple, *The Royal Exchange Assurance* (1970), p. 19. When it commenced business in 1719 the Company was still making use of the powers of the Mines Royal; and it did not acquire its new title until 1720 when it was granted its own charter.
7. GR, 1739–53, p. 49.
8. Ibid., pp. 307–9. The issue surfaced again in 1753 and 1755.
9. Ward, *Lives of the Professors*, p. 193.
10. AC, 1714–21, ff. 160v–1v.
11. GR, 1753–67, pp. 63–5, 152–3, 168–71, 176–7, 181–4.
12. Ibid., pp. 220–7, 237, 243, 245–6.
13. Ibid., pp. 317–18, 323–31, 336–7.
14. 8 Geo. III c. xxxii.
15. GR, 1767–73, pp. 133, 148–9.
16. Willson, *Collyer's School*, ch. VI.
17. Ibid., pp. 96–101.
18. Ibid., p. 105.
19. Ward, *Mercers' School*, p. 23.
20. The title of ch. VI in Willson's book.
21. Willson, *Collyer's School*, pp. 77–8.
22. Ibid., p. 82.
23. Ibid.
24. Ward, *Mercers' School*, p. 25.
25. Ibid.
26. There is of course much information in the Acts. McDonnell's two works provide a convenient summary. His *Annals* takes the story up to Charles's dismissal. The subsequent High Masterships have to be followed in his much earlier *History* (chs XVIII and XIX). (There was a decline in numbers between 1790 and 1804, but a full recovery had occurred before Roberts resigned.)
27. AC, 1687–93, pp. 167–8.
28. AC, 25 June 1772 (an instance relating to Trinity Hospital Greenwich).
29. AC, 1742–7, pp. 16–21; GC, 1747–9, pp. 187–9.
30. GR, 1767–73, pp. 79–81; AC, 1 May 1771, 24 March 1773.
31. AC, 1714–21, f. 38.
32. Imray, *Mercers' Hall*, p. 380.
33. 1808 By-laws.
34. By-laws 4 and 11.
35. By-laws 2, 3 and 6, 9, 14.
36. For the former see p. 100 and for the latter see Imray, *Mercers' Hall*, pp. 299–300.
37. Ibid., p. 300.
38. AC, 19 August 1767.
39. For Winn see AC, 1747–51, pp. 38, 2 (for 1750); GC, 1749–51, pp. 198, 278–9.
40. AC, 27 October 1756.
41. For the general picture see ch. VII of the author's thesis on 'The Government of the City of London, 1694–1767' and J. R. Kellett's valuable article on 'The Breakdown of Gild and Corporation control over the Handicraft and Retail Trade in London', *Economic History Review*, 2nd ser., x (1957–8), pp. 381–94.
42. The figure for 1739 is calculated from a printed *List* of the Company (THG 1/116/345) and the other figures are given in a Book of Lists of Members, 1732–1808.

43. See Doolittle, 'Government of the City of London', ch. II, and Kellett, 'Breakdown of Gild and Corporation Control'.

44. AC, 20 December 1792, 16 May 1793, 28 March, 20 June 1794; GC, 27 and 29 March, 25 April 1793.

45. By-law 19.

46. The figures are taken from the Book of Lists. The sub-totals are:

Linen drapers	12	Hosiers	5
Mercers	8	Woollen drapers	3
Drapers	7	Hatter	1
Silkmen	5	Calico printer	1
Journeyman weaver	1		

47. There is an article on Lombe in the *Dictionary of National Biography*.

48. For the background, see P. Earle, 'The Female Labour Market in London in the late seventeenth and early eighteenth centuries', *Economic History Review*, 2nd ser., XLII (1989), pp. 328–53.

49. Brief but authoritative biographical details on all these men are given in the *History of Parliament* volumes for 1715–54 and 1754–90.

50. For the details see Imray, *Mercers' Hall*, pp. 361–3.

51. Sir John H. Clapham, *The Bank of England: a history* (1944), pp. 15, 26.

52. L.S. Sutherland, 'Sir George Colebrooke's World Corner in Alum, 1771–3', reprinted in *Politics and Finance in the 18th Century* (1984), ch. 20.

53. *History of Parliament 1754–90*, edd. L. Namier and J. Brooke (1964), pp. 200–1.

54. Supple, *Royal Exchange Assurance*, p. 45.

55. P. M. G. Dickson, *The Sun Life Office* (1960), p. 53.

56. AC, 1693–1700, f. 114–v.

57. Ibid., f. 115.

58. AC, 1728–35, ff. 11v–12v.

59. AC, 11 September 1761.

60. AC, 1700–7, f. 33v.

61. Ibid., f. 35v. See also Elkanah Settle, *The Triumphs of London* (1701).

62. AC, 1714–21, ff. 154v–55, 159v, 161v, 164, 167v.

63. The entries in AC 1735–42 are confined to ff. 8v–9.

64. See Imray, *Mercers' Hall*, p. 335.

65. GC, 16 October 1761.

66. AC, 1 November 1782.

67. The Aldermen were Hedges, Sir Joseph Woolf, Sir Charles Cooke, Richard Levett, Sir Francis Porten, Lombe and James Townsend. Details are given in Beaven, *Aldermen*. There were in fact *seventeen* Common Councilmen who served in these years, but five were in office for only a year or two. The names are taken from lists in the Corporation of London Record Office.

68. GC, 14 September, 5 December 1770; AC, 3 October 1770; receipt book of new bonds, 27 January 1771; Imray, *Mercers' Hall*, p. 339.

69. Details are given in the General Committee minutes for December year by year.

70. GC, 26 February 1799. The totals were:

Estates not in settlement	537	14	0¾
Estates in settlement	7,391	13	4½
St Paul's School Estate	1,089	7	4½
	£9,018	14	9¾

71. GC, 27 June 1766 (fire at Montreal), 29 August 1766 (fire at Bridgetown, Barbados), 30 July 1779 (Society for the Propagation of the Gospel), 29 April 1785 (charity children at St Paul's Cathedral), 2 November 1785 (the London Hospital), 31 January 1794 (extra clothing for troops on the Continent), 26 January 1797 (the London Hospital again).

72. GC, 25 July 1793; Imray, *Mercers' Hall*, p. 340.

73. GC, 21 September and 24 November 1797; Imray, *Mercers' Hall*, p. 340.

74. GC, 1802–7, p. 173.

CHAPTER IX

THE EARLY NINETEENTH CENTURY

1. GC, 17 March 1803. The Select Committee's two main reports, together with minutes of proceedings, are to be found under reference 1/17/9.

2. GC, 15 December 1804.

3. GC, 9 May 1805.

4. GC, 27 November, 10 and 23 December 1806.

5. GC, 19 December 1805, 6 March, 3 and 29 July 1806.

6. GC, 6 March 1806.

7. GC, 5, 11 and 18 February, 3 and 17 March 1808.

8. GC, 1 March 1804.

9. Aldermen Nathaniel Newnham and Thomas Newnham: GC, 15 March 1804.

10. GC, 9 May 1805, 26 March, 24 April 1806. (The case itself is at CEP, 4/6/894.)

11. GC, 26 June 1806. The opinion is at CEP, 4/9/897.

12. GC, 14 August 1806. The opinion is at CEP, 4/9/898.

13. GC, 21 August 1806. The joint opinion is at CEP, 4/9/899.

14. GC, 9 and 30 June 1808. The three dissentients who signed a formal protest were Thomas Newnham (again), William Holmes and William Clarke.

15. GC, 18 August 1808. The House Warden was Nathaniel Hillier.

16. GC, 21 July 1808.

17. GC, 9 January 1812. (The dissentients were William Holmes and Thomas Newnham.) See also AC, 23 January 1812.

18. AC, 17 and 24 February 1814.

19. AC, 12 February 1818.
20. Select Committee Report dated 6 September 1803.
21. AC, 6 July, 17 August 1809.
22. AC, 25 January 1810.
23. AC, 26 January 1810.
24. AC, 10 June 1814.
25. AC, 23 May 1816.
26. 58 Geo. III c. 22.
27. AC, 7 and 22 March, 14 and 18 April 1922.
28. McDonnell, *History*, pp. 390–1.
29. Ibid., ch. XX.
30. AC, 20 June, 22 December 1817.
31. AC, 20 and 21 April 1820.
32. AC, 25 and 27 April 1820.
33. AC, 1 and 18 May 1820.
34. Imray, 'The Mercers' Company and East London: an exercise in urban development', *East London papers*, IX (1966), p. 24.
35. This section is based on the full account in Willson, *Collyer's School*, pp. 113–20.
36. Save where otherwise indicated, the author has relied on Ward, *Mercers' School*, pp. 25–30.
37. GC, 12 April 1804. AC, 10 May 1804.
38. AC, 2 June 1865. See also Imray, *Charity of Richard Whittington*, pp. 81–2.
39. This section is based on ch. 5 of Imray, ibid.
40. GC, 1745–7, p. 244.
41. AC, 29 May 1831.
42. AC, 2 February, 8 March 1832, 31 January, 7 March 1833.
43. Jean Imray's draft typescript Memoir on the history of the Gresham lectures has been of considerable assistance for this section. It is the source of the statements which follow unless otherwise indicated.
44. GC, 5 July 1804.
45. AC, 17 March 1837.
46. Palmer, *Discourse on the Gresham Foundation* (1837), p. 29. Palmer (1802–58) was Gresham Professor of Law from 1836 until his death.
47. K. I. Garrett, 'Miss Hackett of Crosby Hall', *Guildhall Studies in London History*, I (1974), pp. 42–54.
48. See Burgon's comments in *Gresham*, II, pp. 495–8, 524–7.
49. Garrett, 'Miss Hackett', p. 50.
50. 1 & 2 Vict. c. 100 (section lxxxix). See also p. 113.
51. AC, 26 March 1841.
52. AC, 17 February 1843.
53. GR, 31 March 1826. It is easy enough to reconcile this figure with the £22,410 given as the Company's half share of expenditure between 1820 and 1826 (Book of Costs of Rebuilding Tower and Repairs at the Royal Exchange: 1820–6, Gresham Estate Papers, 4/61/166), but why *Royal Exchange Extracts* (p. 65) refers to £33,500 for 1819–25 is a mystery.
54. Supple, *Royal Exchange Assurance*, p. 150.
55. AC, 31 January 1838.
56. GR, 6 February 1838.
57. GR, 20 February 1838.
58. AC, 6 March 1838.
59. The author has referred to the use of the coal dues as security for loans to effect various civic schemes in 'The City of London's Debt to its Orphans', pp. 56–7. See also B. R. Masters, *The Chamberlain of the City of London* (1988), p. 58.
60. GR, 1 June 1838; AC, 6 July, 5 October 1838.
61. See the provisos to sections i and lxii in 1 & 2 Vict. c. 100.
62. AC, 5 October 1838.
63. GR, 19 April 1839.
64. There is of course much detail on the competition in the Gresham Repertories and Acts of Court.
65. AC, 2 June 1840.
66. AC, 19 June 1840.
67. AC, 27 October 1840. John Horsley Palmer (1779–1858) was a director of the Bank of England, and had been governor between 1830 and 1832.
68. AC, 15 October 1841, 17 February, 3 March 1843.
69. AC, 17 February 1843.
70. See Diamond, 'Irish Estates', pp. 160–72 and Curl, *Londonderry Plantation*, pp. 132–3.
71. AC, 11 October 1831.
72. AC, 8 December 1831.
73. AC, 15 and 23 December 1831.
74. AC, 23 April, 25 June 1834.
75. AC, 30 July 1834.
76. See the summaries in Diamond, 'Irish Estates', ch. XIII and Curl, *Londonderry Plantation*, pp. 133–52.
77. Quoted by Diamond, 'Irish Estates', p. 229.
78. The figures appear in a letter to *The Times* on 7 April 1876.
79. See O. Robinson, 'The London Companies as Progressive Landlords in Ireland', *Economic History Review*, 2nd ser., XV (1962), pp. 103–18.
80. This is the verdict of the by no means uncritical Diamond: 'Irish Estates', p. 232.
81. Save where otherwise indicated, this section is based on Jean Imray's *Mercers' Hall*, especially ch. 4.
82. Surveyor's Report, 7 March 1811: 4/9/902 (1/228).
83. The initial contract was for £795, but £131 was also paid for alterations to the position of pillars in the ambulatory which were to support the Hall.
84. The total comprised £926 for the repair work, £3,500 for refurbishments, £850 for Chapel repairs, £755 for new furniture and lamps for the Hall and £1,129 for various additional works.
85. GC, 19 December 1811.
86. GC, 9 January 1812; AC, 23 January 1812. The motion (which was designed to 'remove so foul a charge on the conduct of the Company') was in fact defeated by 7 votes to 6.
87. Sutton Papers, Misc. MS 25.27, no. 3. It cannot be established whether or with what amendments the letter was actually sent.

CHAPTER X
PARLIAMENT AND PUBLIC OPINION

1. See the author's *The City of London and its Livery Companies* (1982), pp. 21–8 and G. B. A. M. Finlayson, 'The Municipal Corporations Commission and Report, 1833–5', *Bulletin of the Institute of Historical Research*, XXXVI (1963), pp. 36–52.
2. AC, 19 September, 3 and 10 October 1833.
3. AC, 17 October 1833.
4. AC, 31 October 1833.
5. Memorandum [by the Clerk] dated 11 November 1833, in Nineteenth-Century Papers: Municipal Corporations Commission 1833.
6. AC, 14 November 1833.
7. AC, 17 April, 23 October 1834.
8. Undated cutting in Newspaper Cuttings Book, 1824–39 (Misc. Papers, 1/34/441).
9. *Report of the Royal Commission on Municipal Corporations (England and Wales): London and Southwark; London Companies* (Parliamentary Papers (Cmd. 239), 1837, XXV), pp. 188–9.
10. For the background see the author's *City of London*, pp. 28–36.
11. AC, 8 and 12 December 1843.
12. AC, 23 April 1852. Further information is to be found in the report on expenses presented by the Clerk in the following year: AC, 20 May 1853.
13. GCM, 18 April 1856.
14. See the author's *City of London*, chs III and IV.
15. W. Carpenter, *The Corporation of London as it is and as it should be* (1847), p. 43.
16. AC, 12 December 1833, 17 April 1834. There is a set of papers relating to the case at DEP, 1/33/5.
17. AC, 11 March, 22 July, 18 November 1830.
18. AC, 27 January, 12 May, 21 July 1831.
19. AC, 19 May 1831, 2 February 1832, 31 January, 7 March 1833.
20. See R. Tompson, *The Charity Commission and the Age of Reform* (1979), p. 94.
21. AC, 12 July 1821, 1 June 1826, 24 July 1828, 4 June 1829, 16 and 30 June 1831, 25 April, 12 December 1833.
22. AC, 25 March, 13 May 1824.
23. Tompson, *Charity Commission*, ch. 9.
24. AC, 16 May 1845.
25. D. Owen, *English Philanthropy 1660–1960* (1965), pp. 199–200. For Lyndhurst's speech, see *Hansard*, 3rd ser., LXXXVI, cols 745–9.
26. For example, AC, 20 June 1851.
27. This paragraph is based on Jean Imray's unpublished Memoir on the Gresham lectures, pp. 68–71.
28. AC, 18 November 1859.
29. AC, 20 September, 11 October, 15 November 1861; 10 and 23 January 1862.
30. AC, 17 March, 23 May 1862.
31. AC, 4 and 17 April, 4, 18 and 25 May, 21 and 27 September, 16 November 1860.
32. There is an incomplete transcript of the proceedings and the decree entitled 'Attorney-General and Baron de Rothschild v. Mercers' Company 1862'. The Solicitor's report on the outcome is in AC, 16 May 1862.
33. AC, 9 July 1862.
34. AC, 6 and 23 December 1864, 6 January 1865.
35. AC, 23 March 1865.
36. AC, 19 May 1865.
37. Counsel before the House of Lords Select Committee on 11 May 1865.
38. *Hansard*, 3rd ser., CXC, col. 758.
39. AC, 17 July, 2 November 1865.
40. AC, 2 and 9 February, 2 and 9 March 1866.
41. AC, 2 July (1st Report), 5 November (2nd), 3 December 1869 (3rd), 18 February (4th), 30 March (5th), 6 May (6th), 10 June (7th), 22 July 1870 (final).
42. The decision is reported at AC, 18 February 1870 and transcribed at 3 June 1870.
43. AC, 8 February, 3 December 1869.
44. AC, 28 October, 18 November 1870, 17 February 1871.
45. It is at this point that George Cannell commences his account, 'Resistance to the Charity Commissioners: the Case of St Paul's School, 1860–1914', *History of Education*, X (1981), pp. 245–62. This is a careful and interesting study, though the author evidently did not consult the Company's own records. There is also a long and factually accurate chapter on 'St Paul's School and the Charity Commissioners' in *Res Paulinae*, edd. R. B. Gardiner and J. Lupton (1911), pp. 148–93. The author, R. C. Seaton, was a Master at the School during the latter part of the controversy.
46. AC, 30 and 31 October, 6 November 1873, 16 January 1874.
47. AC, 28 January 1874.
48. AC, 16 January 1874.
49. AC, 6 November 1873.
50. AC, 13 and 27 February 1874.
51. AC, 23 February 1875.
52. *Schemes for the Management of St Paul's School in London and Lord Campden's Exhibitions* (1876).
53. Charity Commission Scheme, 4 July 1879.
54. SPS GM, 27 October 1876, 16 February 1877.
55. R. Palmer, *Memorials: Personal and Political* (1898), pp. 447–8.
56. See J. Lang, *City and Guilds of London Institute* (1978).
57. Sir Philip Magnus, the Institute's driving force in the early years, later recalled that it was Selborne who persuaded the Mercers to participate: Palmer, *Memorials: Personal and Political*, p. 449.
58. AC, 4 May 1877.
59. Palmer, *Memorials: Personal and Political*, pp. 369–71.
60. *The Times*, 7 December 1885.
61. Letter dated 12 January, 1886 in Box 4, shelf 2.
62. AC, 9 July 1886.
63. For example, the expression of 'apprehension' at the £25,000 to be spent on the Finsbury College in July 1886 and the 'protest' at a grant of £1,000 to fit up schools run by the London School Board: AC, 27 and 29 July, 22 October 1886.

64. Magnus quoted in Palmer, *Memorials: Personal and Political*, p. 450.
65. AC, 23 March 1888.
66. AC, 21 and 22 July 1887 (where 'a member' is assumed to be Daniel Watney), 9 July 1888, 6 July 1894, 27 September 1895. (Watney died in 1893.)
67. AC, 13 March, 5 June 1896.
68. AC, 8 July 1898. For the later decision see AC 1 July 1904.
69. Extract from Halsbury's letter in a statement on the 'Mercers' Company and City & Guilds Technical Institute 1875–1905' among Sir John Watney's papers. (Letter not placed before the Court of Assistants.)
70. Statement by Sir John Watney (ibid.) made to General Court, 29 September 1905.
71. Palmer, *Memorials: Personal and Political*, p. 449.
72. For the background see Doolittle, *City of London*, ch. VI.
73. Draft of a letter to the Master dated 10 June 1880, WPP 1/35/387.
74. AC, 15 October 1880.
75. AC, 22 October, 23 December 1880, 21 February 1881.
76. AC, 2 June 1881.
77. 24 and 28 June, 1, 7 and 21 July, 30 September, 2, 7 and 22 December 1881.
78. AC, 26 January 1882.
79. For the Mercers' Return and the prefatory Protest see *Report of the Royal Commission on the City of London Livery Companies.* (Parliamentary Papers (Cmd. 4073), 1884, XXXIX), pp. 1–124.
80. For Counsel's opinion on the point see AC, 24 March 1882.
81. 8 December 1882 (for the resolution) and *Report on the Livery Companies*, I, p. 263 (for the reprinted letter).
82. Ibid., p. 189 (Questions 1684–5).
83. AC, 13 October 1884.
84. AC, 24 October 1884.
85. AC, 3 November 1884.
86. AC, 24 October, 3 November 1884.
87. GC, 17 November 1884, 26 January 1885; AC, 18 December 1884.
88. See a set of papers relating to C. E. Powell's outburst at the General Court on 26 January 1885, in Nineteenth-Century Papers: Freedom and Members (1885).
89. AC, 6 March 1885. The full title of Blakesley's pamphlet is *The London Companies Commission. A Comment on the Majority Report* (1885).
90. S. Gwynn and G. M. Tuckwell, *The Life of Sir Charles W. Dilke* (1918), II, p. 11.
91. AC, 27 July 1886.
92. AC, 29 July 1886.
93. AC, 5 November 1886.
94. AC, 3 December 1886.
95. 4 March 1887.
96. The history of the School by G. W. Olive, *A School's Adventure* (1951), deals only briefly with these years. (It is primarily a memoir of Olive's Headmastership, which began in 1919.) There are a few pertinent remarks in Owen, *English Philanthropy*, pp. 266–7.
97. AC, 9 April 1880.
98. AC, 2 July 1880, 1 April 1881.
99. AC, 28 July, 16 September 1881.
100. AC, 3 April 1883.
101. W. Saunders, *History of the Dauntsey Charity showing how the Charity Commissioners and the City Companies rob the poor* (1887), pp. 22–3. This is obviously partial testimony, but Saunders was certainly well informed. There is an article on Saunders (a local man) in the *Dictionary of National Biography*.
102. For the Master's and Wardens' meeting with a parish deputation, see AC, 20 December 1883.
103. There are extensive documents on the campaign in DEP 1/34/1–332. The Acts of Court of course contain a good deal of information on the negotiations with the Charity Commissioners on the details of the Scheme and representations from the Scheme's opponents.
104. Saunders, *History of the Dauntsey Charity*, p. 27.
105. AC, 1, 7, 15 and 21 July 1887.
106. See J. Collings and J. L. Green, *Life of the Right Hon. Jesse Collings* (1920), II, pp. 220–6 and Q. Bone, 'Legislation to revive small farming in England, 1887–1914', *Agricultural History Review*, XXIV (1976), pp. 653–61.
107. AC, 29 July 1887.
108. Scribbled note of Selborne's remarks at the Court of Assistants on 29 September 1887 (DEP 1/34/9).
109. AC, 21 October 1887.
110. GCM, 18 May 1888.
111. See the Clerk's letter to E. H. Palmer, 13 August 1888 (1/34/38).
112. See *Devizes and Wiltshire Gazette*, 3 March 1887 and Collings to the Clerk, 8 January 1891 (DEP 1/34/391, 395).
113. Copy letter from Collings to W. Bouverie, chairman of the 'middle class' committee, 18 November 1888 (DEP 1/34/25).
114. See Olive, *A School's Adventure*, pp. 17–24.
115. Willson, *Collyer's School*, pp. 142–52, provides a valuable treatment of the episode with which this section deals and incorporates useful information on the 'Free School' campaign.
116. AC, 19 January 1876, 13 April, 11 May 1877.
117. AC, 8 April, 17 June, 1 July, 23 September 1881, 9 and 16 June 1882.
118. AC, 26 July 1882, 16 March, 6 April 1883.
119. AC, 21 March 1884.
120. Cannell, 'Resistance to the Charity Commissioners' and Seaton, 'St Paul's School and the Charity Commissioners' are relevant again here.
121. See, for example, a letter to *The Times*, 5 October 1893. There is a large collection of newspaper cuttings relating to St Paul's School 1890–8 among Sir Frank Watney's papers.
122. The correspondence between Beal and J. G. Fitch, one of the governors, was printed and circulated by Beal in pamphlet form. It is also to be found in SPS GM before the minutes of the meeting on 5 December 1887.
123. SPS GM, 6 June 1890.
124. AC, 28 November 1890. There was a pretence of anonymity, but Clementi was clearly responsible for the letter.
125. SPS GM, 4 March 1891.
126. Ibid., 17 June 1891.
127. Ibid. (Clementi voted against: SPS GM, 22 October 1891.)
128. He had already written to the *Morning Post* on 20 March 1891 and *The Globe* on 23 March.

129. The formulation of the scheme can be traced in SPS GM, 1 April, 21 May, 28 October and 20 December 1892.
130. As witness Lord Selborne's concentration on Clauses 15 and 75 in his advice on the governors' right of appeal: SPS GM, 30 June 1893.
131. A remark made at a meeting with governors on 29 February 1892: SPS GM, 1 March 1892.
132. For his vehement Apposition Dinner and Apposition Day speeches, see *City Press*, 8 July 1893 and Cannell, 'Resistance to the Charity Commissioners', p. 255.
133. See Cannell, pp. 252–4.
134. *The Times*, 6 March 1893.
135. SPS GM, 22 September 1893.
136. Ibid., 26 January 1894. This was in accordance with Fitch's recent advice: ibid., 19 January 1894.
137. Ibid., 23 February 1894.
138. Ibid., 10 May 1894.
139. The governors' views are set out in SPS GM, 25 May 1894. For the Court of Assistants' submission, see ibid., 22 June 1894.
140. SPS GM, 22 June 1894.
141. Ibid., 25 July, 21 September 1894.
142. Ibid., 19 October 1894.
143. Ibid., 3 December 1894. The author was W. Latham, QC.
144. So argues Seaton in 'St Paul's School and the Charity Commissioners', pp. 187–90. By this time Seaton was a Master at the School and his assertion carries weight.
145. SPS GM, 5 March 1897.
146. Ibid., 9 April, 14 May 1897. Sir Cecil Clementi Smith and George Palmer thought that submitting proposals might jeopardise the abandonment of the 1893–4 scheme.
147. SPS GM, 28 July 1897.
148. Ibid., 13 May 1894.
149. See, for example, item (c) in the proposals submitted to the Commissioners in May 1897: SPS GM, 14 May 1897. Subject to the availability of sufficient money to permit the 'full development' of the boys' and girls' schools, the surplus could be devoted to 'the advancement of higher education in or near London'.
150. SPS GM, 13 May 1898.
151. Ibid., 29 June 1898.
152. Ibid.
153. Ibid., 27 July 1898.
154. Ibid., 11 November 1898.
155. Ibid., 20 January 1899.
156. SPS GM 4/8/835.
157. SPS GM, Vol. 10, 1903–6: letters from Clementi dated 29 January 1904 to Court of Assistants and Chairman of the Governors; letters from the Master and Chairman of the Governors to the Auditor dated 24 February 1904 and Auditor's reply dated 30 March, together with enclosed notes and correspondence; letter from Clementi to Chairman dated 27 May 1904 and Chairman's reply dated 31 May; letter from Clementi to Chairman dated 10 June 1904; 21 July 1904, in relation to a letter from Clementi to the Board of Education dated 27 May 1904.
158. Diamond, 'Irish Estates', p. 232.
159. Palmer, *Memorials: Personal and Political*, pp. 368–9.
160. *Coleraine Chronicle*, 26 February 1881. (There is a volume of newspaper cuttings on the Irish estate at Misc. MS 17.21).
161. Diamond, 'Irish Estates', p. 250.
162. *Report of the Select Committee on the Irish Society and London Companies (Irish Estates)*, (Parliamentary Papers (Cmd. 222), 1890, XIV), Question 4033 (the Clerk's evidence).
163. Unidentified newspaper cutting at Misc. MS 1.11.
164. Memorandum dated 28 March 1904: Irish Estate Papers, 5/57/300.
165. GCM, 24 June 1904.
166. For various references to the Association's activities see AC, 14 July 1876, 26 November 1880, 5 May 1881, 1 December 1882, 11 January, 18 July 1884, 13 February, 6 March, 17 April, 1 May 1885, 12 March 1886, 23 May 1889, 18 October 1894.

CHAPTER XI

THE COMPANY AT THE ONSET OF THE FIRST WORLD WAR

1. The figures are as follows:

1822	118	1855	147
1827	114	1860	140
1833	122	1868	151
1837	124	1879	157
1845	124	1892	201
1850	132	1900	212
1910	211		

They are compiled from the General Court Minutes for the relevant years.

2. For the general position see the author's *City of London and its Livery Companies*, pp. 90–2 and Graph II on p. 176.

3. The figures are taken from the Company's return to the Royal Commission on Municipal Corporations and printed in the *Report*, p. 3.

4. A copy of Counsel's opinion is at WPP 1/35/158.

5. AC, 7 December 1849, 1 and 15 February, 7 June 1840. A copy of Counsel's opinion appears in the last entry and also WPP 1/35/157. The committee referred not only to the Whateley precedent but also to a case involving a W. H. Clarke in 1834 (as well as 'other cases').

6. Compared with the 18 admissions between 1813 and 1833 there were 16 between 1850 and 1870 and 16 between 1871 and 1890 (Apprentices bound 1765–1890, 1/11/4).

7. There are a number of documents relating to this case. The most useful are Counsel's opinion (WPP 1/35/288) and the Solicitor's report in AC, 11 December 1840. William Eden was bound apprentice to Nathaniel Clark on 25 October 1832, but the youth fell out with his master and the apprenticeship was ended on 31 August 1836. Eden was subsequently bound to a Mr Macdougal of Cheltenham but fell out with him and ended his apprenticeship with his own father. The Court found the application for the freedom of the Company unsatisfactory and refused it.

8. AC, 20 April 1894. This was a harsher case. An estimable young man, Stuart Gordon Morrison, was bound to James Sutton on 22 April 1887 and served him well for five years, only leaving because Mr Sutton was in severe financial difficulties. He found employment elsewhere but without sanction from the Company. The Master and Wardens therefore ruled against his admission.

9. AC, 22 March, 19 April 1850.

10. AC, 24 July 1863.

11. *Report on Municipal Corporations*, p. 3.

12. See *Report on the Livery Companies*, p. 136. It is, however, significant that none of the membership lists in the latter part of the century list 'freemen'.

13. W. Palmer to [the Clerk?], 11 November 1811 (WPP 1/35/223).

14. AC, 28 January 1813. This was part of a wider debate about the power of the Court of Assistants: AC, 31 December 1812, 14 and 21 January, 18 March 1813.

15. AC, 16 February, 2 March 1877, 25 September 1896, 4 December 1908.

16. For the well-documented case of Richard Collyer in 1908, see Misc. MS 18.8. The Warden with whom Collyer had to correspond was Walter Scarborough (whose advocacy on behalf of the Livery is mentioned at pp. 181–2, 188 and 193). Scarborough told Collyer that he had been through a 'similar experience' himself.

17. AC, 1 September 1814, 30 March 1815.

18. AC, 4 and 11 March 1898.

19. AC, 21 July 1808, 11 June 1812.

20. AC, 12 December 1833, 17 and 24 July 1834.

21. R. v. Powell and others (ex parte Newnham) (1854) in *Ellis & Blackburn's Reports on Queen's Council Cases*, III, pp. 381, 385–6.

22. AC, 6, 13 and 26 October 1871.

23. The Clerk to R. Watney, 28 August 1917, in Misc. MS 18.30.

24. See the resolution in AC, 7 May 1880 and the precedents there cited.

25. Walter Scarborough's printed circular letter *To Members of the Mercers' Company* dated 2 July 1894 (Charters Box 1.2).

26. GCM, 11 July 1894.

27. AC, 2 and 8 November, 20 December 1894.

28. See ref. 21 above.

29. The full title was *Minute of Observations and Suggestions addressed to the Members of the Commonalty of the Mystery of Mercers not on the Court of Assistants respecting the arbitrary functions assumed by that Court* and it was dated 3 November 1856. A copy is to be found at 4/38/46.

30. Ibid., pp. 14–15.

31. Collyer to W. Scarborough (then Upper Warden), 13 October 1908 (Misc. MS 18.8).

32. GC, 18 August 1808. Nothing turns on the point that it was in fact the General Committee not the Court of Assistants which gave Hillier his directions. William Palmer pointed out in 1811 that 'until lately ... the [General] Committee and Court of Assistants were ... composed of the same persons': letter to [the Clerk], 26 November 1811 (WPP 1/35/223).

33. *City Press*, 4 April 1885.

34. A trade directory shows that W. H. Holmes traded as Holmes, Edenborough & Co., manufacturers of British lace and hosiery.

35. In the absence of more reliable information the apprenticeship lists afford the best guide. In the 1820s 12 masters' occupations are listed and in the 1870s 10. The contrast is striking:

1820s	1870s
2 West India merchants	5 stockbrokers
1 wine merchant	3 architects
1 merchant	2 carmen
1 cornfactor	
1 mason	
1 bookbinder	
1 printer	
1 cooper	
1 watchmaker	
1 stockbroker	
1 accountant	

36. Full details are given in Imray, *Mercers' Hall*, pp. 343–50. See in particular N. Davis's account of a dinner in 1899.

37. Misc. MS 18.13.

38. Nineteenth-Century Papers: Freedom and Members (1883). The Liveryman was G. F. Sutton. It is to be noted, however, that his uncle, W. L. Sutton, was shocked by this behaviour.

39. See, for example, AC, 3 March 1882, 15 October 1886, 22 July 1898.

40. i.e. Scarborough in 1894 (see ref. 25 above).

41. See Imray, *Mercers' Hall*, pp. 340–50.

42. Ibid., p. 344.

43. Misc. MS 18.27.

44. For Palmer, see p. 133.

45. For Barnes, Watney and other examples see Imray, *Mercers' Hall*, ch. 16.

46. This remark is attributed to J. Horsley Palmer by John Watney in his account of his lobbying for a Company office in 1870. J. W. Watson was also worried about voting for a member and the Watneys were generally concerned at their increasing numbers. See the letters in Sir John Watney's papers.

47. See, for example, R. C. Lane's letter of application for the Clerkship in November 1906: Sir Frank Watney's papers, A5 (1/38).

48. See the Company's printed volume of returns to the Livery Companies Commission (1882), pp. 146–88.

49. Ibid., pp. 138–40.

50. Ibid., pp. 123–4. The sixty-one names are the same as those listed at pp. 138–40 save for the last seven (together comprising the £1,300 difference between the two figures).

51. *Truth*, 6 July 1905. The instance was recalled in the following year when Watney retired on a substantial pension: *City Press*, 29 October 1906.
52. AC, 21 September 1906.
53. For an account of the out-pensions in the nineteenth century, see Imray, *Charity of Richard Whittington*, pp. 91–9.
54. See, for example, the treatment of Richard Collyer's children at the end of the century: Misc. MS 18.8.
55. See, for example, AC, 25 September 1896 for the cases of H. Paterson, a freeman living in Australia, and R. C. Sutton, a Liveryman. Sutton was more successful later.
56. AC, 28 October, 4 and 18 November, 8 December 1842.
57. AC, 1 June 1883.
58. The figures are taken from the printed lists of members.
59. AC, 13 and 20 May 1870.
60. AC, 3, 24 and 30 June 1870; GCM, 24 June and 30 September 1870; and John Watney's report dated 30 September 1870 (1/78).
61. See the Company's printed volume of returns to the Livery Companies Commission (1882), p. 231.
62. *Report on the Livery Companies*, I, p. 190.
63. Hobhouse, 'The City Companies', *Contemporary Review*, XLVII (1885), p. 10n. George Palmer and Hobhouse subsequently exchanged letters on the matter: AC, 17 April 1885.
64. *Spectator*, 7 July 1885.
65. *Truth*, 6 November 1884.
66. This appears in Scarborough's circular letter (cited in ref. 25 above).
67. Taken from an unidentified newspaper cutting, Misc. MS 5.1.
68. These observations are recorded by Imray, *Mercers' Hall*, p. 313.
69. Ibid., ch. 16.
70. See the reports on the Clerk's duties and emoluments at the beginning and end of Sir John Watney's tenure: AC, 29 July 1875, 12 October 1906.
71. Imray, *Mercers' Hall*, p. 312.
72. *City Press*, 15 and 29 December 1906.
73. AC, 9 February 1832.
74. Imray, *Mercers' Hall*, pp. 246–51.
75. William Barnes represented Cheap Ward, 1849–60 and Nathaniel Clarke Bishopsgate, 1828–31.
76. Beaven, *Aldermen*, II, pp. xlv–vi.
77. See the author's *City of London and its Livery Companies*.
78. AC, 18 October 1832: a reference to the Company's custom 'for many years past' not to join in the procession on Lord Mayor's Day.
79. For the views of the City Solicitor (albeit of a Liberal persuasion) in 1834, see the author's *City of London and its Livery Companies*, pp. 33–4.
80. AC, 17 September 1835.
81. This and the following paragraph are based on Imray's typescript Memoir on the Gresham lectures. Relations with the London Institution are examined in Janet Cutler, 'The London Institution, 1805–1933' (Leicester Univ. Ph.D. thesis, 1976), pp. 145–50.
82. For a modern account see N. Harte, *The University of London 1835–1985* (1985), pp. 146 *et seq.*
83. See the account in AC, 8 December 1908.
84. Memorandum prepared by [Walter Scarborough] at the request of the Master and Wardens for the information of the Court of Assistants: AC, 15 January 1909.
85. Newspaper cutting apparently dated 1909 (Gresham College and Lectures, Box 1.7).
86. See the correspondence and papers, early 1909 (ibid.).
87. Imray, *Mercers' Hall*, pp. 322–6.
88. Ibid., pp. 323–4.
89. Ibid., p. 109.
90. AC, 20 March 1894.
91. See Ward, *Mercers' School*, ch. 5.
92. i.e. G. H. Blakesley in 1899 (MSP, 4/F1/520).
93. AC, 19 February 1909. (The proposer may have been Walter Scarborough.)
94. MSP, 4/F1/446 (notes of a Court of Assistants meeting held on 14 May 1909).
95. Ward, *Mercers' School*, pp. 57–8.
96. AC, 20 September, 18 October 1912.
97. Beaven, *Aldermen*, II, pp. xlv–vi.
98. See G. D. Ramsay, 'Victorian Historiography and the Guilds of London: the Report of the Royal Commission on the Livery Companies of London, 1884', *London Journal*, X (1984), p. 162.
99. Dorothy Kynaston's typescript Reminiscences, dated August 1971 (Misc. MS 31.11).
100. Imray, *Mercers' Hall*, pp. 323–6.
101. Ibid., p. 323.
102. Ibid., pp. 95–117. In addition to the main works, some £2,250 was spent on the Chapel. Ibid., p. 122.
103. Scarborough's circular letter (cited in ref. 25 above).

CHAPTER XII

RECENT TIMES, 1914–59

1. AC, 17 May 1918. The Liverymen were Richard Collyer, C. F. P. Hodson, J. R. T. Longden, W. Powell, A. E. Rayden, D. W. Watney and Reginald Watney. A copy of the circular itself, Charters Box 1.1 (papers removed from Powell's copy of the Charter and Ordinances).
2. GCM, 21 June 1918.
3. Acting Clerk to Powell, 28 June 1918 (Charters Box 1.1).
4. A. E. Rayden to Master, 6 September 1918, ibid.
5. A. Palmer to F. D. Watney, 27 September 1918, ibid.
6. GCM, 13 December 1918.
7. AC, 17 May 1918.

8. AC, 22 March, 12 April 1918. (There was further discussion on 18 July 1919 and then postponement *sine die.*)
9. GCM, 13 December 1918.
10. Sent under cover of a letter from Hodson to the Master dated 5 June 1919 (Misc. MS 18.13).
11. Master to Hodson, 19 June 1919 (ibid.).
12. Paper attached to the letter cited in ref. 13.
13. Master to Hodson, 4 July 1919 (Misc. MS 18.13).
14. Enclosed with letter from Hodson to the Master dated 30 July 1919 (ibid.).
15. GCM, 30 October, 19 December 1919.
16. AC, 15 April 1924.
17. GCM, 3 October 1924.
18. AC, 29 April, 13 and 20 May 1927.
19. In Charters Box 1.1.
20. Ibid.
21. GCM, 22 July 1927.
22. GCM, 23 March 1928.
23. Memorandum addressed to the Master or the Clerk and dated 23 April 1928 (Charters Box 1.1).
24. The same but dated 18 June 1928 (ibid.).
25. GCM, 22 March 1929.
26. Ibid., 21 June 1929.
27. The 'New Blood' redemptioners were:—

Name	*AC reference*	*GCM reference*
C. R. Whittington	13 Sept. 1929	13 Dec. 1929
R. A. Biddulph	22 Nov. 1929	13 Dec. 1929
W. I. P. Serocold	2 May 1930	20 June 1930
P. Winckworth	4 July 1930	19 Dec. 1930
Sir Stephen Bull	10 Sept. 1930	20 Mar. 1931
J. F. Buxton	6 Mar. 1931	19 June 1931
H. A. Caccia	1 May 1931	19 June 1931
G. E. Brownrigg	29 Jan. 1932	24 June 1932
J. W. F. G. Paget	22 Mar. 1932	7 Oct. 1932
C. J. Chevenix Trench	21 Oct. 1932	24 Mar. 1933
R. Chetwood	16 Dec. 1932	23 June 1933
R. McAlpine	23 Feb. 1934	22 June 1934
A. T. Maxwell	23 Mar. 1934	5 Oct. 1934
R. B. Morrish	4 Oct. 1935	20 Mar. 1936
R. R. Blades	1 May 1936	2 Oct. 1936
R. Dawnay	23 Oct. 1936	19 Mar. 1937
T. C. S. Haywood	23 Feb. 1938	24 June 1938
Lord Shuttleworth	1 Mar. 1940	21 June 1940
Lord St Aldwyn	6 Mar. 1942	19 June 1942
A. S. Gilbey	18 June 1945	5 Oct. 1945

28. For a full account, see Imray, *Mercers' Hall*, pp. 135–63. Sir Frank Baines' own report of December 1926 is a mine of information (4/5/3). See also the guide to the restored *Mercers' Hall* prepared by A. E. Rayden (1947). Articles also appeared in *Country Life*, 2 November, 5 December 1931.
29. AC, 16 May 1941; GCM, 20 June 1941.
30. AC, 24 October 1941.
31. AC, 15 July 1949.
32. There is a full analysis of the post-war financial difficulties facing the School (and Colet Court), from the governors' point of view, in SPS GM, 25 April 1947.
33. AC, 4 November 1949; SPS GM, 25 November 1949.
34. Ibid., 8 May 1952.
35. AC, 27 May, 27 October 1955.
36. AC, 17 March 1950.
37. AC, 9 February 1951.
38. AC, 7 July 1950, 26 January 1951.
39. AC, 9 and 23 February, 13 April 1951.
40. AC, 25 May 1951.
41. AC, 18 June 1953.
42. AC, 8 December 1950.
43. Report of the Hall Committee, 12 April 1951; AC, 13 April 1951.
44. AC, 28 January 1954.
45. Surveyor's note of attendance on Hall Committee 6 November 1952: Hall Rebuilding Papers, Box 8, Surveyor's file 19 (Finance and War Damage Commission); draft letter from [the Surveyor?] to the Clerk (following consultation with the Architect), October 1953: ibid., Box 1, Clerk's file 3 (Negotiations with Noel Clifton).
46. Hall Committee Minutes, 2 December 1954.
47. See, for example, the Surveyor's letter to the Clerk, 14 July 1954: Hall Rebuilding Papers, Box 8, Surveyor's file 19.
48. Note of meeting of Hall Committee, 16 February 1956 (£1,068,000) in the Hall Committee Minutes; Architect to the Clerk, 29 May 1956 (£1,049,388): Hall Rebuilding Papers, Box 8, Surveyor's file 19.
49. AC, 15 June 1956.
50. AC, 14 September 1956; GCM, 25 September 1956.
51. Joint opinion of M. E. Rowe, QC and F. A. Stockdale, 13 November 1956: Hall Rebuilding Papers, Box 8, Surveyor's file 21.
52. Clerk to Architect, 18 June 1956: ibid., Surveyor's file 19.
53. Note of meeting of Hall Committee, 22 June 1956.
54. See Ward, *Mercers' School*, ch. 6.
55. Ibid., p. 63.
56. AC, 15 October 1953.
57. Haden to Clerk, 20 March 1952 (MSP 2/24/34).
58. Quoted by the Clerk in a memorandum dated April 1953 appended to a report presented later that year to the Court of Assistants: AC, 15 October 1953.
59. Ward, *Mercers' School*, p. 52.
60. Haden to the Clerk, 22 November 1949 (MSP 2/24/34). The same views were expressed by the Headmaster in a memorandum of July in the same year (MSP 2/24/2).
61. AC, 15 October 1953 (including annexed memorandum by Clerk).
62. Clerk's memorandum of April 1953 (ibid.).
63. AC, 15 October 1953.
64. AC, 15 June 1956.
65. Haden to [Master and Wardens], 6 November 1956 (MSP 2/24/34).
66. Haden to Clerk, 20 November 1956 (ibid.).
67. AC, 28 June 1957.
68. W. R. Lewis to Master, 23 March 1958 (MSP 2/24/2).
69. AC, 14 March 1958.
70. Ibid.
71. Ibid.
72. One of the letters can be found under reference MSP 2/24/2.
73. See the correspondence in MSP 2/24/2.
74. Ibid.
75. AC, 25 April, 2 May 1958.
76. AC, 13 May 1958.

INDEX

Compiled by Hana Sambrook, MA, PhD

Note: Page numbers in italics refer to captions to Figures in the text

N